GIMME SOMETHING BETTER

THE PROFOUND,
PROGRESSIVE, AND
OCCASIONALLY POINTLESS
HISTORY OF BAY AREA
PUNK FROM DEAD
KENNEDYS TO GREEN DAY

GIMME SOMETHING BETTER

JACK BOULWARE AND SILKE TUDOR

PENGUIN BOOKS

PENGUIN BOOKS

Published by the Penguin Group
Penguin Group (USA) Inc., 375 Hudson Street, New York, New York 10014, U.S.A.
Penguin Group (Canada), 90 Eglinton Avenue East, Suite 700, Toronto,
Ontario, Canada M4P 2Y3 (a division of Pearson Penguin Canada Inc.)
Penguin Books Ltd, 80 Strand, London WC2R 0RL, England
Penguin Ireland, 25 St Stephen's Green, Dublin 2, Ireland (a division of Penguin Books Ltd)
Penguin Group (Australia), 250 Camberwell Road, Camberwell,
Victoria 3124, Australia (a division of Pearson Australia Group Pty Ltd)
Penguin Books India Pvt Ltd, 11 Community Centre,
Panchsheel Park, New Delhi - 110 017, India
Penguin Group (NZ), 67 Apollo Drive, Rosedale, North Shore 0632, New Zealand
(a division of Pearson New Zealand Ltd)
Penguin Books (South Africa) (Pty) Ltd, 24 Sturdee Avenue, Rosebank,
Johannesburg 2196, South Africa

Penguin Books Ltd, Registered Offices:
80 Strand, London WC2R 0RL, England

First published in Penguin Books 2009
1 3 5 7 9 10 8 6 4 2

Copyright © Jack Boulware and Silke Tudor, 2009
All rights reserved

ISBN 978-0-14-311380-5
CIP data available

Printed in the United States of America
Set in Sabon
Designed by Nicola Ferguson

*Penguin is committed to publishing works of quality and integrity.
In that spirit, we are proud to offer this book to our readers;
however, the story, the experiences, and the words
are the author's alone.*

Dedicated to those who died while we were putting this book together: Bob Noxious, Bruce Conner, Dirk Dirksen, Johnithin Christ, Lance Hahn, Mark "Junior" Hampton, Max Vomit, Mikey Donaldson, Phil Chavez, Spike, Virginia Fuckette, and Wes Robinson.

PREFACE

From the beginning, this was an unrealistic project. We were given one year and asked to deliver 300 pages; we took three and delivered 800. We could have doubled the number and it would never have been enough. The history of Bay Area punk is too rich and weird and horrible and wonderful, and it is by no means over. Because of this, we have set up www.gimmesomethingbetter.com, where chapters on Powell Street punks, Punk Side Story, Shred of Dignity, Sister Spit, The List, Mad Punx, Incredibly Strange Wrestling, Circuss Redickuless, PyratePunx, Geekfest, and countless other punk permutations may be explored and extrapolated. Memory is all too ephemeral and much is lost through the lens of media. We hope you will visit and add your own voice. We are deeply grateful to everyone who shared their stories with us.

—*Jack Boulware and Silke Tudor,*
San Francisco and New York, 2009

CONTENTS

Preface   *vii*

Introduction by Jesse Michaels   *xiii*

Prologue: Turds on the Run   *xv*

Part I

1 I Gave My Punk Jacket to Rickie   *3*

2 Now I Wanna Sniff Some Glue   *7*

3 Baby, You're So Repulsive   *9*

4 Teenage Rebel   *23*

5 Giddyup Mutants   *31*

6 Holidays in the Sun   *36*

7 You Are One of Our Lesser Audiences   *42*

8 Kick Out the Jams   *55*

9 Fresh Fruit for Rotting Vegetables   *64*

10 No One's Listening   *96*

11 Ha Ha Ha   *100*

12 Beer-Drinking Brothers from Different Mothers   *113*

13 Thank You, Good Night, Get Out   *119*

PART II

14 We Are the Kings Now   *125*

15 Better Living Through Chemistry   *130*

16 Grandma Rule   *136*

17 Blitzkrieg Bop   *142*

18 Gimme Something Better   *153*

19 Berkeley Heathen Scum   *158*

20 Dan with the Mello Hair   *175*

21 Goddamn Motherfucking Son of a Bitch   *178*

22 High Priest(s) of Harmful Matter   *185*

23 Mommy, Can I Go Out and Kill Tonight?   *207*

24 Beers, Steers and Queers: The Texas Invasion   *210*

25 Welcome to Paradise   *222*

26 Island of Misfit Toys   *227*

27 Crossover   *233*

28 Let's Lynch the Landlord   *240*

29 Fucked Up Ronnie   *246*

PART III

30 White Trash, Two Heebs and a Bean   *255*

31 A Chronology for Survival   *263*

32 Sleep, What's That?   *272*

33 Journey to the End of the East Bay   *280*

34 10 Seconds of Anarchy   *285*

35 Two Blocks Away   *291*

36 Ever Fallen in Love   *302*

37 You Put Your Chocolate in My Peanut Butter   *305*

38 Ripped from the Headlines   *311*

39 Rise Above   *321*

40 All I Know Is What I Don't Know   *324*

41 Unity   *338*

42 White Picket Fence   *356*

43 Up the Punks!   *361*

44 Going to Pasalacqua   *365*

45 No Sleep 'Til Hammersmith   *395*

46 Runnin' Riot   *403*

47 Outpunk   *408*

48 My Boyfriend's a Pinhead   *420*

49 Shield Your Eyes   *425*

50 . . . And Out Come the Wolves   *429*

51 I Wanna Get a Mohawk (But My Mom Won't Let Me Get One)   *441*

52 (I'm Not Your) Stepping Stone   *449*

53 Longview *460*

54 He Who Laughs Last *463*

55 Rock 'n' Roll High School *466*

Who's Who *471*

Source Index *485*

Acknowledgments *491*

INTRODUCTION

Punk in the Bay Area started around 1976 or 1977. There were a couple of bands. Mary Monday's "I Gave My Punk Jacket to Rickie" was probably the first record. Whatever you say or do, an obscurist will find something older, so there's no point in trying too hard to nail it down (unless you are an obscurist). Soon after the formative phase, there were more bands. By 1978 there were venues in San Francisco, Berkeley, Santa Cruz and other places that were doing punk shows. In the '80s we had the onset and the decline of hardcore in the original sense of that word. In the '90s we had another 100 derivations. You can read the details in this book.

The oral history format has the great advantage of eliminating The Rock Writer. The Rock Writer writing about punk generally has one aim: to arrogate intellectual ownership of something he or she knows absolutely nothing about. That bullet is dodged here.

The stories that follow are the real thing. Jack and Silke painstakingly sought out and interviewed countless people over the course of two years of nearly full-time effort. Their incredible gift, both in terms of a unique skill and in terms of what they are passing on to us, is that they found people who have a lot to say but haven't said it yet in quite the way they do now. They caught the real spies at a time when those agents were most ready to tell their story—with enough distance to reflect, but not so much that they have lost the sense of excitement about what went down and what is still going on.

Many of the people who speak here are as smart and creative as it gets. That is the nature of people who are right there in the forge when a universe is being hammered out. Also featured are many complete morons. That is the nature of people that show up when there is a lot of loud noise and alcohol available. Everybody will have a different idea of which is which. The stories of the great artists aren't necessarily more fun to read than those of the train-wrecks. And of course, particularly in the early days, most people in punk were a little bit of each.

People will bring their own stories to their reading of this, their own reasons for why it has meaning. For what it's worth, mine is as follows:

It was 2007. I was 38 years old, broke and unhappy. I was driving from Berkeley to Sacramento and a tire blew out. It felt like a juncture where my own history was reaching some kind of summation point. Twenty-five years of punk rock, even a certain amount of success within that world, had led to this. The car was a beat-up Nissan that had 170,000 miles on it. I got out to look for a jack in the trunk. It was raining. I had cigarettes but no light. Of course there was no jack.

Giving up on repairs, I dug around in the debris in the trunk looking for matches. There were old tapes back there. While I was waiting for a friend to drive the 40 miles to the industrial farm belt I was parked in, I started cycling through the cassettes on the weary tape player in my car.

One of the tapes was an old mix a friend had made for me which he had titled "Don't Laugh, Your [sic] Next!" Among other bands, the strains of the Avengers, Social Unrest, Negative Trend and the Dils sputtered out of the dashboard, competing with the rain on the roof.

Once again I heard *the sound*. All was well. When the truth is alive, nothing life or the world or even the self comes up with can touch it. I sat there for an hour, playing that thing over and over again.

—*Jesse Michaels*

PROLOGUE

Turds on the Run

Howie Klein: There was this hideous interlude of corporate rock where the cool Yardbirds turned into Led Zeppelin, and suddenly there was Journey and Kansas and REO Speedwagon, just all this pure garbage.

Jello Biafra: 99.9 percent of the population listened to Elton John and *Saturday Night Fever*. In a way, that music was a major influence on us because we hated it so much.

Dave Dictor: I couldn't go see Marshall Tucker one more time. Allman Brothers, Grateful Dead, the Who, Yes. That arena rock, it was just *numbing*. You were like an ant, with 40,000 other people, and you really felt disconnected from what was going on.

Max Volume: Journey. They were one of the worst.

James Stark: Jefferson Starship, all that kind of shit. Genesis.

Rozz Rezabek: Boston, Toto, REO Speedwagon, Air Supply. Michael Murphy's "Wildfire."

Jennifer Miro: I was in this horrible band in Mill Valley, and we did Doobie Brothers songs. I had to sing "China Grove." It was the lowest point of my life.

Joe Rees: Anything disco. That type of music was part of a big corporate rip-off. It was threatening to take everyone's mind away.

Penelope Houston: It looked like 1973. People were dressed in bell-bottoms and long hair and stuff like that.

Ray Farrell: There was a radio show on KPFA called *Music from the Hearts of Space*. Really fucking aggravating.

Steve DePace: Corporate rock bands of the day like Air Supply and

Journey, the Doobie Brothers, Steely Dan, Rush. These bands were technically superb. If you were a 15-year-old kid, listening to that, you were going, "How do I do *that*? I just wanna be in a band with my buddies and play."

Klaus Flouride: When people say, "What got you into punk?" I say, "The Eagles." Nothing in the mainstream that was calling itself rock 'n' roll was really rock 'n' roll. It was easy-listening music at that point.

East Bay Ray: The music I really hated the most was fusion jazz.

Klaus Flouride: I hated fusion opera even worse.

East Bay Ray: I think that's called musicals.

Klaus Flouride: I think it's called Yes. I had a dream that I was a roadie for Asia one time. I don't know what the hell that was about.

PART

I

1

I Gave My Punk Jacket to Rickie

Ray Farrell: A lot of what San Francisco was about, in terms of local music, was kind of cabaret. There weren't a lot of rock bands.

Joe Rees: The big influence in San Francisco at the time was the Tubes. They used a lot of theater people, 35 or 40 people onstage. I did some performances with them. I played this pop icon of Colonel Sanders. I would dress in a white outfit, and I had a neon cane and neon shoes. "White Punks on Dope" built up to a crescendo at the very end, and I would march in front of the stage and then stand behind Prairie Prince, the drummer, and hold up my cane like Moses.

Johnny Strike: Because of the glam scene, that was what was left over. Bowie and Roxy Music and the Dolls and that kind of stuff. The Tubes were considered the glam group of San Francisco. And we didn't like 'em.

Edwin Heaven: The Tubes were dangerous. When they first started, they had topless girls onstage, people were protesting them. Great bands are dangerous.

Dave Chavez: They were talking about white punks on dope. That's what POD stood for, Punk On Dope. Not the white punks, the Tubes added that. The PODs existed all over, in the Sunset, in El Sobrante and the East Bay. A lot of Hell's Angels came from there, too. In El Sobrante they hung out at the movie theater but they never went in. They would just hang out in front. They posed a lot, and looked really dumb. They wore the Levi's jackets with the wool on the inside. And bell-bottoms, long hair. Most of them were thugs. Total goons.

Bruce Loose: I was a WPOD, White Punks On Dope. We wore big mountain-climbin' boots, and Levi's bell-bottoms. The original grunge fucking Pendleton shirts, all that shit. It was cheap, and it kept you warm in the goddamn fog when you're out wandering around, blazed out of your brains on acid. Like every good San Francisco child should be.

Dennis Kernohan: Jon Hunt and I were working for Berserkeley Records, doing their sound. Jon and Bob Howe, they already had a band called AK47 in high school, Oakland Tech. An MC5 kind of band. They were on it early, this was like '74.

The first punk bands of the East Bay, I'd have to say it was the Rockets, with Eddie Money and Dan Alexander. In '72. This really good punky band. You've heard Eddie sing. Eddie can't sing. They didn't give a shit. It was like an attitude.

Jimmy Crucifix: I grew up in Fremont, man. Before there was punk rock there wasn't a whole lot. We were all rock 'n' roll people. We hung out with bands like Y&T, Mile High, all these weird East Bay bands.

Dennis Kernohan: Patti Smith came through and she was really preaching the do-it-yourself, anybody-can-do-this kind of thing. She talked to all the kids at the shows. She played four shows at the Boarding House and four shows in Berkeley at Rather Ripped Records.

Al Ennis: The first kind of punk act in San Francisco was Mary Monday. She was more in the gay scene. She had red-dyed hair, and was really into the fashion.

Dirk Dirksen: Mary was a topless dancer from Vancouver, who wanted very badly to make an impact in San Francisco.

Al Ennis: She got a rock band together, Mary Monday and the Bitches. I saw her over on Polk Street. She rented out a little place and did her punk thing. She came out with a single at the time, "I Gave My Punk Jacket to Rickie." A little bit hokey.

Ginger Coyote: The Garden of Earthly Delights and the Green Earth Cafe did an occasional show. The Palms and Rose & Thistle had shows but they were strictly rock 'n' roll.

Dennis Kernohan: The first DJs to play punk rock stuff were Richard Gossett and Beverly Wilshire, on KSAN. They'd already been playing all the Iggy and the Ramones.

We didn't have a lot of TV channels then. People used to buy magazines, 'cause a magazine was 90 cents. *New York Rocker*, *Creem*. Andy Warhol's *Interview*. If you were into music, you read all that shit.

Al Ennis: I'd pick up *Melody Maker, New Musical Express, Sounds, Rock Scene*.

Dennis Kernohan: Anybody who says they didn't read those magazines is lying to you. We all read them. They were at everybody's houses.

Jennifer Blowdryer: When I was in Berkeley High, we would bring a bunch of books to Moe's Records for trade, and then I would look through the stacks. I would see a New York Dolls album cover and I would be like, this is the shit. I had that stuff on cassette tape. I'd be in biology class, and I would press one of those old-fashioned flat tape recorders below the desk and put my ear down. I had to listen. Just to keep going, you know.

Aaron Cometbus: Jennifer Blowdryer was reputed to be the first punk at Berkeley High. The first to graduate, at least.

Jennifer Blowdryer: There wasn't any fashion 'cause you couldn't buy peg-leg pants. You had to make them. I scribbled "Anarchy" on a T-shirt and ripped it up. I cut my hair really badly and I lied to my mom, said I got glue on it from a poster. She took me to Macy's and I met one of my first hairdressers. For some reason, I said I want to look like Liberace. I got it dyed silver, a little bouffant, I don't know.

Tim Tonooka: In the summer of 1976 I ended up in Berkeley. Me and my friends would hang out on Telegraph and listen to portable radios. One of my friends was a crazy guy on SSI who'd pour glue in a paper bag and huff the fumes. He really got into the Ramones—ironic, considering their songs about sniffing glue.

Johnny Genocide: In 1976 there were very few of us. We didn't have punk rock stores in the mall. We had to create our world one stitch at a time. The Bagel was the epicenter of our scene.

Rozz Rezabek: The Bagel was down on like Pine and Polk, and all the punk rockers would hang out there. Somebody would always be getting a check from home, or some food stamps, or money or something.

Johnny Genocide: Back then, Polk was a lively gay area where you could dress as crazy as you wanted without being beaten up. At 16 years old, going to Polk Street was an adventure in everything your parents warned you about.

Penelope Houston: There were a couple East Bay bands. The Liars, they were the first ones.

Dennis Kernohan: Bob and Jon and I would go over to Berserkeley's rehearsal space and set up for the bands. They would never show up, so we would play their instruments. Jon started playing guitar, and I started singing. It was weird how it all happened. We were bored, and we had all this equipment. We actually rehearsed for a year and a half, learning songs.

Al Ennis: I was in Berkeley, coming over to San Francisco, but there was *nothing* going on.

2

Now I Wanna Sniff Some Glue

Winston Smith: I had to take some equipment to the Savoy Tivoli in North Beach. They had a narrow staircase that went upstairs, to a tiny little room. I just remember what a dingy dark joint it was, up these rickety stairs. And thinking, wow, they should really make another entrance to this place. Somebody's gonna have a lawsuit about this. The Ramones were there. I'd never heard of them.

Howie Klein: The Ramones were like the Johnny Appleseed of the punk movement. Wherever they went, punk sprouted, and that included L.A. and London. When they first came here, they played the Savoy Tivoli. I was at that show. I was so excited. And I thought, wow, this is going on all over the country. Everywhere they go, they're planting seeds and new bands are popping up.

James Stark: I knew nothing about them. People were like, "You gotta go see the Ramones." So we went to go see the Ramones.

Danny Furious: I tried to get a few buddies to come along but ended up going alone. They played for 10 or 12 people whom I later found out were members of the Nuns and Crime, plus a handful of people who were curious, myself included. Dee Dee was amazing. I left totally inspired and immediately called Greg in SoCal and told him about it and that it was time to start a band and he agreed. My friend Mark Hubbard told me later, he thought I was going to see some mariachi band that night.

Jennifer Miro: I was there and so were some other members of the Nuns, I think Jeff and Alejandro. We all went, and we were all thinking the same thing. I really want to be on that stage, I really want to make my statement.

Johnny Strike: That show was before anybody really played out yet. We were in garages at that point. There were like 50 people there. It was everybody that was in a band. The Nuns were there, and we were there. Seeing the Ramones at the Savoy, we said, "Oh, well, this is for real. These guys are from New York and they're doing it, too."

James Stark: I don't think the set was even a half hour long. They must have played 30, 40 songs. It was pretty mind-boggling. There was a group of people who were waiting for this to happen. With what Crime had been doing, with the Nuns, it was like, here it is. This is what's happening now.

Edwin Heaven: I saw the Ramones with Boz Scaggs and his wife Carmella, Prairie Prince, Michael Cotton, Kenny Ortega. The show we went to, there were a dozen people. They went on, and they performed as if there were 1,000 people. Right away, we looked at each other, and we loved them.

Merle Kessler: Duck's Breath Mystery Theater opened for them. Nobody was paying attention. There was a drag queen on Quaaludes during the break, who stumbled around trying to get backstage. Except there wasn't a backstage, just a curtain covering a brick wall. But she kept trying different places, with a big smile on her face. Moving the curtain aside, walking into the wall. Joey introduced one song: "After seeing Duck's Breath Mystery Theater . . . gimme gimme gimme shock treatment!" Their roadies sneered at my marijuana.

Winston Smith: I had to stay around until they finished to collect the mics and take some amps back. I remember thinking, oh, they're not bad, maybe this will catch on.

3

Baby, You're So Repulsive

Penelope Houston: The Mabuhay was just a little Filipino restaurant that had mostly Filipino acts perform. Ness [Aquino] was trying to bring in people that would do some kind of cabaret-style crazy stuff. To bring in more people to drink after dinnertime. They served really terrible Filipino food. Deeply deep-fried food.

Dirk Dirksen: I moved here in 1974, and was looking to put a nightclub together that would give us the opportunity to document the seminal moment of an artist. The genesis of an artist. My interest was the artist before they got into the recording stage.

In approximately 1975 we approached the owner to give us Mondays and Tuesdays, when the club was dark, guaranteeing him 175 at the bar. We brought in a female guerrilla comedy troupe called Les Nickelettes, a bunch of ladies that worked at the Mitchell Brothers.

They used to do these impromptu appearances at like the opening of the opera. They would dress up in vintage fur coats and then start screaming at the top of their voices, talking about their sexual escapades with sailors they had picked up in the lobby. Shocking the first-nighter audiences.

I convinced the Nickelettes to come into the Mab and do this loose-knit musical revue. They did a midnight show on Sundays, with tacky cartoons, and sang show tunes off-key. They had written a play. Myself and the Mitchell Brothers, under their AKA of H. Hughes, presented the Nickelettes.

That was so successful that the club decided to give us the other nights. We would start at 11 p.m. The On Broadway at that time was a theater, and we would trespass on their soundspace if we started before they were closed. So we had only from 11 to 2 every night.

Joe Rees: Dirk had a background in television production. His big claim to fame is, he worked with Tony Dow, from *Leave It to Beaver.*

Dirk Dirksen: I did a lot of half-hour shows in L.A., followed by associate producing a soap opera on ABC. The first soap opera geared to teenagers, with Tony Dow. From that I began producing concerts in the mid-'60s. San Bernardino, Riverside, Newport—I did the Doors in Bakersfield.

Penelope Houston: Dirksen started having people come in. I think he had comedians as well. And pretty soon he realized that the people who were really drawing crowds were these young bands, playing this outrageously noisy rock 'n' roll. So he just steered it in that direction. But he also mixed it up, he had a lot of real oddball people play. Arty percussionists. Whoever wanted to come up. He wouldn't pay you. The first couple times. But if you showed that you actually had an audience, then he would start paying you.

James Stark: The first couple of Crime shows, and the Nuns, Dirk had nothing to do with those. He came a little bit later.

Jennifer Miro: Terra Linda was a Valley Girl kind of a place. This was a rehearsal studio, 1975. I was in this horrible band and I was singing. Somebody said, "There's this weird band down the hall," and I said, "Oooh, let's go see!" So we went down the hall and opened the door and there was Jeff [Olener] and Alejandro [Escovedo], and Kenny on drums, and Nola, the bass player. Alejandro at that point was still a glitter boy. He had long hair and was wearing red platform high-heeled boots. Nola was wearing purple lamé leggings and purple platform high heels. No one was there. They dressed up for the rehearsal.

Alejandro and Jeff were at College of Marin in the film department, and they were making a film about a rock star. So they had decided to form a band and called it the Nuns.

Edwin Heaven: They formed a band to make the movie, and then the band became a bigger idea.

Jennifer Miro: A few days later Jeff called me up and he said, "Do you want to join the band?" I said, "ME? What am I gonna do?" So he said, "Well, you'd sing."

Johnny Strike: Frankie Fix and I were from Harrisburg, Pennsylvania. When I moved to San Francisco, he did, too. We bought cheap guitars and sat around our apartments. We had little amplifiers, and Frankie had an album, *How to Play Guitar with the Ventures*.

We were big Bowie and Lou Reed fans. We knew we could never play music like that. But we thought we could do our version of it. We had no vocals, it was just guitars. In fact, we called ourselves the Guitar Army. When we'd play with people who had an inkling of musical know-how, they'd look at us like, "Guys, could you tune your guitar at least?"

We were looking for people who looked like us. It was the end of the glam era, so it was just kinda slicked-back hair and black leather jackets, juvenile delinquent look. I was working at a disco at the time, as a waiter, and I saw this guy who looked like he had some rock 'n' roll about him. I said, "We need a bass player," and he said, "Okay."

James Stark: Ron "Ripper" Greco called me and said he's in this new band and they're looking for a photographer. They were looking for a *look*, so to speak. I came down to the rehearsal studio on Howard and Sixth. The whole thing reminded me of the early Velvets shows when I lived in New York back in 1967. Frankie and Johnny were dressed in this basic gay drag, leather jackets. They had poppers. It was a lot of loud noise, but it had something going and I thought, wow, this is pretty cool.

Sometime in '75, '76, David Bowie had done a concert at the Cow Palace, and Frankie and Johnny and their wives went all dressed up as Ziggy Stardust. Their picture was on the front page of the *Chronicle*, maybe the *Examiner*. So they were already into a look. Very style-conscious. They didn't smile.

Chip Kinman: The Dils moved up to San Francisco in 1976. This was even before we played in Los Angeles. We hadn't played anywhere yet. We didn't have a place to rehearse or anything. We just moved up there thinking, well, it's kind of a neat city.

We saw this poster for this band the Nuns, so we went to go see them because we thought the name was interesting. Apparently the owner of the club thought that they were either too loud or weird looking or something. When they went to set up their gear, he sent them away. The owner said, go see them at their rehearsal hall, which was down south of Mission. We were the only ones who showed up.

Jennifer Miro: We tried every club and nobody would give us a show.

Johnny Strike: Our first show was for my barber, a fund-raiser for a gay political candidate at the Old Waldorf. She said, "Why don't you bring your band and play?" She had no idea what we were.

People were dressed up as fruit. I remember a pineapple walking around, that kind of campy stuff. And then, "Oh, now for the entertainment segment, we have this band called Crime."

James Stark: Frankie and Johnny had motorcycle caps, and those white, wife-beater type T-shirts. The gay, rough-trade biker look. I mean, these were two guys that were married.

Johnny Strike: We just liked that look. We had Marshall stacks, and we had 'em cranked. I'm sure it was really loud and abrasive. It was actually pretty good, I thought. It was the first time I ever played live.

James Stark: I remember hearing somebody in the back, said, "Oh, it looks like a David Bowie band." Then they started playing and everybody goes, "What the fuck's going on here?" They played for about 10 or 15 minutes, and people were getting really upset. They pulled the plug, and someone knocked over a stack of amps. That was the beginning of Crime.

Johnny Strike: Then we were supposed to play a place called the Stud. Bisexual leather club. Okay, this was gonna be a real show. So we're gonna do a flyer. What's the most outrageous flyer we could do? Hitler. We took a picture of Hitler, and now I think years later—Hitler, Crime, at the Stud. It was just the weirdest combination.

At this time there was a little bit of a punk scene. There were records coming in from London at Aquarius Records. We had our record in Aquarius. We had recorded a 45, live in one night.

We took our poster all around town. Aquarius said, "No no no no, we're not putting that poster up in our store. In fact, here's your records, guys. We're not selling your records either." Hitler. The Stud called us and said, "You're not playing here. We don't want to have anything to do with this." That made us the most notorious band in town. After one gig.

James Stark: The Nuns played the Mabuhay, maybe in November or December '76. That was the first publicized punk show.

Johnny Strike: We both started about the same time. The Nuns were the first to play Mabuhay, we were the first to put out a record.

Jennifer Miro: When we did the first show at Mabuhay, there was no punk rock. We were the first punk rock band in California. It was actually surprising because there were a few people there. We just stuck a couple flyers on lampposts.

Johnny Strike: We were walking around North Beach one night and saw a flyer that said, "Switchblade at the Mabuhay." We said, "Okay, that sounds kinda like us." So we went to Mabuhay and talked with Ness. And he said, "Oh yeah, they didn't do very good. Ten people came. But the Nuns did pretty good." We said, "Oh, well, we'll do much better than the Nuns. Don't worry about it." And he said, "Alright, I'll give you a night."

Al Ennis: One night I was walking through San Francisco and I saw this magazine, *Psyclone*. It was put out by Jerry Paulson and Dirk Dirksen. It had a picture of Ron the Ripper, the bass player from Crime. I grabbed the magazine, looked through there and found Mabuhay Gardens. And I thought, wow, the Nuns, Crime. These bands look pretty punk. I'll check 'em out. So I went there and I was not disappointed. They really had it down. They just had the punk spirit. There really wasn't much media coverage of other punk bands.

Penelope Houston: I moved to San Francisco to go to the Art Institute. December of 1976. I was 19. The first thing I saw on the street was a poster of a Crime show. I went to the show at the Mab. Entertaining. And then I saw Blondie at the Mab, and I saw the Nuns, and maybe the Ramones. And the Damned came through town.

James Stark: All these guys were really different. Crime had one kind of sound, and the Nuns had theirs. Then you had the bands from L.A. that came up, like the Screamers, who were all synthesizers. The Dils, the Weirdos, and the Nerves. The thing that was a common thread was a raw new sound.

Punk was more like Crime and the Nuns, which is more of a harder, rock 'n' roll sound. And maybe New Wave would be the Screamers or the Nerves, which were more like a pop band. Blondie played the Mabuhay fairly early, and also the Damned, bands like that. Some people said, "Oh, they're punk." And other people were like, "No, they're New Wave." This was a big point of discussion for a few months. There was this dividing line among some people.

Bruce Loose: I was still in high school. I was barely aware of Richard Hell and the Sex Pistols. I was a fevered audience member. I was at the Mabuhay every fucking night at that point.

Al Ennis: When the Mabuhay Gardens started in '77, they used to have tables and chairs. You sat down and watched, like a nightclub. They still had the old kind of cocktail waitresses.

Dirk Dirksen: We broke a lot of rules in terms of what was considered the norm for clubs, like mixing straight and gay audiences on a very heterosexual sex strip. We premiered something like 25 plays of authors who are now very well known. Whoopi Goldberg did a routine which got her on Broadway. So it was a venue that encouraged everything from a woman dancing in a dress that was wired with live electricity and neon tubes, to a guy that used to do full paintings while the band played—and one time he did it on a pogo stick.

The reason I became the MC was that the audience had a habit of throwing beer bottles at the stage, and we were trying to figure out various ways to defuse that. I didn't want anyone to end up being injured. After two days I figured I gotta come up with something. We started with these huge 50-gallon barrels, with oversalted popcorn in them. And I would berate the audience in order to have them get upset with me, and then identify the performers in a way that I might be abusing them. It began welding the two together. The throwing of the popcorn, it was like a blizzard.

Al Ennis: The Nuns had a really good, powerful punk rock show. They were huge. Jennifer would hit the first couple of notes of a song, and the crowd would just go apeshit. It was real exciting.

Edwin Heaven: They were so dramatic. It opened up with Jennifer Miro alone onstage, expressionless, white spotlight on her, and she went, "Lazy, I'm so lazy. I'm too lazy to get laid." This very Nico/Marlene Detrich–esque vibe. She was maybe 18 at the time.

And then these guys came on and they looked like they escaped from Sal Mineo's closet. Black leather jackets, ripped jeans. They went, "One Two Three" *bam!*—and they did "Decadent Jew." Musically it was brilliant. It was dramatic, it had a great, great riff to it, it was sung by a Jew, so we got away with it.

I signed them to a management agreement. I had a feeling they were going to be enormous. I was doing this based on their music and not personality. Coming from a glitter rock band where everybody loves you, the Tubes—they were like family, people had picnics together. This was a whole different vibe.

They started to become really good. The band had a great dynamic. Richie Detrick did that wild gravelly voice. Jennifer would do kinda like a Blondie. She could have had hit records during the '60s. At the end they would do "Suicide Child." It was a dirge about a child who killed herself. "You stole my junk, you stupid punk. You slit your wrists, you fucking bitch." Jeffrey would grab the cord and hang himself. I knew that was a song a label would sign.

Dennis Kernohan: The first band I saw was the Nuns. They were great. They were like the earliest band. I know Crime claims it. They were like an old-school punk band. They could have started in 1970. They were very poppy, real memorable. They were like the New York punks.

Hank Rank: They had a very eclectic look. A mix of ethnicities, genders. They were all over the place.

Jennifer Miro: We were really a snotty little bunch of teenagers. But I really wasn't that confident in those days. I had all these guys coming on to me because I was really young and unattached. It was weird. All these rock stars wanted to date me, so I just kind of closed off. I was really snooty.

Edwin Heaven: I got an investor friend of mine to put money in. We started doing big, gigantic billboards and posters. I went to KSAN and did a 60-second commercial for the Mabuhay, but it would

Photo by James Stark

Too Lazy to Get Laid: The Nuns at Mabuhay Gardens

be 55 seconds from "Suicide Child." The next time they performed, lines down the block. We knew now that this is our club. We could do a show every week there.

Howie Klein: Mayor Moscone's daughter would come to the shows. Everybody in San Francisco society wanted to check out what was going on with this new punk rock thing. The Nuns would have lines around the corner. They were the only band that was able to do that.

Edwin Heaven: Bill Graham wanted to manage them. I had 20 percent of the band. The deal was, they would retain 15 percent and I would have 5. I didn't mind. But they could not perform "Decadent Jew." His family had survived Auschwitz.

Dirk Dirksen: Jeff Olener's song "Decadent Jew" dealt with the stereotyping of Jewish landlords. Jeff meant it to expose the ease by which people get pegged with stereotypes, and that a whole minority therefore suffers. When Bill Graham heard the song he was so enraged. He said to Howie Klein, I want to buy all of their records, how many are there? There was like 500. When Howie rushed to bring them, he thought, "This is a big break!" Bill destroyed all of them and said, "These guys will never work in this town again."

Edwin Heaven: I created a lot of publicity for them. They opened up at the Boarding House for the Dictators, played with the Ramones, Bryan Ferry. I wasn't building a crowd in San Francisco, I was building a record company buzz.

Steve DePace: They had more money than anyone in the scene at that time. Everybody else was climbing into cars and vans to go to the gig, and these guys—they all had brand-new gear. And they weren't making that much money at the Mab, to pay for all that.

Jennifer Miro: We opened for every single famous punk band that came in. Mabuhay was a mob scene. Every celebrity, every punk band was playing there. We went to a party and David Bowie was there. Iggy Pop. Mabuhay Gardens was the spot.

Steve DePace: Their shows were fun. But they were going for that rock star thing, they wanted to plug into that rock star mind-set. Whereas every other band was like, "We're not gonna get signed, are you crazy?"

Hank Rank: My first time at the Mab, Crime came out. And my whole life changed at that moment. I felt like, it's back. I saw Iggy and the Stooges many times, and the MC5 many times. I was seeing

Alice Cooper's first tour in small clubs. When I saw Crime, I thought, "This is the music I love."

They just were tough and very cold. They came out and played 10 songs in 15 minutes, and they were off. No encore, just as abusive to the audience as possible. I was destroyed. I thought it was one of the greatest shows I'd ever seen.

Right after that show, Dirk took the stage and said, "Crime is looking for a drummer. So if anybody out there knows any drummers, they're auditioning." I made up my mind. I have to be the drummer in this band.

I had only sat down at a drum kit maybe three or four times in my life. But I made this elaborate presentation. I made myself over in the image of Frankie and Johnny, and created a whole photo montage, of me in various poses. It ended with a picture of Frankie and Johnny and my picture between them, so that we looked like three brothers.

To make sure that it stood out from the avalanche of responses that I was sure they were gonna be getting, I sent it to them special delivery with the entire envelope covered in one-cent stamps. I later found out from Johnny that it was the only submission they received.

Johnny Strike: It was the picture that sold us.

Hank Rank: We got into the uniformed look, and that became the trademark of the band.

Johnny Strike: We went to where the police bought their uniforms, and were measured. I had a cop badge. Sometimes we wore suits, like detectives, and put our badges on our suit jackets. But the police uniform, that's the one we're famous for. We were in *Gentleman's Quarterly* with that. We were in *Weekly World News*.

Al Ennis: Crime was so exciting. They were very theatrical. The music was rudimentary, but really powerful straight-ahead punk rock 'n' roll. The stage would be black and these sirens would go off, and cherry tops would be going around, and they'd come on in police uniforms and start hitting these chords.

Jimmy Crucifix: One of the first shows I saw at the Mabuhay was the Sleepers and Crime. I was about 18 or 19. I needed money to get back home, so I brought a bunch of pot to sell. I was standing by the bathroom, and a guy in a cop uniform looked at me, and saw me with a fuckin' bag of pot, and I went in the girls' bathroom and flushed it down the toilet. And then I saw him up onstage playing.

Dave Chavez: I thought their gimmick was great. Cops, gangsters, fedoras—one time it was tuxedos. They were just cool. They always had a look. And they spent time with it.

They were the first ones to start the low microphone thing. Where you put the microphone real low so you have to have your legs out when you're playing. They kinda reminded me of Link Wray. His music was much better.

Danny Furious: I loved it when Frankie would wear a candy striper's dress onstage. Crime were so pretentious and lovable.

Jimmy Crucifix: It was like when you went to see KISS, except in the punk rock world. Here was this band playing that couldn't even tune their guitars. But it sounded so good.

Klaus Flouride: Crime were visually such an assault on your senses. Those guys had rubber faces, too. And they would say, "Oh, we're not part of the punk scene. We're above all that."

James Stark: About the third or fourth gig that Crime and the Nuns played, they played together at the Mabuhay. There was a big battle about who was going to be the headliner. They both figured they were the big guns in town. So the compromise finally reached with the poster was that the names would be the same size on the same line.

Johnny Strike: We decided we would once and for all put an end to this competition thing. I remember telling the group before we went out, "Okay, this is it. We're gonna pull every trick in the book." I remembered the old story of Jerry Lee Lewis setting his piano on fire, and went back and telling Chuck Berry, "Now follow that." So we went out, and Frankie was in between my legs playing, we were rolling around the stage. We played like a ten-minute set or something, as insane as possible. We went off, and the audience went on for it seemed forever. We went back and the Nuns were just kinda sitting back there looking at us, "You fuckers."

James Stark: It got pretty intense, because they both rehearsed at the same space. They never had anything good to say about each other. I thought it was kind of ridiculous. If they'd been more cooperative, they could have actually built it into something bigger. It was all crash and burn.

Hank Rank: We imagined that the whole world revolved around us. We imagined these conspiracies and rivalries and all these things that were going on, but most people were pretty much just struggling to do whatever it was they were trying to do. With the Nuns, a lot of our problems were in our own minds.

Photo by James Stark

Rough Trade: Crime's Frankie Fix and Johnny Strike with Howie Klein

Johnny Strike: They still are.

Sheriff Mike Hennessey: I was a young lawyer at the time, working in the county jail. So I was attracted to the group Crime. They looked tough and sinister, and they played loud and fast.

Johnny Strike: We played a gig at San Quentin in police outfits.

Joe Rees: The Crime gig was a part of Bread and Roses, a group that organized a lot of charity events. We showed up and went through this whole routine. They had to let you know your rights, and if you were taken prisoner, they shot first and asked questions later. They couldn't give you any security at all once you were inside the gate.

Hank Rank: This was '77, '78. We were out in the exercise yard in the sun, in these dark blue police uniforms. Sirhan Sirhan was there at the time. A friend of mine was a prison guard there. He pointed to the window where he was.

Johnny Strike: We followed a country and western group.

Hank Rank: There was sort of a demilitarized zone between the stage and the prisoners. There was a rope, and then the prisoners were all behind that. And they really divided right down the mid-dle, blacks on one side and non-blacks on the other. When a black group would play, all of the non-blacks would stand up and move to the far side of the yard. When a non-black group would play, the exact opposite would happen. So when we hit the stage, they all got up and moved away.

Joe Rees: The poster from that day, it was one of those great S&M posters that Crime always put out, of this female dressed in black leathers. A bunch of the inmates got their hands on those posters, flashing them in front of the camera.

Hank Rank: It was a tough crowd. They didn't exactly get the music, and the guards up on the tower with their guns, looking down, shaking their heads. Nobody there knew what to make of us.

Joe Rees: Up on the walkway was a black female guard with a high-powered rifle. She had an afro, and it was bleached blond. You'd think that she was part of the show. Policemen performing the music. Inmates with their eyes hanging out. It was so bizarre.

Johnny Strike: Frankie was so nervous, he was popping Valiums. By the time he hit the stage, I looked over at him and I was like, "Oh man. He's totally out to lunch, he's singing the wrong song." Somehow we pulled it off.

Edwin Heaven: Seymour Stein met with the Nuns, and wanted to bring us into Sire. One weekend we were staying at the Tropicana on Sunset Strip, staying there with Blondie and the Ramones. You would not believe how white everyone was, three o'clock in the afternoon light. We all knew everybody was gonna make it. There was no doubt in our mind.

Hank Rank: The thing to remember was that before the term "punk rock" was codified, there was no coherent look to the crowd. So you still had a lot of holdovers from the rock people. You had rock chicks there with big hair, you had guys with big hair, you had guys with satin jackets, rock gear. And then you had just sort of college kids.

But there was this report on one of the evening magazine shows. It was the first report of the Sex Pistols, footage of them from England. This new thing called "punk rock." It was the first shot of spiky hair, safety pins in the cheeks, torn T-shirts. the first place where people learned how to dress punk. And pogo. The next day, that's what happened. Everybody knew what to do. Those clothes hit town and everything changed.

James Stark: The very next punk show at the Mabuhay, it was like, "Oh yeah. Here's how it works." It changed overnight. And it lost a lot. Because before that, punk could be anything.

Penelope Houston: We saw that, and friends of mine were telling me about punk and describing how people tore their clothes up and safety-pinned them back together. So, without ever having seen a photo or anything, we started safety-pinning signs and Xeroxes onto our clothes.

Rozz Rezabek: If you went to any show at the Old Waldorf, or any-place that had an actual ticket, you'd take your ticket stub and put a safety pin on it. So people would have old white dress shirts with a bunch of safety pins with ticket stubs, from all the differ-ent punk shows they'd been to.

Jimmy Crucifix: When Channel 5 KPIX news first did "Punk Rock Hits San Francisco," they actually put the Mab on. The picture they showed was my friend Mike Trengali from the Street Punks, all wrapped up in Christmas lights, half naked, playing the piano.

Jello Biafra: There were rumors of a scene in San Francisco. I was ready for a new form of rebellion but wasn't aware of what it was or how significant it was. Plus I knew I liked music that hardly anybody else cared about at all. I went there with my friend Mike Ellis from Santa Cruz who was into punk. We just decided Friday night or whatever it was, the Mabuhay. This was fall of '77. So we go there and after we paid to get in we realized we'd gone to heavy metal night.

Metal night is not what metal is now. You didn't have extreme metal, death metal, black metal or very much good metal. It was just the last dying dregs of wannabe stadium rock with a little bit of moldy glam thrown on. And not one good song between the three bands we saw that night.

Some punk rockers appeared at the front of the stage and really began to fuck with the metal bands. One in particular was stick-ing his tongue out and making faces. He was dressed for what was punk at the time, a beat-up old suit and a little skinny tie. Mike recognized him as somebody he went to high school with, at a school for Americans in England. It turned out, yes, it was indeed his friend Russell Wilkinson. But now he'd changed his name to Will Shatter.

He was friendly and said, "You want to be in a band?" "I don't know, I can't play anything!" "I've been playing bass for three days and I'm in a band! We're playing tomorrow night."

That was a house party, a pretty infamous place that I think used to be a printing press on 8th and Howard. That night it was the Avengers and Will's band, Grand Mal, which sure enough sounded like they'd been playing for three days. The singer was Don Vinil who went on to start the Offs. Will and Craig the guitarist went on to start Negative Trend. That was where I found the real stuff.

4

Teenage Rebel

Al Ennis: The Avengers were immensely popular. Penelope was an incredible writer. Almost everything she wrote turned into an anthem. It's melodic, but powerful. Greg Ingraham played guitar, very underrated guitarist. They had the punk look down without even trying.

Jello Biafra: They were way faster and more direct than a lot of what was being called punk throughout the world. They had spiked hair like the British bands did, and paint on some of the clothes. Which was not really something done in New York, except by Richard Hell, who claims that Malcolm McLaren and the Pistols got it from him.

Danny Furious: San Francisco Art Institute was a refuge for lost souls. We liberated one of the painting studios and set up house, complete with stove, fridge, sleeping bags and bags of speed. Hung a "Keep Out" sign on the door. The administration threw us out and turned Room 113 into a storage facility.

Penelope Houston: We started in June of '77. I had friends that had gone to art school with Danny Furious, and he dropped out or graduated or something.

Danny Furious: Penelope came to school every day dressed to the nines, with full makeup and '50s polka-dot dresses, petticoats, high heels and jewelry. She was stunning.

Penelope Houston: Danny said he was starting this band with his friend from Orange County, Greg, and they had stuff set up in a warehouse on Third Street.

Danny Furious: At that point we were just rehearsing old Stones and various other sundry garage.

Penelope Houston: I was hanging out at the warehouse, and nobody was there. The P.A. was set up, and I started messing around. When they came back from wherever they were, I was like, "I'm gonna be your singer." And they were like, okay. So we did one show at the warehouse where we just did cover songs. And then we went to L.A. and the Screamers told me, "You gotta write your own material. You can't do cover songs."

We had a show one week later playing at the Mabuhay for this party the Nuns were throwing. Nobody had ever heard of us. We'd only been together for about two weeks. And in that one week, we wrote like six original songs. A couple of them lasted, "Car Crash" and "I Believe in Me." "My Boyfriend's a Pinhead." One called "Vernon Is a Fag." "Vernon Is a Fag" was graffiti all over San Francisco at that time.

We made it through one song, and the band started playing the second song, and I was like, "I don't even know what song this is. This doesn't even sound familiar to me." They were playing two different songs. And then, after a few measures, they just stopped playing and everyone looked up and said, "What are you playing?" "I'm playing this." "Well, I'm playing that." And then we figured out that the set list had been wrong.

And we went from there. I was an art student, and I was living on my scholarship. Jimmy worked at a restaurant, and he's the source of the song "White Nigger." I don't know if Greg had a job or not. I don't think Danny had a job. He just bossed everybody around.

We all lived together, sharing apartments with other punk rockers. When I did a gig I would take the money and put it in one of my coat pockets in a closet. Like, here's the rent money. Here's some money for the bills, put 'em in another coat pocket. And then when the time of month came around to pay bills or rent, I would be going through all my pockets in the closet trying to find that money.

There was no scene outside of North Beach. The Haight was just dead—burnt-out, drugged-out hippies. South of Market there were a couple places to play, but nothing regular. Some people lived in warehouses out on Third Street.

We played the Mabuhay a lot. Like two nights every month. Once Dirksen realized we drew people.

Edwin Heaven: The Nuns introduced the Avengers at a show in Rodeo, it was a biker club. Penelope was very Art Institute, her fashions were perfectly sliced and cut, safety pins everywhere. Rodeo didn't like the Avengers at all.

Penelope Houston: It was maybe our third or fourth show. This is like when Billie Joe Armstrong was five or something. They were biker types, and they wanted to kill us. Not me so much because I was a girl. They wanted to rape me first. But I remember thinking, "Why are we here?"

Dennis Kernohan: She had just moved here from Seattle, was a freshman at the Art Institute. She came strolling in, in her little pink poodle outfit, with her little skirt and little purse. Next time I saw her she was in a ripped T-shirt, no bra, totally punked out. Ever since that night in the pink poodle outfit I've been madly in love with her.

Joe Rees: Penelope was so gorgeous. She was always this untouchable kind of person. She wasn't sociable. She socializes a hell of a lot more now than she ever did then. In those days she was always the mysterious woman. Every guy in the world would love to have been her partner.

Aaron Cometbus: Penelope is the woman every boy *and girl* in the East Bay grew up wanting to marry.

Billie Joe Armstrong: I got into the Avengers through Aaron. He had these amazing archives and I remember looking at all these old pictures of her.

Sheriff Mike Hennessey: The Avengers were my favorite group, because of their lyrics. Not just punk rock songs, but political lyrics like "The American in Me," "We Are the One." They were just really great message songs for the rebellious youth types. And of course, Penelope Houston was kind of a dream, too.

Dennis Kernohan: Live, they were incredible. When they were at their peak, they were the best band in the whole scene. Bar none. Better than the Kennedys. They made everyone else look like monkeys. Jimmy Wilsey was a lead guitar player playing bass. Greg could play Black Sabbath in his sleep. And play it faster than anyone else on earth. They were definitely a fake punk band. They were a very good fake punk band. One of the best. But yeah, fake, through and through.

Penelope Houston: I don't remember radio being something that we had any access to. Rodney on the ROQ, we did a few times. And then up here, there was one show on KUSF, maybe Howie Klein

Photo by James Stark

We Are the One: Penelope Houston and Danny Furious of the Avengers

did it. All week long you waited for this one show to happen. Once in awhile you could get on it. So we started playing other cities.

Danny Furious: We went up to Vancouver in early '78 to do a show with DOA and the Dishrags. We pulled up to the venue, and this big, beefy, biker type skinhead punk approached our van. Took me by the hand, very politely said, "Hi, I'm Joey Shithead. Welcome to Vancouver!" I nearly pissed my pants.

Penelope Houston: L.A. loved us. They pretended that we were from L.A. because two of our members were from there. We played the Masque a lot, eventually the Whisky. The Go-Gos, X, the Weirdos opened for us. It's funny, all the people that opened for us. How far they went, and how far we didn't go.

Dave Chavez: Negative Trend, I don't know how long they were together. I think it was less than two years. If anything, they were one of the heavier bands. They weren't fast like hardcore became, but they were heavy like hardcore. A very important band, too. They had Will Shatter's beautiful voice that to this day I still think is one of the greatest voices from any of the scenes.

Jello Biafra: Rozz was the most electrifying part of that band. Our local Iggy.

Johnny Genocide: Rozz took the front man persona to the limits, beyond anything anyone was doing at the time.

Rozz Rezabek: I was living with these teenage girls in Portland. I had been hanging out with these people that all listened to Mott the Hoople, Bowie, Lou Reed and Iggy, the glitter kind of crowd. There wasn't really much else. And then all of a sudden the Ramones came up, and we started hearing about stuff over in England. We heard the only place you could even get those records or hear them on the radio was San Francisco. So we had to go.

Me and these three stripper girls, Jane, Pammy and Debbie Sue, headed off to San Francisco together in Debbie's big old '56 Buick. Debbie Sue was able to get an apartment and she had already met up with Craig and Will Shatter, they were in a band called Grand Mal.

Will Shatter was always on. He was always kinda snide and sarcastic. The way he would talk kinda sounded like an English accent, almost like a Valley guy. He was from Gilroy. He never let any of that on. To us, he was from England. But we kinda knew he just went over to England.

So Debbie Sue was with Craig, and Will was with Pammy. Pammy and Will had the couch, and I had a pile of cardboard behind the couch. They were like, "This is Rozz from Portland, you gotta put him in the band."

They were saying, "You can't be in the band unless you get a punk haircut." I had kinda long Peter Frampton hair. I'd fought my dad so long to finally be able to grow my hair out. And I was like, "No, then I'm not gonna do it." Then I did one show with them. I just came in and pushed Don Vinil offstage after about six songs and said, "I'm the new singer."

Danny Furious: They managed to pull off a coup at the Mabuhay that night, Rozz jumping stage mid-show and basically not allowing poor Don Vinil to continue.

Rozz Rezabek: The next time we played, I broke my arm. We played this party with the Avengers at Iguana Studios. All the bands, Dils, Avengers, everybody rehearsed at Iguana Studios for eight dollars an hour. But in the big main room there was a big showcase for Sandy Pearlman, the producer who had just done Blue

Oyster Cult's "Don't Fear The Reaper." We thought it was big and important, because we were all like 17 at the time. But it was not really important at all. He was really there just to see the Avengers.

Everybody was getting entangled in all the microphone cords. I tripped over a cord and broke my arm. I went to the hospital and was supposed to be waiting around for the cast. But we were punk rockers, we were impatient. I wanted to get back to the party and see what Sandy Pearlman thought of the band. So I went back. The arm was all fucked up and got broken again, because I didn't really have a cast on it. I just had these makeshift wraps.

The story got bigger and bigger. It was in *Rolling Stone*: "In the grand tradition of Iggy Pop, Negative Trend lead singer Rozz, a frisky beanpole of a lad, fell offstage breaking his arm to pieces. And his arm was a shattered bloody wreck." And then it got picked up in *New York Rocker*. When actually all I did was trip over a cord.

We thought it was gonna be this big, big deal, playing in front of Sandy Pearlman. It was years after that, before any punk bands got signed to any labels.

The Avengers were really nice to us. They could really play, just gorgeous music. And same with the Dils. Those guys didn't see us as a threat. We were just kinda the California Sex Pistols, destroying and breaking furniture. So those guys put us on their bills, to take the pressure off their set or something. It was a nice little chaotic bit of anarchy.

Danny Furious: Rozz would jump onto tables, knock everyone's drinks over. Just basically being as obnoxious as possible.

Rozz Rezabek: What people liked is that our shows were spontaneous. You went to fuckin' Crime and the Nuns, you knew exactly what you were gonna get. You knew Jeff Olener was gonna pull out his fake teeth during this song. You knew that Johnny Strike was gonna turn on some stupid cop lights on the back of their amplifiers.

But at a Negative Trend show, you didn't know if everybody was gonna smash every table and chair in the joint, cover it with an American flag, douse it with gasoline, and start a fire in the middle of the dance floor. We always ended up owing Dirk money, because of the shit that would get destroyed.

Ian MacKaye: I was quite a student of the West Coast punk scene at the time. Negative Trend, we thought of them as one of the greatest bands that ever existed. The fact that they were San Francisco was just really clear. San Francisco people were really wired. They were jittery, like speed people. And they were kind of crunchy.

Rozz Rezabek: We had a song "Blow Out Kennedy's Brains Again." We'd start sloppin' these big slimy gray cow brains. You could get 'em at any market. You could even get 'em on food stamps. We would use food stamps to buy props.

Bruce Loose: I would always have an interaction with Rozz onstage. Grabbing, pulling him onto the ground, we'd be rolling around on the floor. I did a dance called the Worm at the time, where everybody'd be pogoing, and I'd be lying on the floor wriggling around, trying to knock people over. I got stomped on a lot, but, you know.

Rozz Rezabek: We were like the first punk band to tour the West Coast, and when we went up to Seattle we did not disappoint. The club had this eight-foot painting of Marie Osmond in a wedding dress. When we went up onstage we went crazy, and her painting got a hole ripped in a specific place. People took what we were doing and went with it, and went even nutsier. It was a line of crazy Seattle punks gangbanging a painting of Marie Osmond.

When we got outside of San Francisco, we could still shock and awe people. In San Francisco, people had to go further and further. Some sort of B&D situation where they just wanted to take it further further further. There's no safe word in punk.

Jello Biafra: Rozz was in so much pain he basically left the band to save himself.

Rozz Rezabek: I ended up on a bunch of Percodan and stuff. I was 17 years old. Drinking beer for the first time. I'm taking all these pills, and my arm is all screwed up. Then I started having epileptic seizures. I'd put my head through walls, and waking up with blood in my hair. I didn't think I was too long for this world if I stayed in the band.

Bruce Loose: They were looking for another singer. I went to the Negative Trend singer tryout. Jon Binell was there. Jello Biafra was there. And they did not take him. Because he went, "Oooooohhhhaahhhahh!" I got up and I went, "Idon'tknowwhattosing Idon'tknowwhattosing." So I didn't get the job either.

Jello Biafra: It was a cattle call, so I auditioned, Bruce auditioned, a woman named Stephanie Krieschock. She and I bumped into each other 20 years later at a (Sc)Avengers show. We looked at each other and said, wow, cool—a reunion of the singers rejected by Negative Trend!

5

Giddyup Mutants

Al Ennis: The Mutants had their own scene. As a lot of these bands did. Especially the Avengers and the Mutants and the Offs, they were in San Francisco for a long time, and they knew a lot of people. The Mutants had a lot of really good fun songs.

Danny Furious: I liked the Mutants. Everyone did. They were the B-52s without the catchy tunes. Very charming bunch.

Joe Rees: The Mutants were like the scene band. They were always with the Avengers, always with the Dils. They seemed to be on every bill. It was such a big group of people. You not only get the Mutants, you get everyone.

They had a giant studio right near the bus station. Not only did a lot of the Mutants live there, but also photographer friends, and friends from god knows where. There were 25 to 30 people living in that place, somewhere in sleeping bags. They'd have their practice sessions, and everyone would just have to work around it. If you stayed with the Mutants, it was gonna be a continuous 24-hour party. It was an insane asylum. It was great.

Sheriff Mike Hennessey: I remember seeing the Mutants on Thanksgiving, and they actually dressed up as turkeys and pumpkins. They were kooky and fun and more sort of hard rock than punk rock, maybe, but quite edgy, and good harmonies.

Fritz Fox: The very first show we did, we threw dead fish out into the audience. Each show had a different theme. You know when you see somebody walking down the street with paper sticking to their feet? We thought, "Oh man, that's cool, we gotta do that." So we had a show where we put newspapers all over the stage, and then sprayed the bottom of our feet with adhesive. And then

I saw these big appliance boxes for refrigerators. I said, if the singers got into these boxes, and the audience couldn't see us, and the band's playing, and we're singing from within the boxes, it'll drive the audience nuts. So we did that. And then we did one where we had lights taped on sticks, and mounted these photographic lights and reflectors, and put those on our backs. And had lights shining over our heads. I smashed televisions, and I smashed record players.

In the midst of all of this chaos and stage stuff, we began to actually write some really good songs. Not very many people knew how to play. Brendan and myself were the only musicians that had experience. It was pretty amateurish. But I thought that naivete would lend to the chaotic ambiance, and that it would translate for people.

Dirk Dirksen: I used to tease both the Mutants and Crime about timing their drugs. If we kept them waiting too long, if the sound engineer couldn't get the stuff together, or the drum kit couldn't get set up, then catastrophe would strike. Because the drugs would kick in just at the wrong moment, and they'd collapse on you in the middle of the song.

One particular night at the On Broadway, we said, absolutely no more drinking. We cut the Mutants off at the bar. We didn't know what they'd ingested before they got in the club. But no more drinking until they hit the stage. Security would take booze out of their pockets, go through their guitar cases and drum kits.

We had put out five or six six-packs in various spots of the stage. Well, Sally, the moment she hit the stage, like *Saturday Night Live*, she just picked up this six-pack and went *glug glug glug*, all six of them in less than 30 seconds. Within a song and a half, she was just flying. We had little cocktail tables. She jumped to the first one, the next one, the next one, just kept walking, kicking drinks off the tables.

Fritz Fox: No matter what we played, we left the stage in shambles. So no one really wanted to follow us. Not because we were the better band or we put on the better show. If we played our music well and we sang right, and didn't get too drunk or fucked up on drugs, we put in a damn good performance. There's a lot of them that were just like total washes. You'd be like, "This is a failure."

Photo by Liam Cutchins

Fun Terminal: The Mutants (really) on fire

"CRAMPS/MUTANTS: Napa State Hospital"

Napa's this giant mental institution in the country, far from everything but vineyards and dairy farms. I got up there at around 7 p.m. and something like 250-300 patients, mostly over 30 and of all races, were milling around an enclosed courtyard while San Francisco's Mutants were setting up their motley equipment on a roped-off, open-air concrete stage. The Mutants are a weird-looking conglomerate of oddly shaped people to begin with. . . . They are the antithesis of what a group is supposed to look like.

From the git-go, everyone started realizing that the lunatics were pretty hip. Like they definitely knew what was going on. One Mutant (of the band variety) yelled out, "Anybody got any pot?" And a patient yelled back, "We got thorazine," and everybody (in the audience) cracked up. Hep cats. . . . When the Mutants went on everybody started pogoing immediately. These people came ALIVE with the music, as if it was electricity turn-

ing on a machine. . . . After the first song the whole place was
going NUTS (pardon the expression). Everybody got to do whatever they wanted and half the audience wound up on the stage,
singing, dancing, milling around the singers, and doing their
weird trips. . . .

Meanwhile two patients escaped over a fence and were seen
running down the highway. ("We don't go after 'em anymore.
They don't have any money and they'll be back in a couple
of days.")

—*Howie Klein,* New York Rocker, *1978*

Fritz Fox: We all drove out there in a big yellow school bus. I think
the Cramps had their own bus. They were standing right on
the edge of being launched into superstardom at that time. This
is the way I felt about it: "Oh, what the hell are they doing
here? They're trying to cash in on our gimmick, our idea." The
gig was offered to us. I think that they just wanted to get in
on it.

Joe Rees: Napa State Mental Hospital. Those people were so excited
that someone was interested enough to put on a free show that
they didn't do any preparation, other than, "Yeah, come on
down." These days, you'd have to go through a security clear-
ance, and have to wait a month to get tested for some kind of
disease. There'd be all kinds of lawyers running around.

Fritz Fox: We didn't know what to think, actually. We were outside
on a raised part of a quadrangle, that was adjacent to their dining
area. We had an audience of very uninhibited participants. Like,
they would imitate what they thought we looked like. It was very
strange. Our music is neurotic, or schizophrenic, it's sort of mental anyway. Inmates were just going bananas. Having little epi-
sodes of something that was cloistered in their brains for a long
time. And some of the participants, we triggered them. It was
very intense.

I took acid that day. Along with Sally. I was out there. It started
out, you're picturing that you were made to do this. But there was
drama in that. 'Cause you're up on the stage, singing these songs,
making fun of yourself, and the way you think. And if you're on
acid, looking out on the audience, you don't see things that are
hilarious, you see things more profound and oblique. You go like,
"Oh man—why are we doing this?"

Joe Rees: He looked pretty silly. But he always did anyway. How could you ever tell whether he is tripping on acid?

Hef: I didn't know about the high on acid part. Why would you need to be high? I mean, just doing that should be enough of a high.

6

Holidays in the Sun

Al Ennis: I'd stop by the newsstand, and you could follow it week by week. Sex Pistols sign with this record company. Next week, Sex Pistols get kicked off. Next week, Sex Pistols get signed again.

Rozz Rezabek: People thought it was gonna be like the whole counter-culture '60s thing. People were really threatened and scared.

Jello Biafra: A Denver store called Wax Trax claimed to have had the first Sex Pistols record in the United States, possibly the day it was released. I went to check it out. Right on the front door of Wax Trax was *John Denver's Greatest Hits*, with nails through his eyes and blood coming out.

Dave Dictor: I lived in Austin and I picked up Gary Floyd hitchhiking. He was going to see the Sex Pistols in Dallas. He asked if I was gonna go. I was like, what? That was the first time I ever heard of the Sex Pistols.

Ruth Schwartz: I was going to Santa Rosa to JC and we saw them on the news: "They're in Texas, oh my god, this band's in Texas! We have to go see them when they come to San Francisco."

Sammytown: When I was 12 we were living in Wales, that's when I first heard the Sex Pistols. It was awesome. When I got back to the States, my dad was like, "Hey, the Sex Pistols are playing in San Francisco." It was on the news, and he called me in to watch. He's like, "Isn't that that band that you were telling me about?"

Sheriff Mike Hennessey: I heard that they were coming to Winterland, and dragged my girlfriend—who's now my wife—to see that show.

Danny Furious: I received a phone call in early December from a Mr. Howie Klein, asking if the Avengers were interested in opening for the upcoming Sex Pistols show. Naturally I said, "Yes!" He went on to say we'd only be paid 100 bucks and that if that wasn't okay, there were literally hundreds of bands who would play for nada. That didn't sit well with me but we accepted, of course.

Johnny Strike: I got a call from Bill Graham's people. "Do you want to open for the Sex Pistols?" I said, "Yes, absolutely. We'll take it." Everybody was excited. About two weeks later we got another call. "Well, something happened. It turns out that the Avengers met Malcolm [McLaren] and so they've got that slot, but we still want you guys on the bill. You'll have the third slot." So I went back and talked with the band. It was unanimous. We're not playing.

Hank Rank: We wouldn't open for the Avengers. The Avengers always opened for us. We were the senior band 'cause we formed a good two months before they did. It was a little longer than that. But that was our thinking.

Johnny Strike: Not only did we not play, we didn't go. We completely boycotted the show.

Steve Tupper: Whatever was going on in their brains, I never knew. Crime totally shot themselves in the foot.

Penelope Houston: The Nuns, who did open for us, called me up and said, "Do you want to switch places?" And I was like, "No." We'd only been together six months, and I think that the other established San Francisco punk bands really thought they should be on the bill.

Jennifer Miro: We almost didn't get it. Bill Graham just hated us, but Jerry Pompili was kind of managing us, and he was Bill's right-hand man. And he really liked us.

Howie Klein: This is terrible and I don't know if this has ever been written before. I feel bad about saying this, but I'm gonna tell it. Malcolm McLaren came over to me and goes, "Who's the worst band in the scene?" And I said, "Well, Negative Trend." He said, "They're godawful?" I said, "They're absolutely godawful." He said, "Can they play?" I said, "No, not at all." He said, "Okay, can you find them for me?"

Bill had already put the show together, and Malcolm comes in and says, "We want this band opening for us." He said he wouldn't play if they weren't on the show. So then Bill says, "Okay, you want them on the show? They're the headliner." So Malcolm went for that.

Rozz Rezabek: We were excited because it's true, we *were* the worst band in San Francisco! And all of a sudden we're at the scene of this big swirling controversy 48 hours before the show, where the headline act, the Sex Pistols, is not gonna play unless Negative Trend is on the bill.

    We didn't know if we were gonna play. The night before the show, we took our posters and made this Negative Trend symbol about 30 feet high, on the side of Winterland, with wheat paste. Cans and cans of spray paint. We got it bad. I don't know what got into us. Bill Graham was furious. Furious. He called us a "Nouveau Revolutionary Band."

Penelope Houston: It was sold out. There were between 5 and 6,000 people. The biggest show we'd ever played, and it was the biggest show the Sex Pistols had ever played at that point.

Insane Jane: Me and my foster brother Mike Munoz showed up at 10:30 in the morning in our ripped-up army jackets with Vaseline in our hair. There were two girls already in line, one of them was wearing a yellow, Devo-style jumpsuit. This punk dude strides up and says, "So, you're gonna be first in line, eh?" The two girls jumped up and squealed, "Sid! Sid!" and had him sign a copy of *Never Mind the Bollocks*, which he deeply gouged his signature into. He seemed very happy when my brother told him he was ten years old. Then some dude jumped out of a car and said, "Anybody have an extra ticket for sale?" Sid mockingly repeated what the guy said, then snatched off the dude's wraparound shades and threw them into the street. Sid then took off, saying, "See ya later inside."

Jennifer Blowdryer: I definitely put on my "Anarchy" T-shirt and some horrible off-suede lace-up open-toe boots I'd found in a thrift store, and a slip. A woman on BART called me "sister," thinking I was a whore or something. I was so offended.

Jennifer Miro: Johnny Rotten was hanging around, it was nerve-wracking but it was just *so* cool. There was no punk in L.A. yet. It was so behind San Francisco.

Danny Furious: I remember John onstage alone after their sound check, while I was setting up my kit for ours. He looked like the unhappiest, angriest person in the world. And then in bounced Sid, trying to con me out of the hammer/sickle T-shirt the Dils had loaned me for the show. When I looked up, Rotten had fucked off, so I never had the chance to have my head tore off by him by saying hello.

Bruce Loose: I found thousands of pairs of those glasses that the doctor gives you when they put drops in your eyes to keep the light out. At Goodwill, for like a nickel, I bought 100 dollars' worth, and I scratched "Sex" in one lens, "Pistols" in the other. Filled them in with DayGlo paint, and tried to hand them out. I had a little past shoulder-length hair. These English punks that came along with the Sex Pistols would take them from my hand, throw them on the ground and step on them. Push me on the shoulder. Give me all this attitude.

James Stark: It was one of the most intense, chaotic shows I've ever been to. It was just mayhem. Everybody was jumping and yelling, a constant barrage of flying projectiles. I tried to get up close to take some photographs and it was just impossible. People came from L.A. and up north and from all over. You had a lot of kids from the suburbs.

Gary Floyd: It was a real opportunity for people to strut their punkness. "The Sex Pistols are here, and here we are in San Francisco and we're punks, too, and we have weird hair and we're going to do our shit tonight!" Everybody was just strutting like it was a little parade. It was very surreal.

Sheriff Mike Hennessey: I remember sitting up in the balcony with Beverly. The crowd was loud and obnoxious and yelling. And when the Sex Pistols came on, a lot of people were heaving spit. I knew the music already, because I'd had the album. It was loud, and hard to understand.

Steve Tupper: Up at the stage, you couldn't move at all, crushed in from all sides. As an experiment, first I raised one foot, and then the other off the floor. And just hung there for a couple seconds.

Jennifer Miro: I was dating Brittley Black, who was in Crime, and he broke up with me the night before the show. So I was crying the whole night. I went on first, all by myself, the very first person on the stage, and I was wearing this green taffeta vampire-collared mini-dress with black spike-heeled boots. I was terrified, in the spotlight, and I just stood there, and they cheered. After that, you can't go back to a normal life.

Penelope Houston: There were only maybe 500 punks between L.A. and San Francisco. So who were the other 5,500 people? The crowd was frightening, that's what I really remember about it most. The stage was covered in spit when the Nuns were done. And I walked out and slipped on a big gob. I didn't hit the ground but almost. I was scared. "Everybody, um, take a couple steps back because the people in the front here are turning blue."

Danny Furious: We were nervous. We'd never played for more than a couple hundred, at best. When I hit my snare, the volume from the drum monitor behind me literally knocked me off my stool. I'd never had a drum monitor.

Jennifer Blowdryer: The Sex Pistols didn't play very long. I didn't pay too much attention, 'cause they didn't seem that serious or engaging, so why would I be? I went to the ladies room and there was this woman, Blondine, who had like part dark blond, part light blond hair, and some kind of silver short trench coat, and bright blue eye shadow. I was attracted to that. Really, the stripper in the bathroom made the biggest impression on me.

Penelope Houston: Sid was really not a good bass player. The other members of the band were holding it together. And Johnny Rotten probably knew it was their last show.

Dennis Kernohan: The Avengers blew them away. The Avengers *killed* the Sex Pistols that night. So much so that Malcolm McLaren wanted to produce them.

Howie Klein: I was on the stage for the whole show. People were throwing coins, which Bill Graham and I picked up afterwards. I was going for the quarters, he was going for everything.

Penelope Houston: The Sex Pistols went off to a dressing room up in some offices. We were backstage, hanging out with Negative Trend and some of the Nuns.

Howie Klein: I was watching the Sex Pistols' equipment coming off the stage and it was just a circus. Everyone started leaving except for the same 25 people that would have seen Negative Trend anyway. I felt bad for them.

Rozz Rezabek: We thought we were going to go on. These guys were leadin' us, then the next thing I knew, they were shoving us out a side door. And then we were let back in. Immediately. But our instruments had mysteriously disappeared, and the house lights were up, "Greensleeves" was playing. They said, "Go ahead. You're on!" I was like, "Where are our instruments?"

There was a huge backstage area and we just started destroying stuff. There was like 60 garbage cans full of little Olympia beers, we knocked every single one over. These little six-ounce cans, we were throwin' 'em like snowballs. There was ice about two inches deep through the back area.

There was a hot dog cart, so I asked for two hot dogs with relish and threw them at the first person that had a camera light. There was all the major networks there: ABC, CBS, NBC, doing a live-for-TV thing. Britt Ekland was there, Rod Stewart's girlfriend at the time, so I fuckin' slammed hot dogs right in her face! We were completely rioting, and nobody seemed to stop us.

Ginger Coyote: The Sex Pistols were staying over at the Miyako Hotel and I remember going by there. Rumor had it that Zsa Zsa Gabor was also staying at the hotel and had been partying with Steve Jones.

Jennifer Miro: We were whisked away in a limousine to a party. Sid Vicious kissed me on the head and he invited us all to stay with him in London. He was very polite. There was this long line of people shooting heroin.

Rozz Rezabek: I remember bits and pieces of the after-parties. This one place in the Haight, they were just like knocking down the walls, to the drywall. And Sid occupying the bathroom. He peed his pants a bunch. He was drinking peppermint schnapps. We were like, "Why are all these girls all over him?"

Danny Furious: Sid fucked off with Lamar and other punk junkies to the Haight where he OD'd. The Avengers went to the Mabuhay to very little fanfare. I went home to bed, wondering just what had happened.

Rozz Rezabek: I don't remember anything 'til a couple days later, waking up with really chapped lips on the beach.

7

You Are One of Our Lesser Audiences

Al Ennis: It was a very exciting time historically. You had the assassinations of Moscone and Harvey Milk, then later on after the Dan White trial you had the White Night riots, and all the punks were out there rioting and burning cop cars. You had the Golden Dragon massacre in Chinatown. Tuxedomoon had a song about the Joe Boys, one of the big San Francisco Chinese gangs at the time. You had the People's Temple based here. That was all during the heyday of punk.

It was also the golden age of the serial killer. You had Gacy killing all the kids, you had the Hillside Strangler down in L.A. You had the Son of Sam in New York. There were *songs* about this stuff. A Texas band did a song called "People's Temple." There were bands that did songs about the Hillside Strangler, about Gacy, about Son of Sam.

In retrospect, I think of punk as folk music of the time. Because if you go back to old blues music, old calypso music, Mexican border music, if there was a hurricane, or an assassination, people would put out songs by the next week. This is how fast things were moving. People would come out with songs about all this kind of stuff.

Danny Furious: Beyond a doubt the Dils were and remain my favorite S.F. band. Although originally from Carlsbad they were nauseated by the shallowness of the L.A. scene, and moved to a much more receptive San Francisco. Tony was the smart guy, Chip the pothead. Together with various drummers, they were perhaps the best band in the world.

Chip Kinman: The Dils were one of the few punk rock bands that would play ballads. Most bands wouldn't do it. We thought slowing down was as radical as playing really fast. At that point, it probably was, because everyone was getting faster and faster.

Dave Chavez: Chrome was a band that a lot of people don't remember. It was very influential on bands like the Swans and stuff later. I got to see 'em once and they did the best show. It was like a total magic act. There were puffs of smoke and tin foil wrapped on everything. They disappeared and appeared. There was a lot more multimedia in the early first wave of punk, a lot more ingenuity.

Steve Tupper: The Liars were really great live. They were about halfway between '77 punk and power pop. Very energetic and very poppy and melodic. They would get everybody in the room pogoing every time.

Dennis Kernohan: We had the most requested song on KSAN, "Sudden Fun." It was a minute and a half long. Later, we changed the band's name to Sudden Fun. 'Cause it was our favorite song. We never were trying to get a record. We never tried to do anything, actually.

Al Ennis: Don Vinil was one of the first scene-makers at Mabuhay Gardens. I used to always see him around, and next thing you know, he was up onstage with his band. A lot of the songs the Offs did had a big reggae influence. Later on they brought in a sax player. Very punky.

James Stark: Don worked at a record store in the Castro. You'd go there, and when he was working you could steal all the records you wanted. He'd cover for you.

Jello Biafra: There was a good-natured competition between me and Don Vinil when we were living together. Who would come up with the next new song, and how different would it be from our other songs.

Klaus Flouride: There was a guy that played in the scene, and he had a song called "On the Ward Again." Ralph Pheno.

Dirk Dirksen: Ralph did a record chart, the "Rotten Record Chart," to give the punk scene in San Francisco some legitimacy. It gave the area a real cohesiveness. Ralph at the time was heavily doing ecstasy. Later on, Ralph went outside and took a can of gas and set himself on fire. It was an unfortunate loss.

Jimmy Crucifix: We started a band called the Next. With Brittley Black, who had been in the Readymades and Crime, and me on guitar. Our first gig was with Crime, Pearl Harbor and the Explosions, and Dead Kennedys. We actually brought chickens with top hats and bow ties. Just put 'em on with little rubber bands. We let 'em loose onstage. And we destroyed all our equipment.

Brittley put so much flash powder in his drums and around the stage, it fucking burnt everybody's eyelashes and eyebrows off in the front row. The Mabuhay was full of smoke and chickens running around, *bockbock bockbockbock*, with bow ties and top hats. They closed Broadway Street down.

Sheriff Mike Hennessey: Some groups were just hilarious to go watch. Jennifer Blowdryer. They had great names.

Jennifer Blowdryer: Legionnaire's Disease were kind of funny 'cause they were a couple of Vietnam vets.

Jello Biafra: Part of what made the Mabuhay succeed was, there was none of this standard '70s-bar-band, three-sets-a-night crap. You played your 20 minutes and got off the stage. You just had to play your best material. Or in many cases, your only material.

It was all so new that there wasn't a set regulation way to do things. You couldn't decide how you wanted your punk band to sound by listening to a million other punk or hardcore bands. There weren't enough of them. It wasn't "every band should sound the same 'cause then your friends will like you and you'll instantly get an audience." No. It was, "Every band must sound different from every other band, or none of us are gonna be interested."

Dirk Dirksen: DOA was a bunch of really dedicated Canadians who hitchhiked down for their first gig.

Joey Shithead: It was in 1979, and "Disco Sucks" was getting some play on the local college stations, so we organized this trip down there. Sort of organized. I took the train down, Brad the guitar player hitchhiked down, Chuck and Randy took the bus down. I arrived first 'cause the train was on time.

I met Dirk Dirksen: "Hey, we're DOA." He said, "Okay, where's your band?" "Well, ah, they should be here anytime." He went, "Oh yeah, where's your equipment?" "Well, we don't have any." He said, "You don't have any equipment?" "No. No equipment. Was hoping that we could borrow some." He said, "Are all you fucking Canadians this stupid?" I was like, "Ahhhhh." I didn't know what to say. I was a young puke.

So we played one night with the Avengers, and it went great. The next night we opened for this great old band, Ray Campi and the Rockabilly Rebels. We were like second on the bill, and the place was packed again.

I'd been hanging out with Will Shatter all day. Drinking beer all day long. We went down to Fisherman's Wharf, we'd piss in flower pots in front of tourists. We had a laugh about that. We'd get more beer, blah blah blah.

We got to the gig, and I can't remember what spurred this on, but people were just kinda looking at us like we were from Mars, type thing. Personified the slack-jawed gawker.

Randy Rampage: In the middle of the show there was these three secretary types, out for their punk rock weekend. Sitting on the end of the dance floor at the Mab. They started throwing bottles and glasses at Joe. So he didn't take lightly to that, being the size he was, so he whipped out his cock and decided to piss over the dance floor, onto their table, ya know.

Joey Shithead: I'd been famous for getting a good arc with a lot of distance. When I did that, I knew what Moses felt like. The Red Sea parted, and they ran for cover.

Randy Rampage: He got this huge golden arch going, right? It was like people—"WHOOOOOAAA!" And there was Joe standing there, with this big spray. Right into these girls' drinks. Never got a drop on them. But their drinks were covered, and everything. "That guy pissed in our drinks!"

Well, Dirk was fuckin' goin' mental. The Dead Kennedys were supposed to play after us. They wouldn't let Joe back in the club. Jello said, "If Joe can't get back in the club, we're not gonna fuckin' play." Now the place was gonna riot, 'cause the Dead Kennedys weren't gonna play, 'cause Joe's kicked out of the club. So the bonds were mended.

Joey Shithead: As soon as that was over, they filled up the dance floor again, and went nuts. It was a bizarre thing, but all the people in San Francisco went like, "Oh yeah. DOA's pretty interesting."

Ninja Death: One time Stan Getz showed up wasted to a show by our band, the Emetics. He kept yelling that we needed a sax player. It was obnoxious. Stan managed to drink our whole tab away, then he jumped onstage and played one song a cappella with our punk shit, then went into the Mab alley and got a blow job.

Chester Simpson: Will Shatter and I spent the night in jail when the police raided the Mab. I showed my press pass to the police. They chased me, beat me up, broke my camera, took my film and threw me in jail for obstructing the sidewalk.

A police officer who was in on the raid wrote *New West Magazine*'s "Letters to the Editor." The problem was, he wrote the letter on Police Chief Charles Gainer's stationery and mailed it. So they published the letter in whole.

> I can well appreciate the awe which the raid of Dec. 1 must have struck in the shallow minds of those booger-eating morons who frequent the Mabuhay Gardens, upon seeing 28 of their ilk deposited in my paddy wagon.
>
> —Letter dated January 18, 1979,
> from Sergeant Edward R. Fowlie

Dirk Dirksen: I had my nose broken I think seven times, both ankles screwed up, both my knees, and a broken elbow. So I paid my dues.

Klaus Flouride: I remember Will Shatter being dragged out of the club, and kicking the front door glass through, and giving Dirk a bloody nose, and Dirk saying, "You'll never come back in this place again." And next weekend he's there, and Dirk and him are all being buddy-buddy and insulting each other.

Robert Hanrahan: Dirksen was a visionary showman who enforced his own local version of the record companies' plantation system. He seemed quick to embrace New Wave. But Dirk's Blow Job Machine outside the bathrooms was very cool.

Danny Furious: Dirk Dirksen was a moneygrubbing old carney who saw a buck and chased it. Nothing wrong with that, until he showed his true colors by banning bands that chose to play alternative venues. He wanted to keep the whole thing for himself and his cronies like Howie Klein.

Dirk Dirksen: Howie was there from the beginning. His name at the time was Jack Basher, he had a music column in an advertising paper called the *Progressive*. Cosmo Topper was running Aquarius Records, and he and Howie were friends. Howie and Cosmo had the show on KSAN, *The Outcast Hour*, late at night. Howie evolved that eventually into 415 Records.

Danny Furious: Howie was a scourge on the scene. Being a friend of Jonathan Postal, our original bass player who was sacked for being a complete asshole, he tried to make life hell for the Avengers with bad press, or worse, no press at all. Howie had his own agenda and made out quite well, but I will always see him for what he is, a scumbag opportunist. A no-talent nobody. A con man. The epitome of everything I am against.

James Stark: Michael Kowalsky had been around right from the beginning, he'd been part of the Crime entourage, he was a friend of Ricky Williams, and of De De's. Later on he was part of UXA. But the Mabuhay was very important to him because his home life had been pretty fucked up. He was living the Polk Street type scene. He would hustle. Sell tourists drugs. "Here's some great cocaine." You were lucky if it was powdered sugar.

The Mabuhay scene became very important to people like Michael. There was this one incident where Michael got into a tussle with Dirk and broke his glasses, and Dirk told him, "If you ever want to get back in here again, you gotta pay for these glasses." Michael was a young kid. He didn't have a lot of money. It was maybe 100, 150 dollars. So Michael, very diligently, paid Dirk back. It took him a month or so. And then Dirk let him back in the club.

Joe Rees: The father image. Dirk always liked to play that role. He obviously was older, but at the same time he wanted to play that role as the Bizarro King. Artists, if somebody gives you a theater to perform, you owe them.

Jennifer Blowdryer: I'm glad that there was a tough fag in charge of the club. Because Dirk tolerated me just a little bit, and that's all that I fuckin' needed. And I started performing. I had a lot of anger and I'd been really fucked, and I became the aggressor. I could just let it out, and people thought it was kinda funny.

Sheriff Mike Hennessey: I always loved being there at closing time, because Dirk would get up on the stage, take the microphone away from whoever was performing, and yell insults at the crowd. My favorite one was, "Alright, it's two o'clock. I can't sell any more beer, or make any more money off you, so get out!"

Dirk Dirksen: "Begin moving towards the doors, now. Before we turn loose the police dogs, our tear gas and high-pressure fire hoses. I'm sorry, sir, I can't accept your offer to have sex with me, because I'm already committed. Thank you, good night. Get out."

"I'm sorry to see you're that easily pleased. You should try and show some intelligence and sophistication, and not just accept any slop that's thrown in your trough."

"Tonight's band may not be the best, but you are one of our lesser audiences."

Max Volume: "For the next five minutes you are welcome guests, after that you are unwanted trespassers."

Rozz Rezabek: Ness [Aquino] ran a supper club there. If we came around the side door at Mabuhay at 6:30, Ness would give us

I'm Already Committed: Dirk Dirksen at the Mab

these greasy noodles, that were fried Top Ramen type, like Filipino something. He would feed us all.

Dirk Dirksen: Some of them were too young to actually be in a bar,
but because the Mabuhay served food, we could accommodate.

Jello Biafra: I doubt I would have seen all those great shows or ever
started a band if I'd had to wait 'til I was 21.

Tom Flynn: If you were under 21 they'd put the X on your hand.

Dirk Dirksen: That was the technique to be able to spot them. Out of
that, the huge X's, that became a thing across the country. Everybody had these huge X's, wherever they were doing all-ages
shows.

Ian MacKaye: The Teen Idles went to California in 1980. Dirksen was
letting kids into shows, and he'd put an X on their hands. So we
went back to Washington, to the 930 Club, and we said, "Hey,
we want to see these shows. And we'll put an X on our hands if
you let us in. And if you see us drink, you can kick us out forever." We got the idea from the Mabuhay.

Tom Flynn: Later on they had these curfew shows for minors. You
could be under 18.

Sham Saenz: Being an East Bay kid, going to the city was always kind
of a treat. I'd get onto the F bus with everybody and we rolled it

out to the bus terminal in San Francisco. We all got off and walked up to Broadway whoopin' and hollerin' and drinking 40s and lighting garbage cans on fire and breaking windows, just as much ruckus we could bring. I had to be 11 or 12 years old.

Bonedog: We would panhandle for change to get beer money and to get into the Mabuhay. You went up to the front and you handed Ness a handful of change and you said, "This is all I got." He would count it, a dollar forty two, or whatever. And he'd go, "Oh, come on in."

Dave Ed: I went to On Broadway all the time, upstairs from the Mab. The person working the door would say, "Got ID this week?" "No." He'd wait awhile 'til the line died down. Then he'd look up and down the street to see that there weren't any cops around. "Alright kid, give me your money and get in here."

Audra Angeli-Slawson: My parents owned a restaurant in North Beach, the Mabuhay was three blocks away. My mom would send local police officers to pick me up. They would yell from their car, "Audra, your mother's looking for you." That wasn't really cool. I was like, "Could you pretend to arrest me instead of telling me that my mother's looking for me?" The first time I went to the Mab I was 12. My mother had hired this crazy, coked-out French au pair. I convinced her to let me wear her leather jacket and take me to a show. She thought we were going to the movies. Instead I took her to the Mab.

Sham Saenz: The very first time I went to the city was probably the most memorable. The show was the Dead Kennedys at the On Broadway. We got there and walked in, there was no one onstage. Then all of a sudden these four black guys walked out. At this point I had very little idea that there was punk rock anywhere else in the country. I thought it all happened here. Next thing you know, H.R. stepped out, did a backflip, his feet hit the ground and the band started. It was like the most powerful wall of music I have ever heard in my life. It just blew my mind. It was the Bad Brains. They wore flannel and jeans, but they just fuckin' rocked so hard. That was the first record I ever went out and bought.

Tim Tonooka: After the headlining band played and Dirk announced to get lost, you had to take off running as fast as you could to get to the Transbay Terminal downtown, to make the last F bus at 2:15 a.m. to get to Oakland and Berkeley. If you missed that one, hanging around the terminal until the next bus at daybreak was no fun, because you weren't allowed to sleep there. They had security guards patrolling the place that would poke anyone sitting in the benches that had dozed off.

Dean Washington: One day my buddy said, "Hey, let's go to the Poster Mat over in San Francisco," and so we went to North Beach, strollin' around. The Poster Mat was run by an old man, he looked like one of the Freak Brothers. He had all the classics from the Fillmore, everything that went through Winterland.

We were just hangin' out, and at one point I saw a gal walking this guy. This guy had to have been almost seven feet tall, and he had a collar around his neck, and she literally walked him. I looked at my buddy and I go, "Let's follow them, I think they're going to the right spot." Which took us to Mabuhay Gardens.

I'd never seen anything like it in my life. I was 14 or 15. And it was just unreal. What's with these safety pins, and piercings and whatnot? The alleyway of the Mabuhay, people were hangin' out with not a care in the world. I thought, "Why is the rest of the world so uptight, and not hangin' out like these people are and havin' fun?" I definitely had to go back for more.

James Stark: Posters had been a tradition in San Francisco, from the '60s, the psychedelic thing. Punk rock came along and stepped it up a couple of notches.

Winston Smith: I saw a friend of mine making a poster for the Stranglers. So I started making up posters for bands that didn't exist. They didn't have any date, they'd say, "Friday." And they'd have an address which would not exist. Some of them were up for a long, long time.

Lenny and the Spitwads, Crib Death—there's been a bunch of bands since then called Crib Death. Half Life, another bunch of bands with that name. PTA and the Dipshits. The Infidels. The Cooties. One was called the Anonymous Technicians. I had heard about this new form of execution in the late '70s. Instead of the gas chamber or electric chair, the subject would be wheeled into a room, and three anonymous technicians would insert hypodermics. So I thought, oh, that'd be a great name for a band.

At the time, it wasn't like you could go to Kinko's or anything. It was coin-operated machines, at the library or Rexall. Real crappy paper, bad resolution. But that was part of the look, too.

The Twits: Fake flyer by Winston Smith

Courtesy of Winston Smith

Artistically, it was kind of like sloppy Dada stuff from the First World War.

Aaron Cometbus: I found my first flyer on the way to Hebrew school. Crime, with the Bush Tetras.

James Stark: It was all flyers, word of mouth. There was no outside media. People were really starving for this stuff. It was still a true underground. After awhile there started to be enough people around with different skills and abilities—"Well, let's start a magazine."

Jello Biafra: *Search & Destroy* was amazing. You could open it up to any page and laugh or be inspired. To me it's still the best underground punk zine anyone ever made. Punk was so wide open that the energy connected all kinds of people from different art fields and different age groups.

Even older Beats and avant-gardists like Bruce Conner the filmmaker found a great outlet in *Search & Destroy*. Vale worked at City Lights at the time, and knew William Burroughs. Allen Ginsberg put up the initial seed money to print the first issue. So it meant that the interviews were really intelligent and there was pressure from the first question to say something interesting.

Danny Furious: Vale was an old hippie/activist who was once the keyboard player for Blue Cheer, one of my early faves as a youngster. He was documenting the scene in a rather arty way. I consider him one of the good guys. He never missed a show. A rare individual who never sold out.

Dennis Kernohan: We played their party on a night that an issue came out, and we ripped it up onstage. "Don't buy this magazine, it sucks, it's full of lies!" Vale just started talking to me like three years ago.

Ginger Coyote: *Search & Destroy* was really the first punk zine in San Francisco. I enjoyed it but felt something was lacking. It was a bit elitist and serious. So I decided in 1978 to start *Punk Globe* to help support the bands that *Search & Destroy* overlooked such as the Vktms, No Alternative, Lady LaRue and Mr. A, Mary Monday, Leila and the Snakes, Eye Protection. Along with the people who came to the shows. Sometimes the audience members were more colorful than the bands.

Johnny Genocide: I give Ginger a lot of credit. She gave a lot of bands publicity that never would have gotten any otherwise. All the bands from this period owe her a debt of gratitude.

Ginger Coyote: I loved *Star* magazine. There was also *Rock Scene*. Those were the magazines I centered *Punk Globe* after. I also added a taste of the *National Enquirer* and Bill Dakota's infamous *Hollywood Star*. I also wanted to provide some comic relief. I think people enjoy the gossip because it is not mean-spirited. I always have mentioned people from all walks of life, from Danielle Steel to Joey Shithead.

Aaron Cometbus: I started *Cometbus* in the summer of '81. *MRR* wasn't a magazine yet, but had the weekly radio show, and Tim invited me on. He was incredibly supportive. Then, on the other hand, you had people like Vale, who put out *Search & Destroy* and *RE/Search*. He never missed an opportunity to dismiss and discourage the younger generation. Even in the ads for *Search & Destroy* back issues, he blew his own horn by saying that all present-day mags and bands were just pale imitations. He's telling you how worthless you are, and at the same time he wants you to worship him and pay his rent! His liner notes on the Avengers LP took the cake. "Before the proliferation of a thousand garage bands, hardcore or otherwise." That's how mad it made me—I can still quote it! He said "hardcore" like he was saying "dogshit." You could hear the sneer.

I've met him since. A nice enough guy. But he just couldn't see younger people as anything but an imitation of himself. Contrast that with Tim Yohannan, who said, "Come share your ideas with us. There's a place at the table for you." Two kinds of adults. Obviously, we vowed to do everything we could to not end up like Vale.

Greg Oropeza: The big South Bay fanzine at the time was *Ripper*, where I wrote under the name Sped McGregor.

Rachel DMR: Tim Tonooka, *Ripper* magazine. He's very quiet and very dedicated, documenting not only San Francisco history but the East Bay and South Bay. Years later, I asked him, "How'd you do that?" and he said, "Well, while you were out getting crazy, I was doing a job." He did everything by hand. Sat at his typewriter and typed. I should've been helping him.

Tim Tonooka: The first issue of *Ripper* came in 1980. Initially, our fanzine was focused on the South Bay, but by the third issue its scope was expanded to cover the entire Bay Area. I was largely inspired by *Search & Destroy*, and *Creep*. *Damage* was another great publication at the time.

Ruth Schwartz: I was involved with the gang at Target Video and *Damage* magazine. Every Saturday night they would throw an after-hours party in their warehouse in San Francisco on South Van Ness and 18th. That was the place to be at three a.m. It was this enormous dance party, in the days when it was still New Wave and stuff, so it was all blended, and people wanted to dance and do drugs. I was there every Saturday night.

Joe Rees: It started out as an alternative art space. For performance art, the real strange and bizarro kind of thing. I took that three-story building and put in a professional recording studio. I had a live stage on the bottom floor, and also I did my videotapings there, with an audience. We had events there. We had Jello's wedding, all that shit.

As time went along, I rented out the second floor to some artists. On the top floor I had *Damage* magazine. I worked my ass off. When we organized the Western Front event, we brought in all these bands from all over the country. I would be going from one damn nightclub to the other, to shoot these bands. I found that if I let the bands come there and stay, and have breakfast, they'd play for nothing.

The studio after-hours events, I'd have 200 people in there, packed to the walls. I'd show videos, sometimes I'd have a DJ there. Johnnie Walker, the guy from London, he'd be spinning tunes. People from out of town would come there, just to hang out. It was a real cool scene.

Johnnie Walker: *Damage* magazine had this idea to do the magazine as a radio show. I started doing a monthly hour-long radio show, *Damage on the Air*. A combination of West Coast punk bands, interviews, new records and interviews with visiting British punk acts. We built up to a network of 60 radio stations all over the States taking *Damage on the Air*. It won an award as the best independently produced program of the year.

At the same time I was also taping shows for Radio Luxembourg, until I famously put a record on at the wrong speed. I had a bunch of friends in the studio and we were partying it up, and I said, "Oh fuck, I'll have to edit that later." But I forgot to edit it, so it went out like that on Luxembourg, and that was my last show for them.

Joe Rees: I had a cable TV show in those days, on cable 25 in San Francisco, Wednesday nights. Some of the material would go on there. The irony of the whole thing is that my show, Target Video, followed the Maharishi show. A Transcendental Meditation thing, very low-key and laid-back and spiritual. After about the third week, I came up with this idea. He would be in the lotus position, just seconds before I would come on. So I opened up my show with a machine gun burst, that lasted for about three minutes. I'd have all these images popping in, everything that I disliked, that was going on in the world. But you know what? The Maharishi really enjoyed my show. He thought it was terrific.

8

Kick Out the Jams

Ralph Spight: I'd been playing guitar since I was 12, and smoking pot and listening to metal. I didn't know anything from punk rock. Was sort of aware there was underground shit going on. And one day I was driving around Sonoma, I turned on the radio and there's fucking *Maximum RocknRoll*. It's fast punk rock, and I was like, "Oh my fucking god!" Really aggressive music, lyrics were talking about stuff I could relate to. I just dove in headfirst. On Tuesday nights I would tape the whole thing, and listen to the cassettes.

Tim Tonooka: Rather Ripped Records was on Euclid Avenue in Berkeley. The people who worked there, like Ray Farrell, would turn you on to lots of great stuff.

Ray Farrell: Tim Yohannan came into the store, and this is before Mike Watt extended the John Fogerty flannel shirt thing. It hadn't gone around the waist yet. It was an actual shirt. He was a bearded guy in a flannel shirt, and jeans and boots, who came in to buy records. I didn't trust him. I thought, anybody with a beard who's buying punk rock is obviously slumming.

I'd say, "You're too old to buy this." I was 20, and I wasn't gonna let somebody interfere with this. He tried to get me fired from the store. At one point we realized that we were both from New Jersey, and somehow we started clicking.

Al Ennis: I'd go in there and buy punk records. Ray said, "Do you know Tim?" I said no. "Because there's a guy who comes in here named Tim, and he buys the same records that you do. Next time he's in here I'll introduce you guys."

Tim and I started going over to each other's apartments, and listening to the record collections, and talking about how this thread of wild rock 'n' roll has been going since the earliest days. Tim had a lot of really good rockabilly records imported from Holland. He was working at this shipping and receiving job for UC, and I was studying English literature at Berkeley.

Tim went to Rutgers in New Jersey. His roommate was good friends with Lenny Kaye, the guitarist for Patti Smith. So he had kept in touch with Lenny, and Lenny had put out the first *Nuggets* album, the garage rock stuff.

Finally one day, we were at Rather Ripped and Tim said, "I've been talking to KPFA, and I'm trying to get a radio show going, to play all this punk music that's coming out." I said, "I want to help you with it." And Ray went, "Yeah, I wanna help, too."

Tim went in there and talked management into giving him a time slot. So we just started showing up. April '77. I was 29, so that made Tim about 32. Ray was a youngster, Ray was about 22.

Tim came up with the name. We thought it was a great name. He got it from an old Who motto, which was "Maximum R&B." I had the Maximum R&B poster from *Live at Leeds* up on my wall when I met him.

KPFA was a real funky old studio. The guy on before us had a show catered to prisoners. Sometimes he would have guests on, San Quentin white boys, with the tattoos and stuff. Nefarious-looking underworld types. We'd skulk in with our little bags of records and our leather jackets. But it was really cool. After awhile we started getting fan mail from some of the prisoners, who left the radio on and tuned in to *Maximum RocknRoll*.

We had a lot of people coming in the studio. Sometimes we were just packed in there. Berkeley High, they were digging it. Young kids couldn't get into the nightclubs. They wanted to be part of it somehow.

We would have a little contest between us. We scoured all the record shops all week long to see who could come up with the coolest new sounds. So you hoped that you were the lucky one to find it. Stuff like the Tits' "We're So Glad Elvis Is Dead."

Jello Biafra: I'd seen a flyer at Rather Ripped for the radio show and it listed both known and extremely obscure punk records that they were playing. And I thought, "Oh, this is cool."

Tim and I hit it off immediately. We loved talking records and hipping each other to new ones that we didn't know about. He thought I was good on my feet and a good interview, so he invited me to be part of the show, which I was for three or four years after that.

Al Ennis: Jello was traveling with the Dead Kennedys, and we were glad to have Jello come on. He would have a handful of records from Phoenix or somewhere, and he would get his little segment as well.

We had the Cramps on, which was a highlight for Tim and I. I think the Dils were on. And then whoever else was in town. Sometimes the L.A. bands. All of us at *MRR* loved the fact that so many women were involved in the early days—Mary Monday, Jennifer, Penelope, Olga de Volga, the gals in the Mutants, Pink Section, the Contractions, the Bags, Poison Ivy, Patti Smith and on and on.

Ray and I had more eclectic tastes, the post-punk stuff like Cabaret Voltaire and Throbbing Gristle, these experimental bands that were starting to come out of New York like Suicide. Only if they had a really straight rock 'n' roll beat would Tim want any part of it.

Ray Farrell: Eventually *Maximum* did become more political. Part of it was that Tim was still trying to figure out the context around it. Because we were getting records from the U.K., from all over the world.

Al Ennis: Tim was very, very left-wing. I was left-wing, too, but he was one of these people that was more left-wing than anyone. We used to have arguments about this shit all the time. Tim was a Stalin apologist. Which freaked me out. He told me that Stalin had to kill ten million people because that was the only way he could make communism work. And I said, "Tim, you can't believe this." He goes, "Yeah, everybody in the world was after Stalin. He just did whatever it took to make Russia communist." That's as left as you can get.

We had a meeting. Tim wanted to start going heavy on the politics. Tim and I already had started the East Bay branch of Rock Against Racism. We had the Offs and the Jars at our first benefit, at Berkeley High. But he wanted everything to be more political. He was really serious. He was saying, "So do you want to be part of it? If you don't, I understand. But I don't just want to play punk records. I want to have political people on, I want organization."

I thought, this is not gonna be that fun. I felt like he was trying to get a little too much control. I just dropped out at that point.

Ray soldiered on for several more years. I liked it at first. It wasn't a huge change. They didn't have Trotskyites on for half an hour, with a big spiel or anything. It just started moving in that direction.

Jello Biafra: I eventually met a guy at Aquarius Records, who was instantly talkative and opinionated at the same time, named Jeff Bale. As I got to know Jeff better, I thought, "My god, I know somebody you should meet," and I introduced Tim and Jeff to each other. All those later detractors that thought *MRR* was some communist indoctrination zine—little did they know that I'm to blame for introducing Tim and Jeff, so they could torment those people for years on end.

Jeff Bale: Tim and I hit it off because we both had feisty personalities and liked to shoot our mouths off. He was a little older than me, four or five years. So then I started going on the show.

Ruth Schwartz: Jeff and I started in the same period. Tim sought me out. I was doing a show on KUSF called *Harmful Emissions*. He walked into the KUSF studio one night at like three in the morning and said, "Do you wanna be on *Maximum RocknRoll?*"

Jeff Bale: Ruth was a cool person. She had these engineering skills and she was interested in being on the show. Actually it was kind of funny because me and Tim were about straight-up rock 'n' roll stuff, we didn't want any arty-farty bullshit. And Ruth actually liked some of the arty-farty stuff. That was the one downside with Ruth. But actually it was good for the listeners because it made it more diverse.

Ruth Schwartz: Tim had it very formatted. He coined this term "Schwartzcore" at one point because I was into more difficult music. My job was to prepare a ten-minute set of that type of music.

For many years I taped the shows, edited them with tape and knives, physically put labels on them, and mailed them out to radio stations all over the world. Something like 30 stations. They would get it on a cassette tape with a piece of paper every week.

Jeff Bale: We used to have discussions about how to categorize subgenres, and what was punk and what wasn't punk, and basically the general rap about *Maximum RocknRoll* was that we were purists.

Jello Biafra: Tim also took a hard line early, that rock 'n' roll did not necessarily have to be sexist. He told me one of his favorite recording artists was Johnny Thunders, but he never played Johnny Thunders on *MRR* because the guy was so sexist in most of his songs. There was a way to rock without being cock-rock about it. That was cool, too.

Ruth Schwartz: Jello would come in and do a segment or two at least every other week. He always mixed it up. He's got a massive record collection. He's a crazy collector and he probably has the broadest taste in music of any of us.

Jello Biafra: I was trying to collect every single punk record ever made, I was that into it. I saw Tim's record collection and thought, "Oh my god!" Tim had one after another after another that I never even knew existed. If Sham 69 gave away a special single at one gig in England—he had the record! He was obviously way, way ahead of me. And every record had a green tape spine around it. Which I thought was taking it to extremes. It was an obsession. He probably kept that tape company in business as the scene exploded.

Jeff Bale: That was always grossly offensive to me, that Tim would put green tape on all these records, and just destroy the aesthetics. Tim had to get green tape all the time because he was getting so many records.

Jello Biafra: He told me the original reason for the green tape was that he and his brother were fighting over who owned which record when they were growing up. I think he said Tom was blue tape and Tim was green.

John Marr: It was a particular kind of green tape made by this company called Mystic. Eventually they stopped making it and he couldn't get it anymore. They had all the other colors, but they had sold out of the green. Probably because of his demand.

Sheriff Mike Hennessey: I was a listener, and I would oftentimes tape shows. I met Tim at the Fab Mab. He was a fun guy to talk to, and he invited me to be a guest disc jockey on his show one night. So I went over to Berkeley. I'm not sure if Jeff Bale was there or not, but Ruth Schwartz was there, wearing a very short skirt, I recall. They asked me to pick some songs out, and of course by that time I had a repertoire of law enforcement punk rock songs that I liked to play because it sort of tied into what I did. I was the sheriff. So this was very weird, you know.

I played "I Fought the Law" by the Clash. I remember specifically playing the Dead Kennedys song "Police Truck," which Tim thought was hilarious, because it talks about police brutality. Afterwards we went to some nearby bar and had a couple drinks.

Jello Biafra: Tim and Jeff once left the room during a live broadcast of *MRR* and I started playing country swing. They really flipped out. Tim said to me, "I think you did that just to bug me, Jello!" "Yup, Tim, I did." "Well if you ever do that again I'm throwing you off the show." Another time I played Heino, who is this horrific German oompah singer, as "roots of German hardcore." Tim and Jeff were out of the room, and Jeff came back in: "Are you playing Heino?! Fuck!" and threw one of the classic Jeff tantrums right there in the room. Luckily Tim wasn't there. It would have been worse.

Ruth Schwartz: We used to have fights on the radio because once a year Tim liked to do a "These Are My Favorite Songs" set. He'd bring in all of his Ramones records and play a set of his favorite songs. I would get on the air and tease him because they were on Sire. I'd say, "Woo, hypocrite, you're playing all these major-label albums." He'd be like, "Well, these are my favorite albums." And I'd say, "Well, which way do you want it?"

Jeff Bale: We would talk and joke and give each other a hard time. We had this ongoing banter and we all had strong opinions. We loved giving listeners a hard time. That was part of the fun of it.

John Marr: There was some good music on it. I was never a real religious listener. I was talking about the show once, and someone said, "You've seen Tim around at shows." "What does he look like?" "Oh, he's the greasy little vampire." And I said, "I know exactly who you're talking about."

Aaron Cometbus: Jesse [Michaels] and I had only been doing our fanzine a couple months when a letter arrived. "Keep up the good work," it said. "And if you ever have something to say on the radio, come on by." It was from Tim Yohannan.

I started hanging out there every week. Then one week Tim yelled "You're late!" when I walked in the door. He hustled me into the broadcast booth and put a microphone in front of my face. They were doing a roundtable interview of local fanzine editors, and I was included! That was crazy because the other fanzines were way out of my league. They were, like, serious magazines while I was just a little kid with a tiny, stapled rag.

Ray Farrell: I remember an amazing show, where Tim had Bill Graham up. There was a Clash show that Bill Graham was putting on. And the New Youth organization also wanted to have a people's show with the Clash.

Steve Tupper: I was working with New Youth Productions. It was just a bunch of people in the scene that wanted to do something. Our big idea was to open up some kind of nonprofit performance space. We put on a few shows. We did this semi-underground Clash show. It wasn't supposed to happen.

Ray Farrell: Bill Graham was threatening the people from this New Youth organization, saying the Clash are my band, they're playing in my town, I'm giving them X amount of dollars to play here, they can't do any other show. But the demand was far greater than what could fit into the Bill Graham show. And so a couple of nights later, there was this separate New Youth show. The ticket price was less. The Clash did it, mainly because they were beaten up by all these so-called political organizations to play the gig.

Steve Tupper: I'm surprised Bill Graham even agreed to come on the radio show.

Noah Landis: God, Tim was fucking pissed about that. He just ripped him apart. Like, "Why don't you stick to your corporate shit, with all of your mainstream radio airplay and promotion machine, and leave us alone? You don't have the right to have access to these guys. These bands are for us."

Ray Farrell: There was an argument, and Bill ended up getting pissed off and storming out of the room.

Steve Tupper: Bill Graham was such an arrogant asshole. If he didn't already think that it was in his interest to deal with you, he treated you like garbage. Just as a matter of course.

Jello Biafra: People worldwide have this glassy-eyed memory of Bill Graham as being this wonderful godfather of all that was good about the summer of love and the psychedelic era. But nothing could be further from the truth. By that time, he struck me as this obsessive megalomaniac who wanted a monopoly on all live music in the Bay Area. Even a club as small as the Mabuhay or a hall show like 330 Grove or 10th Street, it was unacceptable. It should not be allowed to exist.

Jeff Bale: We were trying to create a whole underground scene. Both Tim and I wanted to create a vibrant new counterculture that would replace the hippies and maybe even ultimately transform culture and society in big ways. Tim wanted to revolutionize the kids. That was his plan. Even though we were much more cynical than we had been in the '60s, we felt like, why couldn't we generate a whole new youth movement?

Ray Farrell: I didn't really get it. When I played music on the show, I remember Tim thinking that I was escapist, because I wasn't looking for political stuff. I'd go, "Not everybody thinks like that." If your enjoyment of the music is predicated on your political beliefs, then you're painting yourself into a corner. That was something that Tim and those people took to their next steps.

Jeff Bale: We put out a couple of compilations. The *Not So Quiet on the Western Front* was the first one, it was a double album. And we put it out with Jello on the Alternative Tentacles label.

Jello Biafra: Our part of the bargain was to get it manufactured and make sure it got into the record stores. Tim and Jeff put it together. *MRR* had enough of an audience in the Bay Area and in the Central Valley that people were sending in demo tapes as soon as they could get three or four songs together—"Hey, we're a band, too! Play us on the air!" I'm sure some people started their bands with no initial ambition except to get played on *MRR*.

Jeff Bale: It had like 50 local bands. We were trying to put California punk on the map. We thought about it a lot. We picked what we considered to be the best bands of all the stuff we'd gotten. We gave tons of bands their first chance to become known.

Jello Biafra: The hardcore explosion had connected with a much younger audience, both through the music and through skateboard networks. So all of a sudden there were a lot more bands and a lot more people starting bands. Things were just exploding here. As word got out, then the number of people who suddenly claimed they had an existing band doubled. And we had to make it a two-record set.

Fat Mike: The *Not So Quiet on the Western Front* compilation is when everybody found out about what they were doing.

Frank Portman: That was our first encounter with the outside world of punk rock. My first actual band was called the Bent Nails, and was just guys I knew in high school. We sent a cassette that we had recorded to *Maximum RocknRoll*. The song was dumb. By the time Tim Yohannan called, we were not very interested in doing it. They were like, "We really like that one. We're putting together a record."

That comp is awful. How awful it is, is that our song wasn't even the worst thing. A snapshot of a terrible time in music. It was when everything that was cool about punk rock got subverted and destroyed by what ended up being called hardcore. You can see the seeds of it in that record. You speed up the music so it's not rock 'n' roll, you remove the song structure so you don't have choruses. And you draw it from some pseudo-political tract.

Martin Sorrondeguy: There was great shit on there. I still play that comp pretty often. It was just packed with bands. *Not So Quiet*'s great because it really highlighted small-town California punk. Bands from Fresno and the Valley. That was an amazing way of goin', "Hey, man, check all this shit out!" And takin' it to the world.

9

Fresh Fruit for Rotting Vegetables

Steve DePace: Negative Trend, the version I was in, had just recorded for the first time. I was at Will Shatter's apartment down on Third Street. We were listening to the tape. There was a knock on the door. And it was Eric Boucher. He had met Will previously. He walked in the door, and he had his bicycle with him.

Eric sat down, and we listened to the tape. Apparently he was fresh in town. He said to both of us, "Yeah, you know, I'm gonna start my own punk band, I'm gonna call it the Dead Kennedys." I remember thinking, the Dead Kennedys? Who is this nerd? He had the full-on nerd look. Oh god. Nerd in terms of geek nerd, out of place. Most certainly not punk rock. My first impression of him was that this guy isn't gonna do anything, this guy's full of shit.

Bruce Loose: He had waist-length hair, had a fucking sash tied around his waist, and bell-bottoms on.

Dennis Kernohan: Eric was always there. We all knew him. He was a total record junkie. He was at the record store all the time. Every day. He knew when the records came in. He was definitely processing heavily.

James Stark: He'd been around enough and figured out what was going on, and what to do. To me it was always more, he studied the scene and then figured out what to do and then put together a band.

Jello Biafra: When I was just a wild pogoer at Mabuhay, people would come up to me, "Are you in a band? You need to be in a band. You need to find something to do with all this energy." And I was like, "Well, a conspiracy is in the works."

Dennis Kernohan: The guy's an evil genius. He was even more calculated than all four of the guys from Crime. He's so calculated it's ridiculous. I used to be offended by it back then, but now I think he was just smart. He's still doing it. He's made his whole fucking life off this thing. And you have to admire that. He had the most cred.

Al Ennis: The person who did *Creep* magazine used to be a roommate with Jello. Jello would have his door open, and one day my friend told me really seriously, "Al, when Jello listens to a record—*we'll* always pick up a magazine or we'll read the liner notes or something? *He* sits there in front of the record player, and does nothing but just listen to the record." I kinda had him like the old RCA Victor dog, doing nothing but listening. Just the music, baby.

Jello Biafra: Back in Boulder, me and my friend John Greenway, who wrote the original lyrics to "California Über Alles," we were sitting in his bedroom one night blasting punk singles with the windows open. Coming up with names for bands, names for people in bands, names for songs. I took the notebook with me when I came out west.

Originally I called myself Occupant. But then one of my first friends, Larry Shorr, he kept saying, "Hey, resident! How ya doing?" 'Cause we both liked the Residents. I thought, "Oh shit, I better get another name." So I opened up the notebook. I liked the way Jello and Biafra collided in the mind. The ultimate plastic, useless, sugary American product, along with the worldwide symbol of the worst kind of genocide and starvation that might be associated with Darfur today.

Klaus Flouride: I'd been playing on the East Coast and in Detroit. Magic Terry and the Universe was this experimental group that was all tied in with the Warhol crew. Billy Squier was on guitar. I got sick of playing in bands that were basically white guys playing R&B and the whole attitude was, "I can drink you under the table." It just really made me want to puke. So I moved out here.

The Mabuhay was walking distance from the Financial District. On Fridays we'd go there after work for drinks. The rest of the people from the office were cracking up at the bands, and I was wandering up to the front and staring at the Zeros and people like that, and saying, "I like this." I remember seeing the Nuns, Negative Trend. The Avengers. The Zeros were the ones that stood out.

Dennis Kernohan: Ray was in this band, Cruisin'. They played all this '50s shit, they played all the car shows, played at the fairs. Everybody knew 'em. It'd be on the radio: "Cruisin', cruisin', cruisin'," with the echo and everything. They could play. Some of the bands that came up were pro bands who punked it up. There was a lot of that going on.

East Bay Ray: The first band I saw at the Mabuhay was the Weirdos. They were playing "We Got the Neutron Bomb." Right after I saw them, I put the ad out.

Klaus Flouride: He ran the ad in *BAM* magazine. The whole reason for *BAM* existing was, when *Rolling Stone* up and left San Francisco, there was no magazine left that would stroke the Grateful Dead, the Eagles, and Jefferson Starship and all that sort of crap. So this magazine came along, *Bay Area Musician*. And it was nothing. They tried to sell it and no one would buy it. That was probably the worst place, the most disconnected place to advertise for a punk band. It had nothing to do with the punk scene. But basically I looked there and saw the ad.

East Bay Ray: I had a card up at Aquarius Records. Biafra responded. Originally I was working with two singers, and one of them didn't show up on time. Biafra showed up on time. Down on 44th Street in Oakland was a garage where we started it.

Klaus Flouride: Ray had already met Biafra. And then I came over and Ray and I went to the garage and we played. He said, "What can you play?" And, "I dunno." I figured "Peggy Sue" sounded like the Ramones. Sort of. I mean that's what they were lifting. So we played "Peggy Sue."

Jello Biafra: I did "Peggy Sue" with Ray once.

Klaus Flouride: We went through a ton of drummers. This one drummer we did a demo with, Carl Numb, I don't remember what his real name was. The guy didn't want to be in the group. But he was about the best drummer we'd gone through.

Jello Biafra: I was still wavering back and forth and playing with other people, not sure whether working with Ray and Klaus was the way to go. They were a lot older than I was, and there was a lot of '70s bar-band damage to hack through with them. Solos and fills in every possible place were not necessarily the best for punk music.

I brought in a song I'd written called "Holiday in Cambodia" to practice. We played around with it, and they not only didn't like it, they refused to play it. I was crushed because this had never happened before. I thought it was a good song. Then Klaus started noodling around with what became the opening bass line. And I thought . . . Wait! Wait! Wait! Try this! Put all this stuff together for the pre-chorus, the chorus, the bridge and everything, and slow it down and see if it works. And sure enough it did.

It wasn't 'til quite awhile later that Ray came up with that magic guitar overlay. I kept saying, "Ray, Syd Barrett, Syd Barrett." Because he said he'd seen Pink Floyd with Syd Barrett when he was 12, and that made him want to be a musician. So eventually it happened. It was one of the few band-written songs we ever did. I shudder to think what kind of band we would have been if they put in that kind of effort into other songs.

Klaus Flouride: We gave Dirk the demo, but he wanted a picture of the band also. Biafra had met 6025 at the Mabuhay, and asked him if he wanted to pose as our drummer in the picture. So he did. And then he said, "Well, I can play guitar, you know." And we said, "You do? Well, come on and join the group."

East Bay Ray: To this day, people think 6025 actually played drums with us. Not realizing that he just fit in the picture.

Klaus Flouride: We still were looking for a drummer. Ted was the first person who rushed us. That was exciting, because everybody else wanted to do stuff slower. He was really, really good.

Jello Biafra: "You know what would be the coolest name for a band—Dead Kennedys." They still argue about which one of them it was. Maybe they even told me at the same party. It was a guy who called himself Radio Pete, real name Mark Bliesener, who later managed the Nitty Gritty Dirt Band. And the other was Rick Stott, who clerked at Trade-A-Tape and Records, and was also the manager of Colorado's first punk band, the Ravers. What Rick didn't tell me until a few years ago was, it hadn't popped into their heads. They'd heard about another band from Cleveland called Dead Kennedys. They didn't tell me that part.

We started playing as Dead Kennedys. And Ray Farrell at Rather Ripped said, "Hey, that was a great interview you just did in *Cle*." "What? I don't remember being interviewed for them? What is it?" He showed me, and it was a completely different band. I thought, "Oh shit!" So I wrote the leader of the Bizarros, who I had been buying records from, and asked if this was gonna be a problem. He said no, they'd already changed their name, because nobody would book them under that name.

Klaus Flouride: I figured it would last six months, maybe two years. We'd get to go to L.A. once in awhile if we were lucky.

East Bay Ray: We saw a lot of punk bands at the Mabuhay. There was definitely an inspiration, shall we say. I thought that with the trained ability there, we could be the best punk band in San Francisco.

Jello Biafra: It wasn't clear-cut. I was desperately wanting to do something. At first I thought punk was the biggest thing since Beatlemania, or the mid-'60s Rolling Stones. Which meant that the opportunity might close in less than a year.

Klaus Flouride: We all figured out that we liked the Screamers. No guitars in the group at all. But they were so intense. We didn't want to sound like the other groups, definitely. We'd put a weird chord in there, lifted from the Residents' concept. We would take certain things from different things, and just sort of jumble them together.

East Bay Ray: We wanted to rock out and not be so arty that it didn't rock. But we didn't want to be just so rocking that it's boring. Like Bob Seger or something. If you go through and analyze our song structure, it's Beatles and Motown melody. But doing the Ramones thing—that was done.

Jello Biafra: I started bringing a guitar to Ray's, just picking the notes out single-string. Then eventually Klaus said, "Why don't you just sing 'em to us? You sing on key, go ahead and do it that way." And he was able to pick stuff up and then teach it to Ray.

East Bay Ray: 6025 was a big fan of Captain Beefheart. He brought in the song "Ill in the Head," which is like, oh, okay, we got a 13/8 section, and an 11/8 section. You can't really feel that stuff. So we had to write it out.

Jello Biafra: After the majors pulled out, the game changed. Ray was desperate to be on a major label and that was a source of contention. He didn't want to call the band Dead Kennedys because he, said, "The record companies won't sign us." As soon as I started telling people like Negative Trend and the Dils that was the name of the band, the other guys couldn't get rid of it. It had touched such a raw nerve with Ray and Klaus, I realized I was on to something.

Klaus Flouride: Our first show was terrifying. It went by like lightning. We only had seven songs to play. We got an encore, so we did "Rawhide" again. 6025 had never played in a band onstage before. So there he was playing guitar, and he had a curly cord, and some guy came up and wrapped the cord around him. And he was going, "Oh man, what do I do?" I waited for the song to end, and I just unplugged the thing, and unwrapped it around, plugged it back in. He was like, "Oh, okay!"

Howie Klein: It was obvious that they weren't just another band that was gonna come and go. They were something special. I saw that right away. Biafra was an absolute talent. And he had a band behind him that were tight and good.

Klaus Flouride: One of the real early gigs was Sproul Plaza. It was sponsored by the university. The Zeros and us, I think that was it. We were sort of having a war with the guys playing the conga drums around the corner. There was maybe 40 people watching the thing. It was great, we just took an extension cord, set up on the ground and played.

Dennis Kernohan: When they first started playing at the Mab, punk was a big thing by then. People were coming from Hayward and everywhere. The Mab was packed every fucking night. It was crazy in there. Eric just kicked everybody's ass. It was ingenious, I'm telling you.

Hank Rank: They were an energetic band and popular almost immediately. They really ascended quickly. Jello, I always thought he sounded like Katharine Hepburn when he sang. But that was me. I never considered myself a fan but I certainly acknowledge their place.

Penelope Houston: Their songs are good and I liked the lyrics and everything, I thought Jello's voice was irritating. I think there's probably a million people who'd say that.

Klaus Flouride: November 23rd show, the 15th anniversary of the Kennedy assassination. Sun Ra played in the afternoon, and some of them stuck around to see us. Herb Caen wrote an article a couple days before the show: "Just when we thought Jonestown bad taste has reached its nadir, along comes this group called Dead Kennedys." And he knew that just by saying we're trashy, he was doing us this huge favor.

It went AP wire, so then Dirk started getting hate mail and calls from as far away as Texas. That night at the show, they took guns off people at the door. There was the Zapruder film behind us when we were playing, which wasn't our idea. Bruce Conner was doing that. About a song into it, somebody threw a glass. It just missed Ted, and Ted went behind the drums like he thought he was getting shot or something. It was a strange night.

Al Ennis: It took them awhile. Someone put on a show in Berkeley, and it was in an African restaurant down on San Pablo and University. We went down there and got totally drunk, just slam dancing amongst ourselves. There was 16 people at a Dead Kennedys show. It might have been a bad night.

Jello Biafra: We did it with no expectations of being popular or making money. We did wanna put a record out, which meant stashing most of our gig money, even the five-dollar Wes Robinson gigs. We did that for a year, it went into a bank account Ray was running. And then we had money to make the "California Über Alles" single.

East Bay Ray: I put up half the money, and then everybody in the band agreed that we took half the money from the gigs. And we went and recorded it. Ted and I basically were the distribution. We drove it around, stores like Aquarius would take it on consignment.

Klaus Flouride: I wanted a big-hole 45. It was an absurd reason. I wanted it to be able to be played in jukeboxes. I think they did put it in a couple of jukeboxes, and I bumped into them every once in awhile. It was great when we'd come to a town, we'd be eating in some restaurant that people'd drag us to. Then all of a sudden, on the jukebox "California Über Alles" would come on. It was like, okay, see? Because it had a big hole.

Jello Biafra: Alternative Tentacles started as just a name to put out the first Dead Kennedys single. No one else was gonna put it out. We had to do it ourselves. Ray did most of the work putting it together and getting it distributed.

By sheer dumb luck one positive thing happened from the '79 tour in New York when we lost our shirts. Both me and Klaus came really close to quitting the band right then and there. But the promoter at Hurrah, Jim Fouratt, I guess he liked us. Because when Bob Last, who had the Fast label out of Scotland at that time, came to New York, Jim pulled out "California Über Alles" as an example of something that he thought was good that was going on in American music then. Bob Last flipped over it and called us and wanted to release it in the U.K.

This wasn't just huge, it was enormous, because Fast was about the hottest, most trendy label of its time. The first singles they put out introduced the world to the Gang of Four, the Mekons, the Human League and some others. Everyone on both sides of the Atlantic was watching to see who Fast would put out next, and lo and behold they put out "California Über Alles." So here we were beating our heads against the wall trying to get rid of a thousand copies of that damn single, and Last said on the phone, "Yeah we'll probably sell 30,000 in the first day." So obviously that vaulted us into a much higher bracket, especially outside of the Bay Area. And we got to make an album.

Mike LaVella: The first punk record I ever bought, I was at a record swap at a Holiday Inn in Pittsburgh, Pennsylvania. I was buying a Captain Beefheart record, and the guy was like, "You're a weird little kid, I have something I think you're gonna like." And it was the first pressing of "California Über Alles." I took it home and I was like, "Whoa. What's this?"

Winston Smith: I did some artwork for Rock Against Racism, did work for their paper. A friend of mine said, "I know this guy who thinks just like you. But he's a musician, they do a band. Y'all should meet."

She showed me a record and said, "This just came out, it's called 'California Über Alles.'" I sent Biafra a postcard, said, "If you want any more of this . . ." It was a picture of the Zapruder film. He wrote back and said yes, send me more, meet us at the Mabuhay after the show.

We got there just as the show was over. Biafra was hungry, so we found Clown Alley, which used to be down on Van Ness. It was him, his soon-to-be wife and Ray, and the other guys in the band. We scarfed down hamburgers. Biafra I could tell was a creative individual who was kind of a challenging personality. Obviously a deep thinker about stuff.

I showed him a bunch of pictures. He saw one of this cross of dollars I had made a couple years before, a commentary on religion, and Jerry Falwell and those guys making money off it. Biafra said, "This is dangerous, man, we need to use this for our record." He gave me a call a week or so later and said we'd like to use that for our new EP.

Klaus Flouride: Winston's such an eccentric. His juxtaposition of images is great, and generally it wasn't just shock for shock's sake. It all had some sort of theme to it that was driving the point home.

Winston Smith: Biafra called one night and said, "Can you do an emblem for our band, that we can use for our logo?" I had heard their single. At that point, I had seen them a couple of times. I made this DK logo in one night, after going through a bottle of wine. I used the bottom of the bottle to make the circle. And tried to put things on the inside to make it geometrically even. I wanted to make it look Third Reich–ish. Real hard, even lines, something that would be easy to reproduce. I never got a dime!

Ian MacKaye: In 1980 we saw them play, and after the show went backstage and hung out with Biafra. He was super friendly. I remember thinking, oh my god, an older guy. I think he was 22. My conception of punk at that time was really kind of no-frills. We were coming from the world of Bad Brains. Pre-Rastafarian Bad Brains.

Biafra was very theatrical, and his presentation was really considered. I think he probably had his stomach hair shaved in the shape of a cross. Like his little pubic, whatever you call that hair that comes up on his stomach. And he might have been wearing green rubber gloves. It was just weird, you know? But they were good.

Dave Dictor: Biafra is quite a character. He was very inspiring. "Kiss ass while you bitch / But you get rich / While the rich get richer off you." There isn't a more classic punk rock political line out there. And I can say that off the top of my head without even thinking about it. Ingenious.

Klaus Flouride: That first album, people said they liked it, but at the time, we were not the hippest thing.

Martin Sprouse: That was so many people's introduction to punk. You can't even measure the impact of that. Those first singles—huge impact.

Bill Michalski: *Trouser Press*, there was an article about Public Image Ltd. and it had a picture of Johnny Rotten, and he was clutching a bunch of 7-inches. And you could see the Dead Kennedys' "Holiday in Cambodia." I'm like, "What the fuck is that?" So I tracked it down, found it. Okay, that's cool.

Steve Tupper: They were a totally crazy band. It became this ritual where the audience would grab Jello and rip his clothes off and throw him back up on the stage. He would just keep going.

Bruce Loose: Paul Rat put on one show at a warehouse somewhere in the deep Mission. New Year's Eve show, it just happened. Oh, here's a microphone. Oh, nobody realizes it. Oh, I can slip under the stage right now with it, and nobody's gonna see me. I can fuck with someone.

I was under the stage, I couldn't see anything. I waited until they were one or two songs into stuff, and then I started making comments. I was going, "I may be too drunk to fuck, but I can sure eat some pussy!" Stuff like that. Ridiculous. And from what I heard, the sound people were going, "Where is that mic? What's going on? Who's singing that?" They were flipping out all over the place.

East Bay Ray: I don't know if it made much difference in the sound, 'cause it was a pretty crappy P.A.

Max Volume: Dead Kennedys played at the Mab the night before they went on their first world tour. I was very drunk. I was standing in the front row. It was their last song. And Jello says, "Well, I'm getting pretty sick and tired of singing 'California Über Alles.' Is there annnnybody in the audience who knows allllll the words to 'California Über Alles'?"

All of my friends pushed me onstage. I didn't have any time to react at all. I was there on my knees, I started hearing the drums start up, and I saw a microphone handed in my face. They helped me stand up. Fortunately I had an impersonation of Jello Biafra at the time. With the mime show, and pushing against the wind, and all of that stuff. Mocked him mercilessly.

Buzzsaw Bill: With the cord in the teeth.

Max Volume: I asked him about that a year ago, and "No, I don't rememmmber." He blocked it out, obviously.

Jennifer Blowdryer: When I was living with Peter Belsito, he had a zine

Photo © 2009 by Keith Michael Holmes

There's Always Room for Jello: Dead Kennedys at Dolores Park

and I reviewed Jello, and I said something about him doing the same exaggerated movements night after night. Then Marion Kester came along and did an unauthorized book on the Dead Kennedys and used my quote, under the name Jennifer Waters. Jello figured out that was me and was kinda miffed. But it did seem kind of cartoonish. His dad was a lawyer and he was always very hyper-articulate. He liked the girls that had their own brainy, girlish high-camp thing going.

East Bay Ray: I think it might have been *Plastic Surgery Disasters*, we all grew little pencil-thin mustaches and soul patches. That was actually the tour where we actually got the most hate. This is a little bit later, it was like either second or third record, so punk rock was more codified. Sid Vicious with a padlock. That's what you were supposed to look like.

Klaus Flouride: We had all gone on vacation. And we'd all separately, without any planning amongst each other, decided to come back with facial hair and see if we could freak out the other guys.

East Bay Ray: We made it the sleazy lounge lizard thing. We did the whole tour like that, and, boy, it was tough.

Klaus Flouride: We were courted by Polydor. We were courted by all sorts of labels.

East Bay Ray: The Polydor thing, we met this guy Tony something. Like a cigar-smoking guy.

Klaus Flouride: He was in town with Sham 69. We were playing the Whisky. He said, "I gotta talk business with you guys. Come on over tomorrow around noon when they kick you out of the hotel." It was like, sure. We were crashing at people's places.

We met him at the Beverly Hills Hotel, the big pink Beverly Hills place. And the guy was sitting by the pool. He got us up to the room, still wearing a towel. And he was big. He said, "Okay, here's what I picture. I want you to picture this with me. Sit down. Colored vinyl!" This is what he was trying to sell us with. "Colored vinyl! On Polydor! First time we're gonna do it!"

East Bay Ray: We were *very* noncommittal. I had a question or two, well, more than a question or two. Left a message. And the guy never returned the call.

Steve DePace: They started their own record label. They sold a lot of records and they made a lot of money. But they did it themselves. They ultimately became the number one American punk rock band. There was the Ramones, but that was different.

Kelly King: They would totally pack out places. They played Haight Street Fair one time. They were super popular, almost mainstream, almost commercial. Everybody in the United States at one point had heard of Dead Kennedys. Their name just went everywhere. And it was a controversial name.

Howie Klein: The Dead Kennedys were sort of the forerunner of Green Day, in terms of San Francisco. They never signed with a major label, they never made it in the traditional sense of what makes it. Jello never compromised at all. He was what he was and that was it. With some of the other bands, they could say, "Well, you're not the real thing." No one can say that about the Dead Kennedys. Although they did later.

From a conventional standpoint, did they have hits? Of course not. But in terms of the underground audience at the time, they absolutely had hits. "California Über Alles," "Holiday in Cambodia," even when you get down into their catalog, like "Let's Lynch the Landlord." I mean, that wasn't as big, but, yes, that was a hit, too, for the people who heard it. They had a couple of songs that just had that magic moment that you need to sort of be a hit. Jello was an amazing songwriter. And a good performer.

John Marr: Biafra would jump out into the audience. He would run around, knock over chairs, confront people in the back of the room. Back in the '70s this was just flat mind-blowing. Bands didn't do stuff like that. And then a bunch of kids at our high school, who bought the imported records, put on what they called the "Whittler's Ball."

East Bay Ray: Moraga high school.

Jello Biafra: Mark Carges was one of two kids who approached me at the Mabuhay: "Would you ever consider playing a high school?" And I thought, yeah, sure, why not! I wasn't like some of the other bands where they really didn't wanna get outside their own little womb and play farm towns.

Luckily they were very savvy about the whole thing. They were clever. They joined an officially sanctioned club that nobody cared about, called the Whittler's Club. The Whittler's Club got to do the annual Christmas dance. So who did the Whittler's book for the Christmas dance, but us. We knew we'd have to do it under another name, so we called ourselves the Cream-Sicles.

John Marr: In 1978 there was no way a band called the Dead Kennedys was going to play a suburban high school.

East Bay Ray: So we made a logo where the sickle was a popsicle. All the kids knew who we were. This was strictly for the chaperones.

Jello Biafra: Then they expanded it to a real punk show and got Sudden Fun and the Zeros to play as well. Headlining were the Cream-Sicles. We got there, and sure enough it was a festive high school dance. I think Dennis from Sudden Fun probably had the time of his life with all the cheerleader girlie chickies and yarn ribbons in their hair, chewing purple bubble gum. They were pogoing along with everybody else, just enjoying the rock 'n' roll.

John Marr: This was just a spectacular show. Biafra was jumping into the audience the second or third number. The image that remains is the band playing their music while Biafra is being dragged around in the back of the cafeteria. It was great fun. That converted me.

Klaus Flouride: We played something for KPFA. Angela Davis was before us, and she went on for, like, 30 minutes beyond her allotted time. So we had ten minutes to play.

John Marr: This huge stage at Berkeley Community Theater. The [guitar and mic] cords couldn't get them to the edge of the stage, so they invited everyone to come up onstage to see the show. The punk rock kids who were only there to see the Dead Kennedys swarmed up there. This really freaked out the granola types who were running it, so they immediately pulled the plug.

Everyone was scratching their heads, and this guy said, "My fraternity will let them play." So the mob of punks and the Dead Kennedys showed up at the fraternity and set up in the living room and played the show. They played until four in the morning.

Jello Biafra: It was such a ridiculous situation. We were playing a house party, so we treated it like a house party. We played a country-western "Man with the Dogs." We played a disco "Kill the Poor." We played covers of songs we didn't even know, like "The Boy from New York City" by the Ad Libs. I think we played two or three sets.

Sheriff Mike Hennessey: Jello and I met on the campaign trail, 1979. I was running for sheriff at the same time he was running for mayor.

Jello Biafra: I was basically riding to a Pere Ubu show at the Old Waldorf in the back of Ted's Volkswagen. Our first drummer. I was folded in the backseat, and Ted was saying, "Biafra, you have such a big mouth, you should run for president." "No, no, you should run for mayor." Then a lightbulb went off over my head. Why not? I think I will!

So I began mouthing off to everybody at the show that I was running for mayor. People got excited, asking, "What's your platform?" So without thinking about it, I told them, "Ban cars from the city limits." Ideas kept popping into my head. I wrote my platform down in felt-tipped pen, that bled into a wet napkin, as Pere Ubu played five feet away from me.

I mixed and matched the satire and the pranks with stuff I thought was perfectly practical, such as making the police run for election voted on by the districts they patrol. Legalizing squatting in buildings left vacant for tax write-off purposes, which was an epidemic in San Francisco at that time. A lot of downtown was empty. I mixed that with direct slaps at Mayor Feinstein, such as creating a Board of Bribery to set standard public rates for liquor licenses, building code exemptions, police protection, and most importantly, protection from the police. I also proposed erecting statues of Dan White all over town, and allowing the park service to sell tomatoes and eggs and rocks for people to throw at them.

The city was broke, so I also proposed making up the deficit from the city coffers by legalizing panhandling for the city at 50 percent commission. And that the panhandlers should concentrate in Pacific Heights, where Feinstein lived. Her whole campaign was "law and order" and "we need to clean up downtown." I thought, you know, she's right. But let's clean up the other end. The dirty work is all done at the headquarters of Bank of America and Chevron and Bechtel. Therefore, businessmen should be required to wear clown suits between the hours of nine and five. That was the one the corporate media jumped on, and it got all over the world.

His fiancé on his arm, and wearing his campaign wardrobe, a seven-dollar suit from a Geary Street pawnshop, plus shoes a friend gave him for formal occasions. They're serviceable, but a bit large, Biafra says. The candidate, who won't tell his born name, would be a joke except he's too smart.

Jello Biafra, the lead singer in the punk rock group the Dead Kennedys. He held a press conference at City Hall. He then went on to do what he calls "shaking babies and kissing hands." He also went on a whistle-stop tour through parts of San Francisco today on a BART train. No telling how he'll do in the elections, but his philosophy is summed up in his campaign slogan, "There's always room for Jello."

—*CBS 5 (KPIX-TV) newscast, 1979*

Jello Biafra: Only then did it occur to me, how the hell do you run for mayor? Luckily in San Francisco, if you don't have enough petitions you just raise money and buy your way on the ballot. I was getting discouraged. Dirk said, "Wait, don't give up. You have no idea what could be done with this. We'll throw a benefit, we'll raise the money." That's where Dirk really came in. I had just turned 21. I had no idea what I was doing.

Sheriff Mike Hennessey: I can remember being at a big venue someplace in Nob Hill at a candidate's night, and introducing myself to him, and saying, "I'll bet I'm the only one here who has your 45 'California Über Alles.'" He kind of looked at me and he said, "Well, I'm glad you do!" And we became casual friends because we'd run into each other all the time. It wasn't a complete lark. Whether he ever felt he would win or not I don't know, but he really worked hard at being a candidate and made very entertaining presentations.

Klaus Flouride: Hennessey put himself in a very strange position of endorsing Biafra. It was just such a quirky thing to have the sheriff coming out and saying, "Yeah, my vote's going for Jello Biafra." He loved punk rock shows.

Sheriff Mike Hennessey: I recall going to a law enforcement conference in Phoenix, Arizona, and getting the local alternative newspaper, and finding out that Suicidal Tendencies was playing in Phoenix. So I put on jeans and a T-shirt and took a taxi there. A couple of kids in the crowd came over and said, "Are you a cop?" I had a mustache, and shortish hair. Obviously the oldest person there. I told them a half-truth, I said, "Well, I'm a lawyer." Which is true, I am a lawyer, but I didn't want them to think I was spying on them or something. I was just there to enjoy the music.

Jello Biafra: I never went door-to-door, or worked with grassroots to make it a more serious candidacy. Dianne Feinstein is seen nationally as this old-school liberal, but she had far more in common with Margaret Thatcher. She was a mean, hateful witch who didn't even bother to hide her contempt for the disadvantaged. She had that same kind of hatred for people of lesser means that you'd associate with Nixon or Cheney. Or Gavin Newsom.

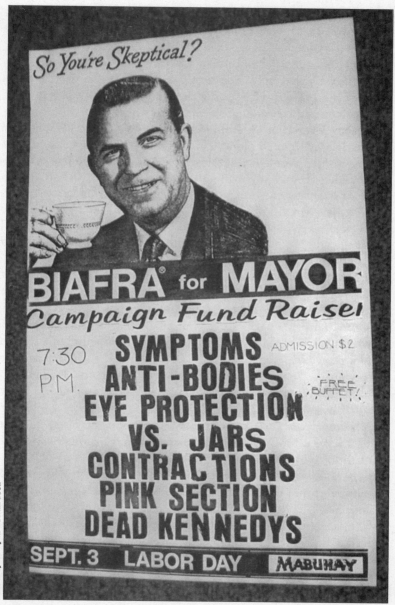

Shaking Babies and Kissing Hands: Jello Biafra for Mayor

Richard Hongisto, when he was on the Board of Supervisors, even called her a cop groupie. Not only did she turn the cops loose to beat the crap out of gay people and punks and cholos and African-Americans, she even had a police radio in her limousine that she listened to for pleasure.

Max Volume: I gave him a ride to his debate with Feinstein. It was pretty hilarious. And by the way, Dianne Feinstein is a fucking cunt. Nothing bad enough can happen to her.

Jello Biafra: After Dan White gunned down George Moscone and Harvey Milk in cold blood, Feinstein became acting mayor, and made a deal with Quentin Kopp, who also coveted the mayor's chair, that she wouldn't run in the regular election if he'd vote to make her acting mayor. Of course she lied, and Kopp was furious and it was a real knockdown drag-out blood feud between the two of them in the '79 election. Neither one of them were pleased that me and the guy that came in third helped force them into a runoff.

Lars Frederiksen: Jello running for mayor, sweeping up the stairs at City Hall. When he had the vacuum, "I'm gonna clean up the streets." I remember that shit. Channel 7 news, man.

Jim Jocoy: I remember watching him debating with the other three or four candidates on TV, with the moderator asking questions. He was wearing this funky, pseudo kind of formal wear, he wore a tie.

Klaus Flouride: Biafra was theater trained, you know. And he knew how to use it.

East Bay Ray: He's a good performer, and he's also very, very good at making, I call them bumper stickers. Taking a phrase—like, instead of saying "complacency," he writes the lyrics to "Holiday in Cambodia," which is about a college student with a five-grand stereo. Bumper stickers, like "Police Truck," or "Let's Lynch the Landlord." That's really great. But the problem with some in the punk audience, is they thought we were writing the Bible.

Klaus Flouride: There were people in places where English isn't their first language, like Portugal. "Kill the Poor" went to number four, something like that. Taking it literally.

East Bay Ray: We weren't trying to tell people what to do. We all have our own political beliefs. Our thing was to try to get people to think.

Klaus Flouride: Eighty percent of the songs were like getting inside some sort of crazed psychopath's head and trying to figure out what made them think that way.

Joe Rees: I went to every one of the damn shows. Jello, my god. He wouldn't shut up. He was obviously a very prolific writer, very astute. That's what really attracted me to the Dead Kennedys. But he always made you a little nervous. It was difficult to talk to Jello in those days.

Larry Livermore: In 1980 a friend of mine tried out to be their drummer and I took him to their practice. I had been up for about three days so I lay down and went to sleep behind the bass amp. But I remember waking up in the middle of this saying, "Hey, these guys really can play." They were really great musicians. You just couldn't tell in those days because the sound wasn't good.

East Bay Ray: We played in Washington D.C. downtown. It was some rental hall, audience was like 500 people, and the cops came in, and said, "Okay, you got too many people here, you have to close the show down." I said to Biafra, "Tell all the people to sit down." And so Biafra said, "Everybody just sit down."

Klaus Flouride: We sang the songs a cappella.

East Bay Ray: It was like a classic sit-in. You had to realize in the middle of D.C., these were like white kids. There's a 99 percent chance that they were the sons and daughters of politicians. So they didn't want to call a SWAT team to come in.

Jello Biafra: The second of the two shows we played there, some rather infamous people from D.C. showed up by the names of Ian and Henry. They'd brought barber clippers and began shaving people's heads by the side of the stage while we played.

Ray Farrell: Dead Kennedys and Black Flag were separate from most bands. Those two bands encouraged kids all over the country to book their own shows. They started to help build that network of places. Basically, those two bands got the promoters of the '80s started by explaining how easy it is.

At the same time, I saw the Dead Kennedys in some small VFW hall, encouraging the audience to pull the toilet out of the fucking bathroom in the name of anarchy. Those were the early days, but that's the kind of shit that would go along with that.

John Marr: After the first few years, it was no longer hip to go see the Dead Kennedys.

Dave Chavez: Their music was New Wave, surfy, kind of accessible. It wasn't hard and mean and angry, even though Jello was doing his best to hold up his end. It was the other guys in the band that wrote really—how would you put it? Very wimpy music.

Steve DePace: Early on, Will Shatter didn't like Jello, and didn't hide it either. I mean, told him to his face, "You're an asshole." One time I was at a show, and Jello was standing right in front of me. Jello turned and said, "Hey, what's up with Will Shatter? What's his problem with me? Why does he fucking hate me? He's always giving me shit." Blah blah blah. I took all this in and I looked at Jello and said, "Well at least he doesn't preach." And he was, "I don't preach! Blah blah blah blah, I don't preach!" And what does he do? Fucking preaches! That's his gig, man.

James Angus Black: There wasn't supposed to be a bunch of egos in the punk scene. The bands and the people are one and the same. Your band played, and then you were a regular person. I never voted for Jello to be mayor. I didn't vote for Jello to be king punk rocker.

He acts like he invented punk rock in San Francisco. He was just a part of it. He really thought he was going to be the benevolent leader of us, and we were all going to follow in his footsteps. Most of the kids involved in that scene had enough of people telling them what to do. They just wanted someplace to hang out and get high and listen to music, and have fun and forget about all the bullshit for awhile. And here came Jello, "*Wha wha wha*, you shouldn't be doing that, you should be more political." He was just another authority figure.

John Marr: They attracted a lot of suburban kids. "Let's have a punk rock night out—let's go see the Dead Kennedys." The hardcore punks didn't like it. But they played some of their best shows for audiences like that. Suburban morons really brought out the best in Biafra.

Murray Bowles: I always thought it was funny, because Jello would have these diatribes against jocks and even songs against jocks, and yet they were the one band out of all punk bands that had all the jocks at their shows. If you're an athlete in high school, you're programmed to be self-confident. You can basically do anything you want. So you went to Dead Kennedys shows. And if you were a misfit, you naturally went to Dead Kennedys shows. But all the people in between were sort of worried about their reputations and not quite sure whether punk rock was cool. They would stay away. So you ended up with punks and jocks at the venue.

Jello Biafra: When the surfers and the skaters picked up on punk and started coming to the shows, we all thought it would be great to finally take this to high schools and teenagers. But some of them brought their high school hang-ups and jock bullshit with them.

It got to the point where at 10th Street Hall shows, specific people, not all of whom were kids, were getting up onstage for the express purpose of getting a running start, jumping off the stage and punching somebody in the back of the head. The same people were doing it again and again.

People out of the crowd said to me, "Is anybody gonna do something about this?" I thought, well, if I don't say something then nobody will. So I wrote "Nazi Punks Fuck Off."

We debuted the song at a 10th Street Hall show that was a little later so people could go see Throbbing Gristle at Kezar first. The crowd went wild in two directions. The people who were sick of the violence were really happy somebody got up and said something. Then the people who it was aimed at of course reacted violently. Sure enough, some dude got up onstage afterwards wanting to argue with me, and he had on a swastika shirt that said "White Power" on the front, and "Niggers Beware" on the back. I couldn't have asked for a better example of what it was we were trying to fight. Nazi skins weren't there yet. It was just people acting like a bunch of fucking Nazis.

Of course it turned out that there were a few ideological Nazis in the scene who were very hurt by the song. One of them even started wearing a swastika armband to shows and a full SS uniform. Then I found out that he'd committed suicide when his wife left him and some of his friends blamed me. And then it got even more violent for me than ever before.

Ray, Klaus and D.H. didn't seem affected by this and didn't really seem to care. But there was times in 1982 when that song came out where I never knew what was going to happen next. I got stabbed at an On Broadway show. Somebody set off dynamite in front of my house and I didn't know who did it for the longest time. It was not good times. I was constantly on the verge of a nervous breakdown.

"SHOOTING THE SHIT"

TIM YOHANNAN: Of all the American bands you're the most renowned. Are you rolling in dough—are you rich rock stars?

JELLO BIAFRA: One of the ways people like the Clash or Devo have gotten supposedly wealthy is that neither of those two bands ever bothered with forming their own labels, or tried to help expedite artwork by anybody else. A lot of our money went into forming Alternative Tentacles records. The purpose of our compilation LP, *Let Them Eat Jellybeans*, was to alert people overseas and wherever to American talent and diversity. With Alternative Tentacles we got out a number of records by other people which might not have appeared—the *Maximum RocknRoll* LP set, 7 Seconds, etc. But not without problems.

TIM: Well, you've still skirted the question of what have you guys done with the large amount of money you made?

BIAFRA: It depends on what you call a lot of money. For example, none of us own houses. We all pay rent and live with roommates. It's not as though we suddenly have gone off to suburbia and bought tract homes. Basically we have been able to live for the past three years on income from the band. So on a day-to-day subsistence and existence level we've risen to that level, which is a lot further than many other people in the punk scene have been able to do, and that breeds a certain amount of jealousy. I take great pride in the fact that we've been able to support ourselves through the band without working 8 hours a day at degrading shit jobs that tax our energy and creativity. We sort of rose and fell in the financial department—at this point the band is pretty much broke.

TIM: No. The reason I bring up the question is—you have 'politically-oriented' punk bands who are accused of preachiness. From my perspective, it's important for bands who are talking or singing politically to practice what they preach, in a sense. Bands who make no bones about being out for bucks I have no expectations of.

JEFF BALE: They have no responsibility.

TIM: Bands who are going out to the public and trying to inform and agitate about political matters do have a responsibility to maintain credibility with the public.

BIAFRA: I didn't come from a wealthy background and I've never mixed well with wealthy people; have barely met any in my whole life. My mother's a librarian and my father doesn't work at all. I'm very proud of him—he works a lot, but he doesn't work any shit jobs, he writes, primarily. . . . People who expect too much of me, who want to lift me to the level of great leader or guru and thus isolate me as a zoo animal—thereby putting me below the level of a human being—I find that ugly. If I got out to other shows, which I do, I don't like getting vibes from some people: "Oh, what's he doing here? There's Biafra the asshole rock star," without ever talking to me. Just viewing me as something to be resented.

JEFF: I think that's inevitable.

BIAFRA: It might be inevitable, but it hurts. I have far more respect for people who walk up to me and say "I think you're full of shit, for this reason . . . ," than sneaking around and stirring up shit behind my back, and refusing to admit they did it.

TIM: But most of the people that Biafra comes in contact with are quite young, and don't have the accumulated life experience that gives self-identity and self-confidence.

BIAFRA: I don't think that age necessarily determines that. Some young people are very self-assured.

TIM: Some, but that's a rarity.

—Maximum
RocknRoll *11, January 1984*

Dale Flattum: I remember reading *MRR* interviews with Jello Biafra. We started getting Dead Kennedys records. Someone brought 'em back from Christmas break. The first two records, they were angry but fun. Like everything's fucked, but we're laughing at it all. They pointed out that you should question stuff, but it's still fun to be alive.

James Washburn: When I was in seventh grade in Pinole, I found a cassette tape on the playground. One side was the Dead Kennedys' *In God We Trust, Inc.* and the other side had the Sex Pistols. I had no idea what punk rock was. "The Sex Pistols, what a cool name! The Dead Kennedys? What the hell is on this tape?"

I played it, and it completely stopped me in my tracks. As anybody who likes punk rock knows, it gets you inside. It does something to you. You can't explain it, it's just there. It either works for you or it doesn't.

The first two albums I've ever owned in my life, was one by Ernie and Bert, and the Dead Kennedys album with the Statue of Liberty on the cover.

Jeff Ott: I got to see the Dead Kennedys a bunch of times. They're probably the first point at which I went, "Oh, you can have a band and play songs and talk more than you play songs." I was like, "That's very interesting. I should try that sometime."

Gavin MacArthur: I went to the Keystone Berkeley and saw the Dead Kennedys. I was 13 years old. I remember being overwhelmed by the density of the crowd. I hadn't even been to any big concerts yet. The closest thing I had been to was my parents dragging me to *The Nutcracker*.

I was really small as a kid and there were a bunch of people doing their little slam thing, moshing in the pit. It looked really outrageous, and me being kind of an adrenaline junkie, I went up onstage and started following people stage diving off of it. They just loved it when kids dove off, really small ones. They'd scoot 'em around the top of the crowd and throw 'em all over the place, and, man, I just had a blast.

Sergie Loobkoff: I don't think any band ever came close to being as intense and interesting. I was a dumbshit kid, I didn't think about anything political. I wouldn't think about what's going on about Cambodia or whatever. Dead Kennedys was actually opening people's eyes. I can't think of that many bands that really did. I don't believe Rage Against the Machine. I think they're posturing. Most bands that play punk rock and talk punk rock politics, are they doing it 'cause it sells records, or 'cause it sounds cool?

Lars Frederiksen: When I listened to a Dead Kennedys record the first time and heard "nigger," I was like, whoa. You didn't say that in my neighborhood. And here it was on a record. These guys didn't give a fuck. "Bragging that you know how the niggers feel cold and the slums got so much soul." I was an 11-year-old trying to figure out what they were saying, but not really getting it, just hearing the words. The word "fuck" in a record. You were like, "How did he do that? How'd he say 'fuck'? KISS doesn't say 'fuck.' "

The Dead Kennedys had the ability, that if you weren't crazy, they made you crazy in 15 minutes. You came in all serene, "I just smoked a joint, I'm cool." Next thing you know, *danana nanana nanana* and you were like, "Ahhhh, I'm gonna kill somebody!" That's what they made you feel like. "Give me something, ahhh! It's like my schoolteacher's on acid and he's yelling at me!" It's rad, you're into it. You're like, "I'm here. Fuck recess. I'll pee right here, I don't need a hall pass!"

I admire Jello. I don't wanna call him a teacher because that's probably not what he would wanna be referred to as. But his music did that. Like, what the fuck is this? Who the fuck's Pol Pot? I'm like ten and I can't listen to a Discharge record unless all the lights are on and my mom's home, 'cause it's scarin' the shit outta me. A nuclear war? What the fuck? Crucifix is saying 1984, the world's gonna end, and I'm just like, "Ahhh, we got two years to live!" I'm 13, I'm never gonna get my wiener sucked. The things you think about, you know. You got Jello screaming in one ear, Sothira's screaming in the next, and you're just like, "Oh fuck. I'm doomed!"

Frank Portman: In the '70s, the Dead Kennedys were tailor-made to appeal to me. Guys who liked Dr. Who and played D&D and listened to Dr. Demento, and liked punk rock—this was like the most awesome thing in the world. The real version of Weird Al Yankovic. This was just fantastic.

I took the bus to the city, and took the streetcar to Tower Records to get the "California Über Alles" single that I'd heard on Dr. Demento. It was two dollars, which was like, all my money. He was speaking to me at that particular time. And I was impressed with his belt buckle. It's famous, it was a star, like a Wyatt Earp kind of belt buckle. He had this cartoon character voice, which I admired.

And then you realize, whoa, he wasn't kidding. He really thinks that Jerry Brown is a fascist dictator, and he really thinks that everybody is Zen fascists, and that there's a secret government underneath these mountains in Colorado that's run by aliens. Wow, he's just a nut. And he's into hemp? That was a real blow to my worldview. It's all down to politics. Which kind of does outlaw humor, other than in particularly directed causes. There's a point where it's, oh, that's not funny. So it's a weird position for a satirist to take. It alienated at least a little proportion of his fans.

Dallas Denery: Of course, Frank is not an impartial critic of Jello Biafra. Because if you look at photos of them, they're identical. I swear to god, in the late '80s he looked just like Jello.

East Bay Ray: The reason we were around so much, and maybe the biggest band that came out of that scene, is 'cause we rocked out. And we wrote good songs.

Klaus Flouride: In the beginning we were also much more insistent on melody. Especially at the beginning. And we sort of let it slip near the end. By *Bedtime for Democracy*, eh, it wasn't hitting quite as hard.

Jello Biafra: It was very hard to get them to jam. But a lot of the jams we did do resulted into songs like "Moon Over Marin" or "This Can Be Anywhere," "Soup Is Good Food" and some of the others. I always longed for more than that, but it was hard.

Larry Crane: Vomit Launch opened for Camper Van Beethoven and the Dead Kennedys in Chico. That was '85. The guys in the DKs were obviously good musicians and fairly open-minded to all kind of shit. But to me, this was a band way past their prime. We thought they were ancient. I was 21 or 22 at that point and these guys were pushing 30 almost. I'm thinking, "Punk bands aren't supposed to be around for more than five years—they're practically dead!" They sounded pretty good, though. I really liked Ray's guitar playing. Jello was a great front man.

Joe Rees: When Jello's mother finally came to San Francisco, she really had no idea what he did. So Jello called me up one day at the studio and said, "I want to bring my mother over. Could we show her some of the videotapes?" That was a big deal to me. So I got everything together. I realized, oh my god, what am I gonna do? I must have a good eight, nine hours of Dead Kennedys here. As it turned out, Jello wanted her to watch eight or nine hours of Dead Kennedys! He made his mom sit in this room, and I played one tape after another. That poor woman. I was getting her a glass of water every once in awhile. We got through at least four hours of it. He did that to his own mother!

Hugh Swarts: Dead Kennedys was one of the only punk bands from here that I'd heard. The whole Frankenchrist thing, the controversy over the Giger artwork, and them getting busted. That was a high-profile thing. It kind of extended beyond.

"SINGER'S TRIAL ON NUDITY IN ALBUM BEGINS TODAY"

—New York Times, *August 16, 1987*

Jello Biafra: April 15, 1986. I was in this flat I used to rent. I heard this tromping up the stairs. "We're police officers. You are under suspicion of distributing harmful matter."

Can you imagine any matter more harmful than finding a cop in your bedroom? And then going on down the stairs in the main part of the place and finding out it's not just one cop, not just two, not just three. Nine cops were busy tearing my whole flat to pieces. I felt like it was a DEA drug raid or something.

There were two cops going through my address and phone book, page by page. It wasn't just San Francisco cops. Three of the cops were from Los Angeles.

I was asking them, what is this harmful matter? There ain't no drugs. There ain't no guns. What it takes nine cops to tear my whole house apart to find is a record album: *Frankenchrist*.

And inside that record album was a painting by Swiss surrealist master H. R. Giger. The guy who won the Oscar for designing the set to *Alien*, designed the monsters. He's done album covers for Emerson Lake & Palmer, Deborah Harry, Magma, Celtic Frost. He's a recognized master. But they really wanted his ass.

One of the L.A. guys was going, "Where's the guy who did this painting? Where is he?"

He's in Switzerland.

[Then-prosecutor] Michael Guarino: I remember looking at the piece of art, and thinking, just on the basis of the insert, we got a great case.

Jello Biafra: I heard drawers opening and shutting upstairs. I plopped down in a chair with nothing but a bathrobe on. Two L.A. cops were circling around me like sharks.

By that time, they'd also raided the Alternative Tentacles and Mordam Records warehouse office space. Couple of the cops were holding up DOA T-shirts, showing themselves off. One of them found the 4 x 6 chrome slide we'd gotten of the Giger painting from his agent in Switzerland.

"Alright, we got it! This is the smoking gun! We've got it, we've got 'em now, ha ha ha ha!"

Forgot to take it with them.

Suzanne Stefanac: When I arrived home, Biafra was sitting on the front steps. He pointed to the rickety front door, with its many glass panes. One of them was broken. "Cops," Biafra said. I was confused.

We went into the house, and it was shocking. The place had been torn apart. Drawers were upended. They'd gone through my things pretty thoroughly.

They'd photographed my phone book, which was pretty upsetting. As a journalist, people had entrusted me with their private information. Open on my desk was the transcript for an interview I'd just done with Frank Zappa, about censorship of music. The pages were out of order. They did find a small film canister with a few crumbs of pot. They left it open on top of the Zappa transcript, to show me they'd found it.

Jello Biafra: Two months later, June 2nd, 1986, me and four other people were all charged by the Los Angeles City Attorney's office with one count each of "distributing harmful matter to minors." I was charged, Ruth Schwartz from Mordam Records and *MRR* was charged, a guy who used to work at Alternative Tentacles and had quit by that time, he was charged anyway. They charged a guy from Greenworld Distribution, who wholesaled to stores. They even charged a 67-year-old man, whose crime against humanity was owning the record pressing plant that stamped out the vinyl and collated the discs. We were looking at a maximum year in jail, a $2,000 fine, because of what we said with a record album.

Suzanne Stefanac: For a year or so prior, Dead Kennedys had been among a handful of bands under attack by the Parents' Music Resource Center (PMRC). Al Gore's wife Tipper had founded the group with Susan Baker, wife of Republican James Baker, who had been Reagan's chief of staff and who later served as George H. W. Bush's secretary of state. It was an odd match with an even odder agenda. The PMRC claimed that lyrics by Dead Kennedys, Prince, Black Sabbath, Judas Priest, Mötley Crüe, Madonna and even Cyndi Lauper were responsible for teenage pregnancy, suicide and violence.

Jello Biafra: The prosecuting deputy city attorney from L.A. went on TV that night, saying, "We feel this is a cost-effective way of sending a message that we are going to prosecute." He deliberately picked an independent, who would have to pay out of their own pocket to defend themselves. Instead of a high-budget PMRC target like Prince or Ozzy, they picked us.

Suzanne Stefanac: Things had been heating up. In protest, some bands were putting their own stickers on albums. *Frankenchrist* was shipped with a sticker that read, "Warning: The inside foldout is a work of art by H. R. Giger that some people may find shocking, repulsive, or offensive. Life can sometimes be that way."

After hearing the story, Dirk Dirksen said that we'd clearly have to launch a defense fund. The three of us founded the No More Censorship Defense Fund. Biafra was adamant that the name had to be baldly descriptive. Nothing jokey or clever. Just to the point.

Even though the primary lawyers on the case worked pro bono, the research, court filing fees, expert witnesses and other legal fees added up to more than $50,000. We got the word out through radio stations, inserts in albums put out by Alternative Tentacles, SST and others, and through journalists. MTV News even played Dead Kennedys' "MTV—Get Off the Air" while making the pitch for the defense fund.

I researched and wrote most of the content in the No More Censorship Defense Fund fact sheet. We told people about the case, as well as other music and art censorship cases. We provided histories of American freedom of expression and the PMRC. We got thousands of letters from people all around the world. Punk kids, their parents and grandparents, even the Ringling Brothers clowns. Most of the money raised came in increments of ten dollars or less. It was an amazing grassroots effort.

Jello Biafra: We finally went to trial in Los Angeles, almost a year and a half after the initial police raid. The smoking gun Michael Guarino thought he had was this handwritten list I'd been keeping, of the different releases we'd put out on Alternative Tentacles.

"Now one would think, Your Honor, that it would be important to show the jury how these people deliberately disseminate material they know is offensive to the public taste. With bands with names like the Crucifucks, and Butthole Surfers. Look at these titles: 'Plastic Surgery Disasters,' 'War on 45,' 'Nazi Punks F-f-f-f Off.'"

He brought the list up to the judge, like a kid bringing a paper to the teacher. Judge looked at it: "Ah ha ha ha ha!" Everyone except Guarino was snickering by now, as he took the list back. Phil Schnayerson [Biafra's attorney] finally asked, "Well, what's the problem? Is that song a little too close to home? 'Too Drunk to Fuck'?"

Michael Guarino: It was upsetting to see Philip Schnayerson so sure of himself, and so sure of the merits of his case. I could start reading the jurors. And I didn't like what I was seeing. I was seeing a lot of various degrees of hatred towards me, registering on faces. I started getting the feeling that this was not a great case, very early on in the trial.

Suzanne Stefanac: Mary Sierra, the mother who'd complained about the poster, testified, as did her daughter, who I think was 17 at the time. The mother claimed that she'd purchased the album as a Christmas present for the daughter, but when her younger son saw the poster, that's when she decided to file the complaint.

Jello Biafra: They didn't charge the record store. Guarino justified this to the press, saying, "Well, they were cooperative, and took Dead Kennedys off the shelves." Wherehouse was the largest retail chain in California. They didn't just ban *Frankenchrist* from the one store in Northridge, they banned every record we'd ever made from all their stores, permanently.

Suzanne Stefanac: There were a number of bizarre moments. Lawyers from both sides played cuts from the album and read lyrics aloud. There was a huge poster with lyrics from some of the songs that they would point to with long sticks, like schoolteachers.

Jello Biafra: Four hours, six hours, eight hours. No jury. Finally, a note comes back from the jury room. "The jury would like a record player." An hour and a half later, out they came. They could only agree on one thing. That they were hopelessly deadlocked, seven to five in favor of acquittal. Charges dropped, case dismissed.

Suzanne Stefanac: It had been exhausting for everyone. Dead Kennedys broke up during the lead-up to the trial. The label had suffered. Biafra hadn't been able to get on with his own work. The PMRC did better. The labels caved and began slapping warning stickers on albums. On the one hand, this only made kids want those albums more. But as predicted, many major distributors refused to carry albums with "questionable" content.

Michael Guarino: That was the turning point for me. From time to time, someone would come up to me and say, "Are you the Mike Guarino that prosecuted Jello Biafra? What were you thinking?" Students were amazed that this person they thought they knew, had been involved in this thing. My son is probably one of [Jello's] biggest fans. He's 22 years old. He would play the stuff so loud that half the block could hear it. He was a huge fan.

Jello Biafra: One of the few silver linings to come out of the trial— Frank Zappa got hold of me and gave me some very valuable advice very early on, something that anybody subjected to the kind of harassment should remember: *You are the victim.* You have to constantly frame yourself in that way in the mass media. So you don't get branded some kind of outlaw simply because of your beliefs and the way you express your art.

I got to visit Frank two or three times at his house in Los Angeles, and those were pretty special times. He showed me a hilarious Christian aerobics video. The women were in their skintight leotards doing jumping jacks. One-two, two-two, Praise the Lord! And of course the bustiest one was in a striped spandex suit, dead center at the front of the screen!

Robert Hanrahan: Like all the other bands I advised, I asked each band member to read the Billboard book *This Business of Music* and for the band to find an attorney through BALA, the Bay Area Lawyers for the Arts. In the DKs case, I may have made a mistake.

> The Dead Kennedys was a punk rock band, which performed together from 1978 to 1986. Together the band created numerous musical compositions and sound recordings. The name of the band was a tribute to the ideals of John and Robert Kennedy. The four members of the band were respondents East Bay Ray aka Ray Pepperell, Klaus Flouride aka Geoffrey Lyall, and D. H. Peligro aka Darren Henley, and appellant Jello Biafra aka Eric Reed Boucher. The Dead Kennedys band toured extensively and recorded six full-length albums, numerous singles and extended-play albums. The song writing was a collaborative effort among the band members. The band's popularity has continued; it sold in excess of 134,000 records in 1998.
> —DEAD KENNEDYS et al., Plaintiffs and Appellants, v. JELLO
>   BIAFRA, Defendant and Appellant; A094272 (San Francisco
>   County Super. Ct. No. 998892)

"BIAFRA'S EX-MATES WIN IN COURT: $220,000 IN DAMAGES ORDERED"

—San Francisco Chronicle, Saturday, May 20, 2000

James Sullivan: I covered the trial for the *San Francisco Chronicle*. The whole thing just felt icky, like taking notes while an old married couple bickered over the pension checks. But the irony—old punk values shriveled up and tossed aside—was just too absurd for words.

Dead Kennedys made their name as America's answer to the Sex Pistols, a group of punks fiercely committed to exposing the bullshit and hypocrisy of modern life—the corporate greed, the class warfare, the "I, me, mine" attitude. And here the band members were suing Biafra over royalties, and Biafra was claiming that they started a pissing match over his refusal to do the Levi's commercial with "Holiday in Cambodia."

There were no winners. Even before the trial was decided, they all looked bad. I guess that's the danger in setting yourselves up as pillars of righteousness. Sooner or later, we're all going to take the low road, and pay for it.

> Kristen Lange was general manager of the label when Ray wanted to see the books back in '97. According to her deposition, a few passages of which were read aloud at the hearing, she found out about a discrepancy between what the books indicated the band was paid and what they should have been paid. When she took the news to Biafra, she remembers him "saying that Ray would go after him if he knew." She says she was told not to break the news to the band. Biafra says Lange misunderstood his orders.
>
> Ray was present during Lange's deposition last August. When he heard how Biafra allegedly instructed her to conceal information, he left the room and cried for half an hour.
>
> —*"Punk Rock on Trial," RJ Smith*, Spin, *February 2000*

James Sullivan: In the end, the jury decided that Jello owed Klaus and Ray and Peligro something like 75 grand for messing around with their royalty rate, and then covering it up. The weirdest part was that the jury bought into the idea that the ex-band members could have earned more money if Alternative Tentacles had continued to advertise for the old albums. What label buys ads for 15-year-old records? It was hard to argue with Jello's argument that it was his notoriety that was keeping the band's legacy alive.

The poor guy looked stricken when the judge read the verdict, like he never imagined he could lose the case. I don't think the other guys were feeling especially victorious either.

Whatever legacy the band had left behind, it was pretty clear it had just been squandered over what essentially amounted to a backlog of petty grievances. If the band left a statue, now it was covered in pigeon shit.

Bruce Loose: Personally, I've not had the best relationship with Jello. He's not had the best relationship with me. We'll leave it at that. I like Ray, and I like Klaus. I connected with Klaus and Ray long before I connected with Jello. It's sad what happened to them. As far as I'm concerned, they ruined a really good thing.

Martin Sprouse: The history became so weird. It was bound to happen that way. 'Cause it was always Jello, and then the three other guys. Even back then. They didn't hang out. You just knew that they weren't a tight group. That behind the scenes things weren't as smooth as it seemed.

Tammy Lundy: The way that they treated Jello later was just so shabby. Jello has his problems. He had a big ego, like most singers do, but what's surprising about that? That's part of the deal.

Dennis Kernohan: The best thing that ever happened to you four guys, and you're gonna fuckin' fight about it the rest of your lives?

10

No One's Listening

Penelope Houston: When you went in, you wrote down your drink order and handed it over the bar. It must have been some kind of nonprofit, 'cause most of us were under 21. They never carded. The Mabuhay was the mainstay, but the Deaf Club, that was Robert Hanrahan.

Robert Hanrahan: I bought a burrito at La Cumbre and noticed a sign on the fire escape across the street. It said "Hall for Rent." I went up the flights of stairs and saw two guys watching TV with the sound off. After a very short while, I realized we weren't going to communicate, so I wrote on a piece of paper that I wanted to rent the place. Bill—I never knew his last name—was a mustachioed, lascivious, cigar-chewing character who apparently was in charge. He wrote "OK & $250," so I wrote "OK."

I rented a P.A. system from the company I worked for, and booked my favorite bands: the Offs, Mutants and On the Rag, who later became Noh Mercy, for the first show.

Penelope Houston: It was kind of amazing. I think they were dancing to the vibrations. The deaf people were amused that all these punks wanted to come in and rent their room and have these shows.

Robert Hanrahan: The social aspect of being able to participate and be accepted was big for the deaf people. They enjoyed being exposed to a different subculture like their own. It was very convivial, no fights or hassles.

Winston Smith: They put their hands on the table and they could hear the music. It was music they could appreciate because it was so loud.

Johnnie Walker: I was in my little corner with my mobile disco rig. We transformed the place, had it packed full of punks going crazy, bands coming up from Los Angeles, stage diving into the audience, the floor was bouncing up and down. You had mayhem at one end of the club, and all these deaf people at the other drinking beer and signing to each other, grinning all over their faces, because they absolutely adored it. They had all the atmosphere, but they didn't have to hear the music.

Ray Farrell: Any other club at the time, people would be snotty because it was either trendy, or because they just didn't give a fuck. What was very unique about the Deaf Club is that the people who ran it were the friendliest people imaginable. I think I saw the Butthole Surfers there on their first time playing in San Francisco.

Robert Hanrahan: In the early days, the commander of the Mission precinct sent a patrol officer to the Deaf Club. He told me that we had their cooperation, as the "punks were changing the face of the neighborhood and appeared to be bringing the crime rate down." But he said if I fucked up he would unleash a shitstorm and close it down. "Understood?" was his next word. And with that I was escorted out to the street by the patrol officer and walked back. Sometimes younger cops would drop in to ask about learning to pogo with the real intention of meeting those "loose and wild" punk women.

Jennifer Blowdryer: It was on Valencia. I remember Russell got queer-bashed pretty badly near there, and someone else got stabbed. When there's a new area it seems like some blood gets shed, initially.

Robert Hanrahan: There was one invasion by cholos near the end of the club's life. The attackers were beaten back down the stairs and out onto the street by the audience. There was also the murder of a transient who apparently was flung out through one of the fire escape doors in the upper floors of the hotel and sailed over the heads of *Thrasher* magazine's Enrico Chandoha and Matty Todd from Pink Section. Matty went into the club and asked me to come outside to talk with the cops, who arrived with paramedics, who waited patiently for the guy to die. While the cop and I were talking, this couple walked over into the street and the guy began to sift his hands through the blood from the transient's head, that was pooling up on the street.

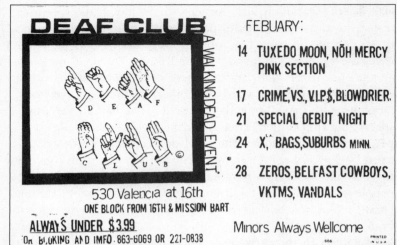

DEAF CLUB

A WALKING DEAD EVENT

D E A F
C L U B ©

530 Valencia at 16th
ONE BLOCK FROM 16TH & MISSION BART

ALWAYS UNDER $3.99

FOR BOOKING AND INFO - 863-6069 OR 221-0838

FEBUARY:

14 TUXEDO MOON, NÕH MERCY
    PINK SECTION

17 CRIME, VS., V.I.P.$, BLOWDRIER.

21 SPECIAL DEBUT NIGHT

24 X², BAGS, SUBURBS MINN.

28 ZEROS, BELFAST COWBOYS,
    VKTMS, VANDALS

Minors Always Wellcome

PRINTED IN U.S.A.

Courtesy of Robert Hanrahan

Good Vibrations: Deaf Club flyer

Jennifer Blowdryer: I had this thick Rhode Island accent and I was mean as a snake. I didn't like the fact that I'd been a reject all my life. I would always be tanked. I used to carry a bottle of Seagrams 7. And then people were kissing my ass 'cause I was in a band. I remember Sally Mutant was backstage, and Timmy said I said, "You've got two short little legs, why don't you walk away on 'em?" People would come up to me years later and be like, "You really upset my friend at the Deaf Club."

Rozz Rezabek: Everybody would end up drinking Bud, because it was the only thing you could order with the deaf people. You'd try and do sign language. But then if you mouthed the word "BUD" they'd understand. That's all anybody ever drank, was Budweiser.

Larry Livermore: The building was old and a little bit shaky. The whole place would move with the drums and the sound of the music, and people stumbling around and jumping around.

Rozz Rezabek: This couple named Joel and Mimi lived next door. The window from their fire escape faced the backstage room. When bands were there, Joel and Mimi would just charge people a buck to come through. People would be crawling through the window into the dressing room. In and out, all night long.

Jennifer Blowdryer: Now you think of people who are so-called handicapped, there's supposed to be this liberalization of using language as if no one's different, but they're actually more protected and segregated now. It wasn't like the deaf people must be separate or something. They were just down and drinking and having as good a time as anybody. They were drinkers, those deaf people. Oh yeah.

Sammytown: They closed it down 'cause pogoing was big, and they were afraid the floor would collapse.

Robert Hanrahan: The deaf community supported the club to the end. Bruce Conner had the last unofficial show there, a private affair that was paid for with an award he received.

Dennis Kernohan: The deaf people there with balloons, holding them up and feeling the vibrations of the balloons to the Germs, all these fuckin' great bands, and using these balloons and dancing around. For a tough old punk, it just made your heart—it gave you that beautiful feeling. They loved the music, and we were making money for them.

11

Ha Ha Ha

Steve DePace: I remember being approached by Ted Falconi at a party in a warehouse somewhere. I was jamming around with some different people. He had seen me in Negative Trend, we had done shows together. He was in a band called Rad Command. He said, "Hey, man, I really like the way you play drums, blah blah blah. I got a thing going with Will Shatter. We want you to come and play drums with us."

Ted came from a band that had broken up. Myself and Will, from a band that had broken up. The original singer, Ricky Williams, was fired from the Sleepers.

Flipper started in '79. There was no talk of how we were gonna style this band, or how we were gonna style the music, or anything. We literally got together in a room, plugged in, and started playing. And what came out, came out.

Ted Falconi: We did a show right outside the Aquarium in Golden Gate Park. And, as all these kids were running out, you know, "Flipper—I wanna go back and see Flipper!" Talking about the aquarium. And Ricky Williams had all these animals called Flipper. So Will was like, "That's the name of the band—Flipper. Ricky will remember it, and it signifies fun."

Steve DePace: Ted was the art school guy. He came up with a logo that anybody could do. It was one continuous motion to do the whole thing. You just had to take your pen off the page to do the fins. That thing was all over the world.

Joe Rees: Ted and I were friends in art school. I never in my life ever thought Ted Falconi would play a musical instrument and perform onstage. Oh sure, he was a frontline, open-minded anti-war guy with long hair. You just never expected any interest in the music scene.

Steve DePace: Ricky Williams was fantastic. What a great presence, he was a great punk rock star onstage. But he was all fucked up on drugs. He lasted maybe six months. We actually kicked him out of the band. He was showing up to rehearsals unconscious. He had these two girls that were his handlers, and they would drag him from place to place. How do you have an unconscious singer?

Bruce Loose: The only reason I'm in Flipper is because I was a friend of Will's.

Rozz Rezabek: The early Flipper shows were really good, when they were kind of like the Grateful Dead of punk. They would do these long pounding dirges, long, horrible anti-groove things.

Joe Rees: Ted's guitar was irritating as hell. But you could always have a good time when you went to a show. You never had to think a lot about Flipper. It was basically a crazy, mad happening.

Ruth Schwartz: Flipper were the first rave band, as far as I'm concerned. Will was a poet. So he was doing poetry over this grunge thing. And it worked for a lot of people. I go back to that stuff now and it's unlistenable. There's a lot of things you go back and listen to now and you go, "They really were good." And then other things you go back and listen to: "Wow, what were we ever thinking?" Flipper's one of them.

Steve Tupper: I first saw them in either late August or early September of '79 at the Deaf Club. Mike from the Tools and I were both total Negative Trend fans. We cornered Ted in the back room and said, "Hey, would you like to be on this record that we're putting out?" And Ted was totally grinning from ear to ear. I don't think they'd even done a demo at that point.

Jello Biafra: Flipper was a very controversial, maybe even dangerous band that still had the attitude of Negative Trend running through it. Where the reason to play music is not to be liked, it's to fuck with everybody. There was no middle ground. People either loved them or absolutely hated them. It got to the point where one way of heckling crappy out-of-town poseur bands, or British record company bands, was to yell "Flipper!" out in the crowd. I yelled that at the Keystone in Berkeley, and somebody punched me in the back of the head as hard as they could. Just mentioning Flipper offended people that bad.

Dave Chavez: I was a big fan of theirs because they were so noisy. You never knew if somebody was gonna be too high, or if they were just gonna play one song, or maybe a couple, or ten. You didn't know. And if they did play one song or two songs, they made it fit the whole set. The scene was so new, it was really like the beginning of the hardcore scene. It sounds funny to say that, but early Flipper shows were some of the most hardcore shows I've gone to.

Krist Novoselic: I met Buzz Osbourne, who was in the Melvins, in Aberdeen, Washington. I heard some of the old-school punks from the '70s, but I hadn't really heard any American hardcore music. I was 18. Buzz was a punk rock evangelist, so he lent me a bunch of records, and one of the records was *Generic Flipper*. I put it on and listened to it, and I said, "God, this is really weird." Just the production value. Is this live? I listened to it again, and then the third time, I rolled over and it just floored me. Oh, this is really art and expression, and ethereal. It actually was an epiphany.

Dean Washington: Flipper's music is filthy and slow to me. I don't wanna nod out, I wanna be, like, teeth grinding. But they were good.

Johnny Genocide: They are the one band I never got tired of. There are layers to their sound that are fascinating to listen to, especially with headphones.

Steve Tupper: The Tools, the Vktms, Flipper and another band that was pretty popular at that time, No Alternative, were all on *S.F. Underground*. The idea was to do this series of 7-inch compilations. Pick one song from four different bands and put them on a 7-inch. By the time the first Flipper LP came out in the spring of '82, Subterranean was pretty much plugged into the whole U.S. indie distribution network. Flipper got this full-page spread in *NME*. We got their *Generic* LP released in the U.K., but it didn't sell worth shit there. I don't know why.

Larry Crane: I lived in Nevada City through high school. My friends used to tape the *Maximum RocknRoll* show. We'd be riding in my car, and one of those shows, my friend said, "You're gonna hate this." And "Earthworm" by Flipper came on. I was like, "Wow, that's really cool!" It was just so textural.

Steve DePace: Will Shatter and Bruce Loose. Those guys were the real deal. They didn't give a shit. It wasn't about, oh, let's play a great show and we'll sell a lot of records. It was about torturing the audience to fucking death. To them, if you walked out, then they did their job right.

Courtesy of Silke Tudor

Mabuhay Flyer: Flipper, The Lewd, and Crucifix

Gary Floyd: When we first moved here, I didn't know those guys. The Dicks were playing at the Mab and Will Shatter jumped onstage and grabbed the microphone and started singing along. I ran over and grabbed him and kicked his fucking ass offstage and said, "Start your own fucking band!" Later on a friend said, "That was the guy in Flipper. He fucking loves you guys, and you told him to start his own fucking band. He *has* a band—bigger than your band." But I had to pull it in, you know. Like, "Well, I didn't like it."

Ruth Schwartz: Most of the people who were really in love with Flipper were pretty messed up. You had to be really messed up to be into it. People who didn't do drugs didn't like it, 'cause who wants to stand around for that?

Jello Biafra: Flipper opening for PiL at the South of Market Cultural Center. My favorite show of all time. Visualize the PiL audience, 3,000 people crammed into a building way too small. I commend Johnny Rotten for refusing to play for Bill Graham. Which meant it was a poorly run Paul Rat show that was way oversold. One person there turned to me afterwards and said, "You know, Bill Graham should have done this show." It was that badly run.

Tom Flynn: The crowd hated them. A huge crowd, all in this big long narrow building. Flipper started, and I thought something was wrong with the P.A. system. I couldn't hear a note the guitarist was playing. I was like, "Is this what they're trying to sound like?"

Jello Biafra: The sound was bad, the crowd was pissed, everybody was in a really edgy mood. There were all these jocks, and people even from Travis Air Force Base, there to see the freak show, 'cause Johnny Rotten was gonna come on.

And there was Flipper, playing their wonderful/horrible music, and people getting madder and madder, trying to boo them off the stage. Most bands would melt, and go off into the dressing room and cry. But Flipper was just laughing at 'em. Bruce said, "Okay, now we're gonna torture you some more." And then would come the next song. Eventually Falconi was playing his guitar, using a Bacardi bottle as a slide, that someone had thrown up there apparently.

The stage was about ten feet off the ground with a chain-link fence. People kept trying to climb up on the stage to pull Flipper off, and falling back on everybody else like the Potemkin movie. Bruce and Will were actually playing soccer, kicking all the cans that were thrown at them back at the crowd. And then finally Will hit his bass on an upstroke, his bass flew over his head, took him with it, he crashed into all of the equipment, and knocked it over. The whole thing was feeding back something fierce, all through the P.A. And Will just paced the stage, dragging his bass and his amp behind him, laughing. It couldn't have happened to a more deserving audience.

Fat Mike: San Francisco punk in the '80s did not have a sound. Out of tune and totally sloppy and fucked up was the San Francisco sound. Flipper, I mean seriously—worst band in America. They may be classic, but L.A.'s got Bad Religion, and the Circle Jerks, and Agent Orange, and Social Distortion. And you have Flipper? What the fuck is that?

Steve Tupper: On a lot of the records, I did the artwork. The album *Generic Flipper*, the bar code, I took it off a can of dog food.

Ray Farrell: I worked for Subterranean. They would come in eating cat food to get advance money, because they spent all their money.

I was at some Flipper gig in San Francisco. Before the bands started, I was standing in the beer line. I wasn't paying any attention, but I kept getting hit in the back, by somebody not being able to keep their balance. I turned around and I saw it was the Flipper guys. Two of them were already drunk, and kind of smacking each other. One of them kept falling into me.

Instead of turning around and hitting him, I made my back very rigid. He got pissed off that I did this, and smacked me in the back of the head. I turned around, and smacked him in the face, and I got hit in the eye, and before I knew it, I was on the floor being held down by three of the guys.

Ted Falconi, it was a hair trigger with violence for him. He was a fucking Vietnam vet that was just like, I'm here to protect my guys. He didn't know what the fight was about. But if the other two guys were gonna do it, then he was gonna join in. They got me on the floor, and a guy was sitting on my chest. Ted said, "Wait, it's Ray!" And I said, "Yeah, I'm getting beaten up by a band that's on the label that I work for. This is fucking ridiculous." I ended up with a black eye.

Steve DePace: I was kind of the straight guy surrounded amongst all these crazy fuckers. There was always some serious drama between Ted and Bruce. Over whatever. One show at the Hotel Utah, I think, Ted and Bruce started fighting onstage in the middle of the show, and ended up out in the audience pummeling each other.

Another night it happened at the Mabuhay, over a girl they were both dating. Before we even started. The place was packed, all these people were watching Bruce and Ted fight. And that was the show. The fight went offstage somewhere, and it was me sitting there in front of a full crowd. They came back up and we did one song. We had a 45-minute set. The first half hour was the fight, and the last 15 minutes was "Sex Bomb."

Bruce Loose: Steve, he's a good embellisher. I don't know if we were into direct fistfights. There may have been supposed things that

Gone Fishing: Flipper

looked like punches thrown, but there were never any punches that landed.

Tom Flynn: I saw Flipper with Dead Kennedys and Circle Jerks. Flipper only played three songs. Then Dirk Dirksen came out onstage for some reason, and Will started punching him. It was a huge fight, and that was the end. A bunch of their sets ended in fights. I can remember someone saying to me once, "They gotta figure out another way to end their shows."

Steve DePace: We played 4th of July down at the Farm. Bruce had just had his kid. He collected up dozens of these dirty, shitty diapers, brought them to the show and started lobbing them into the audience. He decided that was the punk rock thing for that particular night. So these shitty diapers, what do you think happened to them? They started coming back onstage. Shit diapers.

Johnny Genocide: Bruce is an amazing person. You have to peel back the layers to see the brilliance of his mind.

Steve DePace: There was an episode in Ann Arbor, Michigan. Oftentimes audience members came up onstage and would dance around, stage dive, whatever. This girl was up onstage, a bunch of people around her. This guy kinda literally bumped into this girl, thrashing around. The girl fell backwards and the guy fell on top of her, and it was right in front of my kick drum. And they just started fucking, right there. They're like, well, here we are, let's do it. One couple ran off after the show and went to Reno and got married. And are still married.

Steve Tupper: After we'd done that one Flipper song on *S.F. Underground*, I was thinking, "Jeez, we need to do a live recording of Flipper because the studio stuff doesn't capture it." Bruce and Will both had this very dry, sarcastic humor thing going. We went through scads and scads of board tapes and picked out some of that outrageous in-between song patter and put it on the records.

They were doing quite well. They were getting a lot of national airplay by that time. People around here knew what to expect. But they would hit towns cold, and no one would know about them except by hearing their records on the radio. People would show up, and then just get all this total disdain, hurled at them from the stage. That alienated a few people.

Steve DePace: The first national tour we did, we came through New Orleans and played in the French Quarter somewhere. The bartender was this hot chick who introduced us to kamikazes at three in the afternoon, while we were sound checking. We went off and had dinner, more kamikazes.

This particular night was just Kamikaze Drunken Mess Night, for us, onstage. We were so bad. Most of the audience left. There was probably ten people in front, they were the hardcore fans and we ended up just going, "You guys play." We handed our instruments to them, they started jamming, and we went to the bar.

Bruce Loose: When we were on tour with GWAR, we left them in New Orleans. On our way back, we stopped and drank a bunch of Hurricanes. It was a really hot day, and we started having a squirt gun fight on the street, which turned into having the police coming, an art gallery smeared with mayonnaise, a water pistol being pointed at the police, and then Ted being held with a gun on the top of his head, facedown on the ground. Over a water pistol.

Ted Falconi: Only one time it was really bad, and that was in Jersey. Steve and I pretty much killed this quart bottle of tequila backstage. After about the third song I was making myself seasick. I started asking for somebody to play guitar. I had this line of kids. I was like puttin' it on, they'd play for awhile. Take it off, put it on the next guy, they'd play for awhile. I was sitting on the side of the stage, in front of the drum riser. It was okay.

Steve DePace: There were times when Will or Bruce either couldn't do a tour or left in the middle of a tour. Bruce did that to us one time, he just up and left, and we had half a tour to go. Even Ted left us in the middle of a tour one time.

Krist Novoselic: That was the thing with Flipper. They had a few shows scheduled in Seattle, but they were all canceled. Word was, they could never get it together to take it up that far north.

Steve Tupper: Flipper started going on extended breaks in '82. We were trying to record their second studio LP. It took about a year. They did like two LPs' worth of basic tracks. And then Ted wanted to live in L.A. for awhile, and Bruce wanted to stay in New York for awhile. It was getting difficult to get people together. There were too many drugs around.

Steve DePace: In San Francisco, people didn't do cocaine. That was the rock star drug and we were all anti–rock star. So it was speed. It was cheap, it lasted longer. Heroin was cheap. Acid. Those were the big drugs of the day. And booze. Punks weren't into weed because it was hippie.

Rozz Rezabek: We were so down on that. Somebody would light up some pot, everybody would be like, "What the fuck you doin', you fuckin' hippie? Get that shit out of here!" It's really funny because a lot of those guys are now practically Rastafarians.

Kelly King: Definitely a lot of heroin in the city. A good friend of mine, Nina Crawford from the Vktms, a great singer, really great band, and she was a junkie. There was a lot of that going around.

Bruce Loose: The drugs and the type of music that got influenced from those particular drugs killed the true heart of the San Francisco punk scene by 1981, '82. Up to '83, maybe. But then I'm thinking more of Flipper.

Jello Biafra: I guess I made a decision early on. I could either do what Will and his buddies were doing and spend my money on speed— I just couldn't handle it as well as those guys seemingly could—or I could spend it on records. Which one would make me more happy long-term? Records, of course.

Rozz Rezabek: I can remember Will doing this. Back then, you could take these things called Vicks inhalers. Get about 20 of 'em, bust 'em open. They had this big chunk of ChapStick type stuff in there. You'd get some acetone down at the hardware store, pour it on that in a glass baking tray, and then set it in the window. It dries out, after about a week of sittin' in the sun. And that's all you really had to do.

Steve DePace: I don't know why or how, but I drew the line in the sand for myself as far as drug use went. Because I saw around me people going very rapidly from drug use for fun and yuks, to being really fucked up, to being desperate, and robbin' and stealin' and lookin' like shit, to dying. That happens fast. And I guess I was smart enough to go, wow, man, if it can take you from having fun one night to being dead in a year, or six months, or three months, I better not fuck with that shit.

Kelly King: They weren't like a regular band. They were just wasted, so wasted. Bruce would always be doing heroin and the other ones were always wired.

Steve DePace: I saw three guys in my band die. It affects your business, it affects your playing in the band. It affects everything. It goes from, you're in a band, you're making music, this is great, this is cool, we're playing shows, to, so-and-so's too fucked up to play, or to rehearse. Or he's passed out on the chair over there. Or he's been up for a week, and he's crashed, there's no waking him up. But we have rehearsal scheduled. Well, when you're on drugs you don't think about a schedule. It's all one big day. There's no time, there's no day.

You've got a tour planned. Well, Dickhead doesn't want to go on tour, he tells you the day before. And he makes up some excuse. But the real reason is, he doesn't wanna leave his dealer down the street. And if he doesn't feed his habit every day he gets sick. We would just threaten to go anyway, and he would go, "What do you mean? Oh no, you're gonna leave without me, okay I'll come." Like you're gracing us with your fucking presence.

Kelly King: Ted was a total speed freak. Ted would stay up for days. They drove my van for a long time. We'd get back to the warehouse and they'd just disappear. I'd always have to load back in by myself. Too much drugs, man.

Bruce Loose: We went until Will died.

Steve DePace: Will used to flip back and forth between dope and speed. So if he got too strung out on heroin—bang, I'm gonna go to speed now. There's that three days of hell you go through while you're detoxing? Well, Will discovered that if you just bang speed, that overrides everything. And he would do that. He would be a speed freak for awhile, and then he'd start banging dope again, and then he'd start banging speed again. How long can you do that?

Rozz Rezabek: One time Will came over to where I was living, all tweaked up. This was probably in '87. I'd given him my address. Out of the blue, he came over with big saucer eyes, like eight in the morning, with a basketball, and said, "You wanna play basketball?"

We went and played at this little hoop. It was on a Saturday or Sunday morning. He was so godawful, it wasn't even funny. I got the feeling that he was walking over to go see me, and he saw a basketball sittin' on somebody's porch, and stole it. I know it wasn't his because he didn't know how to play. That was the last time I really got to spend time with him.

Steve DePace: The sad thing is, he was actually sober. He had cleaned up. His girlfriend was pregnant with their child and the plan was, he was gonna move to Marin somewhere and live a regular, normal life. He was working a day job.

Rozz Rezabek: I was real close with Jean and Nina, who were two of Will's best friends. I was hanging around with them. They would keep me in touch. "He's up in Gilroy." I guess he'd been all clean. Then he came back to San Francisco.

Steve DePace: This happens all the time with junkies. When they go to do it one more time, they remember, well, I used to do this much, a few months ago. Let's do that. And now your tolerance is gone. And you do the thing you remembered you used to do, and it kills you.

Bruce Loose: It's hard. I can't speak about this. It's too personal, it touches too many people's lives. I was a good friend of Will's. It was really sad what happened to him. I'm really sad for all the people that were around him. And the path of lies that got left behind were very hurtful. That's all I have to say.

Rozz Rezabek: We all heard, Will's dead. It was like, oh god. And then, "Who's gonna get together some sort of memorial?" We had an impromptu thing, a bunch of us up on the top of Twin Peaks. Bruce was there. It was really cold and windy. We couldn't get any of the candles to stay lit because it was so windy. It was bad.

We did a little lame version of "Kum Ba Yah." We all huddled in small groups. It was like, "Will's dead. Punk rock's over. What do we do now?" We all just stood around there for an hour, and nobody knew what to say or what to think. We all kinda sensed that, wow, this was the end.

For a lot of us, Will was the guy. He was always on. It was like that old saying, girls wanted to be with him, guys wanted to be like him. All of us, any quality time you got with Will, I cherished it. I still miss that guy. He was the greatest.

Danny Furious: Will's death was definitely a tragedy. He was one of the finest minds I've ever encountered.

Kelly King: They took a hiatus for awhile. Then my friend John started playing bass with them and they got back together and they did *American Grafishy*. I did a short tour with them.

Steve DePace: We played Gilman once that I remember. If I'm not mistaken, it was 1991, Green Day was the opening band that night. With this guy who was playing bass for us, John Dougherty.

He had this '69 Harley chopper that he built from scratch. With the coontails coming off and the whole nine yards. He rode that thing right into the club, with his girlfriend on the back, and parked it next to the stage! He's gone. Heroin overdose. The Flipper school of punk rock drug abuse.

Bruce Loose: In the real physical history, we did not go out there and do that much. As compared to like, Black Flag. Who was practicing, touring, touring, touring, every fucking day. It's wonderful to be in a band. But there's a little more to life than just that monster, on the road 24/7, 365, you know? I'm sorry. I went and fell in love a few times, had a child. As far as I'm concerned those things are more outstanding and longer lasting than that little hardcore scene ever was. Or my memories of it.

Andy Asp: We did play a show with Flipper at Gilman Street, which was pretty insane. I remember during a song, Bruce Loose running to the snack bar and saying, "I need a fucking beer, where's a fucking beer?" I looked at him and said, "It's all-ages, there's no beer." Just the look on his face was like, "What the fuck are you guys doing here?"

Bruce Loose: I remember doing those shows. That Not Flipper show was the first thing that was breaking me out of basically becoming crippled. That was really my coming back, trying to continue my career as a musician, as a creative person.

Steve DePace: It's a miracle Bruce is around. Over the course of time, it's gotten worse and worse. He wrecked his pickup truck. That put the injury over the top and really fucked him up. And that ended our career in 1994.

That whole thing with Cobain and Nirvana, it was well known that they were big huge fans of ours. And I knew that Krist had

had a couple of bands and wasn't doing anything at the moment. Thurston Moore of Sonic Youth was curating a concert in England. He wanted us to come and play. I told him, "We don't have a bass player. I was thinking about Krist Novoselic." And he goes, "Brilliant, I've got his phone number, I'll call him."

Krist told me, "Flipper was the band that influenced me and inspired me to be in a rock band." He was honored by the invitation to come play with us. It was meant to be a one-concert little mini-tour and then see what happens. And that's what we did.

Scott Kelly: Flipper broke every fuckin' rule in the book. If it was there, they broke it. I mean, purposefully. Destroyed every fuckin' rule there was, and so, as a result, we had this wide-open palette.

Kriss X: I still think that they are the worst band on the planet.

12

Beer-Drinking Brothers from Different Mothers

Dave Chavez: Jak's Team is something that's been going on since the '70s, since the beginning of punk rock pretty much.

Nosmo King: Everybody was forming their cliques. We skated and listened to punk rock. Everyone else went to art school. I had been a surfer skater. I quit surfing because I got tired of trying to find my clothes.

Dave Chavez: It started with four guys in Petaluma—John Marsh, Tom Scott, Kevin O'Connor and Biff, whose real name is Chris Wilkinson. Jonathan [Nosmo] from the Toiling Midgets was probably the next person to join. Then Paul Casteel from House of Wheels and Black Athletes.

Paul Casteel: My first experience with Jak's Team—we were playing a show at the Sound of Music with Toiling Midgets, and the back window popped open and these five guys with skateboards piled in through the window. That was a recurring situation.

Dave Chavez: You would see 'em at the Mabuhay and they had these long police flashlights. And they'd be sneaking into the girls' bathroom, trying to look under the stalls. Just total juvenile delinquents.

Zeke Jak: Jaks were the cool guys that everybody looked up to. They had vests. You could identify them. They were all good skaters. I started hanging out, skating, trying to improve as much as I could. I would skate China Banks. I loved doing psychedelic skating, back in the day. I was so focused, I would nail every trick. Speed kind of came into play after the psychedelics, and once again I found myself down at the Embarcadero, skating all night long, for days and days. It was always about street skating because we didn't have parks here. It was punk rock and street skating.

Nosmo King: We are "beer-drinking brothers from different mothers who will ditch any date to go out and skate." We didn't even have colors back then because we couldn't decide what we wanted to look like. Biff had this suede leather jacket with "Jak's" in studs and I had this sir jacket, which was really cool, that had "Jak's" on the bottom in electrical tape. Well, it looked kind of cool.

Zeke Jak: A sir jacket is like a gas station attendant jacket with a mandarin collar that all the cholos wore in the Mission a long time ago. They're not really cool.

Paul Casteel: There was the Dish up on top of Hunter's Point. We used to go up there almost every night after shows and have parties until the sun came up. The Dish was a small reservoir bowl with a lip you could do tricks off of. It's real archaic by today's standards of public skate parks. If you went there during the day, you'd have bottles flying at you.

Nosmo King: It was, "Oh, these white skaters want a skateboard park. Let's put it in the most dangerous neighborhood in the city." But that didn't deter us.

Bill Halen: You always put your favorite bands on the back of your vest. My favorite bands at that time were Flipper, Verbal Abuse, Black Athletes and Crucifix. The Black Athletes appeared on the first *Thrasher Skate Rock* comp.

Paul Casteel: The logo "Absolute Music" was something Kevin O'Connor came up with. He was looking through the dictionary one day and he found "absolute music." It's music with no preconception. It's just spontaneous. It's been part of the colors since then.

> Absolute Music: n. self-dependent instrumental music without literary or extraneous suggestions
> —*The New Shorter Oxford English Dictionary*

Nosmo King: And 43? It's always been a magical number. Look at Nascar, what do they start off with? 43 cars. It just comes up all the time. It's like 4 plus 3 is 7, 3 minus 4 is 1. It comes up in the Bible all the time. And Jak's Team, we love to give 43 percent. A lot of people give 100 percent. I get a job, I'm just going to give you 43 percent.

Zeke Jak: Numerology by Nosmo King.

The Exception: Chi Chi at Dolores Park

Paul Casteel: Dave Chavez and his brother Joel are East Bay Jaks. I skated Dave's ramp in his backyard that was made out of tin cans and street signs. The ramp went right up the side of the house, so we would use his mom's windowsill as the coping to do tricks off of. It was 12 feet off the ground. That was the Berkeley punk scene.

Dean Washington: It was like, "Holy shit, it goes up the side of your house!" After you spoke to the mom, you walked along the side of the house and this ramp was so caveman-like. It was the most insane thing I'd ever seen. I thought, "Awww, this thing looks reeeeally dangerous." And it was. The transition was just so fast, but I'm thinkin' I can do this. I dropped in and I slammed so fuckin' hard. So I watched him do it and I did it again and *bam!* "I think I'll just take some photos and watch you skate the bowl." Really, that ramp was legendary. It's in lots of books on coffee tables, and in old *Thrasher* issues.

Paul Casteel: It was kind of like a family. Tales of Terror used to hang out there a lot. The Jaks would hang out there.

Nosmo King: We started recruiting. We were hopping trains up to Portland and Seattle, collecting members. It didn't matter if you were black or white. You could be stupid or drunk, but you had to be honest.

Paul Casteel: Drinking beer is a big part of being a Jak, but there's clean and sober Jaks and there are gay Jaks. There's Jaks all the way to Canada and Hawaii.

Jimmy Crucifix: I was actually on the Jak's Team in L.A. with Tony Alva and that whole gang, but you got this thing on your back that says "Jak's Team." There was some guy down in L.A., he did something to somebody in a gang, and me and a friend were skating down the street and we had the colors on and this gang of people, man, kinda fuckin' racked us up. So later on that night we went to Santa Monica pier and threw the colors off. Ever since then, I don't put nothing on my back.

Bill Halen: Jimmy Crucifix was the first person I met in San Francisco. Jimmy introduced me to Paul Rat, and through Paul I started working with Dirk Dirksen at the Mab and On Broadway, doing the lights and the stage. When I took over the Tool & Die in '82, I started bringing in bands from Los Angeles, from Boston, all over. I never charged more than three bucks. Some nights we would have ten bands. The best deal in town.

Dean Washington: The Tool & Die was this dank basement on Valencia with brick floors. They drilled holes in the basement so they could pour in sand to soundproof the room. There was only one way out—a little, tiny, narrow, steep stairway.

Bill Halen: There was no room for a stage because the ceiling was maybe six and half feet high. I had to wrap the stanchions in foam to keep kids from breaking their heads open.

Steve DePace: Just a tiny little fucking sweatbox. You had to be punk rock to play that place.

Ray Vegas: The toilet was at the top of the stairs and it would usually back up in the course of the evening. Someone would flush it and water would just flow down the stairs.

James Angus Black: No air, people smoking like crazy. If there had been a fire, forget it, everybody dies. The Tool & Die was a death trap.

Dean Washington: You had a room packed full of people who hadn't showered for Lord knows how long. By the time you got home, if you had a home, your parents would be like, "What's that smell in here?" "Nothing, Mom, Dad, what smell?" "It smells like cigarettes, wet ashtrays, booze, and an array of other things. What did you do last night?" "Oh, I just spent the night over at Nate's house." "Well, sweetheart, where does Nate live?" Nate lived in the trash can on the side of a bar.

Bill Halen: I met the Jaks. Nosmo, Paul Casteel and Tom Scott. Nosmo was a pretty boy, one of those guys who would try to steal your girlfriend. But, oh god, he was funny, and just a great skater and a great bass player.

Nosmo King: We would steal beer from the Tool & Die. We were with a bunch of cute girls and it was after two and we were broke— Jaks are always broke—so we opened up the hatch in the sidewalk in front of Tool & Die. It wasn't even locked. We stole four or five cases of beer, took 'em to Dolores Park, drank 'em all, and went back down to get more. I told Bill later, "Man, really sorry about ripping you off."

Bill Halen: My Jaks teammates were all beer-stealing bastards. We did a couple of *Thrasher* shows on the top floor. They brought in JFA.

Nosmo King: It was skater-friendly. We had a ramp, a little half-pipe that could be moved around up there.

Dean Washington: By the time I got there, I was never in any condition to skate. My buddy Max Fox, who sang for the Boneless Ones, got a bright idea once. We had been skating all day so he still had his knee pads on. He ran and dropped to his knees, but the knee pads just ripped down. So he slid—oh, how he slid! You could see little pieces of flesh embedded in the brick. It was like, "Ooooh!" That was fuckin' cool.

Bill Halen: We always thought the cops were coming. We were so paranoid. We would take all the beer cans and shit out to the street in plastic bags. Then we'd go back upstairs. But we'd want to do some more speed, right? Because we were starting to come down and we had another show to do. Oh fuck, wait, did anybody see my bag? And someone was like, "Yeah, I hid it in a beer can because I thought the cops were coming." Dude, you hid the speed in a beer can?! So we'd have to go back outside, pull all the bags back into the Tool & Die, pour them out over the floor, and search through all the cans. Of course it was in the last bag. So we'd do the rest of the speed and set up for the next show.

Jimmy Crucifix: I spent a lot of time there. Tool & Die was like hell. It was crazy partyland.

Toni DMR: Everything was just off the fucking map. Nothing was just like, "Oh, we're going to go to the park today and then we're going to a movie." It was like, "We're going to slam a bunch of dope, we're gonna go to a hardcore show, we're gonna kick some fuckin' ass and we're gonna be really obnoxious." I mean, Carol was sharpening needles on the back of a matchbook!

Jimmy Crucifix: When everyone left we listened to Judas Priest, the Scorpions, all that shit. Our getting-high music. Everybody had their pick. It would be me, Nicki Sicki, Bill Halen, Courtney Love, Mike Ness. Everybody's done dope at the Tool & Die and everyone had their getting-high music. 'Cause it had to be just right. Me and Bill would put on the Scorpions and do our drugs. Then Courtney Love would do her drugs and listen to Fleetwood Mac or something.

Bill Halen: It started with a little bit of meth, a little bit of heroin, and then, as the '80s went on, it became more and more heroin. We were staying up all night. For days and days.

Jimmy Crucifix: Then we'd go skateboarding at five in the morning. At the Dish out in Hunters Point—Paul, John Marsh and the whole Jaks gang—listening to the drive-by shootings as the sun was coming up. The after-hours were fucking hardcore.

Bill Halen: If I hadn't been so strung out on drugs, I might have done a better job with the club. After Tool & Die went under, I lived in L.A. for a year, hung out with Tony Alva and some of the new Jaks down there. That's what we were into back then. We were indestructible. Unfortunately, a lot of us didn't survive it.

13

Thank You, Good Night, Get Out

Ian MacKaye: The first time I played Mabuhay Gardens, we went to go see that show the night before, Dead Kennedys and Circle Jerks and Flipper. And it was a pretty fucking phenomenal gig. That was the show where the Circle Jerks brought up all these Huntington Beach skatepunk kind of dudes. The first stage diving kind of stuff in San Francisco. Legendarily. It was a totally insane night, the kids were just going nuts. Ted Falconi from Flipper—I think he hit Dirk with his guitar, and punched another guy in the face. Dirk had a bloody nose. There was so much carnage.

Bruce Loose: A lot of the first generation of punkers left San Francisco. There was all these bald-headed fuckin' violent motherfuckers that were not thinking at all. They weren't having fun doing drugs, they weren't fucking in the bathrooms, they weren't even thinking mischief. They were just beating the shit out of everything. And they didn't care.

Paul Casteel: After the *Quincy* punk rock show aired, and the *CHiPs* punk show, almost overnight the scene changed. These kids would show up with their heads shaved, Circle Jerks bandanas on their brand-new boots, chains all in the right places, pants pegged up, jackets covered in spikes with some English band like GBH on the back, which they obviously had never seen and probably never heard. These kids were at their second show and ganging up on people that have been around forever.

Winston Smith: Clubs said nope, we can't afford it. Our insurance won't cover punk bands.

Penelope Houston: Nobody could afford to record an album or manufacture one. It was always just singles.

Jello Biafra: I felt horrible that there was never gonna be a proper Avengers album. They could have made at least three. They had that many good songs. The Dils could have made two. The Sleepers could have made two, and Negative Trend, UXA, who sort of got to do theirs eventually, one each. The Mutants, probably two, maybe three. But nobody was putting them out, nobody was signing them.

Dennis Kernohan: It was too early. The music industry was not ready for it. Besides Howie Klein, the real industry people couldn't get their mouth around the dick of it, you know? They kept missing it.

Hank Rank: Howie Klein was the most powerful punk rock critic. And he pulled a lot of strings, had connections, pointed people in directions, made opportunities for some bands, and got bands coverage and other bands not. Howie was very smart, very ambitious. He exerted a huge influence over what was going on.

Howie Klein: The Nuns had a little bit of a chance, it's why I started 415 Records. We put out their record. And I had great reaction to it. But it wasn't enough for anybody to make any money from, especially not a major label.

Jennifer Miro: A lot of the problem was that later we had these drug dealer managers that ended up in exile in South America. It'd make a great movie, I'm telling ya.

Penelope Houston: So sad. By the time their first record came out, it was more like Jennifer and this other guy, the bass player, had taken over the name the Nuns.

Hank Rank: Crime recorded some songs and went to L.A. to take it around. I remember being in one guy's office and he listened to it and said, "This is not a song." I said, "What do you mean?" And he said, "Well, it's just, it's not a song." That was pretty much the response.

Howie Klein: No one was gonna sign Crime. I mean, let's be real.

Johnny Strike: And then heroin. I was doing it more and more. Frankie started doing it, Hank luckily had a bad reaction to it. These coke dealers at Berkeley Square Records started managing us and paying us like $100 each a week. Things started falling apart. I quit and I ended the band at that point. This was '81, '82.

In the '90s, Frankie decided he wanted to get the band back together again. Me and Hank, neither of us were interested, so he got Brittley and Ripper and some other guy on guitar, all on dope. Hank and I saw their first show at the DNA.

Hank Rank: It was sad. It wasn't well promoted. Frankie was all into the look. He didn't play guitar anymore. He was changing his costume all the time. He got locked out of the dressing room. He was up there, you could see him pulling on the door, trying to make a fast change between songs.

Fritz Fox: The company that the Mutants signed with was based financially on the sale of cocaine. They gave us a little money and they always had coke. We were very naive. Our record came out and the record company went bust. We found ourselves in debt.

The band started, little by little, to disintegrate. I was in the height of my drinking era. I started climbing up on speakers on the stage and jumping off. The first guy to leave was Brendan. And then Dave left, and John. And Paul. That left Sue and Sally and I. We recorded some new stuff. And it got very sad, very depressing. So the band broke up. That was 1984.

I was on the skids. I was living on the docks. I was living in my car. Then I got a job as a motorcycle courier with a friend of mine. I started my own company. I was really in a drunken, drugged-out stupor. I lived on a sailboat. Got drunk a lot. It was kinda screwed up.

Howie Klein: I had the feeling that if the Avengers had better technical help, they would have sounded better. The songs were there. They were great. Penelope's great. It just sounded a little bit too troublesome for a major label to deal with it.

Danny Furious: The Avengers were frustrated and tired of playing to the same 300 people. Greg and I had an argument during a rehearsal and he walked.

Penelope Houston: We replaced him with Brad Kent from Vancouver. Also known as Brad Kunt. But basically after six months with Brad, we felt like we'd hit some kind of glass ceiling. The momentum wasn't there anymore. We weren't going to get signed.

Another thing was, Danny and I were a couple and we had just started falling out. Danny got pretty heavily into drugs. Jimmy joined up with Chris Isaak. Greg had little bands for a few shows, then he got out of the music scene completely.

Danny Furious: I had been serving time with Joan Jett. We went to Europe and my dissatisfaction with the music I was playing, coupled with my ever-growing drug addiction, had me quitting the Blackhearts. When my visa ran out, I hightailed it back to S.F.

Jimmy had been putting together a band with Chris Isaak. I was the original drummer, but I chose to continue my career as down-and-out junkie. My bullshit took me back to Orange County, where I met Mike Ness, having the same "interests" as me. I ended up playing with Social Distortion for a short time. Those are the last gigs I've done.

Penelope Houston: Danny ended up moving to Sweden in order to kick the drugs.

Howie Klein: So, of course, what was the first one to break out of here? It wasn't Romeo Void. It was embarrassing. Pearl Harbor and the Explosions. So it was more like New Wave rather than punk rock.

Jello Biafra: Unlike England, where even the Exploited had chart hits and played on *Top of the Pops*, American punk stayed underground and got more and more angry and more and more extreme. And in the artier areas, more and more bizarre. The extreme side eventually morphed into hardcore. Which was something completely alien across the Atlantic. Also volatile, because it had no expectations of becoming commercially popular.

Danny Furious: Punk was passed on to the next generation, for better or worse. Bands like Black Flag toured and toured and toured and eventually people started to listen. The original bands were all but forgotten.

PART
II

14

We Are the Kings Now

Rachel Rudnick: The bus would go from Berkeley to San Francisco. Its last stop, before the Bay Bridge, was the New Method warehouse.

John Marr: New Method was on the Oakland–Emeryville border.

Tim Tonooka: It was dicey. Along the way you'd walk past a liquor store with husky transvestites hanging out in front of it. Then you'd go into an industrial building, up a flight of narrow stairs, into a warehouse space where the walls were covered with egg cartons. The air was stale, with meager ventilation from only a few windows.

John Borruso: It was where clusters of people lived, rehearsed and made art before the live-work concept had been rendered meaningless.

Sothira Pheng: It was this big old brown brick building and there was a huge sign that read "New Method Laundromat." There were older artists, but nobody older than 30. Ironworkers had a huge metal shop downstairs and this open space full of junk. We had the whole upstairs, this big sprawl.

Jimmy Crucifix: I was completely into the New Method thing. It was a bunch of artists but it was a lot of tweakers. I was tweaking then. Tweakers were different back then. It was kind of nonchalant. Brittley Black used to walk around with a suit and a tie and a pen holder that said, "Hello, my name is Brittley," but instead of pens, it held orange syringe caps.

Sothira Pheng: Crucifix was the first band that used the spot. It was 100 bucks a month and nobody could afford it. We probably lived there for about six months, but it seems like years. That's how explosive it was.

Me and Matt put up flyers saying we were looking for band members. This was about tenth grade. We had our first gig with Flipper, January 3rd, 1980 at the Sound of Music. At the time, Flipper were already old guys. They were great. Their sound, their attitude, and their style—it was perfect for that time and space. But they didn't speak to us, to our generation. There was no excitement.

Jimmy Crucifix: Crucifix was hardcore punk. The kids were fuckin' beating each other up out there. No more pogoing and throwing popcorn like they did at the Mabuhay. This was like throwing bottles, getting kicked in the face.

Sothira Pheng: The '77 crowd was scared. They were running for their musical lives. We were the Kids. We felt we were the chosen ones, like the Three Musketeers—me, Matt and Chris.

Jimmy Crucifix: I think Sothira's always been political because he was from Cambodia and went through a lot of shit.

Sothira Pheng: At the height of Nixon's strategic bombing of Cambodia—the secret wars—there was a major attack by the communists in Phnom Penh. Massive shelling, I totally remember that. My dog was shitting all over the place. So my father got stationed in Taiwan and we got refugee status. We went to some kind of refugee camp in Pennsylvania, then we came to San Francisco. My parents went from diplomatic treatment to having to show up for welfare.

I was born in Cambodia, but I didn't use the Cambodian thing. I never have. Crucifix was never a race band. We weren't the "black band" like the Bad Brains or the "Mexican band" like the Zeros. We were always Crucifix. We became heavily involved in our own political thought.

> *From dehumanization, to arms production,*
> *for the benefit of the nation, or its destruction,*
> *power is power, it's the law of the land,*
> *those who live for death, would die by their own hands.*
> *Life is no ordeal, if you can come to terms,*
> *reject the system, which dictates the norm,*
> *from dehumanization, to arms production,*
> *for the benefit of the nation, or its destruction,*
> *it's your choice: Peace or Annihilation!*
>
> —"Annihilation," Crucifix

Jimmy Crucifix: They were the real unit, those three guys. I liked them all a lot. I went to see 'em play at the Mabuhay and it was so weird. Sothira was just laying around on the stage.

Sothira Pheng: Mohawk, knee-high boots, the spikes, the leather jacket—that's how I remember Jimmy.

Jimmy Crucifix: When I first got into Crucifix, I felt like an old man. They had a song called "You're Too Old" and they actually dropped it 'cause I was 22 by this time. I was probably the only one that could really play in the band, even according to them. I showed 'em what to do and it was fun. I thought they were doing a good job.

Sothira Pheng: Punk rock became our lives. We were living it 24/7. Paul Rat was one of the few people who actually recognized that we had something. He got us some great gigs. You name it— Black Flag, Bad Brains—we were on the bill. I can't believe he did all that stuff for us. He was our manager until we found out Matt could do just as good a job as him.

We were expected to open up and basically let the headlining acts do their thing, but we'd come on and start breaking all the microphones. They'd get all pissed, these older geezers. That's when we started our own gigs at New Method—shows had to be under five bucks and all-ages.

We were literally the center of attention. By '82, we all adhered to the British punk scene and style. Exactly as Discharge dressed— spikes, leather jacket, Doc Martens boots, mohawks. It took months to assemble the jacket, paint it, put the logos on it. And the logos were bands and albums that we loved, Discharge, GBH, Crass. It wasn't an advertisement. It meant something. It was an interpretation of what the English were doing. I even had my name painted on my jacket à la Johnny from *The Wild One*. We knew it was an iconic thing. We stood out apart from everybody else, we had our own look. People would say, "Here comes those Crucifix boys."

Jimmy Crucifix: People used to laugh at us.

Sothira Pheng: One time we went to play a gig with Black Flag and they started calling us "Exploited!" As teenagers, those were fighting words. It was like, "We love you guys and you made fun of us?"

Jimmy Crucifix: They got into Crass and the vegan deal, and everything kinda changed. They got into the whole political thing. They went from studded leather to jean jackets painted with black acrylic paint.

Photo by Murray Bowles

The Kids: Crucifix at the On Broadway

Sothira Pheng: We went on tour in '82, John Loder from Crass had never even seen us, only heard about us. He flew from London, came to see us in Boston, and signed us.

When we got back from the tour, everybody was congratulating us. We are the kings now. We had tried Alternative Tentacles and they pooh-poohed us. The difference between us and the Dead Kennedys is that we thought we were punk rockers. The Dead Kennedys were playing in a punk band. We had that flag waving. We were more punk than punk.

We created our own genre, our own pool that rippled out and created those satellite bands like PLH, Trial, Atrocity, A State of Mind. They were like our little siblings.

Jimmy Crucifix: Matt's brother John Borruso was in Trial. Some of them started PLH. Peace, Love and Happiness.

John Borruso: There were members in common with Trial and Atrocity. It was all very cross-pollinated.

Jimmy Crucifix: When they started going that direction, it was like, oh, we're into peace, love and happiness. It's like, man, I still wear leather coats. I'm still into drinking and doing drugs. Peace and love—that's cool, but I already went through that whole '70s thing with my sister. I really can't play this music. I can't preach something that I'm not into.

Sothira Pheng: You can only be in a rock 'n' roll band for so long before you become an activist. *Maximum RocknRoll* championed MDC. I thought MDC was a great band but we were local boys and we were basically ditched. Between '80 and '84 we were almost totally ignored. By the age of 20, I felt that was as far as we could go.

15

Better Living Through Chemistry

Welcome to Barrington, kids! Please keep your hands and arms inside the ride at all times.
—*Graffiti at the entrance of Barrington Hall*

Scott Kelly: Barrington was one of those mind-blowing experiences. I had never come across a place like that before. It was supposed to be a college dormitory and there's a 40-year-old biker fixing his fuckin' Triumph in the front room, just tweaking balls. As far as I could tell, no one that lived there went to school. I remember thinking, "How does this happen?"

Ray Farrell: It was a Berkeley campus housing unit. Everybody played there. All the bands from L.A. Anyone that had a San Francisco gig would come to Barrington.

Dean Washington: Dead Kennedys, Flipper, Black Flag, you name it—right there in the dining hall.

Jason Lockwood: They would lose power so the room would go dark, which was great. You would be thrashing around, floors painted with beer, with people slipping every which way.

Scott Kelly: We were walking down the hallway one day, and this guy with a big vial of liquid acid said, "Want some acid?" I say, "Sure." And he sprayed some fuckin' liquid acid in my eye. By the time I hit Telegraph I couldn't even feel my legs.

Nosmo King: A guy goes, "Okay, we've got a keg on number three and four. If you're into speed, that's on five, and there's acid on six." I was still in high school then and I was thinking, "Wow, this is what college is like?"

Jason Lockwood: It was a co-op. Nobody was responsible for anything, because everybody was.

Dan Rathbun: It was a four-story building, a block long. And off of each hall were like 13 suites of rooms and each suite had anywhere from three to five bedrooms and a bathroom.

Nils Frykdahl: I was going to school at Berkeley and wanted to live in the co-ops. I went to the co-op office and they had a little catalog. All the co-ops had little pictures and descriptions of their gardens and other attractive things. When I got to Barrington, there was no picture, no description, it just said, "We suggest you visit for yourself." I said, "Yeah, what about this place?" And they said, "Oh, you don't wanna go there. Everybody just leaves."

Rachel Rudnick: My first punk show was probably '82, '83 at Barrington Hall. I was 12 or 13. It was Trial, Atrocity, Deadly Reign, and 13. I remember going up these dingy staircases and there was a big shit in the middle of a step, and I thought, "No dog is stupid enough to do that."

You can't fistfuck with nuclear arms
—*Graffiti from Barrington Hall*

Dean Washington: My buddy Adam had a gutter rat named Lucifer. He became semi-domestic. The rat was huge. Lucifer drank EKU beer, which was really strong. Lucifer inhaled pot all day. As long as someone was smoking, he wanted some. He'd act a fool in his cage if you weren't blowing a cloud his way. Back then, Adam was a heavy doser of acid, so he'd give Lucifer hits every now and then. Lucifer was pretty much the devil himself, really.

Jason Lockwood: The cops would raid that place constantly 'cause it was just rampant with drugs. When the cops came all the windows toward the parking lot would fly open and drugs and needles would come sailing out of the windows. It was just ridiculous.

Dean Washington: They'd have "wine dinners" and the house would vote on what the theme drug was gonna be for the party.

Nils Frykdahl: That was the euphemism for our acid parties, "wine dinners." It sounded very respectable.

Anna Brown: We went to lots of wine dinners. I remember coming out of there with Katie once and we could not find the car, we were so high. We had to walk home.

Scott Kelly: The hippies paved the way for the whole drug market in Berkeley. When you can go to the high school where Jimi

Hendrix played, it gives you a different perspective on things. LSD was a huge part of our very specific scene because of the availability and quality.

Nils Frykdahl: Berkeley Bob lived in the closet of the study room. Berkeley Bob was a very sweet guy, but a schizophrenic or something. He had really involved conversations with himself. Like three-person conversations in different voices. This was supposed to be the room where you were gonna work on writing your papers or whatever, and, from the closet, you heard, "Listen! Don't you tell him not to talk." Which implies three people, you know.

There were little quotes from Berkeley Bob all over the walls. There was a whole mock Cult of Bob with the older members who had degenerated into pure stonerdom. They had recorded Bob at one point on a cassette and had memorized long chunks. They would sit around [bubbling bong sounds], and go into it, something like, "Uh, 2315 Dwight Way, don't you tell him not to talk. Listen, this isn't the only pig iron in the business . . ." They would fire off these Bob rants in unison. Initially I was very impressed with those guys. But they listened to the Grateful Dead all the time.

> You're persona non grata in my hippy van, bitch
> —*Graffiti from Barrington Hall*

Jesse Luscious: I had been squatting in West Philly so I was pretty used to a really radical living situation. I felt really at home. Onng Yanngh was, I don't really know what you'd call it—the entity, the symbol, the embodiment of the house. You'd see it on stickers everywhere. I would call it a religious icon but I don't know if the people who lived there would. You still see it every once in awhile. People from bands have tattoos of it.

Fraggle: There was that pagan organization, OBOD—Order of Bards, Ovates and Druids. They had a bunch of parties there. They would have their ritual bell-ringing, and there would be a band playing, and naked people walking around covered with red paint.

Nils Frykdahl: Wes Anderson came to Barrington with his punk band Slaughter of Small Animals. One of the party coordinators had brought some skinned goat heads from a Chinatown butcher. Skinned and mounted on stakes on either end of the stage. It was a gruesome spectacle.

Dan Rathbun: This was Halloween.

Nils Frykdahl: And my brother Per, in an inspired moment, went up and started French-kissing the goat heads, and ended up ripping the tongue out of the head with his teeth. It stopped the band. He grossed out Slaughter of Small Animals. This was a hardcore band from Oakland.

Dean Washington: Everyone looked forward to summer, because the actual students that went to school would leave and sublet their rooms. All us punks would have full control of the building. So it was the Barrington Compound. We had a full kitchen, and we made meals—well, when we weren't grinding teeth, or something else.

Nils Frykdahl: The Acid Rain Ensemble was the official name of our band. We started out playing Barrington's wine dinners, which were big costumed affairs, so we dressed up in ridiculous outfits right from the get-go. Not necessarily good costumes, but certainly face paint and garbage bags or whatever we could come up with. That often spilled over into class. I remember meeting each other in the morning, "Hey, let's wear garbage bags to school today." And then we'd see each other between classes wearing garbage bags. Or wearing spikes up to the elbows in music class, just bristling. I hope that people are still doing retarded stuff around the UC Berkeley campus.

Dave Chavez: Black Flag with Dez, Flipper and Sick Pleasure. That show was just insane. Somebody kicked in my speaker while we were playing and I got really upset. I had steel-toe boots on. So I just started kicking these bikes until they wrapped around a pole. It was in the air, the violence of the night. Everyone was acting like that. Everybody was pissed off and wanted to throw something. I'm surprised that nobody lit the place on fire. It was the craziest show probably of its time in Berkeley.

Kareim McKnight: A friend of ours got killed at Barrington. We believed that he was pushed by the cops. This was around the time that Bush Sr. was visiting San Francisco. He had helped us organize for that protest.

Nils Frykdahl: There were protest movements going on, some of them had their zines based out of Barrington. So there was the political edge and there was the musical, artistic edge, and some extra sort of edge because it was surrounded by this new conservatism within Berkeley.

Kareim McKnight: For a long time, Barrington Hall was at the center of the anti-Apartheid movement. We would meet at Barrington and organize, fill containers with gasoline. It was the '80s, no one went anywhere without a can of spray paint.

Nick Frabasilio: The first issue of *Slingshot* was published at Barrington, as were all issues of the *Biko Plaza News*, *Slingshot*'s forerunner, during the anti-Apartheid sit-in.

Robert Eggplant: *Slingshot* gets its name from the Palestinian resistance people shooting slingshots against heavy artillery weapons.

PB Floyd: The first issue was just one sheet of 11 × 17 white copier paper, folded in half. It was raw and militant, with handwritten headlines and hilarious seditious graphics. *Slingshot* looked like it was put together in the backseat of a getaway car after some really cool revolutionary act.

Robert Eggplant: One of the fights that the Slingshot Collective was involved with, besides diversity in education and homosexual rights, was trying to save Barrington.

> During the fall [of 1989], with the war on drugs in full swing, students held a smoke-in on Sproul Plaza that attracted 2000, the largest event of the semester. Barrington Hall, a student co-op that helped organize the smoke-in and that had long provided a haven for activists and organizing efforts . . . was threatened with closure from a vote within the co-op system. There had been several other votes over the years to try to close Barrington and in November, the referendum passed.
>
> —*The People's History of Berkeley*

Kareim McKnight: My friends at Barrington put out flyers and showed up at Sproul Plaza with shoeboxes full of shake joints. Of course, this massive crowd formed. It was a big spectacle. My brother was on the way to class and ended up on the front page of the *Daily Cal*, smoking a joint with a latte in his hand.

Nils Frykdahl: There were always a lot of threats in that direction. Every year, "Oh, the council is voting to close . . ." And we'd all get up in arms and we'd go around to other co-ops and bring guitars like, "Hey, we're from Barrington Hall and we're here to sing some songs for you guys tonight while you eat dinner." As a goodwill gesture.

Kareim McKnight: The Barrington kids came around to all the other co-ops to make their plea. They were very emotional. I remember one kid saying, "Look, if we get killed, it's on your hands."

Nils Frykdahl: People really had exaggerated notions of what was going on there. They'd say, "Do you carry a gun? I hear everybody carries guns and it's really dangerous." Or, "I hear everybody's addicted to heroin." There was definitely plenty of drugs and plenty of ruined lives. So from the point of view of parents, it was a bad place.

Kareim McKnight: The neighbors sued. They had a lot of documentation about the shows and the parties, people throwing washing machines off the roof.

> Finally in March [of 1990], a poetry reading was declared illegal by police who cleared the building by force. A crowd developed which built fires and resisted the police. Finally police attacked, badly beating and arresting many residents and bystanders and trashing the house. Eventually, the house was sold to a private landlord.
>
> —*The People's History of Berkeley*

Kareim McKnight: I was told the police formed a gauntlet and beat all the kids as they ran down the hall when they came to throw the squatters out. I went to the courthouse to support all my comrades. We cheered when they were brought out in their jumpsuits. I was so sad to see it close. It's a pathetic piece of nothing now.

Dean Washington: Barrington Hall was like a rainbow in the sky, when you walked through that door. It was a beautiful place.

> Time is a crutch, eat mandarin oranges
> —*Graffiti from Barrington Hall*

16

Grandma Rule

Sham Saenz: All the girls in DMR wore these jean vests. That was their colors—jean vests that said "DMR." Durant Mob Rules— Carol, Natasha and the twins.

Jason Lockwood: They were the meanest people on the planet. They were just awful and they won't deny it.

Noah Landis: Toni and Rachel ruled the scene. These two tiny, His-panic-looking punk rock twins. Tiny! The scariest people I'd ever met. Some jock asshole would say something wrong and they would just charge him swingin'.

Rachel DMR: We hung out a lot. It sounds hokey now, but we were just kids. Durant and Telegraph was our stomping grounds. Sil-verball was the center of it. On the second level above Leopold's Records, La Val's Pizza and a coffee shop.

Jason Lockwood: Runaway kids would hang out at La Val's and eat leftover pizza. The girls' bathroom was destroyed, almost solely the work of DMR.

John Marr: Silverball Gardens was a pinball hall. A lot of punk rock kids worked there.

Kate Knox: My boyfriend Dave Chavez, who played in Code of Honor and Verbal Abuse, he worked at Silverball. I remember sitting behind a desk with him and all of a sudden he ran out from be-hind the counter and busted this little kid. He had a quarter with a string on it, trying to play extra games. That was the first time I remember meeting Noah.

Noah Landis: Basically I had drilled a hole through a quarter and at-tached it to a piece of thread. In some of the machines it would

Courtesy of Rachel Royce

Scene Monitors: The DMR Twins on Telegraph

work. One time it got stuck and I was sitting there struggling with it—it was a lot of work to drill a hole through a quarter, I didn't want to lose it. The guy busted me. Kate pointed at me and laughed. She just thought it was the funniest thing she'd ever seen.

John Marr: Apparently you could buy controlled substances from the change guy.

Noah Landis: He carried it in those little fuse boxes. He would sell us the trimmings that came off the sheets of acid for like 30 cents a hit.

Rachel DMR: There was a whole skater crowd, too. About half of us skated.

Toni DMR: With skateboards as weapons you don't have to be a strong, tough bitch to knock someone out. You just have to fuckin' swing your arm.

Rachel Rudnick: The EBU. And the BTU. They would hang out.

Dean Washington: Now, the BTU guys and my EBU guys didn't always agree on things. There'd be times when there were physical acts of violence. Not always, but on a few occasions.

Jim Lyon: East Bay Underground was made up of people who skated and hung out at Blondie's Pizza. Dean Washington is the founder. He was our social calendar.

Ray Vegas: East Bay Underground were just a bunch of drunk skater dudes, but they were mean guys.

Patrick Tidd: BTU stands for Berkeley Trailers Union.

Sammytown: They were like the local biker gang, but they rode mountain bikes. They were like street thugs that rode bicycles.

Kate Knox: They were kind of the counterparts to DMR. Total drinker, fuck-up, get-crazy kinda guys.

Toni DMR: We were linked to BTU vicariously, through Rachel.

Patrick Tidd: I met Rachel on Durant hanging out. I would see Rachel at shows. She and Toni were pretty out of control back then. Rachel on the run all of the time, Toni on the run half of the time. Those two got me in a lot of fights. I guess I fell in love with Rachel when I first met her.

Dean Washington: The DMR girls were nightmares. We didn't look at them like they were hot chicks. They were a manly little bunch.

Rachel DMR: We had big mouths—

Toni DMR: —and steel-toe boots.

Rachel DMR: I had a chip on my shoulder. I was angry and pretty violent, and I drank a lot and did a lot of drugs and so did Toni. I look back at the anger and violence. It was almost primal. There was a rage that was almost existential. Like you've been getting beaten down your whole fucking life and then, *bam!*

Dave Ed: They were kinda scene monitors. Just completely fearless. I saw them fight sailors all the time at the On Broadway.

Jason Lockwood: I watched Carol beat the crap out of people. Like a boxer. No wasted motion.

Paul Casteel: The twins were sort of poster children for abuse. I think they were runaways for that reason.

Carol DMR: There was a *People* magazine article about their abuse. I was in court as one of the witnesses when they were goin' through all that. They flew in witnesses from Indonesia.

Rachel DMR: We had been abandoned in East Oakland as kids because our parents were drug addicts. We were discovered by neighbors and put into a foster home where we were abused. Then we were adopted when we were seven by a family. We lived in other countries earlier in our lives, but mostly we grew up in Berkeley. Our father was a professor of kinesiology. He was also a pedophile. Basically our father kept us locked away, until we finally rebelled at 14.

Carol DMR: DMR started because a 13-year-old got raped walking home. We got together as a group of girls and made rules. The first rule was nobody walks home alone. That's how it started. DMR was about sisterhood and trying to keep some type of order.

Rachel DMR: The DMR girls consisted of Carol, me and Toni, Aileen Sullivan, Tasha Robinson, Emma Clarkson, Cathy Schulz, Kathy Harris, Wendy Orem, Robin Woolsey, Sarah Archbold and Kris Connolly.

Carol DMR: We had these rules, like you can't throw the first punch, one-on-one only. And to be in DMR you had to get in at least one fight.

Rachel DMR: We were some fuckin' psycho-assed bitches! We didn't always follow our own rules.

Rachel Rudnick: Rachel had a mohawk, Toni had the catwoman, which was a double mohawk that had bangs in the middle. Natasha had the skater bangs and the flannel and carried a skateboard and talked shit.

Sham Saenz: Carol used to wear black eyeliner that dripped down her face. She was half black and half Jewish. I didn't even know what a Jew was until I met Carol. She had a little red afro and a Star of David bleached into the back of her head.

Anna Brown: She once kicked someone's ass while she had a peace sign shaved in her head. She was nice to me for some reason.

Paul Casteel: They were little fashion fascists. If there was some new girl in the scene that they didn't know who was dressed a little bit too preppy, they would try to scare her off.

Dean Washington: These chicks from Orinda were *smokin'*. But the DMR was not gonna be okay with those girls.

Carol DMR: Skimey hoes and sketchy wenches! If you were dressed like a sketchy wench or a hoochie, if you were wearing a short-short skirt and fishnet stockings at the show, you were basically making women look more objectified. We always wore pants and our jean vest, flannel shirts and sometimes a bandana. We just tried to look like cool people instead of what we considered slutty girls. So as soon as we saw somebody like that—we didn't just start fuckin' with them—but it was a lot easier when they did something wrong.

And if any girls start messing with your guy or even the guy that you're interested in, that was it. I remember one fight that happened in Barrington Hall. I had a crush on Pat Rat forever but he didn't like me like that. There was some girl that he hooked up with in the bushes and came back in the show . . .

Toni DMR: She had to go to the hospital. It was really fucked up.

Rachel DMR: I've always felt bad about that one. We got into some pretty stupid fights protecting each other, or so we thought. We made mistakes. We terrorized people.

John Marr: I will say this, they were *really* dedicated to the punk rock scene.

Toni DMR: If you were from out of town, part of a skate crew or a hardcore crew or surfing crew or whatever, you were welcomed by us. We'd take you in and give you a place to stay. You could eat our food—you couldn't fuck us, but you could hang out with us—and you would be safe. You would never be stuck without bus fare.

Sham Saenz: Carol and Natasha were some of the first people I met. I was 10 or 11. I trusted them. You just got a sense that they cared for you. Carol worked at a hamburger shop on Shattuck and I'd go in there 'cause I was always on the streets and poor.

Noah Landis: My sister, who was two years older than me, was already good friends with the DMR girls. For whatever reason, they liked me. I was lucky.

Sham Saenz: They were kind of like the grandmas of the scene. You know how if you bring a friend over to the house, your grandma wants to know, "Who is this guy? I don't know his family." That was how those girls rolled. They wanted to know who you knew, where you were from.

I was sitting in the lobby at Ruthie's Inn. I don't know what had happened, but Carol basically walked in and there was a dude there, and Tasha had a skateboard, and they just beat the shit out of this guy in the doorway. One of them with the board, the other with her fists. Grandma rule.

Dean Washington: Carol and the DMR girls booked some great shows. NOFX, Jodie Foster's Army.

Sham Saenz: The best shows, and you always knew that if you were paying them for a show it was going to the bands.

Carol DMR: Tasha did all the flyers, some of the art was tasteless, especially the one for Jerry's Kids. But she could draw anything. She started tattooing back then and she did some album covers— Special Forces. She moved to Nicaragua. Whenever we go visit her, the phone is ringing off the hook because she still takes all the new punk rockers under her wing.

Rachel DMR: Patrick and I got married and I had my son around '84. I just hung up my leather jacket and took care of that kid. I didn't want him to see the drugs, the trauma, the homelessness, and stress, but I retained the good parts of punk—the camaraderie, the love. Punk really saved my life. At the time I was completely out of control but it saved my life. Those people I met, they are still my core.

17

Blitzkrieg Bop

Jeff Bale: There was a period in the mid-'80s where it was really unpleasant going to a punk show because there'd be a face-off between factions of skins and punks. You never knew if you were going to end up in a brawl. It was like a tempest in a teapot because outside the scene, nobody really gave a fuck.

Orlando X: We were all getting along fine. We would go to shows and hang out together, punks and skinheads, and then suddenly they decided they wanted to be racist and Nazi skinheads. It was the strangest thing.

Lenny Filth: You didn't know who to trust. Some skins were cool, some skins would cut your laces, take your boots.

Dave Dictor: By late '83 and '84, there were cracks. Skinheads who had been our good friends and buddies, all of a sudden were talking about white power and niggers and fags. What the fuck are you guys talking about?

Scott Kelly: Before I came up here, I had my head shaved and was hanging out with skinheads in San Diego. It was a totally mixed-race group but right around '83 or '84 the White Aryan Resistance started to get involved. Tom Metzger and all those people came out of San Diego. A bunch of the guys started going super-hardcore white pride, and the other guys started falling off.

Sara Cohen: I was a hardcore proud American skinhead punk rock chick and I was a fuckin' Jew. This was before Tom Metzger and his clan came out and started recruiting my friends. There'd be skinheads at every show, and more and more of them would be Sieg Heiling. Those of us who didn't want to take part in that scene, because of ethnicity or because it was just so fuckin' retarded, we had to go our separate ways.

Dave Dictor: I do think there was a backlash against the very politicalness of *Maximum RocknRoll*, Dead Kennedys, MDC. To a certain degree, we were mouthy and we were telling people what to do. I mean, all of us—Jello Biafra, Tim Yohannan and, to a certain degree, myself. I thought everyone needed to know what I knew.

James Angus Black: You can't have any kind of socialist community with a bunch of National Socialists. They have no politics at all. They're just about violence. So it was inevitable they would ruin everything.

Jason Lockwood: It would've never happened in the U.K. But in the U.S., the skinhead scene came out of the punk scene. The BASH Boys were the first skinhead gang, which honestly was like a joke.

Everyone was really into Sham 69, pre-Nazi skinhead-era bands. We were sitting around at our friend's apartment in Upper Haight and we were talking about starting a band, and we were coming up with names. Somehow the words "Bay Area Skinheads" came out of someone's mouth. Hey! BASH! I don't remember who said it. It was me, Curtis, Terry and Bob. That was it.

We were trying to emulate British skins. We had Fred Perrys, 501s, suspenders, Doc Martens, laced sideways. Bomber jackets. We could look very dashing on some days. But nobody had any racist leanings until somebody got ahold of the Skrewdriver album. It had a dramatic effect.

Curtis is Sicilian, he's a very dark-skinned guy. Bob Blitz is German, but he grew up in San Francisco. Terry was from San Jose and I was from Berkeley. So we weren't by default very racist people. But I grew up in Oakland in black neighborhoods, which in one respect made it easy for me. I used to get jumped constantly as a kid. So I kinda made it like, oh, I can hate those people, no problem—they used to beat me up! It was a weird slow transformation. After awhile, one day everyone was chanting, "White power."

Dean Washington: There were a couple of key names out there that you really wanted to stay away from. It was like your parents telling you about the Boogey Man.

Kurt Brecht: Dagger was a real tough guy. We were terrified of him. You'd see him in the pit and he would be just destroying people.

Jason Lockwood: At my third or fourth show, Marc Dagger came flying off the stage, and he was so much bigger than me, when his hand hit me he gave me a cut on my lip *and* my upper brow at the same time. We had all known each other forever.

Marc Dagger: Me, Jimmy, Beau, Bags, Dickie—we were pretty much the founders of the S.F. Skins. We were never really an organized gang or anything. We were just a bunch of assholes who loved to drink and fight.

The first person I met after I hit San Francisco was James Black. Big Jim. He worked in a bar South of Market and he became the roadie for a whole shitload of bands.

Then I met Beau, Jimmy Mange and Bags. I was pretty much homeless and hanging out downtown. They were with a little street gang down there—just a bunch of crazy motherfuckers. We'd hang out in the Tenderloin, bum change, get beer, go to the park, get drunk, beat people up—stupid shit like that. We were a bunch of fucked-up kids. Basically just tweakers.

James Angus Black: I'd seen Dagger around and he scared me. But the more I watched him, the more I thought, this guy is like Luca Brasi from *The Godfather*. This is a man of intense power and passion and unbelievable physical strength, wandering around looking for trouble. But he has no focus, he has no one to guide him. I don't want this guy as my enemy. I'd much rather have him as my friend.

Marc Dagger: I came from Texas. I was in juvy down there and I split, hitchhiked to L.A. and met Jeff 4-Way from Bad Posture. I hung out with him for a couple of weeks before I got run out of town by the cops and made my way up to San Francisco. That was 1980.

I was probably here about six months, when I met Spike up on Polk Street. I thought she was cool as hell looking. She was all dressed out in chains and spikes, and her mohawk was up. You could tell, man, she was not somebody you wanted to mess with.

Tammy Lundy: Spike was an iconic figure. So much so, when Kriss X came on the scene, she completely copied Spike's look. We used to call her Spike Jr. because she used to do Spike drag from top to bottom.

Marc Dagger: We just kind of clicked, you know. We was never apart after that. She was in the scene way before I even hit town. She used to hang out at Target Video and the Tool & Die. She took me to all those places—Mabuhay Gardens, the On Broadway.

That's when I started to get into punk. I was already pretty frickin' crazy so I fit in with that crowd.

James Angus Black: Almost a year later, I ran into Marc on the street and he was all punked out with this big mohawk. And he says, "This is my girlfriend, Spike." That was the first time I'd met her and, boy, she did not want anything to do with me. But she saw that Marc loved me and respected me so she set about giving me a punk rock makeover right away. Cut my hair, made me cut my mustache, changed my clothes, my shoes, everything. She also knew I had a truck. And anyone with a vehicle, willing to drive people around the punk rock scene, was in.

Tammy Lundy: Spike was like a whole lot of women on the scene who were afraid to expose their intelligence, but she was absolutely not stupid. And she was in the center of *everything*.

Ninja Death: I met Spike when I was 15 and living in a squat one block from the Mab. She was security and overseer of bullshit at the Mab. She worked with Dirk, Hobbit, and Michele Rebel.

I was an orphan after my mom died, and I became a ward of the California court. Spike would always ask me to come over to her and Marc Dagger's house if I was hungry and wanted a place to stay.

Marc Dagger: Spike and I used to have hellacious brawls. It was one of those things, you know, two people like each other but can't stand to be with each other. Neither of us would back down.

James Angus Black: Spike was way stronger, way badder than Dagger. I'd fight him before I'd fight her.

Tammy Lundy: Dagger was a bona fide idiot and a violent, racist asshole. I never liked him. Spike may have known another side of him. She probably did.

Marc Dagger: I was called Marc Hardcore before I got named Dagger by the cops. I was tweakin' one night and the cops pulled over 'cause I was walking down the street with this cane with this eight ball on top. They opened up the cane and it had a sword in it. So they put me up against the wall and started pulling knives out—I had like about 21 knives all over me and most of them were double-edged daggers. So I went to jail. Got out and I was down at Mabuhay Gardens one night, and these two cops came walking up and were like, "Hey, look at him. Come here, Dagger. What's up, Dagger? Got any knives, Dagger?" Everybody was looking and snickering as they searched me. After that, I couldn't get rid of the fucking name.

Kriss X: I remember when Dagger got the offer to sing for Urban Assault. He was like an excited little kid flying all over the house, like a bull in a china shop.

Marc Dagger: We played with Sick Pleasure, Bad Posture, DRI. We played with everybody, but we played with the Fuck-Ups more than anyone 'cause we got on really well.

We did a tour with the Fuck-Ups. We played Fender's Ballroom in L.A. and we were at the T-Bird Rollerdrome when that big riot jumped off. We were pro-American hardcore and Wattie from the Exploited was up there and the first song that comes out of his mouth is, "Fuck the U.S.A." So we filled up this big cup full of piss and threw it in his face. Then he started talking shit and everybody stormed the stage. By the time we got outside, there were riot cops everywhere and it just jumped.

We also played with MDC when they got to town, but we didn't really see eye to eye. They were so political and we didn't give a shit. They started doing their hair pink and we just thought that was frickin' killing the dark punk rock style we were into. All of a sudden it switched. All the bands became fuckin' politically motivated. We were not into that crap.

Jason Lockwood: The S.F. Skins were really funny because their whole conversion from punks to skinheads was just shaving their heads. For awhile they used to make fun of us: "Why don't you dress like American skinheads?"

Marc Dagger: If you were a BASH Boy, you were just lower in the pecking order. We wouldn't beat you up or anything, but we'd give you a hard time. They were the juniors.

The only way you could become an S.F. Skin was if you had cojones, man. You were gonna prove to us that you were a bad motherfucker before you were even gonna fuckin' hang out with us. A lot of the BASH Boys—you'd get into a fight and they'd disappear. They'd run. You'd never see an S.F. Skin run, ever.

Jason Lockwood: Marc Dagger talked shit, but there wasn't any real animosity. We intermixed freely and looked out for each other.

I actually helped a group of skinheads try to kill a guy. The S.F. Skins tried to jump Jeff Asshole in Piss Alley and take his leather. Jeff always carried a knife. He was scrawny, but a very scrappy guy. When they tried to jump him, he cut Bob's face from the back of his cheekbone to near his lip. Everybody was after him after that. I love the logic: We tried to jump you and rob you, and since you defended yourself, we're going to kill you.

Somehow, people found out that Jeff was down in the Pit drinking. The Pit was a construction site but construction had halted. It was just a big hole and it was there for years. A lot of bad fights happened there.

Everyone went down there to beat up or kill Jeff. No one thought about the fact Jeff would almost certainly have something sharp on him somewhere. Terry Bash tried to get him first, but Jeff's really quick—he's got a natural springiness to him. He snapped out like a little pit viper and cut Terry's forehead wide open, blood all over his face.

Ace Disgrace charged in and knocked Jeff over. Ace was a big guy but Jeff just went off like a Tasmanian devil, swinging with that straight razor. He eventually broke the knife on the back of Ace's head and left a maze of cuts because Ace wouldn't let go. Terry started kicking Jeff in the head. Jeff was really lucky to come out alive. Jeff's a good friend of mine. We laugh about it now and again.

Silke Tudor: When I first started hanging out at 13, 14, there were a few badass punk chicks that really fucked with me—I've got some good Tenderloin scars. But after my wannabe skinhead boyfriend shaved my head, that pretty much stopped. Well, Audra hunted me for awhile but that was because she was sleeping with him, too. We were just getting wasted, hanging out with thugs and behaving very very badly, but there was no philosophy behind it. My childhood boyfriend was black and Portuguese. My younger brother is half black. I hated his father but I fucking loved that kid. When I was 14 and he was four, I would dress him up in little boots and braces, and take him to hang out with my punk friends. That's how little any of this had to do with race. It was fucking violent, though, no doubt about it. Very violent.

Audra Angeli-Slawson: Skinheads went hunting for trouble. One night, it was like every skinhead for a 100-mile radius had planned to meet at the Farm and rush the door for some show. I was already inside when they rushed the door. It was really gnarly, just crazy. They were beating up people that I knew. I got kicked out along with the rest of them. We went back to Skinhead Hill.

Jason Lockwood: It was Hippie Hill originally. The park that's at the end of Upper Haight before it drops down into Lower Haight.

Audra Angeli-Slawson: There were about 40 skinheads from everywhere and they were all pissed off because their plan had been foiled, or whatever, and they were just looking for trouble. We got some beer, and four or five of them found some people on the hill to beat the shit out of. Me and my boyfriend were flipping out, yelling, "Do not fucking hit this person anymore! Stop—you're gonna kill them!!" It was really bad.

David Solnit: There was a handful of people who would fuck up a show and 300 people just wouldn't do anything to stop it. All the more sensitive, creative, positive-minded people stopped going to those shows. It was ludicrous.

Jello Biafra: One day they had a touch football game, punks versus skins, in Golden Gate Park. The real badass semi-organized skinheads hadn't really hit the scene yet. They were starting to turn up but it hadn't really gotten bad, so I thought, oh, what the fuck. I was the worst athlete in my whole school, but I never minded being knocked around in gym class. It was kind of what pogoing was about. So I played football with the skinheads.

Jeff Goldthorpe: The midsummer punks versus skins football game did not clear up the problem. Punk audiences and the clubs in the Bay Area were pulling back from the scene because of the mounting problems with the skins.

Fat Mike: Marc Dagger was interviewed by Tim Yohannan on *Maximum RocknRoll* Radio. That was hysterical. The guy made no sense at all.

"PART TWO: S.F. SKINS RESPOND"

Tim: Well, it sounds like, as people said last week, on an individual basis and when you guys are sober, you're really nice guys. Yet, I've seen you all of you going off in situations that were totally . . . your reactions were totally out of hand, and people got hurt. Why do you think so many people were calling in last week saying, "I don't want to go to shows anymore because of a lot of stuff that's happened to me or my friends"?

Marc: I'll answer the question that you just asked. You know, a lot of times we are really nice guys when we're sober, and we take a lot of crap from people that we shouldn't take . . . because we don't have to take it. You talk about politics. Personally, I don't believe in politics. They're gonna blow us up, and what are we gonna do about it? What is our little vote going to do about it?

—*Tim Yohannan,* Maximum RocknRoll *18, October 1984*

Marc Dagger: I ended up ripping the microphone out of the wall. Tim Yohannan and all those guys hated our guts 'cause we were just a bunch of violent fucking assholes. But they wanted to politicize everything.

James Angus Black: I called in on that show because Dagger is my best friend and Tim Yohannan was getting the upper hand. I wanted to get in Dagger's corner. But, even at that time, it was obvious the skins were going to break up the scene. I agreed with Jello on that completely. I wouldn't tell him that.

> As of July 16, there will be no more punk shows at the On Broadway in San Francisco . . . [C]onstant damage to the O.B., rising violence, bands demanding too much, people sneaking in, etc. has led to the end of an era here. Dirk feels that "trash has taken over the scene." Yet 85% of the people are as good as ever, but the few have become fascist and no one is standing up to them.
>
> —*Tim Yohannan,* Maximum RocknRoll, *July 15, 1984*

Marc Dagger: Peter Jennings interviewed us once. We were on *World News Tonight* 'cause we were getting a lot of notoriety for what we were doing up in the Haight. He was talking about gang violence and skinheads coming to America. It started some stupid media sensation. I stayed out of it 'cause I didn't want my face on the TV.

We had a reputation because a lot of black dudes used to come up to the Haight from the Fillmore District and mug people, rob people, and stab people and stuff. It got to the point, man, where every time we saw them, it was a boot party. And the cops liked it. They turned a shoulder to it because we were taking care of a problem they obviously couldn't deal with.

They stopped coming up from the Fillmore District 'cause a couple people were found dead in the park. So we were basically running the frickin' place. Then some of the storefronts were targeted because gay dudes owned the pizza place. When we started fucking with them, the cops started coming down on us. Because they owned the buildings and we were running off business.

Carol DMR: I remember some terrible band was playing at the Sound of Music and Terry got his throat slit. They had done something shitty to some black guys outside and the guy came in and slit Terry's neck from ear to ear.

Steve DePace: The Sound of Music was the first club that popped up beyond the Mab. It was a transvestite strip bar on Turk Street.

Carol DMR: Terry didn't die but I'm glad I wasn't there because this was somebody I knew and I used to hang out with. Before he became a Nazi skinhead.

Jason Lockwood: I got kicked out of BASH. Dramatically. My cousin got jumped on Broadway by a bunch of thuggy hip hop kids. We called them stubbies. Instead of fighting, I just got him out of there. So I got kicked out. I had to fight Terry Bash on Skinhead Hill.

They actually wanted me to fight Jimmy Mange but I knew that Terry was not as good a fighter. I knew if I got into a fight with Jimmy, he was gonna maul me. And if I got into a fight with Terry he would just hit me a couple times. It worked out perfect. As perfect as it can be if you wanna completely shed all your self-respect. I wound up running because it was all the S.F. Skins and all the BASH Boys and I was certain I was gonna get killed.

I was never much of a fighter. I wanted to be a tough guy so desperately. I went through so much torture trying to be the guy that gets into fights. But I hate it. It terrifies me.

Marc Dagger: I had to leave town 'cause I had warrants. Me and Spike and Bags stayed in New York with Harley from the Cro-Mags, Agnostic Front, a whole bunch of different skinheads that we used to take care of when they came to San Francisco.

Spike ended up getting pregnant and she didn't want to be on the run. She wanted to go back to San Francisco to have the kid and be near Carole Lennon and her friends.

Tammy Lundy: Carole Lennon owns Lennon Studios on Capp Street. Everyone recorded there. She was like the mother figure on the scene. Which we desperately needed.

Ninja Death: When Aunt Spike and Marc broke up, she came back and had her treasure, Little Marc. She got a huge house on Baker Street and she immediately moved me in to be with her and Little Marc. This is where she started to actually shine. She always woke me up for school and got me on my way with a killer breakfast.

Marc Dagger: I had to keep moving. I had a murder warrant, an assault warrant, and a probation violation—all of which got dismissed when they finally caught up with me in Texas and shipped me back to California. I ended up getting a year and a half on the probation violation.

Audra Angeli-Slawson: But things got really weird with Bob Heick. Bob Blitz. Nazi Bob. He became a full-on crazy white supremacist.

Carol DMR: Bob was a total nerd kid. We probably made fun of him. Six months or a year later, he came back with his boots and braces and he was a Nazi. He founded the American Front, and began working with Tom Metzger and the White Aryan Resistance. These were the same type of kids that got their lunch money stolen. These are the same type of kids that become cops.

Martin Sprouse: This was above and beyond the Marc Dagger skinheads. This was the weird and organized Nazi skinheads.

Patrick Hughes: They used to march down Haight Street on May Day during the late '80s.

Jeff Goldthorpe: Bob Heick made a name for himself in the neighborhood by kicking in the window of Bound Together anarchist bookstore.

Patrick Hughes: Skinheads actually firebombed the store in the spring of 1989. I was working there and living behind the store so I was there to put out the fire. The White Aryan Resistance claimed responsibility.

Sara Cohen: SHARP [Skinheads Against Racial Prejudice] grew up to combat all that shit. Everything just got so political. Shows were more like rallies than punk rock.

Silke Tudor: A lot of us were uncomfortable with where things were heading. In private, even some of the guys admitted how fucked up it all was. But when we were at Baker Street, it was a different story. It is all so embarrassing. Unconscionable. I hope the way I live my life now makes up for some of that shit back then, but I really wish I had been less angry and fearful. I wish I had stood up.

In August, 1987, Greg Withrow, former president of Aryan Youth Movement had his hands nailed to a six-foot plank, after publically denouncing his former comrades. The summer of 1988, skinheads made a very high profile appearance, protesting outside the Democratic Convention in Atlanta. Later that fall, they made some appearances on sensation-drenched talk shows, first on Oprah Winfrey's and their grand finale on Geraldo Rivera's, where they pummeled the host before millions of viewers, making skinhead a household word.

—*"Nazi Skinheads: The Hate Behind the Headlines,"*
Cary Tennis, Calendar Magazine, *January 1, 1989*

Portia: One day, Little Marc referred to someone as a "nigger," so Spike packed up their things and moved north to start over. She ended up living in a small town in Idaho for 11 years, working as an EMT and a volunteer firefighter. Delivering babies, saving lives. Just like you'd expect. And Marc grew up.

Marc Dagger: I have seven kids. I'm a grandpa now. I'm still not smart enough to walk away from a fight so I don't go out a lot because of that. My kids need me out here.

Portia: Spike was murdered while trying to break up a fight between two of her nephews in Mendocino County in 2008. All her favorite bands played at her memorial. Bad Posture, the Fuck-Ups, Verbal Abuse, MDC, the Lewd, Naked Lady Wrestlers, Fang and whole bunch of others.

Ninja Death: I found out what happened to Aunt Spike from Johnithin Christ, of Code of Honor. He was her best friend. She was and always will be the only real family I ever had. She taught me how to skate, drink beer, cook, bake, sew, put on my makeup and never forget who I really was. She gave me *me*.

Jason Lockwood: You don't realize how bad you really felt as a kid until you look back and think, why would I do that if I didn't feel terrible? Music really does influence you. I was a nervous wreck as a kid. So I would put on headphones and those waves of sound would white everything out.

I would pick up the stylus and drop it back on the song, over and over again like an OCD pattern. It was so dramatic, like a sensory overload, overpowering everything that I was terrified of. There was such a beautiful reckless abandon to the punk scene. I think that sound conditioned me to use music the way that I do now. If I need to be calm, I listen to chick rock. Horribly unabashed chick rock.

18

Gimme Something Better

Rachel Rudnick: Social Unrest was probably the best hardcore Bay Area band. They had really good catchy songs, anti-American songs, anthemy sing-alongs. Their singer Creetin was kind of the Bay Area version of Mike Ness. The girls loved him. He eventually came out of the closet, a lot of broken hearts there.

Danny Norwood: Punk saved my life in some way. Because I was literally going to hang out in Hayward and work at the local radiator shop.

Jim Lyon: I went to Tennyson High School with four members of Social Unrest. I remember Danny and Jim playing a lunch show at school. The band was called Leather Nun. I was nicknamed Tape Recorder because I would make up songs and make them listen to them on my tape recorder.

Bonedog: Besides Social Unrest, there was no scene in Hayward whatsoever. They had the full-on band T-shirts and spiked hair and studs and all that. Nobody else at the school looked like that. They were outcasts.

Ray Vegas: My first show was actually a Social Unrest show at the Mabuhay Gardens. James Brogan—who became the guitar player for Social Unrest and later started Samiam—he took me to see them, and that was it for me. It was Social Unrest and the Naked Lady Wrestlers.

Creetin K-oS: I remember going to hang at the Mab one night and seeing this teenage boy lying on this cool old Cadillac. He was my age, about 15 or 16 at the time. He was totally decked out in punk garb, although not looking like the rest of the crowd of the day. He probably didn't know the right people to get in the club, given his age. He seemed content smoking his cigs and blurting various nasty remarks at tourists and passersby. I was floored. That is when it all clicked for me.

Bonedog: I started talking to the kids in my high school, and they told me where they rehearsed. I'd go down in industrial Hayward and watch Social Unrest rehearse every Tuesday and Thursday for years.

Danny Norwood: We rehearsed in a storage place. Where you could actually drive your car in. We were the only band in there. And we brought carpets and soundproofing stuff. It was actually the first place I ever lived after I left home.

Jim Lyon: I would sit in front of their garage door and listen to them writing the song "Making Room for Youth."

Creetin K-oS: It was an accident or destiny that I joined with Social Unrest. I knew a couple of the guys from school. I did not even know if those guys liked me or just thought me a poseur. Bob, their first singer, ran into me in Sacramento one summer. He was not happy with SU and was going to quit. He thought we should start a band. At the end of the weekend, I called SU to tell them their singer quit and I wanted the job. We were packing the Mab in less than a year.

Jim Lyon: Kevin Reed, who would become the vocalist for Teenage Warning, lived down the street from Creetin K-oS and Maire, their drummer's girlfriend. I ran away from home and rented a couch from Creetin for $100 a month. The house always had Nina Hagen or Siouxsie blaring out of the speakers. We would raid vegetable gardens in Hayward and bring them back to the pad to have Creetin make dinner. We lived on apples for about a month.

Danny Norwood: When Creetin first joined the band, he sounded a lot like Johnny Legend, but he developed his own style, which reminds me of something Middle Eastern. We started pretty much like the Ramones, and then we got faster and faster as we got to be better musicians. He is kind of a shy guy, except for when he gets onstage.

Creetin K-oS: I will be the first to admit Mr. Rotten was a big influence on how I sang punk rock. No hiding it. He was a hero and a villain. I loved the whole U.K. sound.

Greg Oropeza: When the South Bay scene finally took root, it was mostly made up of aging New Wavers and lots of young skaters.

Danny Norwood: We did the Agnews State Hospital in Santa Clara. All the state hospitals were looking for entertainment back then and no one else wanted us to play. Our other guitar player at the time, Doug Logic, had a nervous breakdown. It just weirded him out, playing in front of the mentally challenged. There was some LSD or mushrooms involved. South Bay punks came to the show and the attendants were very friendly and gracious. We were pretty well behaved except for the LSD. We didn't exploit them. But it was a little bit unsettling.

We played with MDC a lot, with Flipper sometimes. Flipper would always stand back there and mock us the whole time. They were probably four years older than us, and thought we were pretty much just run-of-the-mill. So every time we'd finish up a song, they'd go, "Onetwothreefour!" Every time. "Onetwothreefour!" Anticipating.

Ray Vegas: Social Unrest was the first real band I was in that people came to see. When we were onstage there were 200 people at the Mab, or at the On Broadway. I'd never see girls. They were always in the back 'cause everyone was thrashing. They were all dudes. But when we were on tour, there were girls.

Danny Norwood: We hit the road with U.K. Decay in '81 and played a lot of shows with the Dead Kennedys. They'd take us out of town with them on weekend stints. They were good people. Their manager Barbara Hellbent became our manager at one point, and East Bay Ray produced our records. We were friends with Jello's then-wife. She helped us with our marketing and sales.

After *Rat in a Maze*, Jason Honea took over for Creetin. We had a really successful tour in Europe in '87.

Ray Vegas: It was really weird. Once you crossed into East Germany, there was one little shop on the main road, but you couldn't get gas, so people were pushing their cars through the border. Me and James had to drop our pants at the border. The women guards laughed at us. These lines and lines of cars and we're standing there with our pants down to our ankles, five punks in front of this dirty van.

But Yugoslavia was a really big show. We were a good release for them. All the cars looked the same and all the buildings looked the same, totally gray. It was industrial. The kids ran machinery and they all worked in factories.

When we pulled into the parking lot, all these people were

looking in the van windows. People were just hungry for it. I can't say we were the first band to go play there, but it sure seemed like it. People were just way into it. We got letters from people thanking us for just coming out.

Danny Norwood: This guy came to the show and had a sweater that his mom made. She had knitted "Hüsker Dü" into it, because you couldn't buy punk shirts. It looked great.

Ray Vegas: When we were in Spain a guy came to our show with our logo knitted into a sweater his mom made for him, too. Crazy.

Danny Norwood: Being a punk at the time, you doubted what our government said. Part of the allure was to see if it was really as bad over there as Reagan was saying it was. It was poor. And we got stopped randomly a couple of times for papers—that definitely was true.

Ray Vegas: But the people we met there were nothing like that. They were just like us.

Billie Joe Armstrong: I didn't get into Social Unrest until the last show they ever played and I thought they were just great.

Danny Norwood: I had to take a break. To regain that freshness I was seeing in younger bands. Taking a break meant I moved away. I moved to Czechoslovakia. Then I moved to the mountains. There was a big period I was just disconnected from it all.

Ray Vegas: When Social Unrest departed, I was in the next incarnation of Attitude Adjustment.

Danny Norwood: In '95, when we started playing again—that was a weird time to come back because it was almost like, "Oh, you're riding the Green Day wave." Then we recorded with Billie in his basement. Billie basically recorded, engineered, and produced it.

Billie Joe Armstrong: Noah from Neurosis came over and helped me set everything up. He had a lot more knowledge than I did. They recorded downstairs and my wife was totally pregnant. She went into labor the day after they finished recording. So that was the sound that was coming up through the floor.

Danny Norwood: We took a hit for that because those people who read "produced by" thought, "Oh, they're trying to be . . ." That's where I saw the Tim Yohannan backlash against Green Day. Billie's a very cool guy.

We play shows in Southern California, and there are moms and dads there who are ex–punk rockers, who grew up in my era. Now their kids are in bands and they are there with their video camera—still kind of punky looking—filming their new hardcore offspring.

Ray Vegas: You can't help to be concerned as a parent. We know what we did when we were that young and we're lucky to be here now. They're doing all the same stuff. It's like, "Oh, my gosh."

Danny Norwood: Punk made me reeducate myself. I read more and paid attention to politics. I went back to school. There were a lot of negative things, too, but mostly it pushed me in a good direction. It inspired me never to be ignorant. That's about as simple as it gets.

I love my family, but I can see the difference between my immediate family and my cousins. In Hayward, I went to school with 20 cousins. They stayed and had kids and got a job in a local factory. That whole suburban thing. It's not like they admire me because I was in a band, but I got out of California, I waited to have a kid, I just did something different. Punk taught me I could do something other than pay bills, something that might even mean something.

19

Berkeley Heathen Scum

Sammytown: There's the term "army brats." We were all university brats. A lot of our parents were professors at Cal Berkeley. My dad teaches forestry. Turner, the guitar player from Special Forces, his dad worked at UC. Toby Rage, who was a local fixture and roadie for everybody, his dad was a professor. As far as parenting went, there was a lot of crazy ideas. "Let them make their own mistakes and be who they are gonna be." A lot of us didn't have any fuckin' boundaries.

I started drinking and smoking weed when I was 11. Started dealing drugs. Started to get arrested. I ended up in juvenile hall, and went to jail. GTA [grand theft auto], vandalism, just basically being a kid, running amok. Mainly it was crimes of fun. Steal a car, run around and crash it, shit like that.

Tim Armstrong: I'd known Sam for a long time, 'cause we're Albany. First time I ever seen a punk rocker was Sam. I'll never forget it. We were up on Gateview, the next street up. Just dorky kids hanging out. He came out of the hills—earring, short spiky hair, colored—and walked by, didn't even register that we existed. I just watched him. And I went, "That kid is fucking cool. Wow." He was probably 15.

Sammytown: I was the only boy in high school to have my ear pierced. I had purple hair and I was already starting to get tattooed. In three months I got jumped four times by the jocks. I dropped out of the ninth grade. My parents were like, "What the fuck?"

Speed was the drug of choice back then by the punk rockers, and a large percent of the population shot up. Especially in the

East Bay. There was a lot of young kids all running around shooting speed and eating acid. I started using heroin when I was 15, and I remember being very much looked down upon in the punk scene because I was the only one.

Tim Armstrong: My brother Greg was a drummer before he joined the army. He was in a band with Sammy. A bunch of Albany punk rockers in a band called Shut Up. Very, very regional, very specific. Shut Up had a song called "Fuck All the Albany High School Jocks." I was stoked that my big brother was rolling with these guys. And Sam went on to join Fang.

Tom Flynn: The first band I was in was Fang, in Connecticut. I got here, and then about a year later, a friend that was in the band moved out here also. We decided to be a duo. One of us would play drums and the other of us would sing and play guitar, and we'd switch.

It was a weird band. We liked being minimal. But also, I wasn't good at meeting people. The only place we could play was the Sound of Music.

In 1981 we played Texas, played Kansas City, drove all the way up to New Haven, and played in Boston. Two people and a station wagon. We looked pretty unassuming. Nothing abnormal. Just a couple of young guys.

I was afraid if we got a bass player, I'd have to play what they wanted to play, and I wanted to be in control. I put a note in Universal Records and it said, "Drummer wanted to jam," something retarded. "Sex Pistols and Flipper."

Sammytown: My best friend Joel Fox, the drummer from Subsidized Mess, went and tried out for Fang.

Tom Flynn: We told Joel to join. Sam said, "You really need a singer. I can sing."

Sammytown: I was an arrogant little fuckin' bald-headed 15-year-old brat. Tom was like, "Come back next practice and we'll try it out." And so I came back and he said, "Here's some lyrics."

Tom very much had a cynical take on things and so it sort of set the tone. "Skinheads Smoke Dope" was more about hippies than anything. Even "Destroy the Handicapped"—Berkeley was probably the first city in the world to ever need handicapped ramps. It was such a PC place. I was very much anti-that. Not on purpose or with any kind of agenda, but because growing up when and where I did, that just came out.

Noah Landis: I was going to Berkeley High and Fang was like "our band." In some ways I felt really lucky to have them. Because they were for us and they were just amazing and unique and funny. They didn't take themselves too seriously. They always put on a great show. For what punk rock was, when I first found it, Fang summed it up. In terms of attitude.

Hef: Tom had a very unique style of playing the guitar, and the songs were written around his guitar. It was punk in that it was rebellious and different and all that, and it was hardcore. But musically it was very slow.

Dean Washington: I was at every single Fang show. Some of 'em were more memorable than others, and some were total and complete blackouts. Beer and speed induced. "Yeah, that was a great set!" You didn't hear a fucking single bit of it. "You guys *ruled* tonight!"

Tom Flynn: At some point I realized, "Oh, we really have a following." It was kind of weird. I was used to playing places where no one would show up. It never got to be huge. A big show was 200 or 300 people.

Paul Casteel: Fang's probably the best band out of the East Bay. It reminded me of a Penelope Spheeris movie: kids all on the run, squatting somewhere, staying at somebody's house while their parents were out of town. It was an ongoing cutting class, drinking and drug spree. It was cool and it was authentic.

Rachel Rudnick: Loved Fang, they touched me heart. "Skinheads Smoke Dope"—I know a skinhead who was very excited, one time he was smoking dope during that song. "Destroy the Handicapped"—they would always pick somebody with a disability to come sing that. "Berkeley Heathen Scum" was considered the anthem by a lot of people.

> *Well Berkeley's full of heathen scum*
> *I should know I am one*
> *I'm a drunken junkie bum*
> *Then there's those Berkeley bitches*
> *Think they'll go from rags to riches*
> *Hang out on University*
> *but now they've got my herpes*
> *You give them enough cash*
> *They'll do anything you ask*
> *They'll take it*

They'll take it up the ass
Then there's those Berkeley bad boys
Don't know how to use their dicks as toys
They only use them to pee
So I taught them something kinky
Now they're fetid virgin killers
Mother rapers and hooker thrillers
They'll bend you down to your knees
Steamy mucous is set free

—Tom Flynn and Sam McBride,
"Berkeley Heathen Scum," 1984

Aaron Cometbus: When the album with "Berkeley Heathen Scum" came out, Orlando said, "Some records shouldn't have lyric sheets."

Sammytown: We started playing a lot and touring. I was 16 and in Tulsa, Oklahoma, and it was 18 and over. So I had to sit in the van until we played. And then after, I would have to go and sit in the van.

Tom Flynn: We wanted to put out a record and I was scared someone else would fuck it up. I thought about Universal Records. They put out the first Crucifix. But I didn't think they were really *cool*. They were older, wouldn't really understand our music. I had money saved up. So I said, "Fuck it, I'll do it myself."

I lived on Bonar Street in Berkeley. So these friends of mine would send me letters to "Boner Street," and they would get delivered. So, Boner Records. It wasn't trying to be a record company, it was just a way to put out the first Fang record. I thought maybe ten people would buy it.

Hef: I was a long-distance trucker at the time. I was in a punk rock record store in Denver and saw *Landshark*, their first LP. I had seen the band, so I bought it. The Fang guys were over one time and they were looking through my records, and they were like, "Wow, he has our record and he doesn't even know us."

Fat Mike: *Landshark* is, behind the Operation Ivy record, the second or third best record out of the East Bay.

Gavin MacArthur: I got their album in the seventh grade, and I remember that song, something about getting to fuck Brooke Shields. "The Money Will Roll Right In." I just thought that was the greatest song.

Aaron Cometbus: Fang were the most Berkeley of all Berkeley bands. They sung about local stuff and Sam was always working delivery for Blondie's Pizza or taking vocal lessons at Laney College. The dead-end sort of nutty stuff that was the essence of Berkeley life. Sam never liked me, probably because I was an annoying little runt.

Later, I did the East Bay scene reports for *Maximum Rockn-Roll*, and almost every month, I wrote that Fang had broken up, because some member had told me so in a huff. Sam was understandably pissed that I didn't check the facts with him. Finally we came to a reconciliation of sorts. He said to go ahead and write whatever I wanted. So of course I began to make up the craziest things. From then on the scene reports were a lot more interesting. "Fang drummer gets a sex change." "Sammy teaching preschool." "Fang bassist run over by ice cream truck." They got a lot of condolence cards for that one.

Bob Noxious: I liked Fang a lot but it was hard for me to admit it because they were our competition. Fang had the East Bay and the Fuck-Ups had San Francisco.

Murray Bowles: They had really catchy songs.

Tom Flynn: We were political personally, but I didn't think we were a political band and I didn't really like political bands. Just

Photo by Murray Bowles

Sammytown at Eastern Front

seemed really boring to me. Writing songs about Ronald Reagan: "I hate Ronald Reagan." There's our song! It just seemed dumb. Do these people really feel a deep emotional response singing about Ronald Reagan?

Sammytown: Tim Yohannan asked us about the lyrics to "Fun with Acid," and he kept trying to steer it towards something about Vietnam. We were like, "Dude, no, it's just about being fucked up and paranoid on acid."

Tom Flynn: People figured any band from San Francisco was ultra-political. Fang was not like that at all. People were kinda surprised when we'd go around the country, that we weren't a typical *Maximum RocknRoll* type band.

Sammytown: We were like number three in Penn State on the college radio station. What does that even mean? There'd be all kinds of kids that knew the songs. We'd look at each other thinking, "This is fuckin' crazy."

Tom Flynn: In '84 we put out another record called *Where the Wild Things Are*. And then we went on tour again. And I quit at the end. In the fall of '84. It wasn't any fun anymore. We couldn't write a good song. It just got to be a pain.

Sammytown: He was tired of me. We went on this big U.S. tour. My girlfriend had three kids, and was living in Tom's house while he was on the road. We were fucking strung out on heroin already. I was like 16. So he comes home to his house, and his singer, his singer's girlfriend are shooting heroin in the bathroom while these three kids—I think he was just like, "This is fucking off the hook."

Tom Flynn: I really thought that I'd quit and the band would end. But Sam said, "If you quit the band can we go on?" I said, "Whatever, that's up to you." And eventually they decided to keep going, which hurt my fragile ego.

Kelly King: Bill Collins was playing for Fang. He was the only person that could copy Tom Flynn's style almost perfectly. It was excellent.

Sammytown: I did a lot of drugs. I started dealing acid. I made my own blotter. I would get crystal and put up 20,000, 100,000, 50,000 hits at a time. Going on tour made it really convenient because we'd hang out in town for a couple days, I'd find the local pot dealer and ask, "Well, what about acid?" I'd end up mailing acid all over the country.

I remember going through Nevada and taping our pot underneath the fucking body of the car because the drug laws in Nevada were so intense. It was '85, I got busted in Texas with a roach worth of weed and I had to spend three days in jail. So I moved the band to Europe for awhile in '85.

The last few tours, I ended up kicking on tour. I would just deal with it. "Yeah, Sam's got the flu." I'd go out and play shows, they'd think I was punk rock 'cause I was running, puking offstage. But I was fuckin' kicking heroin.

We played with Operation Ivy in some weird valley outside of Las Vegas, way out in the fucking middle of nowhere. This band called the Atomic Gods had somehow gotten two flatbeds that they'd stacked back to back, and just left them out there because it made a good-sized stage. They would bring a generator truck, and charged by the carload because there was only one road in and one road out. All these punks would come and they'd bring three-wheelers and four-wheelers. There was vast quantities of fuckin' Everclear and punch and acid, and guns.

Tim Armstrong: Everclear and Mountain Dew. He had a fuckin' can of this drink, man.

Sammytown: I only remember bits and pieces, but at some point I'd been riding this three-wheeler and I think I fucking rolled it. I staggered out and somebody came up and handed me a big fuckin' handgun, like a .44 or a .357.

Matt Freeman: They were shooting targets. So someone had the bright idea, let's have Sammytown shoot targets, too.

Sammytown: We were out there behind the stage and the Oppers were trying to play, or were about to play. They saw somebody giving me a gun and they knew how fucked up I was.

Tim Armstrong: We were all behind them. And he was out in front of us about ten feet.

Matt Freeman: With a real gun, okay? And he just—*bam!* Totally missed the target. The whole crowd just busted up laughing.

Tim Armstrong: He turned around and went, "Who the fuck's laughing?" We were just like "AHHHH!!!" and we scattered.

Matt Freeman: We literally dived behind the end of the car. All of us, me, Tim and Dave Mello, all crouched down. We knew Sammy was no joke. It was, like, not funny at all. It was pretty intense.

Sammytown: I was just too wasted to even fuckin' play. It was a few days later before I was actually coherent enough to talk again.

I think it was that same tour, we played with Crimpshrine in Baton Rouge or someplace. There weren't a lot of East Bay bands that toured. I don't know if it was Aaron, or some other guy in Crimpshrine—we ended up giving each other tattoos. That was kind of a moment. The next generation. It was, "Wow, you guys are now out here on the road. Some other hometown East Bay idiots dragged themselves out to this godforsaken fuckin' place!" It definitely was cool seeing the young kids coming out. We'd done many tours by then. I was probably 19 or 20.

We were supposed to go back to Germany to record. It was cheaper for Tom to fly us to Germany and record over there. I'd been dealing a lot of drugs and acid in Germany. My girlfriend over there had been dealing for me. She ended up getting busted. Then Interpol wanted me, and they knew I was supposed to be coming to record. So we had to scratch that whole trip to Europe.

We ended up recording in San Francisco, and by that time the habits came home. Drugs were always a huge part of the scene. But it wasn't really until '87, '88, '89 when heroin exploded. People started dropping like flies. It was a really sad time for the early punks. Will from Flipper died. And John, who ended up playing in Flipper after Will, died as well. I got real strung out. I never ripped anybody off or ripped my friends off. But given what happened that's hardly the worst thing you can do, obviously.

Tom Flynn: Some Fang shows they played without a singer. They had other people onstage. They had one guy singing off of the lyric sheets.

Sammytown: I started concentrating on dealing. I had people all over the U.S. It was probably 95 percent mail order. I made 30 grand in a month, and I'm 22 or 23, thinking, "I'm making more money than my dad."

James Angus Black: I did a U.S. and partial Canada tour with Fang. That's the only time in my entire professional life of roadying that I took a band to the wrong place.

Everybody went to sleep in the van and I thought we were going to Roanoke, but we were actually supposed to be going to Chapel Hill. Me and Petey went to a party,

Artwork by Michael Girvin. Courtesy of Tom Flynn

The Money Will Roll Right In: Fang logo

where we met Dixie Lee. She was like, "Oh, you're here with Fang? I love Fang. I'm going to go see them on Thursday. Is Sammy in town? You got to take me over to meet him."

So we introduced them. They hit it off and she followed us to Chapel Hill, then back to Roanoke. At the end of the tour they got together. It was all fucked up.

Sammytown: She started dealing for me and she went from buying like 100 to 500 hits every couple weeks to 10,000 hits every two weeks. She had a good head for business. I moved her out to California.

She wasn't a drug addict. I was a fucking mess. I kept telling her, "Oh yeah, I'm gonna quit, I'm gonna quit." And I had no intention of quitting. I felt that if I was a drug dealer and I wanted to spend all of my money on drugs, then that was my god-given right.

She had came from hardscrabble Virginia, she lived in a boardinghouse with her mom. I think it just ate her up to see me blowing tens of thousands of dollars on fuckin' heroin. Because she was talking about investing in a legitimate business and trying to parlay all of this money into legitimate things.

And I thought, "Well we've got a fuckin' nice apartment, I just bought a new Triumph, you got a nice car, what?"

I never thought I was gonna live to be 18. So the future was not in my plans. But to placate her I went down to Los Angeles to ostensibly clean up, and left her in charge of my business. I was parking cars at a Renaissance Faire. Great place to go to kick drugs! I was working in the parking lot and shooting heroin. And coke. So I really wasn't getting clean. And she knew it.

I'd started hearing rumblings as I was coming back that she was foolin' around with other guys. This guy in Texas was one of my best customers. He would come and get 20 to 50,000 hits sometimes twice a month. She couldn't get that kind of quantity at the drop of a hat. So that's why I was coming back.

I got back early and I was at the house, and the guy from Texas had shown up. The phone rang and it was this guy from Salt Lake City, and he was acting really weird towards me. I'm like, "Dude, what the fuck is going on?" He said, "Hey look, I don't know what the fuck's going on out there, but she said that you've been burning people, and that you're out of your fucking mind, and that she's moving to Texas, and that if I want to keep doing business I should do business with her." And he unwittingly let me know that she had started a bank account in South Carolina.

So that's how I found out that she'd basically been bad-mouthing me to all of my customers I'd set up over years, and had planned on taking my business and moving to Texas with my best customer. I took off.

About five o'clock in the morning—I'd gotten a bottle of whiskey, I was getting all wasted—I decided I was gonna inform them about this. And I came back to the apartment, parked the car underneath the big picture window. I saw this guy from Texas coming out of my bedroom, he was pulling his boxer shorts up. So at that point I lost it. I fuckin' chased him.

He got away, and she didn't.

"DIXIE LEE CARNEY/JUNE 14TH, 1965–AUGUST 6TH, 1989"

Dixie Lee Carney was found murdered in her apartment on August 6th, 1989, 4 months after she had moved to Oakland, from Roanoke, Virginia. In Roanoke, Dixie formed a punk rock band, "Pretty Pathetic." Although the band did not stay together long Dixie became a devoted fan of punk rock music. Her home served as a stopover for most of the bands to come through the area. She put up such bands as Verbal Abuse, F.O.D., Ugly But Proud and GBH. She was a well known figure in "the scene."

Dixie moved to North Oakland in April of '89. Although her stay in California was short, her generous and peaceful nature earned her many friends.

On August 6th, 1989, three friends visiting from out-of-state found Dixie's body in her apartment. Autopsy reports verified that she had been strangled. To think that she had suffered such a violent, savage death has brought unspeakable horror to her numerous friends and relatives. Although the police and FBI have been investigating this crime, they still have not found the suspect responsible for her murder.

Dixie Lee Carney was loved by all and is sorely missed. Her death has left an enormous void in the lives of her loved ones. Our only comfort is to keep her memory alive and to hope for the capture of the fugitive responsible for her murder.

We are looking for Dixie Lee Carney's boyfriend, Sam McBride/ Sammy-Town/Slammy. He was the singer of Fang, and has numerous tattoos including: Spiderman on right upper chest, penis on ankle, skeletal hand, gun being shot, fetus, nuclear cloud and Chinese symbol on arms. He was last seen with a shaved head, and may be growing hair and a beard. . . .

There is a large reward for information leading to the arrest and conviction of the suspect responsible for her murder. Please help us!!

—*Maximum RocknRoll 77, October 1989*

Tom Flynn: Someone called my roommate and told her, "We just called Dixie's house and a policeman answered, said 'Homicide.'" Whoa. I didn't know what was going on. I found out that day.

Hef: I got a call somewhere around noon from Patty Wagon, who used to be a well-known KALX DJ. She said, "Did you hear what happened? Dixie's dead, and Sam's missing, and they're looking for him."

Tom Flynn: I wasn't expecting it, but I could see that happening. They say she was his girlfriend, but I think she was more of his exgirlfriend. I don't really know the story. Who knows.

Hef: Sam had been strung out on heroin for at least six months before this happened. When we were living at Madonna Inn, we were constantly trying to get him off of heroin. Not that I have any training in psychology or psychiatry, but I would say he would have been considered clinically insane. You could barely hold a conversation with him, he was that strung out.

Tom Flynn: People were mad at him, that I knew. Because they knew her. The band had already broken up, so they were not in good circumstances.

Sammytown: I left the apartment that morning and was on the East Coast within 24 hours. I took all the money. There was quite a bit of it. I did slide back into the Bay Area for a short period of time before I went to Alaska. But when I was here, the last thing I was gonna do was go to a punk rock party.

Paul Casteel: The scene had died down. A lot of people who had been around, like me and Sammy, we had all gotten into drugs. I can say that about myself. I was a mess then. That whole thing happened without me even realizing it.

Tom Flynn: The *Current Affair* people came to my house, and talked to my roommates. I didn't want anything to do with them. I was in the bathroom, running water, while they were trying to do the interview. And the guy came over and said, "Don't you know what's going on here?"

Maury Povich: Dixie Carney grew up in Roanoke, Virginia. Like most other girls, she had a mother who loved her dearly. And a life that should have been full of promise. But somewhere, it went tragically wrong for Dixie. She got involved with the strange world of punk rock music. She followed her boyfriend from a punk band out to California. And it was there she died, according to our reporter John Johnston. And while her mother grieves, the mystery remains, in this punk rock death.

—"Punk Rock Death," *A Current Affair*

Rachel Rudnick: They did a two-part series on it. The first one was what he did, and he was at large. And the second one was a follow-up saying he was still at large.

Jesse Luscious: He was on the run. And we were like, he's in Kenosha, Wisconsin . . . he's in Alaska . . .

Gavin MacArthur: It was unbelievable. But it was sad at the same time, because I knew he was really fucked up. Now he's killing somebody? Ahh shit.

Sham Saenz: This is a super-sensitive subject in the scene. Sam McBride is not the first person I've known who's killed someone. Honestly—I grew up in Oakland.

As I understand, a lot of people had turned their back on him. Dixie Lee was the sweetest fuckin' girl on earth. And basically Sam admitted in a court of law that he asphyxiated her to death with a pillow. That was fuckin' pivotal. A slap of reality that we were not invincible. A lot of us could no longer go and pretend that it didn't make a difference.

Sam was the best when I was a kid. And that's why I have to say that I'm kind of still loyal to the guy who was my friend to me growing up. I can't turn my back on him. I remember the guy he was before he started using. And I know what drugs turn you into.

Noah Landis: I was used to violence and seeing people go to prison. But I wasn't used to seeing people killed in ways like that. I saw how it affected my friends. How it affected Dave Chavez and Kate Knox and Steve Chinn, who were in the Fang family and in the band.

Sammytown: In some ways I thought it might have brought a lot of people together. They started talking more. They probably conversed. There were people who were telling the cops where I was.

Marcus DA Anarchist: Kate Knox knew his girlfriend really well and she won't have anything to do with Sammytown. Anytime she sees him, she's fucking raging pissed. And I don't blame her.

Hef: Kate is in a lot of ways queen of the scene. And I'm not saying this with any negative connotation, it's just the factual way it is. A lot of people follow her lead, especially some of the younger punks. She said, "I'm done with him. As far as I'm concerned he betrayed all of his friends." She refuses to forgive him. There are a lot of people who are like, "We don't want anything to do with Sam."

Sammytown: I ran for a long time. I got a job up in Alaska, working in a screen-printing place in Anchorage. I kicked heroin up there. I knew I couldn't be strung out, on the run. Then I got a phone call, "They know you're there."

I went to the airport and it was snowed in. I waited 24 hours before they could actually start flying out of there again. And that was long enough for the federal marshals to get set up and be waiting for me.

I knew I was busted. I walked in that airport and I just knew. They were pretty slick about it, actually. This middle-aged couple had like fuckin' carry-on luggage and shit. Another guy who was a federal marshal was working at the newspaper stand. I have to give them credit.

And then I was back in Oakland, in county jail. I found out who would still talk to me. And who would have absolutely nothing to do with me.

Bill Halen: I was living back in Buffalo, and I was watching *America's Most Wanted*, and they were saying, "The punk rock singer for the punk rock band Fang." And I am like, Sammytown? No fucking way. I got freaked out. I talked to Sammy on the phone: "What the fuck? How did you land in jail? You really need to be thankful that you have this second chance. Make the best of it."

Sammytown: I was sitting in North County Jail and *Current Affair* had the follow-up, after I'd been arrested. I was sitting there in the pod. My public defender had told me that it was gonna be on TV. So I actually made sure to set my watch. I sat there next to some old black guy, we were watching TV. He stood up and said, "Yo, that's McBride on TV! Come over here, check it out! That motherfucker's on TV!" That really helped me, you know. 'Cause usually I'm the only white guy in the fuckin' tank. I was in county jail for about 16, 18 months, fighting it.

Lorraine: By the time he got arrested, Johnny Puke and I had hooked up. Sam and Johnny were best friends since they were like 12 or something. Somehow Sam got the word on the street. We would go visit him every Wednesday and Sunday.

Sammytown: They finally offered me an 11-year manslaughter deal and I took the deal. Went to San Quentin, was in Soledad for awhile. Very few people came to see me while I was incarcerated.

Hef: Sam and I would write each other. He would call me sometimes from prison. The first time I talked to him, he said, "I didn't do it." And I said, "Sam, you know what? Everybody knows that you did it."

The next time he called me up he said, "Yeah, okay, I did it. I'm sorry. It was an error and I realize there's nothing I can do about it now. It's done. It's not like I can bring her back to life." He sounded like he was sorry. Probably for a whole bunch of reasons, including his life. But I never got the feeling that he was totally repentant.

Jimmy Crucifix: These people made these flyers, "WANTED: Sammytown." They put 'em up in Lennon Studios. I tore 'em down, I just thought it was ruthless. When there's drugs and alcohol involved, who knows? You could have been in that position.

Sammytown: I was gone from '89 to '96. I was in Soledad when Nirvana started getting radio play. I heard them on the radio, it blew me away. And then Rancid. Tim and Matt were in Rancid—they were little kids! I was hearin' it on the radio, it was awesome.

Toni DMR: As far as I'm concerned, he did his time. Shit happens if you're a junkie. If you're going to mess around with that shit, that's the fucking risk you're going to take. I feel really bad about what happened, but I wasn't there.

The last time I had seen him was at an NA meeting that Pat Tidd dragged me to. Sam was there, and I was like, "So Sam, did you do it?" "Oh, I can't talk about it." And I was like, "That's okay, I don't fucking want to know anyway."

Lenny Filth: People bitch about the time he served, and to me, it's like he served his time that our judicial system gave him. You don't ask for more because you did something wrong. You take what you get. He didn't get out early, he did his fuckin' time. What's he supposed to do? Ask to stay?

Mike Avilez: Back then I was living in L.A. I didn't know about the murder until I moved up here. I was working at Rasputin Records in early '96 when he got out of jail. He came in with long hair, looking like a biker and fresh out of prison. And he said, "I'm trying to find a band called Green Day that covered one of our songs."

James Washburn: Green Day covered a few Fang songs. Courtney Love sent Billie Joe all of Kurt Cobain's Fang albums, 'cause Billie's from Oakland. Think about how influential Nirvana was, and then look at what was in his record collection. Fang spread that far. Fuckin' badass band. With a dude that did some weak-ass shit.

Bucky Sinister: I ran into him in L.A. one time, and he was all like, "I'm Sammy, I used to play for Fang." I said, "Why would you ever tell anyone that? Everybody knows what you did. People did not forgive you for that. You might have done your time, but people are still mad about that shit. Why don't you just say you're Sammy? I never would have known."

He started getting really defensive and shit. He's not a very big guy at all, and we were kinda getting a little into it. Someone else came over and calmed me down. It was like, "Dude—I mean, she wasn't my friend, but I still think you're a scumbag. What are you thinking? I don't care if you were on dope or not."

Sammytown: I tried to get my parole transferred. But they wouldn't let me. They made me come right back to where I got into trouble. I had to reintegrate into society. A lot had changed. Tattoos, Hot Topic. Everything became something else. I do think that it doesn't cost now what it cost us. But the jocks and the rednecks and the assholes are still out there. I started connecting with people who were in the scene. A lot of people were urging me to do it.

Johnny Genocide: When he got out of the hands of the California penal system he started playing music again.

Sammytown: I thought it was going to be different. I had a booker that was booking us. And then he changed his group of friends and he wouldn't book us anymore. One of the roadies, he had a lot of feelings. And we talked. It was hard. I don't know if it helped or made it worse. But at least we had to deal with it.

You have to go on. You go to prison and you can still go out and do things. I felt if I had to be here, if they wanted to find me, I'd rather say, "Here I am. If you got a problem let's talk about it." Or however you choose to approach it.

Johnny Genocide: People reacted in near-violence, making death threats, picketing the shows, throwing bottles at him.

Fedge: I went to the first show back. It was at the Trocadero. They played with the Dwarves. It was a really tense night. People in line were like, "I want to fuck that guy up. That dude killed his girlfriend." Like, do you know the guy? Did you know the girl? No, you're just some 15-year-old kid who heard what his brother said.

Sammytown: When I got there George Lazeneo grabbed me and pulled me in the office and said, "Dude, we've gotten ten death threats for this show."

If somebody's gonna kill me I'd rather see it coming. I'd rather have it happen here, instead of just walking down the street at random.

Hef: He got out of prison, he was doing deliveries for a flower shop or something, and a guy who owned an electrical company got him in as an electrician's apprentice. For a blue-collar job it's one of the best ones you can get. He had a wife and two kids and he had this nice job. And he started doing heroin again.

Of course they're now divorced. She moved back with her family in Sacramento. My wife is a totally mellow person, she's not into any kind of violence at all. She heard this and said, "These people are toxic. I don't want anything to do with them anymore."

Fat Mike: I saw Sammytown at a show at the Pound and he was like, "Hey, Fat Mike." I said, "Hey, Sammy." And I kind of gave him the eyes down. He was like, "What's the matter?" I said, "My wife says I'm not allowed to talk to you." And he said, "What? I murder my girlfriend, I'm an asshole for life?" And I was like, "Well, yeah, that's how it works. You're an asshole for life."

Mike Avilez: When I got married, Sammy was our pastor and Fang played at the reception. The whole band was onstage and he said things like, "Do you promise to wear your red wings?" We did a tour with them in 2004. That's when I really got to see another side of him. It was unfortunate he was still doing drugs at that time.

Kelly King: A lot of people still to this day hate Sam McBride. It was a terrible fuckin' thing. And if it was my daughter I would have eventually found him and killed him. But that's his life and his karma and his deal. I didn't see him for a long time and didn't communicate with him. But I never hated him.

Rachel Rudnick: I saw him play a couple Fang shows a few years ago in Seattle. They creeped me out. None of the old members were there. All these new guys playing.

Tom Flynn: Sam's the only one close to being an original member. I saw them once. And all they played were songs from all those records that I was on.

Jimmy Crucifix: I started playing with Fang. There is a whole new fan base, a whole new group of kids. It's weird, man.

Tom Flynn: It's almost more popular now than it was. It never really tapered off. As far as CD sales.

Rebecca Gwyn Wilson: To this day, Sam is a chick magnet, which I find bizarre. It seems like some girls have this Richard Ramirez attraction to him.

Aaron Cometbus: They were around for a decade and didn't spend the entire time killing people, you know? So I think it's kind of unfair, especially to the other band members, that that's all they're known for now.

Dean Washington: He has a killer stage presence, and that's what people like. Your band can be lousy as hell, but if you've got a singer with tremendous presence, he'll literally have the crowd by the throat. Hypothetically speaking. Not that he'd *do* anything like that!

Tom Flynn: He seems grown up. He's still a punk but I think he regrets his crime.

Sammytown: A lot of the things that were really important, they're still really important. My friends, and the family I choose. Watching out for each other, and taking care of each other. And not buying into society and the bullshit, the fuckin' crap that we get spoon-fed every day. I still question everything. My beliefs haven't changed at this point, and I don't really see them changing. I'll be a punk rocker 'til the day I die.

20

Dan with the Mello Hair

Aaron Cometbus: The first punk shows in Berkeley were, I believe, at a place called the Dew Drop Inn on San Pablo Avenue, put on by the False Idols. But that was before my time.

Buzzsaw Bill: And then we changed bass players, so it was a different band. A different band has to have a different name.

Jello Biafra: I kept seeing this name Naked Lady Wrestlers on bills and thought it was a traveling troupe of women who wrestled naked. They even got booked at the Stone. I thought, yeah, this must be a wrestling thing.

Buzzsaw Bill: We recognized a lot of similarities. Punk rock is to music what pro wrestling is to real sports. It's a matter of entertainment.

At the same time, we were watching these wrestlers on TV. It was so cheesy. And yet so entertaining. Of course the wrestling was horrible. But the talk, oh my god. So we were trying to come up with a name for a band.

Max Volume: We got it from a sign on Broadway, where it said, "Naked Lady Wrestling." Across the street from Big Al's.

Buzzsaw Bill: One of those strip clubs.

Max Volume: Our first gig was at the Mab, a big gig with the Dead Kennedys.

Buzzsaw Bill: We had our personas. It always pissed Dirk off that we would never be out of character.

Max Volume: When we were getting onstage, he said, "Next up, ladies and gentlemen," and then he leaned over to me and said, "What's the name of your band again?" And I said very quietly, "The Naked Lady Wrestlers." And he said, "Next up, the Naked

Lady—" And I started yelling at him in the other mic, going on about how I was gonna plant a shoe factory in his ass and, "What are you gonna do with the world's greatest guitarist?" etc., etc., etc. I started yelling about how "nobody cares about all these bands playing their Campfire Girl chords—we'll dump them like yesterday's garbage," etc. That was our first gig.

Buzzsaw Bill: The epitome of cool was to play a song, and then go right into the next song, and then right into the next song. And not say anything. So Naked Lady Wrestlers would talk for 15 or 20 minutes, about how great we were.

We got our music, adapted by Mr. Volume from TV shows. Our stage act was definitely from Georgia Championship Wrestling. We ripped off a lot of the speeches from religious shows.

Max Volume: One of my favorite speeches, and this is from the last night of the On Broadway, "You know, I saw a cheap imitation of the Bolshoi Ballet out there. I want you people to know I don't appreciate dancing at all. Nobody dances on my dime! You wanna dance, you go to a disco."

Buzzsaw Bill: If a mosh pit would suddenly break out in front of us, we would stop. And proclaim there would be no dancing while we were playing. People needed to pay strict attention.

Klaus Flouride: Naked Lady Wrestlers, probably the funniest fucks in the whole fucking thing. The punk community just hated them!

Johnny Genocide: Max Volume is the most talented guitarist on the face of the earth, period. This band is one of my top five all-time favorites. They were so ahead of their time, their music went over most people's heads.

Johnny Bartlett: The guitarist was this amazing surf guitarist. I talked to the guy, I said, "Those songs sound so familiar, but I can't really place 'em." And he's like, "Well, you know, our main influence is Hanna-Barbera theme songs."

Jason Beebout: They'd play the *T. J. Hooker* theme song, they were really good at that one.

Max Volume: It was a great, great TV show theme song. I think people weren't giving it the proper amount of shrift just because it was on TV. There's a lot of anti-television bias in this society. I don't particularly like it.

East Bay Ray: People that were too much into punk didn't get that they were punk.

Klaus Flouride: They were making fun of them! And people don't like that: "I'm doing my punk band and this guy's making fun of me. And he doesn't even look like a punk, he's dressed like a god-damn soldier."

East Bay Ray: Punk's an attitude, not an outfit. Where's the rulebook on punk? Naked Lady Wrestlers were a great punk band, even though they didn't sound punk or look punk. They just destroyed certain preconceptions.

Buzzsaw Bill: I think it was the fact that we'd go out there and tell 'em how great we were. That wasn't very fashionable.

Max Volume: The guitar solos got on people's nerves, too. Eventually, we started to do drum solos in every song.

21

Goddamn Motherfucking Son of a Bitch

Johnny Genocide: The Fuck-Ups were always this underdog band. They weren't good looking, didn't care about writing trendy songs or what people thought of them. They were the essence of the punk spirit.

X-Con Ron: My favorite Bob Noxious story: They were at the On Broadway, Bob was up there onstage lecturing the crowd, giving them shit. Leslie, his girlfriend, came up and said, "Oh, shut up, Bob. You know you like to lick my pussy nice and clean all night long, so shut up!" He just turned beet red. It was one of those punk rock moments.

Al Schvitz: "Lick the pussy clean." That's the real deal.

Bob Noxious: Everyone would ask us, "Where's the Fuckettes? Did you bring the Fuckettes?" They loved it.

Jimmy Crucifix: Victoria and Leslie. French girls. Very scary.

Bill Halen: They were sisters. Little girls with leather jackets. If anybody bumped into them, they would kick them in the shins really hard.

Bob Noxious: If you went to see the Fuck-Ups you didn't know if we were gonna be drunk or if we were gonna start a fight on the first song. All the politically correct bands didn't like us. We did everything we could to be bad. Fuck, got our name in the paper, you know?

I grew up in Mountain View, California. For lack of anything else to do, we'd go up to San Francisco and eat acid and go to these three-dollar shows that had the Dils and the Avengers and the Zeros. The first time I saw the Dead Kennedys was for like a buck down at the Temple Beautiful. I just fell in love with it. We cut our hair. We started a band called the Undead with Joe Dirt, and went up to the city one night to play a show at a gay bar. I never went home.

Joe Dirt was in Society Dog. He came up with the name Fuck-Ups and I thought it was the greatest name ever. I have it tattooed 11 or 12 times all over my body. It's just a little hard to get into a kiddie pool, you know, with my kids.

Leslie Fuckette: We grew up in a nice little house outside of Paris and went to terrible nun school for 12 years. My parents uprooted us and moved us to the States when I was almost 18.

We became the Fuckettes because the Fuck-Ups were playing the Sound of Music in the Tenderloin. You had to be 21 to get in the show, unless you were in the band. So we did backup vocals on one song.

John Marr: The Fuckettes traveled in groups of three. One totally drunk and two supporting her.

Leslie Fuckette: Me and my sister Victoria and our friend Virginia. We all lived together with Bob. We didn't want to work so we collected GA.

Dave Dictor: There were a bunch of scams you could get by on in San Francisco. General Assistance was one. You could clean buses four days a week for the city. For 25 hours a week. They would give you $310 to $312 a month, and then you could get food stamps on top of that.

Leslie Fuckette: We all lived in a van for awhile, then we lived in a storefront on 18th and Guerrero. There was no hot water, no kitchen.

Bob Noxious: Leslie was my girlfriend and pretty much the ruler. She was like four foot eight—very small, very frail build, but tough. Her sister was considered the cute one 'cause she'd get really dolled up. Virginia was considered the butch one 'cause she was a little overweight and cut her hair really short. So we had the brains, the brawn, and the ugliness, you know? But they were real good people.

John Marr: I always thought the Fuckettes were the San Francisco equivalent of the DMR, only rougher.

Fat Mike: That's what was different about San Francisco. There were girl gangs up here. There were more girls fighting here than in L.A., or anywhere I'd ever seen.

Rachel DMR: We respected the Fuckettes. San Francisco was their turf.

John Marr: They all became closely linked with the skinheads.

Marc Dagger: The first time I met Bob Noxious he was fucking drunk and he was walking down the street, singing to himself, and bouncing off the walls. I thought he was the coolest motherfucker I ever met. He always had awesome wrist bands. He made them and sold them around the scene.

Bill Halen: I did the stage at the Elite Club for Public Image, and the place was just packed. People from all walks of life came out, but most of them stayed in the periphery. Because when the pit started rotating, Bob Noxious was out there raking faces with his studded armbands.

Marc Dagger: He would make spikes that were razor-sharp. Even if you just bumped against somebody, you were going to rip up their clothes. We were told to take off our gauntlets in the pit 'cause they just caused too much damage.

Dean Washington: I remember leaving the Mab and this El Dorado pulled up to a red light, and Bob looked over and said, "The gorillas got a night pass," or something like that. A night pass! Before you knew it, these five gangster goons from Big Al's Strip Club were on our back. And we were as big as toothpicks. So the chase began, from Broadway and Montgomery all the way down to the bus depot. Then all of a sudden Bob flung himself in front of a Muni bus. The bus screeched to a halt right before it ran him dead over. When it pulled off again, we saw Bob onboard waving and smiling at us. It was just unbelievable.

Bob Noxious: I was never good at fighting. If I got in a fight I would get beat up. Unless it was fuckin' five on one or something like that, I almost always lost. It was still fun. It was better than going to see Poison or something like that.

Ian MacKaye: I quite liked the Fuck-Ups. I thought the record was good. But they took deep offense to Minor Threat. We did a show at the Tool & Die and somebody set off four strings of firecrackers. That little tiny room was just filled with smoke and noise. I had my soda onstage, and I remember going to pick it up, and it was heavier than when I put it down 'cause one of their crew had spiked it. For them, it was a joke.

Bill Halen: One night Jimmy and I went to see 45 Grave at the Elite Club. And there was Bob Noxious. I hit Jimmy on the shoulder and said, "What is Bob doing up there, man? He's up to no good." So Dinah Cancer came out and started singing, and the next thing I knew, Bob came running across the fucking stage and she went flying out into the crowd. She was unconscious, lying on the dance floor. A couple of bouncers grabbed Bob, punched him, and kicked him out.

Bob Noxious: I picked her up and jumped off the stage. It was like a stage dive with the singer.

Bill Halen: She was just lying there. A player for the band jumped out and took her in his arms. I was like, "Oh my god, Bob, what the fuck?"

Bob Noxious: I got really drunk and I just happened to go out that night. I vowed to kick anyone's ass who came from an out-of-town band. That's what kicked all that off.

If anybody came from L.A. we'd fuckin' do something to sabotage their set. I remember seeing the Circle Jerks at the Savoy Tivoli and they were the greatest thing I'd ever heard. They just ripped, man. And bands like Agent Orange and fuckin' Social Distortion. How am I supposed to hate those guys?

Photo by Tim Tonooka; courtesy of Ripper

Bob Noxious with Virginia and Leslie Fuckette at the Tool & Die

Klaus Flouride: They were so nihilistic, it was sort of absurd. They said they had it out for us and, specifically, Biafra.

Leslie Fuckette: We were the real punk rockers. The Dead Kennedys were more poseurs, frankly.

Ian MacKaye: I was attacked onstage. We came back to do a show at the On Broadway in '83, it was us, 7 Seconds, and maybe MDC. While we were playing, I was blindsided by a bald person. Two of them, as a matter of fact.

Bob Noxious: Leslie had really short hair and the way she wore her clothes, she looked like a little guy. She walked up onstage and he started punching on her, thinking she was a guy. So I went onstage and started punching on him.

Ian MacKaye: Bob had told that woman that he would tackle Dinah Cancer of 45 Grave, and he did. And so in return, she was gonna do the same to me. But she didn't get me off the stage. I ended up basically slugging it out with two of the Fuckettes and Bob. Onstage, in front of like 1,500 people.

Bob Noxious: That, uh, got a little bit of press, but not that much.

Leslie Fuckette: Sure, the Fuck-Ups had a reputation, but so did Sick Pleasure, Verbal Abuse. So did all those guys.

Bob Noxious: We always played with Urban Assault, Sick Pleasure, Code of Honor or Verbal Abuse. The tour we did with Verbal Abuse was probably the best one. Nicki had it all mapped out, it was a really good experience.

Dave Chavez: We went on tour for four and a half months. Our driver was Bob Noxious. It was so awesome. We'd get to towns, and because of the Tim Yohannan–Bob Noxious feud that was going on in *Maximum RocknRoll*, he was more famous than we were.

Bob Noxious: Tim Yohannan didn't like us at all.

B: Basically, a lot of people who listened to us at first . . . you can't judge a book by its cover. And people, when they first heard our record, they thought, basically, that "White Boy" was a racist, anti-black song. What it is—it says right in the song—"White Boy, you're a minority," and that's how we feel, you know. The San Francisco punks, which is what we're singing right here, is there's not too many of them and they've got to unite. I think that's basically what the song says.

MRR: It also says, "White boy gonna get a gun, white boy gonna kill." What's all that about?

B: That's the anger built up deep inside everyone. Some people are gonna relate to that; some people jump right off and say, "Well, hey, you know, what is this? This is wrong to say things like that." Well, you know, you go to war, fuck, you're gonna have a gun. That's just a bit of anger in all of us, I guess. Everybody lets it out.

MRR: That anger inside of you, where does it come from?

B: Mostly, just being oppressed as in a sense of, I'm not a boat person, where I've got to come to another country. It's like, you take a lot of shit in your life, and you wanna do what you wanna do, and that's the way I feel.

—*"Bob Noxious of the Fuck-Ups," Tim Yohannan,*
Maximum RocknRoll *8, 1983*

Bob Noxious: We were blacklisted. "White Boy" was a song about walking around in the Mission District, being the only white boy, and always gettin' yelled at, spit at. Tim Yohannan said, "If it's not a racist song, why didn't you call it 'Punk Boy?' " Well, 'cause "Punk Boy" sounds gay.

Dave Dictor: The Biafra–Tim Yohannan world really didn't know what it was like to live that way. They would say, "Those guys act racist," and I'd say, "Sometimes they have a racial attitude but it's not deep." It was like, you get jumped by people coming back from the soup kitchen or some girl gets threatened in an alley, and something gets ingrained in you, this tough thing.

Food stamps were 85 percent African-American. We were in the city fighting for that piece of cheese with these people. To them, we were cutting in line. The food stamp workers weren't much more sympathetic—"You're a white kid from the suburbs. Why don't you go home to your momma and finish your college and get a real job?" We had to deal with prejudice on that level.

Bob Noxious: I was hanging out with skinheads and people that were affiliated, but I never joined. I was always an independent.

Dave Chavez: Before he got involved with any of the skinhead people, he was just Bob, a drunken, white-trash kinda guy. I think that was all a front, that whole thing.

Bob Noxious: I lost a lot of friends. It was such a waste. Sean died of AIDS, alone and basically homeless. He was always into shooting up and screwing all the girls. Really unsafe.

Leslie Fuckette: The drummer Craig had a melanoma on his neck, and three months later he was dead.

Bob Noxious: A lot of people OD'd, just went out and never came back. It happened to me a couple of times—I'd turn blue and people would have to walk me around and throw me in the fuckin' bathtub full of ice. I met my wife in Boulder Creek. When her mother died and left her a bunch of money—like over $100,000—we did it all. So when my mother died, I said, "Take the money. I already spent all of yours." She bought the house, so now I can go piss on my own lawn if I want to.

22

High Priest(s) of Harmful Matter

Dave Dictor: It was spring, summer of '82, the first issue of *Maximum RocknRoll*. I was on the cover.

Ruth Schwartz: Issue Zero was the one that went into the double album, *Not So Quiet on the Western Front*. It was Jeff and Tim and a few other people that published that first one. They had a blast, so they just did another one.

Jello Biafra: One thing that really impressed me about Tim was that, unlike most people in the scene, he was organized. If he decided something was going to be done, it got done. "Let's expand the radio show into a magazine." And it didn't just become a magazine, it became a magazine that came out on time every month from day one, instead of a few sporadic issues for ten years. He was very good at that.

John Marr: *Flipside* would come out maybe once or twice a year depending on their mood. *Search & Destroy* only lasted 11 issues. *MRR* came out every month. And is still coming out.

Jeff Bale: 20,000 circulation. Something along that line, worldwide. And it was coming out like clockwork.

Ray Farrell: It was a natural development because Tim was getting so much coming from people. Bands that had played through that town, they'd go back to their town in Kansas or Corpus Christi or wherever it is, and they said, I wanna be able to do something here. Even if it's a real small-time version of it. *Maximum RocknRoll* gave the impetus to a lot of bands around the country, to create their own thing going on. I thought it was great.

Murray Bowles: I would meet Tim at shows and he would buy pictures from me of whatever happened a week or two weeks ago. And

Maximum RocknRoll #1 featuring Dave Dictor of MDC

then use those in the magazine. I carried around old boxes of photos with me at all times. I just took whatever was recent and printed up the good stuff.

Ruth Schwartz: We wanted to change the world. We wanted to spread DIY attitudes, and we wanted the people to rise up against their oppressors and party! And do right and do better. Everything that was published in the magazine was about that. It was what punk rock was all about, makin' noise and bein' crazy and changing the world every day. Without letting corporate culture have its way on us.

"SCENE REPORT BAY AREA"

Bands in the Bay Area continue to multiply faster than we can keep up with, and here's how it adds up. In San Francisco proper, the most popular bands in the punk-H.C. scene seem to be the DK's, Flipper (probably much to their chagrin), Code of Honor and MDC. All have albums out by now (as has the Lewd, whose present status is in limbo). Up and coming bands include Bad Posture, Fuck Ups, Domino Theory, and Free Beer (ex-Revenge). Other newer bands these days are Juvenil Justice, 5th Column, and Urban Assault (not the So. Lake Tahoe gang). No Alternative reformed, War Zone mutated into Vicious Circle, with Jeff joining remnants of the Fried Abortions to form Lennonburger. Impatient Youth still exist, but rarely play. Arsenal is off to the U.K. to record for Crass, and the Undead are rumored to have had stakes driven through their hearts. The Tanks, Hellations, GOD, and Wild Women of Borneo all have something in common. And then there's the Pop-o-Pies, who trucked here from New Jersey.

The East Bay scene has finally come alive, as have all the suburbs. The demographics of the scene show a shift to the outlying areas, and a constant drop in the average age. We have no accurate statistics on any possible drop in I.Q. Crucifix, now veterans, are joined by Deadly Reign, Intensified Chaos, Fang, Ghost Dance, and Shut-Up. From the North hail the great Naked Lady Wrestlers (formerly the False Idols), Pariah, Karnage, Demented Youth, and UXB. And from the Eastern fringe, Social Unrest continues to hold sway, although they too hardly ever perform. They are joined now by Vengeance, Anti-Social, and everybody's favorite most-hated band, Church Police. And the Southern flank is brought up by the Afflicted, Whipping Boy, Killjoy, and PLH. I'm sure that by the time this paper goes to press, there'll be 10 more new ones, but next issue for them.

—*Tim Yohannan,* Maximum RocknRoll *1, July 1982*

Sheriff Mike Hennessey: It had very small print and was very hard to read. But it was a great way to find out about other groups. I remember as a result of *Maximum RocknRoll*, going to see DOA, who I ended up really liking.

Klaus Flouride: Their magazine was so obsessive-compulsive, as much type as you can fit in a small place.

Jeff Bale: A lot of people didn't like us because they thought we were too opinionated. They didn't like our politics. We didn't like their bands. We had a lot of power in the punk scene. If we liked something, it became hugely popular. If we gave a band a bad review, that band might have gotten popular anyway, but we really hurt them a lot. It wasn't like we were trying to hurt people, but we were expressing our honest opinions.

Tim Tonooka: Tim Yohannan was a nice guy, with good intentions. He was deeply concerned that kids might think incorrect thoughts unless they were provided with carefully selected correct information. The idea of someone setting themselves up to be a self-appointed authority that needs to do other people's thinking for them—because left to their own devices, those other people might come to the wrong conclusions? The underlying mentality is elitist and condescending.

Jeff Bale: Me and Tim lived in a house in Rockridge in North Oakland. We had lots of visiting bands staying there, so we might've left a bedroom open so people could crash there. A house full of albums, and in my case, books, and that's pretty much it. A stereo. The magazine was made in the house.

John Marr: At one point they almost filled the entire three-flat building. Two roommates upstairs, two roommates downstairs, and then two big rooms to use for the magazine. It was like a little bustling economy.

Jeff Bale: A ton of people have been shitworkers over the years. That was Tim's idea. He didn't want to call them slaves, they were basically people who volunteered. And so the term "shitworker" just seemed like a funny punk way of expressing that. Tim and I were volunteers, too.

John Marr: I did it for three years. I don't know if this is a secret or not, but shitworkers got paid. If you were showing up every week, Tim would give you 20 bucks a month to cover your carfare and stuff.

Jeff Bale: The other cool thing is we'd turn bands on to other bands. Like DOA'd be stayin' at our house and we'd turn them on to the Pagans, this punk band in Cleveland they'd never heard of. We had listening parties and we were playing records all the time.

Kamala Parks: A girl I went to high school with said, "Oh, do you want to go do some work on *Maximum RocknRoll*?" And I said,

"You can just do that?" That was such a bizarre concept to me. So I became a shitworker, doing things like the layout. They'd have food, so that was the other draw. I was a scene reporter for awhile.

When I lived with my father our phone number ended in 7588. One day I figured out it translated to "SLUT." I would tell people, "525-SLUT, that's my phone number." Someone was writing up my scene report one day and they said, "What's Kamala's phone number?" Tim said, "Oh, it's 525-SLUT." So it got printed, and I got some really weird phone calls that month from perverts.

At a certain point, I stopped going to as many shows in the Bay Area because my mother had moved to Sacramento. Tim was like, "Well, you can't be the scene reporter if you're not at the shows." And he basically fired me, as much as one can be fired. So there was a certain unilateral decision-making that was going on under this coat of "Aren't we this collective, great thing." Tim was in charge, essentially, and what he said went. I understand in another respect, because coordinating people to work for free is not an easy thing to do, and you have to be tough.

Tom Flynn: There was a real struggle with trying to run it as a communal magazine. But overall, he was a dictator. I wish he had just admitted that.

Kamala Parks: I felt like there was more of a purpose to it. But it had its flaws. Why do people keep coming away with this bitterness about their volunteerism? Because Tim modeled *Maximum RocknRoll* and all these other enterprises on his incredibly cushy position of being able to earn a full-time wage while working very few hours. For most of us that's not possible, to work at a part-time job, and live.

Jeff Bale: We started sponsoring gigs at the Mab. We had DOA. 7 Seconds would come down from Reno.

John Marr: Dead Kennedys played one of the shows. A bunch of Midwestern hardcore bands played. We were very adamant about these being all-ages shows. It started at six and was over by ten.

Jeff Bale: We really felt like we were bringing people together, and catalyzing and stimulating an international punk scene which had previously been pretty separated, in many respects. We exposed unknown bands and unknown scenes and unknown magazines. If there's any justice in the world, 90 percent of the world's punk rockers would be thanking *Maximum RocknRoll* for all the shit we did for them.

Dave Dictor: Tim was a very passionate person. He had so much energy to get the scene going. A lot of things we take for granted. Not to say that punk wouldn't have succeeded without him, but the magazine just became this focus. It set up all these networks, and became this intelligent voice, to crystallize the punk anger and frustration—and "Why are these young people doing all this crazy stuff?"

Jello Biafra: From the beginning, all the record reviews had addresses in 'em. I would frantically write off to anybody whose record I'd never seen, to see if I could get it off 'em. It was especially exciting when we got something from a foreign country. People started finding out they could get a review in an American zine if they sent their records to *MRR*. And it worked beautifully. We keep in touch with many of those contacts to this day.

Jeff Bale: Somebody would write from Brazil and say, "Here's the scene going on," and we would publish it. So everybody would know about Brazil.

Jello Biafra: Scene reports started coming in from countries only Dead Kennedys had visited, like Finland and later Italy and Holland. Those were the first places where people actually got the American hardcore thing.

Jeff Bale: By virtue of even publishing these things, we created this whole synergistic network of exchange. We expanded the punk rock scene in the Bay Area and all over the fucking world by a factor that I would say is incalculable.

Jello Biafra: These scene reports would be peppered with that country's politics. You could learn how strong the squatters' movement was, and how successful it was on the European continent. Another report would come in from Italy where the local city government actually shut down a squat using tanks! Sometimes you would also get reflections by people from Europe who had visited the U.S., and came home and detailed how shocked they were at the homeless population in "rich America."

John Marr: Tim completely dominated the magazine, especially in the early years. He was the one who worked the hardest. It was very much his political vision. He had worked on this magazine in the '60s called *All You Can Eat*.

Jeff Bale: Tim was a communist, that's just a fact. Like all communists, he was a great organizer. He was really into Maoism. He became a Maoist in '71, and always sort of retained that. Tim was a very smart guy, very intelligent, but he kind of stopped reading about politics in a serious way by the early '70s. He had what I would call fixed political ideas.

John Marr: Tim was a ferocious competitor. Every Wednesday night for years, Tim played Risk. I think there may have even been an NPR or alt-weekly piece on the Risk game. It was this real big thing. If the Sex Pistols had played on a Wednesday night, they probably would have said, "No, sorry, we gotta play Risk."

Martin Sprouse: The Risk game wasn't some youth revolutionary, political party type of thing at all. People have the wrong impression. That guy had his politics, but he was way too anti-authoritarian to be part of anything.

Larry Livermore: He was shorter and louder-mouthed than I expected. When he found out I lived in Ann Arbor, the main thing he was interested in was if I had this extremely rare record called "Just Like an Aborigine" by the Up, who were the third band of the MC-5/Stooges trio that worked with the White Panther Tribe. And I thought, "Geez, he's just a dorky record collector."

Fat Mike: Tim Yohannan was always kind of weird. I went to Sizzler twice in my life, in San Francisco. Both times I went, he was there.

Aaron Cometbus: Tim had annoying qualities, but they were not the ones that everyone assumed from their ideas about *MRR*. Tim didn't read, as far as I could tell. He didn't eat vegetables. And I never once saw him at a demonstration.

John Marr: *MRR* made pretty good money. There was a waiting list for ads. Tim thought it was important to keep the advertising rate somewhat low. Tim was not in it for the money. But Tim benefited from it by being the publisher. You had the home office. The magazine eventually owned a car. But it wasn't like using money from a 1/16 ad from this little western Massachusetts hardcore band to fund his summer vacation to Barbados.

Sheriff Mike Hennessey: I'd run into him at Giants games. He was a Giants fan, and I can recall being out there with my daughter, who was nine or ten at the time, and seeing Tim Yohannan. I said, "Samantha, I want to introduce you to a real punk rocker right here."

Frank Portman: I was totally shocked to hear he actually agreed with my contention that hardcore was not as good as non-hardcore. Because he championed it. His reason was political. He had this clearly delusional but sincere idea that since that was what was happening, you could use it to bring the youth into this force, to gather the threads of the old counterculture and eventually overthrow the government.

Ian MacKaye: When I first met him, I didn't get the sense that he's an all-ages show kind of guy, but I think what Tim started to recognize is that the punk energy that he really had an affection for, felt connected to, was something that was ultimately what the kids were up to.

Noah Landis: He was really excited about young people doing new things in music. The way the East Bay punk rock scene started to grow—he was more thrilled than anyone to see that kind of stuff, and he jumped right in the middle of it. He spoke truth to power. He was the first person I met who was all about finding and making and taking advantage of the pathways of communicating the right shit.

Rachel DMR: Tim didn't like us. I remember him being a little softer toward us as he got older. But he never said hello. We didn't fit into his mold, the activist punk movement—the vegetarians, the peace punks, the people that were thoughtful about what they were doing.

Toni DMR: Rachel and I didn't buy into that whole intellectual fucking crap. We'd spent our whole childhood surrounded by the upper echelons of academia. We didn't watch TV. We were well read. So fucking what?

Carol DMR: I spent the night at the *Maximum* house with this band, Vicious Circle. When Tim found me in the house that morning he flipped out: "There's no girls here!" We didn't do anything.

We went to *Maximum RocknRoll* shows and they went to our shows. Ruth was always cool, Jeff Bale was rad. But Tim, our whole presence must have bothered him. The women that he always dated were modelesque, mousy girls. They were always really younger than him.

Ruth Schwartz: He was an old fart. He'd end up trying to date 20-year-old women and we'd be like, "Tim, how are you going to meet women your own age?" And he'd be like, "I don't know! I'm only around 20-year-old women! I don't know what to do." I just used to feel sorry for him.

Dave Dictor: Couple times Tim helped us out, with thousands of dollars. We got arrested in Canada. They charged us with "weapons dangerous to public safety." Which meant we had a crowbar in our car. They were trying to say that we were thuggy youth going around with shaven hair, with pipes and clubs in a van, creating menace. It was a two-year sentence. They had charges on my bass player and my guitar player. The bail was $2,000 each.

I left the police station in shock, like, "How am I gonna get $4,000?" Went to the house I was staying at, the promoter and the people that were hosting us, and started making calls. To raise $4,000, you find out who your friends are very quickly, in 1982, when you're in a punk band in Canada and half your guys are in jail.

I called my mom, she sent me $1,000. And I got some money from Ruth Schwartz, from Mordam Records. But I had nowhere else to go. So I called Tim Yohannan. He sent me $2,000. And he wasn't rich at the time. *Maximum RocknRoll* grew into whatever, but at the time it was a lot of money. We ended up paying it off. We nickel-and-dimed half the money back, and then he let it slide 'cause the magazine started taking off. That was very, very cool.

Chicken John: I got Tim Yohannan to send me $300. It was during the first Circuss Redickuless tour. I just called him from the road and I was like, "Tim! I'm dying out here. Got any money? I am totally fucked." He sent it to the club in Atlanta. It was like a FedEx pack with 300 one-dollar bills in it. Not even in a bundle, just stuffed into this FedEx pack.

Martin Sprouse: I grew up in San Diego. Pat Weakland, Jason Traeger and myself started our own fanzine called *Leading Edge*. I was writing scene reports for *MRR*.

I came up here for the very first time to visit in '84. I was 18 at the time. We stayed at the *Maximum* house. Jeff Bale and this woman Erica lived there. Jeff was drinking Coke and listening to Twisted Sister. He was trying to say they were punk. Painful!

We'd been reading the magazine since the second issue. I remember how thick it was. Seeing politics and punk, done pretty smart, and also seeing a dead guy laying in front of Bechtel in a suit, with a flag over him—I was like, "Fuckin', that's great!"

Aaron Cometbus: They tried to get a ton of punks to show up outside of Bechtel for a photo shoot for the *MRR* cover. Only one did, so they took a picture of him lying down, draped him in an American flag. Pretty smart.

Ray Farrell: The magazine and the radio show were like the entry points. For many kids, punk may still be a rite of passage for them. They get into it, they maybe have difficulties with how their parents are raising them. A lot of those basics—how you take care of yourself, how you find a way to be happy without a lot of the trappings of a capitalist society—that's a lot of what *Maximum RocknRoll* helped kids to start to understand.

The hippie movement was certainly not successful in that. The message I remember as a kid was that it was a freeloaders' society. Whereas punk rock was more like, there's a working-class system in place, and you have to think about what you have to do to survive. *Maximum RocknRoll* made it more fun, because the message by itself is kind of depressing. Punk lowered the age when you start to get disgruntled with everything. It used to be, life is shit after 17 years old. Punk rock brought it down to 13.

Kurt Brecht: We found it at a punk rock record store in Houston. *Maximum* was like our bible. It was our connection with the worldwide punk scene.

A. C. Thompson: Everyone across the country was reading. In 2006, I wrote a book about the CIA. It's a direct link to something I started researching in eighth grade, because I read Noam Chomsky in *Maximum RocknRoll*.

Andy Asp: *MRR* was sort of the Internet of its time for punk rock. In Humboldt we were really isolated. But I sent records to Mexico City punks. I got letters from Croatia. To be a punk in Yugoslavia or Colombia back then, writing letters was pretty ballsy.

Lenny Filth: You could order records that you couldn't get in your normal stores. You could see interviews from bands across the country, or across the world. It gave you an opportunity to read about what other people are thinking, someplace else in the world. Why they started playing music, and what they're doing it for.

Adam Pfahler: When *Maximum* got a little bit older, the columnists were starting to get into it with each other. People were always getting mad at each other up here about something. Calling bands out, calling each other out.

Ian MacKaye: The letters section was such incendiary, squalid gossip. It was a total pissing match. The columns were maddening. I can remember being really infuriated by things.

Audra Angeli-Slawson: You either read it or you went to your local record store and bothered the shit out of the poor guy behind the counter about every stupid little thing.

Rebecca Gwyn Wilson: I had seen *Maximum* in Hawaii. It reminded me of Dr. Bronner's soap and the *Oxford English Dictionary*, because you needed a magnifying glass to read it. At first I was intimidated because I thought, "Wow, these people are really smart, and socially conscientious."

Chicken John: At the time, the scene reports were all written very, can I say, laconic? It was just like, "This band played and then this band played. They rocked. Da da da. This band is not punk rock so therefore they are kicked off the island. And then we all danced around. Blah blah blah." It was dumb.

I started writing New York scene reports that were like stream-of-consciousness creative writing. I'd turn in 1,500 words about driving around New York in the Letch Mobile, this ridiculous old Pontiac station wagon covered in graffiti and food. Bugs buzzing around it. Shit like guitars screwed to it. The Letch Mobile—smell it while you can.

Tim would send me these little postcards. They were so Tim Yohannan. It's like, *Maximum RocknRoll*, the fun punk rock music magazine where everybody has colored hair and STDs! And here's the fucking leader of the movement, right? The guy who's in charge—his postcard is a blank gray piece of paper with a computer-printed *MRR* label on one side, and on the other side he's written in pencil, "Hope you don't mind editing."

I still have every fuckin' issue. That and my collection of soiled GG microphones. They're in the same box.

Blag Jesus: There was not much punk rock in Chicago. We had heard about that magazine and we followed it, and so we went out there and played our music on the radio show. There was ten other bands standing there, and they all wanted to play their music.

Fat Mike: In '84, I went to Italy with my dad. He went on business. I brought my *Maximum RocknRoll*. When I was in Italy, I found a guy who was in Florence, and I just walked up and knocked on his door. I got his address from the scene reports. "Hey, I'm a punk rocker from America." His name was Stefano Bettini. So we had some beers and I taped some music, and his band was playing the next night. And I got to see a basement show in '84 in Italy. You could do that back then.

Mike LaVella: My band did one tour, we made it to California. We went to the *Maximum* house, and I was like, "This is it?" In my mind I guess the house was gonna be like some condemned building. We went in, and Tim interviewed us. Everybody was so nice.

Ruth was like, "This is where you get a cheap burrito." We were literally like, "What's a burrito?" The only time I ever heard of a burrito, there was one in the *Bad News Bears*.

Jennifer Blowdryer: Tim Yohannan was a big fan of the Blowdryers, and so when my first book came out, he approached me about writing a column. I was like, sure. No one ever gave me opportunities. Tim said something about how I was more grounded in writing than in person, and that kinda hurt my feelings a little bit. But he loved to laugh. He always had a big smile, he liked chaos.

When I would travel, the one or two nutty people in town would know me. I'd be in Chicago doing a Smutfest, and some schizophrenic would say they knew my name from *Maximum RocknRoll*. It was more global than anything else I'd ever engaged in.

Tim had a theme issue for April Fool's Day, where the columnists all made fun of each other. I wrote a column as if I was this girl Katie O'Dowell. She got in the office and read mine before I could read hers and then wrote a super-mean one to me. I was like, "I don't wanna be part of another sick family, and this is sick shit. I'm outta here."

Bill Michalski: When I lived in Baton Rouge I used to take photos at shows all the time, and I thought, "Oh, this'll be great. I can work for *Maximum RocknRoll*." But very shortly after moving out here, I realized how cliquish it was. And how exclusive, and what a cool-kids club it was. I really didn't wanna have anything to do with that.

Bill Schneider: I'd read *Maximum RocknRoll* while I was in L.A. but it seemed like it was on another world. It was kind of intimidating. It really wasn't until I moved up here, and then all of a sudden it had a face. You were sitting there in a meeting with Tim Yohannan and all the people who had articles you'd read. And everybody was arguing about whether the toilet paper was recycled enough times. You were like, "Wow, this is cool!" It seemed real, and it felt like it was mine.

Ben Sizemore: I was in this band Econochrist and we were from Little Rock, Arkansas. Basically we all just wanted to leave the South 'cause it sucks there. Once you figure out there's not a wall around it, you're free to go. California had this kind of allure, the Bay Area in particular. We saw *Maximum RocknRoll* and we loved

Moe's Books

2476 Telegraph Ave
Berkeley, ca 94704
(510) 849-2087

Transaction #:00203101
Station:register 2, 4   Clerk:ADMINISTRATOR
Saturday, February 27 2010   7.09 PM

SALES:
  1@   8.00 -   8.00
  Remainder
  1@   7.00 -   7.00
  Remainder
SUBTOTAL   15.00

TAX:
  Sales Tax   @9.7500%   1.47
TOTAL TAX   1.47

GRAND TOTAL   16.47

TENDER:
  Charge Card   16.47
TOTAL TENDER   16.47

CHANGE $0.00

*Five day return with receipt, store
credit only*

00203101

all these bands, like Christ on Parade, MDC, Crucifix, the Dicks, the Offenders, stuff like that. We knew some of those bands from Texas, like MDC and the Dicks, had moved to San Francisco. So we were like, "We could fuckin' just move to the Bay—those guys did it."

Greg Valencia: In Santa Fe, there was nothing to do. We were on our way to jail. We all broke into houses for money, did stupid, stupid shit. A couple of the other dudes that I looked up to had *Maximum RocknRoll* around. It opened up a whole new thing to me. Interviews, everyone's trading demos, it was awesome. It had so much to offer for kids who didn't have much. We came out here in '91 to play three shows. It was like being in a candy store. The record stores. Punk rock girls. We never wanted to leave.

Adam Pfahler: Jawbreaker started playing shows in Hollywood. But then we looked at *Maximum RocknRoll*, and it was fuckin' blowing up here. So we played Gilman and I think we filled in the next night at the Covered Wagon. We met so many cool people that we admired. It made you feel like, if you're gonna do it independent style, this is how it should be done. There was something for everyone here. You could be into taking pictures and have something to do in the music scene. Or you could be a musician, or you could be into writing your own zine like Aaron [Cometbus]. We just packed up and moved here.

Martin Sprouse: Me and some friends from San Diego and Reno all happened to be at the *Maximum* house at the same time. We were all getting along, and Tim presented this idea. He was always scheming to do the next thing. And he said, "I want you three guys to move in here, take over the magazine. 'Cause I want to open a club." Jason and Bessie were into it but then it fell apart. So I just moved up here. Late summer '85. Tim had just found that house on Clipper Street.

Ben Sizemore: I considered that place a palace. They had this really nice house in Noe Valley with this killer view. We all lived in the ghetto in Oakland, so we'd go over there and be like, "What the fuck? These guys are like yuppies. This place is so clean."

Adrienne Droogas: Before my mom would let me move into the *Maximum RocknRoll* house, she had to come out and meet Tim Yohannan. It was funny. Tim was like, "I have to meet your mom?"

Cammie Toloui: I ended up moving into the house and being one of the zine workers there. There was four bedrooms, and a huge rumpus room in the basement where all the records were. The main floor had the magazine zone with the computers.

Adrienne Droogas: Bands constantly coming and going, getting interviewed, stopping by. You were constantly walking in the door and going, "Hi, I'm Adrienne and, this room full of people from Sweden, hi, nice to meet you all. I'm gonna go in my room now."

Cammie Toloui: Tim smoked like mad and the place always had an ashtray smell. I just have these nauseating memories of getting up in the morning and the smell of the trash that was full of rotting beef and egg foo yung.

Chicken John: His laugh was like a goose, sort of a honk. The sweatshirts never fit him right, or he washed them in hot water. Cigarette in the corner of his mouth. The guy was a fuckin' cartoon. You could dress up like him for Halloween.

Cammie Toloui: He was definitely a father figure for me. There was this point where I was this wild punk rocker and fell in love with this even more wild punk rocker in the Soviet Union. We went on this long tour with his band and got married and then came back to America and I got pregnant. I called up Tim and was like, "Guess what, Tim? I'm gonna have Max's baby!" He was sooo mad at me. Like, "Cammie, you have no money. Max is an alcoholic." Just laying it out for me like a dad would. He pretty much didn't want to talk to me after that.

Adrienne Droogas: Tim worked in the mornings and would come home at noon, and do *Maximum* 'til 10 or 11 o'clock at night. He'd delegate, other people would be responsible and did their thing. But weekends, Saturdays, Sundays, it was just what he did.

Matt Wobensmith: Tim lived like a Spartan. He slept on a twin mattress in the basement. He never bought anything for himself.

Martin Sprouse: It was weird. Tim always told everybody that I fired the entire staff of *Maximum* the minute I walked in the door. 'Cause it was very loose, and depended on a large group of people to put it together. They had work parties on Sundays and some people typed, some people laid out, some people did this. I had a totally different working style. I'm a very focused, workaholic person. It looked really fuckin' sloppy to me. I was such a little anal graphics guy. And slowly the work parties disappeared.

John Marr: Someone characterized Martin as the son that Tim never had. They were very, very close. Martin introduced a better aesthetic for the magazine. I started to do my own zine, so I just drifted away. But I probably would have never started my own zine if I hadn't been a shitworker.

Martin Sprouse: We had those discussions at *Maximum*. What is punk? Why isn't this band getting reviewed? All the time. It's been happening since the beginning, and it'll go on forever. I still have that side of me. It's really embarrassing. It makes my girl-friend crazy 'cause she just loves music. I love music, but I got this other weird side that's like, "Nah, that's bullshit."

People liked *Maximum*, people hated *Maximum*. There was a revolt since issue three or four. People started hating it early on. 'Cause of the political side of it. Hate mail every single day. "You fuckin' motherfuckers"—you know. "That wasn't punk" or "That's not how it was." Some of it was valid criticism, some of it was corrections, some of it was just fucking people bitching about things.

Maximum funded a lot of things. End of the year we'd give money away to people. A lot of the contributors or shitworkers. We gave money to different organizations. One year we picked 20 fanzines. A lot of money, to good things.

Jeff Bale: There's a lot of things about *Maximum RocknRoll* that were fucked up, and now especially I feel that way.

Jello Biafra: Going after people, from very early on, in the magazine, and calling people on sexism, racism, and homophobia triggered one hell of a backlash. From the East Coast to the Midwest. When the magazine had barely gotten off the ground.

Jeff Bale: It came from Tim. We weren't gonna cover any homopho-bic bands, we weren't gonna cover any right-wing bands, we weren't gonna give publicity to any bands that we wouldn't re-view, like skinhead records, or Skrewdriver.

Tom Flynn: *Maximum RocknRoll* assumed everyone was racist and homophobic. Irony or sarcasm was totally lost. People assumed that everyone else was a moron.

Jeff Bale: There was obviously some relationship between local emanations of the punk scene and the general milieu in the Bay Area. We were at KPFA, the most PC fuckin' station in the whole world. In retrospect, *Maximum RocknRoll* reflected all too per-fectly the sectarian, intolerant left-wing milieu of the Bay Area. To complain that homophobia is bad—I mean, gee whiz, is there anybody in the Bay Area, except for a few fringe elements, who doesn't agree with that? If you really wanna be a badass fuckin' revolutionary, go down to Alabama and start peddling these views. Don't just sit in your comfortable little Bay Area house drinking your cappuccino and getting all morally righteous.

Jello Biafra: Who was the lucky band that got to go on tour when everyone was crying, "Commie faggot, you're trying to indoctrinate us!"? Dead Kennedys. And me in particular. I was the one who did most of the interviews. I was starting to get asked all over the country, "Isn't Tim Yohannan a communist? Isn't this just a front for some kind of communist cult or something?" As if everybody's fragile eggshell minds would suddenly become little Tim zombies if we dared to read his magazine or liked the same bands that he did.

Larry Crane: God bless Tim Yohannan's heart, he was one of the sweetest, nicest guys, but he started this thing that became really fuckin' rigid. Punk rock, man. Jesus Christ, anybody could do it. Just get up there, it's all attitude over rules. All of a sudden it became the same kinda rules that made dinosaur rock gross. Less interesting than Foreigner.

Bucky Sinister: The thing that really got to Tim was that I pointed out to him that he'd been running book reviews of corporate books, books that came out on Warner's press. He wouldn't review records out by Warner, because they were corporate. But he'd review the books because they were about the Sex Pistols, or whatever. He never forgave me for that.

Scott Kelly: I remember having my opinion of Agnostic Front completely shaped by *Maximum RocknRoll*. We went to New York and became friends with Agnostic Front and hung out. As we were taking the ferry to New York, Roger [Miret] was like, "Every time I see the Statue of Liberty all I could think about is my father and how much it meant to him to come to this country. And that's why we fly that flag. Because I wouldn't be able to do what I'm doing if I was still in Cuba."

As we got to talking more, he was like, "So, you know your buddy Tim Yohannan? What's that guy like?" And I'm like, "He's pretty intense but he's actually a really good guy." And he's like, "Well . . ."

Roger got in some trouble for some shit, went to prison, I believe it was a drug thing. But the reason that he ended up going for as long as he did was because the district attorney brought out *Maximum RocknRoll* and said, "Look, this guy's the leader of a Nazi skinhead movement in America."

I remember going, "Man, that's some irresponsible, fucked-up shit that happened to him." Agnostic Front's not Nazi. Roger's Cuban.

Jello Biafra: The first place I ever saw the term "grunge" was in *MRR*'s record review section. Long before it got glued onto the Seattle bands by the industry.

Ian MacKaye: Another thing to credit to Tim—the term "emo."

Jello Biafra: I don't know whether that was Tim or Martin Sprouse who first came up with "emo." Originally they slapped it on Embrace, Ian MacKaye's almost forgotten transitional band. Embrace were really important. The lyrics were personal like Minor Threat, but starting to take on worldly concerns like Fugazi. Plus it was very emotional. Supposedly he even cried onstage.

Ian MacKaye: This is the genesis of that term. In 1985 Rites of Spring and Embrace were playing in D.C. People were talking about metalcore, and a lot of jokes about all the different cores that were out there. Brian Baker, who was the bass player in Minor Threat, coined the phrase "emocore," which was emotional hardcore. It was an insult, it was pejorative. So he used that term in an interview with Dag Nasty in *Thrasher* magazine. Somehow Tim picked up on it. And he just fuckin' went to town with it.

He would write these reviews and call us "emocore," "emo," whatever. I was of course infuriated. Since when is punk not emotional? It'd be like saying, "chai tea." It's a redundancy. Chai means "tea," so chai tea is "tea tea." Tim really hammered that term in, as an insult. He beat it into common usage. And like every other thing, like the word "punk," eventually people started using it.

Dave Dictor: Tim could be very dogmatic in what should go on, and what shouldn't happen. I had arguments with him. He even sometimes sandbagged me.

Frank Portman: There was a transcript in *MRR*, an interview with MDC.

Larry Livermore: They denounced Dave for selling out the scene because his band had flown from one gig to another, instead of driving in a van. And so they got Dave for an hour-long debate with Tim.

Dave Dictor: We made $8,000 in ten gigs in a tour in 1986. And Tim started saying, "Bands like MDC are selling out their roots." He didn't relate to what it was like to be in my shoes, being in a band, trying to feed five or six people, keep my people out of jail. Arrested at the border, held at the border. Two, three, four times.

Tim, what are you writing? You don't know what it's like to get an engine for your van. And I realize you work 70 hours a week, and you're a slave to your zine. Well, I'm a slave to being a punk. I'm on the road, I'm living at other people's houses. When I get home I'm right at the food stamp line.

"Everyone should work at least 20 hours a week." But there weren't 20-hour-a-week jobs, when you're going away on tour for three months and you'll be back in three months.

Tim could see there was going to be a day where there was going to be Green Days playing Woodstock, and Blink 182s, showing off their 15-car garages, grinning like idiots, with a funny mohawk. He was laying the groundwork for that.

But at the time, $8,000 for ten gigs from D.C. to San Francisco? By the time you get home, there's $2,000. There's $400 apiece to pay my month's rent. And I've gotten someone pregnant, and having to deal with these other realities.

"I hear what you're saying, Dave, I still disagree." Later on, I said to him, "You've always picked on us. You picked on DOA and 7 Seconds. But Dead Kennedys are making more on one tour than we make in three years, and you don't mention them. What's going on?" He was silent about it for a year or two or three, and then, instead of getting more understanding of what it takes to be in a band, started picking on Dead Kennedys.

Jeff Bale: Tim was not a person who believed in freedom of speech. I was. Elements in the punk scene were being excluded. So I started giving them a voice in my column. At a certain point Tim just said, "That's it, I'm not tolerating that kind of stuff, and you can't do that if you want to write for the magazine." So I said, "Fuck you. I'm not writing for any magazine that's gonna try to censor what I say." That was the end of that, pretty much.

Larry Livermore: It was a big dispute within the magazine, where Tim fired Jeff Bale. A number of people said, this is advertising itself as a magazine for the community—that means there should be a variety of community viewpoints.

Jeff Bale: When I got out to Berkeley initially, I thought, "Oh, this is so liberating," because finally I'm somewhere where being anti-establishment in a certain way is not considered heresy. But it took me a few years to realize that actually the Bay Area is no better than anywhere else in terms of tolerance. In fact it's worse. It's like fucking Stepford people. It's mind-numbing, and even worse than that, it's censorious.

Matt Wobensmith: Jeff Bale is very reactionary in some ways. Benzo-diazepines were created for people like Jeff Bale. Xanax, Klonopin, Ativan, get some, man. He's so angry.

Ruth Schwartz: Jeff is one of the most massively opinionated people I know. It wasn't just a column. I mean, maybe in Jeff's eyes it was just a column, but the column was just the last straw. So it became The Thing.

Larry Livermore: That argument came down to a mass meeting of pretty much everybody involved in the magazine, over 50 people. This was whether this was a community magazine or Tim's magazine. And the vote came down in favor of Tim's magazine.

Jeff Bale: I blame myself for not seeing that it was going to go in that direction. And even to some extent contributing to that process. Oh, I blame Tim much more, but I blame myself for allowing myself to go along with it for so long. I wasn't very clever. I got caught up in the spirit.

I would still go over to the *Maximum* house, and Tim and I would sit there and listen to records, and we'd go out to gigs and drink and have a good time. But as far as the magazine, no.

Ruth Schwartz: I was Tim's business partner, I owned *Maximum RocknRoll* for eight years. So I did the books, I did all the tax returns. And I worked for two years for Rough Trade as their buyer. We had a big stormy protest in there and walked off the job, so I decided to start a new distribution company.

Biafra had just lost his shirt down in L.A. A distribution company cut him off, and didn't return any of his product. They called me one day and said, "We've located our stock in a warehouse, and how quickly could you sell these for us?" It was like—*boom!* Tim loaned me a thousand dollars to get a UPS account and rent a space, and get a phone line put in. He told me I had a year to pay it back. When the year came up, I wrote him a check. But he said, "No, no, it's okay."

Jello Biafra: Alternative Tentacles and *MRR* were the original two clients of Mordam distribution. When Ruth started it, with Tim involved, I knew this was the way to go. Rather than holding my nose and signing everything to Enigma and quitting Dead Kennedys because I didn't wanna be on Enigma. This was a great option. So we grew together for many years that way.

Tom Flynn: They had big arguments. All the labels would get together in these official meetings. They had to have their policy about selling to major labels, selling to distributors that are owned by major labels. Some wanted to sell as many records as they could.

Steve Tupper: I think it got dark when Tim began trying to give orders. He demanded that everybody agree to stop making CDs to make a statement against how the industry was going.

Jello Biafra: Then Tim came out with, every Mordam label should pull all their stock out of every chain store because all chains are politically incorrect. Except for Tower, because he liked them. Because they stocked punk singles early on. The room was silent.

I thought, "Wait a minute—are people actually gonna knuckle under and agree to this just because Tim is ordering us around like a general? Fuck that!" So I spoke up, "Look, not everybody is as spoiled and elite that they can live in a big city where there's choices. Or a college town where there's a cool independent store. I know what it's like to come from a cultural desert where you really have to hunt for something cool that will change your life. And I want my stuff in those stores, just because it may be the first time people blunder into anything that will hip them to how evil those stores could be. Somebody has to be the gateway drug, and it should be us."

Ruth Schwartz: Blacklist Mailorder was another *Maximum* offshoot. It was a retail outlet, in the back of the Mordam warehouse. Nobody was doing real mail order, and doing it well. Nobody could get the records that we were reviewing in the magazine. And so we wanted to become that source, simply as a service. We were buying records from all over the world and mail-ordering them.

Basically Blacklist broke even. We sold things as cheap as we could. It was the eight-to-midnight crew in there every night, it was insane. I agreed to do it as a not-for-profit. Running something like that with volunteers—oh my god. It's very hard to build motivation. After awhile, people who gave a crap moved on.

Danny Norwood: I was involved in helping start Epicenter. They had the record store going and Blacklist Mailorder was in the back.

A. C. Thompson: Epicenter was in a huge second-floor walk-up on Valencia Street and 16th Street. There was a back room where all the records were kept, because punks would just steal them. Then there was a bunch of couches, a pool table, bulletin boards for people to post their various things, and an area for bands to play. There was a zine library. For awhile there was a switchboard. If you came to town and you needed to get connected with some kind of service, whether you needed housing, a ride, or an STD test, we had this list of references for people.

Ruth Schwartz: Epicenter was a record shop, but Tim was trying to make it into a community center.

A. C. Thompson: Epicenter was never really about being a business. It was about having a place for people in that scene to hang out. There were so many smart, crazy people there all the time.

Floyd: After Blacklist Mailorder folded, Epicenter was never able to find a suitable tenant.

Kegger: They used to put on a lot of queer shows at Epicenter in the early '90s. Until it flooded. Assfort from Japan was playing. Everyone was getting rowdy and this young punk kid jumped up and grabbed on to the sprinkler system and it broke. Me and friends tried to save the library by throwing the fanzines up on top of the shelves.

Floyd: We couldn't operate as a show space after the flood. That really shot a lot of the enthusiasm. There was a small loyal core to the end, but not the manpower to keep it going.

Ruth Schwartz: Tim didn't want to make any money. He was a communist at heart. Money was the root of all evil. I'm okay with people making a living. I don't care if they make a living off of their art, I don't care if they make a living off of their DIY businesses. I think it's okay. And he didn't. He thought it corrupted it automatically.

Maximum RocknRoll paid for the house and the utilities, and he would defend and justify that. I thought it was more honest to just admit that *Maximum RocknRoll* paid Tim Yohannan. By giving him electricity and computers, and a bed to sleep in, and his car and his gasoline, and all these other things. And that it was dishonest to say nobody gets paid. If somebody gets paid, then everybody should get paid.

It's one of the punk rock tenets of that genre of people. We spawned this PC attitude that money is inherently bad. I have my detractors as well. I think people do bad things with money. But I don't believe that it is inherently bad.

He was a very talented capitalist, actually. But at a certain point it just becomes hypocritical. He was like, "It's okay, I'm giving it away." "But you're not giving all of it away." Sometimes he just had more money than he knew what to do with, and he would justify different ways of getting rid of it. I argued with him in a kindly natured way on that point for many, many years, until the end when it got nasty. Then we couldn't even talk to each other anymore.

23

Mommy, Can I Go Out and Kill Tonight?

Jason Lockwood: When I was a kid, you were basically forbidden to publicly enjoy the Misfits.

Kelly King: The Misfits came to town. There was big hype about how great they were. They were from New York. They had that foot-and-a-half-long piece of hair hanging down in the front.

Tom Flynn: It was 1982. It wasn't the first time they came. It was the first time they came here as the starring band.

Kelly King: At the Elite Club, which is now the Fillmore.

Tom Flynn: It was a big audience, maybe a thousand people. One of those nights where there were six or seven bands on every show. They started playing, and immediately started yelling at the audience. I remember Glenn Danzig said something like, "I can see why they call this the land of the homos!"

Greg Oropeza: "The city of buttfuckers!"

Kelly King: "S.F., you're a bunch of faggots!"

Tom Flynn: I had liked the Misfits. Most people at the show were into it as much as me. When he said that, I was like, "What a moron!"

Toni DMR: They were being really hostile, hocking loogies, kicking at people. They kicked Rachel in the head with their steel-toe boots.

Kelly King: They just got rained on with beer cans. Somebody hit Danzig in the eye with a can full of beer.

Tom Flynn: They had only played three or four songs.

Kelly King: The drummer jumped off the stage and attacked Tim Sutliff, of all people. He was pretty much the smallest kid there. Tim was just covering up his face and backing up and that guy Doyle took his big ol' guitar and just swung it down with both hands like an ax and broke it over Tim's head.

Jello Biafra: They left him in a pool of blood. The worst thing I'd ever seen at a show in my life by far.

Toni DMR: I saw Tim's head split open. His skin split and flapped down to his ears. Split his entire fucking head open. You could hear the collective gasp of everybody, "Oh my fucking god!" And then all hell broke loose.

Kelly King: I totally freaked out and attacked Doyle. I jumped onstage and landed on top of him, but he was a muscle guy and just pushed me off. Then Wes Robinson and all his security guys grabbed me and the band disappeared backstage. I was just completely hysterical. I had done coke and I was drinking heavily, smoking pot—so I was totally out of control. They were holding me against the wall, saying, "Okay, just settle down, just settle down." And finally I was like, "Okay, I'm cool." They let me go, so I ran back onstage and started kicking in the drum kit. They grabbed me again and Wes was complaining that he was going to have to pay for the broken drums.

There was a big pool of blood. I smeared my hand in it and wiped it on my leather jacket. I don't know why. I was just completely out of my head. I ran to the back of the club and Tim was there. They were holding towels on his head. This big security guy put his hand out to stop me and I grabbed his fingers and bent them over backwards. They finally had enough and shoved me outside onto the sidewalk, and it was raining. I just sat down against the wall and started crying. Somebody handed me a Lowenbrau Light. I chugged it and got into the back of Sam McBride's car. I held on to that empty bottle all the way back to Berkeley. I had never been so freaked out in my life.

Tom Flynn: They came back out onstage—just the singer and bass player and drummer. And they started trying to play again, but then people just started throwing bottles. Danzig looked over and said, "Well, fuck you guys," and left.

Toni DMR: I think they ended up locking themselves in a room somewhere.

Rachel DMR: We were hanging out in the back alley by the church, waiting for them to come out with their equipment. But they got wind there was a mob out there ready to kill 'em.

Kelly King: I think Tim's mom sued Wes, but she never tried to press charges. The Misfits got away with it. Wes never had to pay for anything and Tim almost got killed.

Greg Oropeza: This led to a ban of the Misfits, an informal agreement between bookers.

Jello Biafra: *MRR* went after him about it and put a rather nasty cartoon about them about the incident, changing the Misfits infamous hairdos into penises, drooping across their heads. Mr. Danzig is not known for a sense of humor.

Tom Flynn: KALX used to play the Misfits all the time. After that show I'm sure they had some sort of board meeting.

Aaron Cometbus: It wasn't just that the Misfits bashed in Tim's head. They had also busted into an exhibit at KALX, which at the time was located in UC Berkeley's Lawrence Hall of Science, and stole a bunch of skulls, which totally jeopardized KALX's existence. Then they spray-painted a bunch of "Fuck you, Berkeley faggots" stuff on the sidewalk outside of Universal Records. They added insult to injury.

Jason Lockwood: Timmy Sutliff wound up being my best friend. We would hang out between the tennis courts behind the junior high. That was one of those hangout spots for the East Bay punks. One day, Tim pulled a two-inch sliver of wood from the guitar out of his scalp. It was months after he'd gotten out of the hospital.

Greg Oropeza: We had a show at Club Culture in Santa Cruz with Samhain. I was one of the promoters, but had no idea it was Danzig's band. When he walked in, I had a fit. I was yelling, "No way, they're not playing!" pleading my case to my partners. Danzig came up to me and asked if he could talk to me down by the river for a few minutes. I thought maybe he wanted to brawl, but he just wanted to have a beer and explain his side of the story. We sat on the banks of the San Lorenzo River and he explained that the night at the Elite Club was the worst night of his life. He said he was horrified by his bandmate's actions, and would never play with him again. He said it was all an act that went too far and regretted it deeply.

Kelly King: I was bummed out for years that nobody did anything. Doyle could have killed him. He's lucky he didn't.

24

Beers, Steers and Queers: The Texas Invasion

Dave Chavez: Sick Pleasure was the first hardcore band in San Francisco.

I got a call from Mike Fox, who wanted to do a hardcore band "like they're doing down south." That's the way he put it. Nicki Sicki and a friend were out here from Texas. Mike had met them in front of the Mabuhay, on the sidewalk.

We were just mesmerized by Nicki, the way he looked. He was really thin and his eyebrows were shaved off and his hair was spiked. He had half a mohawk, it was just like a half head. He had a really crazy look in his eyes.

We asked him to go behind the mic and he just made this squawking sound. Like a toucan or something. "Waaaahhhh!" It was really loud and grating and we were like, "That's it." We didn't even care if he could play a note. He just had the look and the really weird voice.

Nicki Sicki: We got the Sick Pleasure name from a jacket I had. A picture of a syringe on the back and the name above it.

Dave Chavez: Nicki wrote about the life he was really living, so it had kind of a Chicken Little effect. Here's this little guy in this big world, living on the street. I think one of the lines was, "My only friend's my knife." There was a real street thing to it. "I Just Want My Parents to Burn" is about a kid from Texas who actually burned up his parents in his house. It's just something that happened in Nicki's neighborhood. I don't think the songs were as nihilistic as people took them to be.

Nicki Sicki: I'm not saying my lyrics are good or bad, but I do write

Photo by Tim Tonooka; courtesy of Ripper

Just an American Band: Verbal Abuse at Berkeley Square 1982

what I know, and live what I write. You don't write lyrics like "I've got herpes" to impress people.

Dave Chavez: When I was young, I really liked R. Crumb comics and that in-your-face, fuck-you attitude. Not really political. That's what I saw in Nicki. Sick Pleasure had that kind of obnoxious slant.

Nicki Sicki: When we were on tour once, I farted so bad Dave quit the band and got out of the van in Wisconsin with his bass and started walking home to Oakland.

I quit Sick Pleasure 'cause I was about 16 or 17, and my girlfriend had a kid. We shot speed every day and nobody worked. I was scared I'd kill the kid or something.

Dave Chavez: I turned 20 right around the time the band was breaking up. Mike just immediately started Code of Honor with Johnithin Christ, the singer from Society Dog. I started playing with Code of Honor at their fourth gig, but I didn't really get along with the singer too well. I didn't understand what he was trying to sing about. What it was, was Scientology. Mike was into Scientology. It was very strange. But a lot of people thought that Code of Honor was gonna be the next big thing—the guys from *Flipside* told me we were gonna be the biggest band in the country. I was just like, "Yeah, whatever."

After Nicki left Sick Pleasure he went back to Texas and started Verbal Abuse. It was like a continuation for him. Sick Pleasure had been a little too psychedelic and weird for Nicki. He wanted something more straightforward.

Nicki Sicki: No one was really playing fast in Texas. This was right before the Dischord thing started.

X-Con Ron: Texas hates us because MDC left, Verbal Abuse left, DRI left, the Dicks left.

Nicki Sicki: We came out to play in San Francisco and decided to stay. Every time I've been in the same city as Dave we end up together. I love that guy.

Bob Noxious: When the Texans started coming out here that was really, really good, man. It brought a lot of new blood into the scene. I liked them.

Greg Oropeza: Ribzy once played a basement party in San Jose with Verbal Abuse. The only light in the whole basement was a single bulb hanging over the drum set. Right in the middle of a blazing set, Verbal Abuse's drummer hit the bulb with his drum stick, plunging the basement into total darkness. They kept playing without skipping a beat. It was one of the raddest things I had ever seen.

Nicki Sicki: I've never done a band with anything more than the idea of having fun, and when it stops being fun I move on.

Dave Chavez: Verbal Abuse is Nicki Sicki. He wrote all those songs on bass. The Verbal Abuse that we did without Nicki Sicki doesn't really count. But he left. Again. Both times we had a good thing going, it was really building momentum, then *whoop*—singer disappears.

Nicki Sicki: They tried to give me 25 to life for fucking speed. I ended up with five.

Dave Chavez: Nicki is what he is: He's a true unique entity. That's why I still love playing with him.

Tammy Lundy: The best show I ever saw in my life was the Punk Prom at Armadillo World Headquarters in Austin. It was the Dicks' first live show and they blew everybody away. Gary dressed in a nurse's outfit and pulled liver out from under his dress. They had some friends dressed in skirts who came around with trays of cocktails and served them to the crowd.

Gary Floyd: Later on, I stopped doing all the drag stuff, and the liver and the shit in the panties. But the reputation was already there. People always say, "I saw you in Cleveland and you were dressed up like a nurse and had a watermelon in your ass." But I never dressed up on the road. I just nod. It's hell being a legend.

Dave Dictor: Gary attracted all kinds of people and he brought the freak out of these people. He was just so out there and liberating and ahead of his time.

X-Con Ron: Gary Floyd had a strong influence on Dave.

Gary Floyd: I always thought that being gay, maybe people thought I was prissy or whatever. But I wasn't very prissy, I was just this fucking loudmouth drunk.

Tammy Lundy: The Dicks just ruled. They wrote the ultimate anthem of all time, "Dicks Hate the Police." Back in the days when we all had homemade T-shirts, ours said, "You can kill us but we'll be back in a couple of days," a line from "Pigs Run Wild."

X-Con Ron: The Dicks are like our mentors. As Al says, our "sister band." Thank god they were there.

Gary Floyd: There were two Dicks, the Texas Dicks and the California Dicks. We came out here on the big Rock Against Reagan tour with MDC, and the rest of the band decided to stay in Texas. I wasn't going to do that, so the band broke up. I really wish I had done things differently. But I came back out here with our manager Debbie Gordon and we reformed the Dicks. The California Dicks did "No Fucking War" and "Hope You Get Drafted."

When we did our first reunion show, after like 20 years—me and Pat and Buxf—we played at the Eagle here in San Francisco. It was so unbelievable. We hadn't played since '86 and it was packed. We were totally shocked that everybody knew the words to the songs. One of the bartenders said, "In my whole life, I've never heard a crowd of people screaming, 'Shit on me!'" It was a really wonderful moment.

X-Con Ron: I lived about three blocks from Raul's in Austin. Dave had moved down from New York and had already been in a band called the Solar Pigs. But he had a different idea.

Dave Dictor: There must have been 30, 40, 50 bands in the scene. I hooked up with Ron, and our first songs were cover songs. Talking Heads, Sex Pistols, Ramones.

X-Con Ron: At first the band was called the Reejex. Then it became the Stains.

Tammy Lundy: I was the poster maker and the girl at the door with the cigar box. I looked about 12 years old and Dave was chasing me around Austin. I got into a bunch of shows free. I was also the biggest slut at the time and very, very proud of it.

Dave Dictor: In the summer of '79, John Wayne died. Immediately, I wrote "John Wayne Was a Nazi" with my friend Frank Mares. Frank would play bass with us on and off.

We tried to give the song to all the bigger punk bands in Austin. Ty Gavin from the Next said, "It's a good song but I just don't think it's me. You should play it." I'm thankful to him. Here was one of the big guys from the Austin scene, saying, "Go for it! You should have your own band." We worked on a single and had it out by early 1981.

> John Wayne killed a lot of gooks in the war
> We don't give a fuck about John anymore
> We all heard his tale of blood and gore
> Just another pawn for the capitalist whore
> He was a Nazi
> But not anymore
> He was a Nazi
> Life evens the score
>
> —"John Wayne Was a Nazi," MDC

Dave Dictor: I started writing people and sending them my single. We sent "John Wayne" to *Creep* magazine, but Mickey Creep was on holiday. So Jello Biafra opened his mail. 'Cause they were roommates and, of course, Biafra was a record collector.

He put it on and immediately called Tim Yohannan. Next thing you know, Yohannan called me up and said, "I've had you number one for eight weeks in a row on the *Maximum RocknRoll* Radio show. We love it! Biafra loves it!" Biafra? Of the Dead Kennedys? Wow. I was in Austin and I didn't know any of this.

Jello Biafra: I called Dave and said, "Look, you wanna play with other radical bands? Why don't you come out here and play with Dead Kennedys?" At first he didn't believe it was me.

X-Con Ron: We were number one on KPFA on the West Coast and ranked number 37 or some shit like that in Texas. So we were like, "Let's get the fuck out of here."

What really inspired us to hit the road was seeing Black Flag play Raul's in Austin, and watching Greg Ginn squeeze into a 16-inch crawlspace in the back of the van as they drove away. I mean, fuck.

Dave Dictor: We finally went out and played with the Dead Kennedys at the Mabuhay Gardens. And we played with Flipper, and we played with Black Flag at the Cuckoo's Nest.

X-Con Ron: We met the Fuck-Ups and the Fuckettes at the soup kitchen.

Dave Dictor: They took us back to their place and they said, "Stay an extra week. We're gonna do a show at the Sound of Music." We started out with three gigs and we ended up playing six. Getting in that van to come home, it was like, "Man, we gotta move out there. There is a whole world going on in California."

Tammy Lundy: The Dicks' bass player Buxf Parrot named them MDC. There was already a band called the Stains in L.A. So Buxf said with his usual laconic drawl, "Well, maybe you oughta call it Millions of Dead Cops."

We were a little worried that the new name would close doors for us, but it was the opposite. When I started booking for the band, after they moved to California, putting Millions of Dead Cops on the flyer was part of the draw.

Dave Dictor: Cops would come to shows with our albums and ask us to sign them. Or we'd be on the street after the show and they'd turn the sirens on and come over and go, "Take a picture of me and Dave and three street punks." In front of the Millions of Dead Cops marquee! Then they'd just get back in the car, turn off the light, and go away. You'd be like, "Did that fucking happen?"

When we arrived it was like the Toiling Midgets scene, the Avengers, the Dils. It was cool meeting them. We went to all these parties, but that first wave of the San Francisco scene—that '78, '79, '80 art-rock scene—was kind of dying.

The Kennedys came out of that early S.F. scene, but they drifted towards Tim Yo's world. It was much more college educated and politically oriented. They read *The Nation* and could talk about Ralph Nader and what Coca-Cola was doing to this country. They had all that knowledge, but not a lot of street cred. MDC had both. We knew what it was like to stand in a soup kitchen line with the Fuck-Ups and Sick Pleasure.

Tammy Lundy: They played every place they could. One night, they played the Sound of Music for eight dollars.

Dave Dictor: We were also at that point 23, 24, 25—or I was. A lot of the other people were 16, 17, 18. So people gave us respect. We weren't weird or confrontational. But we really felt we were changing the way people were thinking. I had political thoughts about how the world could be less fucked up, less multi-death corporate, less polluted, more Age of Aquarius. It seemed like more and more kids were getting involved with that.

Ian MacKaye: MDC stood for lots of different things—obviously, Millions of Dead Cops. The second most notable one was Multi-Death Corporations. I remember getting into a tremendous discussion, almost argument, about the narcotics trade with Dave and them. Because they were involved with so many kids in San Francisco who were basically runaways strung out on drugs. I used to think, to what capacity are drugs not a multi-death corporation? I mean, drugs are like the most ruthless profiteering corporation I can think of, practically.

Tammy Lundy: Everything that I did with the band happened in five years, but every day was just jam-packed. We went on the tour that never ended—it started as three months and ended up being 19—raiding grocery stores along the highway. Frank couldn't play bass worth a fuck, but he was an amazing shoplifter. We did the U.S. and Canada. Ron is called X-Con Ron for getting arrested in Toronto for half a joint. Which wasn't even his.

We all went to do Europe with Dead Kennedys on Jello's invitation, only to find out that the rest of the band didn't know. In England, Dead Kennedys said they would give us 50 pounds a gig, which wasn't much even back then. When they hit the mainland, they said they couldn't afford to pay us anymore.

My mother sent money. Dave's mother sent money. Ron pulled something out of his ass. And we went with them on our own dime. We were sleeping in people's basements and eating the cheapest food we could get, which was difficult because all of us were vegan. Then in Nuremberg, we caught sight of Dead Kennedys in this four-star hotel, eating in a really fancy restaurant.

They had been pleading poverty, but I think tension had been building because our styles were really different. We were really fast. MDC would get people so worked up that when Dead Kennedys first came out, it would take a few songs for the crowd to get into it again. Of course they did because it was the fucking Dead Kennedys and everyone was there to see them, but there was still some tension.

So we waited for them to come out of the restaurant and we confronted them. Jello was very uncomfortable because it was his band. He always wanted to ride with us, anyway (the saying in the van was, "There's always room for Jello"). Ray and Klaus were shouting all kinds of abuse. East Bay Ray said, "You guys are a fart in my living room." But we could always give as good as we got. We actually got thrown out of the hotel, which was fun.

Dave Dictor: We played for the Pope in 1987, on the roof of my house. He came right up to the Mission Dolores Chapel and we jumped on our instruments and played "This Blood's for You" and "Multi-Death Corporation." We all had Pope hats with eye patches.

The police grabbed us and said, "You wanna fly? You wanna learn to fly?" Then they brought us down to my apartment. Just "Millions of Dead Cops" flyers everywhere. You can imagine. The Secret Service did their whole thing. "You got guns?" I explained, "No, we're peace punks. I've been an angry Catholic since John F. Kennedy was shot." They turned us over to the San Francisco police, who were like, "Fuck those guys—we've been working with those fuckers all week."

We also went to Russia. We got hooked up with some squatters who had Polish punks coming through via the Saint Petersburg–Helsinki route. And we pulled it off. We played Minsk, we played Leningrad, we played Moscow, Saint Petersburg twice. It was incredible. It was six months after Yeltsin faced off soldiers surrounding the Russian White House with a tank. There was such a headiness. We had 1,000 people at every show, throwing jewelry and little trinkets at us. People wanted to meet me—"You are a big star of the American music." I'd say, "I'm a soup kitchen celebrity."

These train rides—it was like *Doctor Zhivago*, seeing those yellow fields of grass and wheat. When we played Minsk, the cars were old, the streetcars—it was still 1950s Khrushchev. It was very eye-opening. We were being fed fear—this build-your-bunker-in-your-backyard thing—while they lived the reality of breadlines.

I took off a few years from the band between '95 and 2000. I got hooked up with drugs, then I got away from drugs and got my teacher's degree. Now, for every month I'm on the road I need to take a month or two off. For my personal life.

Tammy Lundy: Ron grew up in Caracas, Venezuela. He lives there when he is not on tour with MDC. Mikey Donaldson toured with MDC until 2007. His liver just finally gave out.

X-Con Ron: Our best friend and the best damn bass player ever passed away. Punk rock will never be the same without him.

Dave Dictor: My son is 23 years old, he does not watch TV at all. When he was 13, 14, I'd say, "Let's watch MTV together." I was trying to fill up time because my son and I didn't live together for the first 12 years of his life. One day he said, "I hate MTV. MTV is trying to get me to be something I'm not. I'm never gonna be as skinny and pretty as 95 percent of the people they show on MTV." And it really hit me. That's our culture: Drive a Volvo. Look like people on MTV where everyone's pretty and packaged and no one is struggling to pay their gas bill. It took him saying how phony and how vile MTV was, to make it hit home.

That's what punk rock's about. Not trying to fit into that disco world or arena rock world, where everything's about money. Where you buy people, you buy love, you buy Acapulco, you buy everything, and you do it by getting over on the world. I know we're all monkeys chasing coconuts, but one person's freedom and liberty is another person's oppression.

Kurt Brecht: A lot of people didn't even acknowledge us as a San Francisco band. We were a really hardworking band and we were on the road a lot. But, for somebody growing up in the suburbs, it was so cool to be in the city. I just fell in love with San Francisco.

Bob Noxious: When DRI came out, we thought, "These guys are so fucking weird!" They had mange haircuts. Totally weird.

X-Con Ron: We called it the Chemo Cut. They were the guys who started that.

Dave Dictor: DRI were from Houston.

Kurt Brecht: When we had our first gig we didn't even have a name yet. We were practicing in my parents' house in my bedroom. Every day, my dad would come home from work and pound on the door, yelling at us to turn it down: "You dirty, rotten imbeciles!" It kinda stuck. He wanted royalties later.

DRI got to be one of those bands that opened for every big act that came through Houston, like Dead Kennedys, Minor Threat, MDC, the Dicks, Butthole Surfers.

Dave Dictor: We said, "You gotta come out to San Francisco." You could play to 150 punks in Austin and Houston for the rest of your lives, but there were 500 kids out here on any random weekend.

Kurt Brecht: Then one day Tim Yohannan called my parents' house out of the blue. Nicki Sicki, the singer of Verbal Abuse, had given Yohannan our demo tape and he really liked it, and he said, "I want you guys to come out to San Francisco. I think you'd do really good here." They were setting up an all-Texas band gig at the Tool & Die. It was MDC, the Dicks, us and Verbal Abuse. I traded my P.A. for a van and sold pretty much everything we had just to get gas money to get there.

Bob Noxious: Their songs were so fast. It was really different and everyone was just blown away.

Tammy Lundy: I remember Tim Yohannan saying, "What do they feed you out in Texas?" For awhile, MDC billed itself as the fastest band in the world, but it was a contest between DRI and MDC. Spike from DRI used to stand out in front of the On Broadway with their first record and say, "22 songs in 17 minutes!" That's how he sold them.

Kurt Brecht: In San Francisco, all the bands were do-it-yourself bands. I learned a lot. It always blew me away that everybody was so nice. Bob Noxious and the Fuckettes taught us about faking the little bus transfers. They had every color of transfer, with every number and letter, on their wall. We got stolen phone cards from Verbal Abuse. MDC took us on tour with them.

San Francisco was a good place to live in your vehicle between tours. It wasn't hot, so you didn't wake up sweltering, like in Texas. The main thing you had to worry about was a bathroom and what time the soup kitchen served.

For awhile I was living in a tree in Golden Gate Park. It was crazy to sleep on the ground, 'cause anybody could just come up and stab you or whatever. Up in the tree, I was fairly safe. The branches grew together like a natural bed so you could lie down. It was like my house. They would drop me off there after the show. I even had a cat. I guess somebody had just dumped him out there. So I brought him up in the tree and he slept with me and I fed him.

X-Con Ron: Then DRI did their crossover thing and fuckin' hit the big-time.

Kurt Brecht: MDC wanted to put our 7-inch out on a 12-inch. So we did that. Then Metalblade came around, so we were on the same label as Corrosion of Conformity and Slayer and a lot of those metal bands.

Mike Avilez: In the mid-'80s I was a metalhead. I saw DRI open up for Slayer in '85 and that was the ticket. The crossover scene from '85 to '87 is basically what got me into punk rock.

Kurt Brecht: People said that we single-handedly ruined punk rock forever. By polluting it with metal.

Dave Dictor: It was here in the Bay Area that it crossed over.

Kurt Brecht: Before that, the punks had their shows and the metal-heads had theirs. In San Francisco, the Stone was where all the metalheads went, and the On Broadway or the Mab was where we went.

Kelly King: Broadway was the border. It was completely separate. You were metal or you were punk.

Toni DMR: You weren't even allowed to listen to AC/DC.

Tammy Lundy: DRI really did something different. They didn't care if people called them traitors. It's what they wanted to do and they did it well, so good for them.

Kurt Brecht: The metalheads started coming to the punk shows and it was violent. Especially with the Nazi skinheads who, for some

Courtesy of DRI; artwork by Kevin Bakos

DRI EP 1984

reason, really liked our music. They'd beat up anybody, but they'd really go after the metalheads.

Aaron Cometbus: DRI had this song "Violent Pacification," and there was this huge skinhead dude who'd always be there to sing the "Violent" part, then Kurt would sing "Pacification." It was comical, but the guy was also pretty scary looking.

Kurt Brecht: It wasn't just San Francisco. It was all over the country. It got real bad. Certain tours, we'd have to stop almost every night to break up fights. But after a few years, it became accepted that you were gonna see people with long hair at shows. And vice versa.

James Angus Black: The second tour I roadied for DRI was in a *bus*. It was high class.

Kurt Brecht: We finally got a manager after playing at the Olympic Auditorium with Suicidal Tendencies. Pretty soon he had us traveling around in tour buses. We just couldn't believe it. After living in that crappy van for so long, we had a real tour bus and we were playing packed shows every night.

Some punks approached us and said, "You won't be able to come back to us if it doesn't work out." That's pretty heavy. Like, how many years do you have to suffer and live in your van and eat at soup kitchens before you're allowed to step foot in a tour bus? Back in the old days, we were starving, living off government cheese. I see pictures of myself back then. I was like a concentration camp victim or something.

James Angus Black: That one tour was the zenith. And they were back in the vans again.

Greg Valencia: DRI was the first punk band that I heard that was really punk. There was a big black metal scene in Santa Fe. We were all metalheads. DRI opened my eyes to a lot of things.

Kurt Brecht: Until Spike was diagnosed with colon cancer we never really slowed down. It had been one tour after another for 25 years. And we never had to do any cover songs.

25

Welcome to Paradise

Bob Noxious: The beer vats were down on 15th and Florida.

Dave Dictor: It was a brewery that had been abandoned—this six-story structure with these tremendous beer vats. The top ones were open. They'd mix the beer there, and then they'd drop it down through a piping system to the other vats, where they would store it as it would brew or ferment, or whatever beer does.

X-Con Ron: It really was too good to be true. As soon as we got here we found out about the beer vats, went over and got jackhammering.

Paul Casteel: You paid to have someone come blow a hole in a vat for you. The people who owned the building would charge you $150 to install this door—this big hatch—on a beer storage tank and that was used as your home or rehearsal space. These things stunk like vinegar. The open ones were like 30 feet deep.

Tammy Lundy: I paid $25 a month for my air shaft. It was between floors so you had to climb a ladder half a story. It was exactly as wide as my arm span and 40 or 50 feet long.

Gary Floyd: MDC ruled the Vats because they were the ones that got it all started. Our bass player Sebastian Fuchs lived at the Vats. So we hung out and practiced there.

Dean Washington: You had to *really* know somebody to get into the Vats. It was like bein' invited to the White House. I don't think there was anybody that played San Francisco at that time that didn't squat and hang out there.

Dave Dictor: We weren't the first people—there were five to seven stragglers already—but we were the first band.

Kurt Brecht: MDC and the Dicks were there. I think Verbal Abuse was. And then we started living at the Vats in our van. Just camping out there, eating canned foods.

Jason Lockwood: It was such a weird place. You never felt quite safe there. Especially when you stayed at night. There were a lot of junkies.

Sammytown: I stayed at the Vats all the time, especially before I had a car. After shows, everyone would go to the Vats or to the Fun Terminal, the Mutants place. We were all on speed—we were all fucking kids so it's not like we slept anyways.

Ian MacKaye: Minor Threat stayed there with MDC in 1983. And there were these 14-year-old kids, most of 'em were girls. I remember five or six of them. They were basically four days up, four days down. If they weren't begging for change to buy speed, they were speeding out of their brains, or they were just fuckin' flat out for four days. They had one-quarter the waking days of the rest of us. I remember thinking, clearly, this is a bad situation. I think they were being taken advantage of. I just couldn't reconcile—how can you all profess to be so concerned about the state of the world, when, right here, there is a problem?

Kriss X: This was in the midst of a big speed binge for a lot of us. I remember being in Spike and Dagger's vat—Terry and a couple others were there as well. We all got high and then the cops came into the vats with the dogs. They came directly to the door of Spike's vat and were pounding. It was locked and we were all quiet as church mice, ready to shit our pants, not knowing if they would kick in the door or just go away. We waited for what seemed like hours.

Bill Halen: One guy had a ship steering wheel as a handle, for his round doorway. It was beautiful inside. He broke up a bunch of furniture and pulled it into the vat. Then he put it all back together inside. Some of the vats were very cool.

Marc Dagger: We lived up in the yeast culture room. It was actually not a vat—it had a window in it and we had running water. Me and Harley from the Cro-Mags ran security at the Vats. If you didn't pay your rent we'd do an eviction party on you—throw all your stuff out. And if you were there, you'd probably get whipped. The owners of the place let us live up there for free as long as we made sure everybody got their rent paid and no crap happened.

Toni DMR: The last time I saw Harley, Spike and Marc had a going-away party for him. He was tripping on acid and fell in a vat and got stuck. At his own going-away party.

Paul Casteel: I remember one night Bob Noxious and Marc Dagger fell in a vat somehow and they were fistfighting one another. It went on for like two hours because no one would throw them a rope or help them get out of the thing. Every time they came out of their stupor, they would just start pounding one another. The crowd up above treated it like a chicken fight, cheering them on. It was the entertainment for the night. It was like a gladiator scene. These guys were best friends and they were beating the crap out of each other.

Toni DMR: I'd been up for a week and Spike put me to bed. I remember opening one eye and seeing Victor Harris and Nicki Sicki making pancakes over some butane camping stove. It was so weird.

B. A. Lush: Laundry was not really available at the Vats but we found boxes of sausage wraps. Cases and cases of them. And they were perfect for socks. Vats socks. Clean socks were a godsend.

Jason Lockwood: There used to be a barber chair inside the ground floor of the Vats. One night, I had consumed some freakish amount of acid. I came to, feeling really disoriented and unnerved. Sitting right there, it was like you walked into an insane asylum they were never gonna let people out of. It smelled like old, stale beer. I still get angry when people spill beer on me because of that smell.

B. A. Lush: We were lucky. We were on the fourth floor, with the bathroom. Other people had to pee in bottles.

Marc Dagger: The Vats were right across the street from the Hostess factory.

Jason Lockwood: The smell of the bread factories. We used to run over in the middle of the night, bolt people over the fence, and one person would throw bread over. They were all there on racks getting ready to be shipped.

Marc Dagger: We were all tweakers—so the sugar high, it was great.

Nicki Sicki: The soup kitchen was down the street, so you could basically live for free.

Kriss X: There was a dominatrix that lived up on the top floor who used to throw these amazing parties.

Bill Halen: Upstairs, there were a bunch of bikers making a mess. Some very scary shit. You didn't venture up there unless you knew somebody.

Tammy Lundy: We thought the Vats were owned by this wannabe biker guy, but it was actually owned by his mom. Every Wednesday night, his biker friends would come by and throw somebody out. That was their Wednesday night activity. They were called the Uncles.

Marc Dagger: I had this little rat named Darby, 'cause I loved the Germs. Until I learned that Darby Crash was a frickin' cock smoker. Anyway, he used to live in the couch where Harley slept. When we were moving out, we picked up the couch and there were tunnels chewed through the frickin' foam. We found bags of speed in there, money, everything. This rat was just like the person he was named after. He was a little pack rat speed freak.

Jason Lockwood: I remember bleach-spotting jeans in the hallway 'cause it was all tile. If you leave bleach on your skin long enough, you will learn it gives you a mild chemical burn. Say, if you put on damp jeans that you've just bleach-stained. By the end of the day you'll have red patches on your legs where the bleach was.

Tammy Lundy: January 2, 1984, was the day the Vats burned down. I have a Vats Rat tattoo to commemorate the day.

Marc Dagger: There was one room downstairs where everybody threw their garbage, like old mattresses and old furniture and crap. Some dude wandered in there and passed out. I guess the guy had a cigarette.

Kurt Brecht: I was sleeping in the vat right next to the one that caught on fire. I turned the light on and it was all full of smoke. I felt the door, which was a round, hobbit-hole kind of door, made out of wood, and it was real hot. We made the decision to just open up the door and make a run for it.

Bob Noxious: The walls in the vats were coated in six-inch-thick rubber.

Mark Dagger: That's probably what killed the guy, just breathing in that smoke. It was nasty.

Tammy Lundy: Robbie Cryptcrasher, who used to play with Cause for Alarm, saved my life. He used to wear a gas mask on his belt. It was just punk rock kitsch, but when everyone started choking, he put it on and it worked. Robbie was dragging out his girlfriend Michelle, who was already unconscious. He had to drop her down half a story. I slid down the ladder and landed on Michelle. Then he hooked one arm under each of us and pulled both of us out and kicked the doors open to great cheers.

Marc Dagger: We threw shows in the parking lot every week while they were destroying the Vats. They had this huge crane up there with a big ball on it. Probably took them two months longer than they planned to tear that building down, because we kept fucking up that crane.

Kriss X: I heard that there were bodies hidden in the walls when they tore the place down. I wouldn't doubt it a bit.

Jason Lockwood: I had some of my favorite experiences in the Vats. There was a lack of structure. Spaces like that don't exist in the Bay Area anymore. The land is too expensive. We're too packed in. There's no no-man's-land.

26

Island of Misfit Toys

Dave Dictor: When the Mab and On Broadway got too hot, and [Mayor] Feinstein closed down Broadway after the Democratic Convention and all those riots—we had to go into the warehouse districts. The Farm was the perfect place at the perfect time.

Andy Pollack: The Farm started around 1974 by Jack Wickert and Bonnie Sherk as a big multi-dimensional art project. Back then, it was abandoned buildings. The park next to it was the ruins of an old dairy. It was envisioned as a working farm in the city. We had goats, chickens, ducks and rabbits, and gardens and compost piles. We did tours for kids during the day. There were cows. It was a beautiful vision, actually.

The Mime Troupe did benefits there. We had Make-A-Circus rehearsing there and all these little art groups that put on plays. We did reggae and blues shows, but the punk shows were the most consistently successful.

We weren't really a club, we were a community center. It was all-ages, we served food. We didn't have a liquor license, but I'd let people do insane things, like after-hours parties where they sold alcohol to minors. I wasn't running this thing like a business. I was running it like a spaced-out hippie. So it wasn't about money. It was about staying open so the kids could see the animals.

Carol DMR: It was in a pretty shitty part of San Francisco.

Steve DePace: But you didn't have to worry about cops kicking you off the sidewalk like on Broadway. And it was a big space. They had a big stage, big room, great P.A. You could fit a lot of people in there.

Andy Pollack: Our legal capacity was 299 but we would fit close to 1,200 in there.

Steve DePace: Everybody played there—DOA, Flipper . . .

Andy Pollack: . . . 7 Seconds, Circle Jerks, Agent Orange, Black Flag, Dead Kennedys, Bad Brains, Verbal Abuse, MDC, RKL, DRI, Polkacide . . .

Nosmo King: Our drummer got community service for playing those shows.

Adrienne Droogas: I don't think that the Farm carded. I don't think the Farm cared about anything.

Day at the Farm flyer

Kate Knox: They always had huge all-day shows at the Farm, with 10 to 13 bands.

Andy Pollack: "Day at the Farm" was 18 bands in one day.

Kate Knox: And it would get so hot, it would actually rain inside. Because, basically, it was just a big metal building. You were like, ewww, that's everybody's sweat raining on me.

Zeke Jak: It was cold sweat and dirt and manure dripping down on you. When you got home, you were covered in dirt. You would blow your nose for the next three days and your boogers were black. It was so gnarly.

Aaron Cometbus: I was looking for the bathroom downstairs once, and opened a door to a room full of goats.

Andy Pollack: We actually dehorned the goats because they would spear people. We had a goose that would attack people, and a killer black rooster called Darth Vader. He finally drew blood from some baby and we had to eat him. There was a certain amount of peril. We also had rats. People would go rat killing. They would take shovels and kill rats and throw them up onto the freeway. A pretty punk rock situation.

The very first show I did as director of the Farm was in 1983, a birthday party for a local guy from the Mission. I was very naive. The guy said, "Don't worry, I'll do security at the show." And two people were shot and killed in front of me.

B. A. Lush: A lot of the minority groups that hung out in the park thought the punks were gang members, so they would take our presence as a challenge on their turf.

Audra Angeli-Slawson: We left the Farm once and the car was surrounded by Mexican gang members. It was weird, they let us get in the car and then they came after us. Their pit bulls locked jaws on the tires and they punched through the back windows and were pulling me and Mari Cunningham over the broken glass, like, "We're gonna fuckin' rape and kill you!" They beat the shit out of the dude we were with. It was nuts. We fought for our lives and drove off with the car doors swinging open. Fucking crazy shit!

Dean Washington: Occasionally, you'd see someone stickin' a needle in a vein behind a bush, or you'd see people pissin' in bottles, leaving them where any thirsty person might find it. Never pick up a half-full beer off the ground and drink it.

Andy Pollack: I had this anything-goes attitude. Like, we're here for the community, do what you want, whatever happens is meant to be. Looking back at it now, maybe it was a lack of ego formation or something.

Oran Canfield: I could never figure Andy out. He wore cardigans and argyle socks and was a lawyer. It was very weird. There he was running this thing, surrounded by weird punks and hippies and all these people that didn't fit in anywhere else.

Andy Pollack: I started doing more shows 'cause we needed to make money. Paul Rat was the main booker and he really knew what would draw.

Dave Chavez: Paul Rat was a kind soul. He was a guy that was into the scene, wanted to be part of it even though he couldn't play an instrument. He was older and he had a little bit of money stashed away. He started up CD Records, which did all the *Rat Music for Rat People* comps, some of the better comps of that time. He also was the guy that booked the On Broadway and did the door. So he was a very visible character.

Andy Pollack: We would just pack 'em in. My theory was, you pack 'em in one side and they come out the other side if it's too crowded. There were only two toilets. For a thousand people. The guys would pee in the animal yard but, in the downstairs bathroom, people would shoot drugs. Did I know that? No. Did I pay any attention? I didn't even know people on my staff were shooting drugs.

One time Paul Rat overbooked a show. The Circle Jerks were headlining and we could *not* fit any more people in. There were hundreds of punks on the street and in the park. The riot police lined Potrero Avenue.

Kate Knox: The Farm used to be like L.A. It would sometimes have three pits. It was just insane.

Chicken John: The Farm was more violent than anything I'd ever seen. No one was there to have fun. It was a terrible place to enjoy music. The sound system was awful. You had to cross that big field. The first thing I thought was, "There are so many people here, there's so much money here. They could hire a security person or two." I found out that there were ten.

Andrew Flurry: We didn't always have money to get in. I went with Silke once and she had a bunch of cheap metal bracelets around her wrist that she used to barter with the doorman. I lost her in the crowd almost immediately. It was intense. I loved it but I was a little fucking kid and it was intimidating. I think the band said, "We are the Mentors. You are going to die." The next time I saw Silke she was sitting on the stage behind the band.

Andy Pollack: The only time we ever had real violence was with the local kids from the Mission. We had a rap show and people sued us because they got stabbed in the park. In the punk shows, people got their heads split open, but it wasn't from violence. It was from jumping off the stage and hitting the floor.

Silke Tudor: Just getting there was an adventure. The approach. Who was in the park? Was it going to be okay? Or was it going to be a fucking hassle? It was like an amusement park ride, but it was real life. And we were the freaks. We were part of it. Part of the excitement, the oddity, the tension, the violence, the sex, the complete abandon. Once you were inside, it was like being swept up in a vortex. All that noise, sweat and smoke. Arms and legs flailing, music blaring, the floor shuddering. You just let yourself go and hoped for the best. Surfed the chaos. I don't remember much about the shows themselves, just the heart-pounding adrenaline.

Andy Pollack: By 1987 there were 20 people scattered around. I started putting people all over the place, filling up all the crannies. People were sleeping in the day care center at night, plus we had developed live-work spaces in the back which were kind of legal.

Oran Canfield was part of Make-A-Circus when he moved into the Farm. He was this incredibly talented young juggler, just very personable and beautiful. His dad is that famous author of *Chicken Soup for the Soul*—just the father from hell. I met his mom and she said, "Well, he's in the circus and we don't want him to travel back and forth from the East Bay." It was ridiculous, really. He lived in building C. He had a bed back there somewhere.

Oran Canfield: I was nine. I was sharing a room with a night nurse, just a normal person who lived there. There was the main building with the stage and the preschool and the kitchen. This guy Bruce lived in a fucking animal cage downstairs—he was always practicing drums. There were weird, dark passageways that led to building C, where I lived, which was a hangar. The other hangar was Mark Pauline's SRL, Survival Research Laboratories.

Dale Flattum: There's always been a strange noise scene here, but one of the things that really influenced us was Survival Research. They were like, "Aww, you play in a band? That's neat. We build robotic machines and set the freeway on fire."

Oran Canfield: These crazy people with mohawks and pink hair, wearing clothes they made, building robots that were destroying each other and shooting fire. It was nuts.

Zeke Jak: You could sneak into the Farm by scurrying across SRL's roof and climbing in through an open window. I didn't make it that far. I got up on the roof and this metal dude saw me and followed me up. I was trying to be as quiet as possible, but he started stomping across Mark Pauline's roof, being totally obnoxious. I heard Mark and Matt Heckert yelling, "Hey! Hey! Who the hell is up there?" I ducked behind a big metal vent just as they climbed up. They were yelling, "Get the fuck off our roof! Now!" The longhair returned with, "Fuck you!" I couldn't see it but I heard them hit the guy with a fucking flamethrower. I'm not kidding. I could smell hair and fuel and the dude was fucking screaming as he jumped off the roof. They came out into the park and hosed him with a semi-auto BB gun.

Oran Canfield: The second year I was in the circus, I decided to sleep in the preschool right underneath the performance space. I couldn't sleep, so I went upstairs and the place was just jam-packed with every weird punk in San Francisco. I didn't know what the hell was going on but I loved it. I loved the energy, I liked being away from my mom. There weren't any fucking rules, no structure. I didn't have any relationships with other kids, but I was kind of a responsible, little-adult kind of kid. It was a fantasyland.

Andy Pollack: I wasn't the only one who cleaned the bathrooms, but I tell my friends nothing will ever upset me after that. We'd be cleaning 'til three or four in the morning and then there'd be an elementary school coming in at nine a.m.

Julie Generic: A lot of fuckin' mopping. There were perks though, for sure. We all had carte blanche at the On Broadway and the Mab. All the clubs swapped out guest lists. Even if those clubs were past their heyday, it was still a lot of fun. We also used to get comp tickets for the York Theater. They would play classic punk movies, and we'd smuggle in beers. Like they didn't know.

Andy Pollack: The Farm was a legal place of entertainment for only three years. We probably did 300 or 400 shows. I stopped being the director at the beginning of '87.

Dave Dictor: I'm sad that the Farm only lasted as long as it did. We had some great shows and great times there. I remember just feeling awful when it went down.

Andy Pollack: I knew that it had to be the coolest place in the whole world, but I didn't go to other clubs, so how would I know?

27

Crossover

Wes Robinson has been putting on punk gigs in the Bay Area for 4 years now. He started with a little hole-in-the-wall in Berkeley called Aitos, doing great intimate shows with the likes of the Dils, Avengers, DI's, Controllers, etc. For awhile he was a mainstay in the East Bay chapter of Rock Against Racism, perhaps the only one who did not lose his sense of humor during all the internal squabbles. He later moved on to medium-sized shows at Ruthie's Inn and the Elite Club, but for some reason, as of late, has been hell-bent on do-or-die (usually die) extravaganzas like the Eastern Front, Summer Slam, and Discharge at the Oakland Auditorium.

—*"Wes Robinson—For a Good Time, Call (415) 841-2678,"*
Cliff Carpenter, Maximum RocknRoll 3, 1982

John Marr: Wes Robinson had the reverse Midas touch. In 1982 he had this bright idea to book this English band Discharge at the Oakland Auditorium. They weren't the Sex Pistols. The Oakland Auditorium is like a 5,000-seat place. It was up on the marquee: "Thursday! Discharge!" You walked into this enormous room and waaaay at the other end was the stage with this tiny cluster of people. That was Wes Robinson.

Tim Tonooka: But the first two Eastern Front shows were fabulous.

Kate Knox: Wes Robinson started these. They were down in the Aquatic Park. It was just dirt fields back then. Now it's a Frisbee golf course. They were a reaction to Bill Graham's gigantic "Day on the Green." We used to call 'em "Day on the Dirt."

Jesse Michaels: The first Eastern Front was DOA, the Lewd, Flipper,

Photo by Murray Bowles

Dust Bowl: Eastern Front at Aquatic Park

7 Seconds, the Fix, TSOL, Sick Pleasure and a couple other bands. That was one of the first shows I saw.

Wes Robinson: Immediately after the first Eastern Front show I retired from music. Then I started getting involved again, and suddenly there was another one. Both shows lost money—but I only lost half as much money on the second show, 'cause everyone snuck in the first time. It was a big party, an expensive party.

Kate Knox: The next Eastern Front was with Black Flag, Code of Honor, the Meat Puppets, the Dicks, Los Olvidados, Suicidal Tendencies and St. Vitus Dance. I think the third or fourth Eastern Front was sponsored by Miller or Budweiser. They had these trucks of beer. Somebody broke into the beer truck and wheeled away all the kegs on skateboards.

Dean Washington: Twelve hours of music, outside, and trucks of beer show up just fit for stealin'. What could be better?

Kate Knox: I didn't have any money to get in and so I traded Wes Robinson a couple hits of acid and he put 'em in his wallet. Two or three weeks later, I saw him at Ruthie's and he was like, "Oh, fuck you, Kate. I got arrested and I forgot that I had the acid on me until I started getting booked. So I pulled it out of my wallet and I swallowed it, and then they put me in jail for the weekend." So he sat there and tripped in jail all weekend long, going, "Fuuuuck."

Rachel DMR: Ruthie's started around '83. That became the center of the East Bay punk scene. It was originally a blues club. I never understood how Wes Robinson convinced the owners that they could make any money. Most of us were underage. We didn't have money to buy beer. We'd go steal it and go drink it in the parking lot across the street.

Dave Dictor: East Bay was a little bit more like L.A. in that the kids actually grew up within ten miles. They knew each other in high school. In San Francisco, we were like immigrants. We were ready to move away from our hometowns and get far away from mother's milk. It was a lot easier to keep that East Bay scene together because those people grew up together, they worked together, looked after each other. It was the nature of their tribe. That's one of the cool things about the Ruthie's scene.

Wes Robinson: My first effort was a dynamic headliner from Washington D.C. called the Bad Brains. I had brought them to the West Coast to do a concert at the Elite Club and they were still in the area.

Rachel DMR: People would drop through the roof instead of paying at the door.

Dean Washington: I can remember a Suicidal Tendencies show. The place was just packed. There was no way to get in through the front door, but a few of my buddies remembered that skylight. My buddy broke his ankle. The cops got called.

I think that was one of my favorite shows at Ruthie's, not only because I dogged my way up to the extra mic, but because the pits were really violent. You could kick the shit outta anyone and get away with it. Not that you were there to hurt anyone, but it felt so good after the show. Those really violent pits were probably the closest thing to having really, really good sex.

Wes Robinson: Ruthie's was another example of a unique social change that had taken place in many American metropolises, post–Civil Rights movement. Black communities and ghettos were delighted, captive support for nightclubs such as Ruthie's Inn and the Elite Club.

Sham Saenz: The first thing that always hit me was the smell of clove cigarettes. In '83, '84, you'd go to the On Broadway, the Mab, Ruthie's Inn, and it always smelled like clove cigarettes.

Adrienne Droogas: When I was 16 years old a friend of mine asked if I wanted to go to this punk show. I was like, "What's that?" It was at Ruthie's Inn. When we got out of the truck, she goes, "Oh my god, I've locked my keys in the car." There were people with mohawks and studded jackets all around us, just completely punked out. I was wearing white moccasin shoes and some Lee jeans or something. I grew up in Pleasanton. I didn't know what was going on.

We asked, "Who knows how to break into a car?" and every single punk said, "I do." Within half an hour, we had 20 people surrounding the truck, five trying to break in, one of my friends was makin' out with somebody in a bush. There was a beer bong, people were smoking pot. It was perfect, you know?

Paul Casteel: You had to watch your p's and q's at places like Ruthie's. It wasn't like San Francisco, where you could get away with wearing a clown suit.

Wes Robinson: The image switched from multi-colored hair and art school, thrift shop montages to T-shirts, jeans, and low-cut Chuck Taylors. The only hair worn by these freshmen carriers of the torch was a mohawk, occasionally seen amongst the shaved head. These kids brought new energy and vitality, and redefined the movement.

Cinder Bischoff: The bathroom was just insane. Live sex acts. People shooting up. You name it.

Kelly King: Black Flag came to Ruthie's and Henry Rollins was singing. Everybody hated Henry because he was the new guy. I had a bad attitude and I was going up front and trying to spit on Henry. He just kept opening up his mouth and pointing in so I could make the shot. I had to respect him after that.

Noah Landis: I saw some guy get his faced kicked in with a steel-toe boot outside Ruthie's. It made a popping sound that I heard across the street. The kind of violence that was happening back then was scary and real. It will never be as exciting and creative, and innovative and original, as it was back then either. But it'll also never be as dangerous.

Sammytown: For awhile, Fang was the house band at Ruthie's. We would play every week.

Jeff Ott: I went one weekend and saw Teenage Warning with the Faction, Fang and Social Distortion. Mike Ness of Social Distortion was so high on heroin, he kept falling down. Again and again. It was totally sad.

Jason Lockwood: Shammy lived a block away.

Sham Saenz: I remember particularly one night Wes Robinson was like, "Look, man, if you want to hang out it's totally okay with me." I had to be like nine or ten years old. But I knew his son from school. He said, "Go across the street, clean up the parking lot and you can come in." So that's what I did.

Jason Lockwood: The really young kids would hang out at Shammy's house and drink, then go to the show.

Aaron Cometbus: They got black light ink to keep people from faking the hand stamp and sneaking in. So we went out and bought black light ink. Actually, that made it even easier because as long as it glowed, they wouldn't look very close.

Leslie Fuckette: Wes loved the Fuckettes. We would go over to Ruthie's on Monday or Tuesday night and he'd have plates of spaghetti waiting for us with garlic bread. He really loved the punk rock kids like they were his own kids. He hated all the hassles, but he really never gave up. He was a really, really good man.

Wes Robinson: At the same time, I was dealing with these longhair metalheads. The lead singer of a local heavy metal band called Exodus came in to pursue bookings at Ruthie's. They were no longer welcome at the Keystone because their fans were too rowdy.

Kate Knox: Ruthie's Inn was *the* venue that started crossover. That was the only place in the United States, as far as I know, where metal bands and punk bands actually played together rather than fighting each other. Wes was like, "Fuck it, let's see what kind of money I can make off of this."

Dean Washington: Slayer didn't have a place in L.A. to call their own. No one would book them in L.A. But Wes Robinson would put Slayer at Ruthie's Inn. What Wes did was allow us to say, "Fuckin' right, I love metal!" Because when there wasn't a punk show goin' on, you'd see those same punks at a Slayer or a Metallica show. It was violent, there was a pit, we were gonna listen to it all. Heavy hard, and fast.

Ray Farrell: Wes Robinson was an interesting guy. I think he was in his 40s when he was booking those gigs. He had come from a jazz and blues background. He was into putting different bills together. He wanted the jazz experience, he wanted the black experience, he was interested in hip hop to a degree. If Wes Robinson could put Ornette Coleman and Crass on the same bill, he would do it. To him, all those audiences could be combined and he was taking a lot of risks. He genuinely seemed to like it for what it was giving to the people.

Wes Robinson: Exodus was the number one band behind Metallica. Ruthie's was suddenly a Mecca for this music, and every weekend the place was packed to the rafters with headbangers. Metallica moved to El Cerrito and were regulars at the club. Slayer and Exodus quickly became house bands. There was Violence, Forbidden and Heathen. Stone Vengeance was an all-black band. I was sure they were the only all-black thrash band in the world. They were true rockers from the Hunters Point ghetto in San Francisco.

Dean Washington: I didn't always like Wes over the years but he turned out to be a really good friend. There weren't a whole lot of blacks that were involved in the scene. We had Darren, who came over from England who drummed with the Dead Kennedys for a period of time, Eugene from Whipping Boy, and of course, Orlando. There was basically a handful of us.

Kurt Brecht: Yeah, Wes Robinson was kind of a shady character. He always owed us money so he let us in for free.

Kate Knox: He was known for ripping bands off.

Hef: When you walked in the front door, there was a ticket window on the left side. Wes was usually there selling tickets. It got to the point where my friends and I would just go there and stand at the window and stare at him until he'd say, "Okay, okay, you're robbing me," and let us in.

Rachel DMR: Wes had his own demons to deal with. I'm sure there was many a time when he didn't pay out the money he should have, but I think most people in the scene were guilty of similar things at one point or other.

Wes Robinson: I was a hopeless methamphetamine junkie. What had been a weekend thing became a daily routine. By the time I got to sleep and recovered two or three days, I was ready to start the madness all over again.

Crack cocaine brought me to such a desperate low that one night I got on my knees and begged god to help lift me from the despair of depravity. God sent my youngest son. He came to my apartment and, looking deeply into my eyes, asked me to quit the drugs. I learned to stay away from bars and parties where heavy drinking took place.

A young hip hop promoter seized the opportunity to present a super hip hop extravaganza, featuring talent from two rival sections of East Oakland. One group gathered in the parking lot across the street. The other group held fort inside. The kids in the parking lot were suddenly flashing guns like cowboys. The man operating the searchlight in front of the club ducked for cover.

The police responded in force. The days of Ruthie's Inn were numbered.

Rachel DMR: Wes wanted to do a Ruthie's Inn documentary before he died. It was really disappointing because people who should've been there, that should've contributed, didn't. I was really upset. Here's the one person who gave us a chance, you know. It was hurtful to hear so many people bad-mouth him and not step back and realize where they came from.

Dean Washington: The bottom line is, had it not been for Wes, the Berkeley punk rock and/or metal would not be what it is to this day. He did what no one else would do and some of those bands are huge today. Slayer, Metallica. I honestly don't think it would have ever happened had it not been for Wes Robinson.

Kate Knox: Absolutely right. Slayer's still playing Fang and Verbal Abuse and Sick Pleasure songs. I think it had a huge effect.

28

Let's Lynch the Landlord

Jeff Goldthorpe: Polytechnic High was originally squatted in late 1982.

Portia: Polytech was a huge abandoned high school on Parnassus Street near the Haight-Ashbury district. It was rumored that it was abandoned due to asbestos. Many different types of people lived there. Some hobos, some skins and the punks.

It was left without ever being emptied. There was still chalk left on the chalkboards, and costumes in the drama room. The lights still worked and there was still running water. But all of the toilets were plugged up and the bathrooms were unusable.

Audra Angeli-Slawson: You would go to a room and squat there for awhile, and then somebody would shit in the corner or something, so it would fucking reek and you couldn't stay there anymore. So you would just close it up and move on to the next room.

Portia: At one point, we were all in some room on the roof. The last place that I recall everyone staying was the drama room. The police used to raid Polytech and arrest people for trespassing.

Jeff Goldthorpe: The *Bay Guardian* ran an article on squatting in San Francisco, detailing the activities of the recently formed Squatters Anonymous. The group made it clear that, unlike some East Coast squatters who had moved into empty government-owned buildings in order to negotiate legal residency, they viewed illegal squatting of privately owned property "as a solution, not just a tactic."

Hilary Binder: I had heard about squatting from friends of mine in New York and Europe, and went to San Francisco with a friend from the D.C. yippie scene. The Democratic Convention was coming up in San Francisco that summer.

We went to a meeting of people who were interested in organizing a counter-demo. Jim Squatter and Peter Plate were both present. Jim did most of the talking. Peter was this mysterious character. He didn't say much but he had this presence of someone who really had something to say.

Courtenay Dennis: Peter Plate used to speak at the anarchists' bookstore. He kind of looked like the singer for Midnight Oil. He always wore a black beret and carried a big shoulder bag. He was super eloquent. I remember feeling like I was a little too dumb to be there.

Mike Tsongas: Jim Squatter was a Greenpeace activist and very involved in the squatter movement.

Hilary Binder: I had found an apartment in San Francisco and was just about to sign the lease. Jim said I should check out his squat. He gave me the inspiration. The idea that something like this could work if I had enough energy to do it.

So I went walking around the city, looking for places that were abandoned. I found HOLC on Sixth and Folsom. I went in and stayed there for a few nights by myself. At the Mabuhay Gardens, I ran into a young punk woman who needed a place to sleep. I invited her to stay and that's how it all started.

Jeff Goldthorpe: The Hotel Owners Laundry Company was nicknamed HOLC or "hole-see."

Courtenay Dennis: It was an old laundry service plant.

Hilary Binder: The Vats and Polytech were models to us. But there was a lot of drugs and drinking. They were basically a bunch of musicians and youth. Predominantly, the people involved with HOLC were anarchist identified.

Jeff Goldthorpe: Many of the squatter activists evicted from the Vats moved into HOLC. There were two rules: no shooting drugs, and everyone had to work.

Hilary Binder: There was a goal to provide housing and to do something with it as a public space. We had community dinners every week or two.

Mike Tsongas: Most of the meals came from dumpster-diving. You could find all kinds of fresh vegetables in the dumpsters behind Safeway. It was amazing what we found.

Julie Generic: If we dumpstered a crate of tomatoes, it was spaghetti night.

Hilary Binder: We also started a free-food program. We raised the money through donations, then would drive over to a distribution warehouse in Oakland sponsored by a church. We would load up the car with near-expiry vegetables and fruits for 15 dollars. Drive back to the city and set up a free distribution stall somewhere. First we did it from the HOLC, then on Sixth Street, and near Church Street. We kept the program going for a few years.

Mike Tsongas: They were actually doing so many wonderful things. Everything was very positive and very inclusive.

Julie Generic: We had a big room that had 15 mattresses in it, and we all slept on those mattresses. We had movie nights once a week. It was fucking genius. It was so fun. We showed underground movies that people had made, stuff from Crass and PLH, political movies.

Courtenay Dennis: Everybody was really into MDC. They came over a lot. And the guys from the DKs and the Dicks came over. And Kurt from DRI. People would play music and have debates. Listening to those people who were older than me talking about what was wrong. So many of them were really bright, politically astute people. Hilary certainly was.

I always felt like it was Hilary's place. She was the boss. She looked kind of dykey. She wore shirts with the sleeves cut off, no makeup—sort of a hippie punk. She was like a weird grumpy mom. She was very outspoken and she had a temper.

Julie Generic: Hilary was a self-righteous bitch. I know she was a well-intentioned person, but she always fucking hated me because I didn't know what the hell I was doing, and she felt like she had to tell me what to do.

Aaron Cometbus: She was kind of hot.

Courtenay Dennis: The summer of '84, that was when the political punks were really the most visible.

Julie Generic: HOLC was home base for Rock Against Reagan that summer. They pulled one of the big school buses inside. All the sound equipment was there, the crew—everybody was staying at the squat.

Hilary Binder: A lot of people were in and out, from Rock Against Reagan, yippies I knew from New York. They were doing the West Coast tour, and then going down to Texas for the Republican Convention counter-demonstrations. We had meetings up the wazoo to figure out what we wanted to accomplish. We met with more established organizations, and with the whole DIY scene of anarchists and punks. I went to the Rainbow Gathering in Mount

Shasta that summer to drum up body support from the Love Family.

Jeff Goldthorpe: HOLC was also a part of a broader squatting activism. They held meetings at Bound Together, St. Anthony's Coffeehouse, the Hotel Harold and HOLC, where new sites would be discussed.

Hilary Binder: We did consultations with the homeless people on Sixth Street. I was encouraging them to go inside this abandoned apartment building. They were really against the idea because "that's illegal." Eventually they did occupy the building, but they didn't want to go as far as stealing electricity. By that point we had learned how to get electricity from the street lights.

Julie Generic: A group of people branched off from HOLC and created the Women's Squat, which was on 20th and South Van Ness. The whole process of creating that squat was really cool. They created a safe sanctuary for women. I was never into segregating the sexes, but it was good.

Jeff Goldthorpe: A high proportion of European nationals heard about HOLC through political squatter networks.

Andrew Flurry: The squatting symbol was a circle with a lightning bolt arrow going through it. People would draw it everywhere, I'd see it on signs all over town.

Courtenay Dennis: Hilary had that symbol tattooed on her arm.

Hilary Binder: San Francisco has a long history of free clothes and free food, from the Diggers on. You could eat pretty well if you knew the schedule of all the kitchens. Whether it was the Cauliflower Collective or the Coltrane Church or the Krishnas. I became friendly with the Haight-Ashbury Soup Kitchen. I learned how to make bread in coffee cans. They were really great, openhearted people.

Courtenay Dennis: Tree's House in the Mission was a restaurant run by these hippie people, with a big room and long benches and a garden. We all worked over there and they had these theme nights for the soup kitchen. Oh my god, it was a magical thing.

Julie Generic: Tree's House was awesome. People who volunteered there would dress up for that week's theme. So the girls would wear crazy Tahitian outfits and the guys would paint themselves up. You would see people in a grass skirt. The whole process of feeding people was like a tribal group experience. It was cool and kind of weird.

Jeff Goldthorpe: The HOLC squat had avoided any major police harassment during the Democratic Convention. But they were finally evicted in mid-October 1984.

Hilary Binder: It wasn't a surprise. We were told the day they were coming. We barricaded the squat. I wasn't there when it got busted. People believe someone opened the door for the cops. They didn't have any trouble getting in.

Julie Generic: They kicked us out of there. Articles appeared two days in a row in the *San Francisco Chronicle* and *Examiner*. We took all our mattresses and our cooking stuff and plants out onto the sidewalk. We drew windows and a clock on the wall in chalk, and made it homey. After we got kicked off the sidewalk, a bunch of us went to an abandoned funeral parlor half a block away. We got kicked out of there, too.

John Borruso: Trial did a show in front of City Hall in support of squatting rights, December 8th, 1984. As I recall it was a special lineup with Roddy, then of Faith No More, performing with us.

Andrew Flurry: Rock Against Rent was my first real punk rock show. I only remember the Dicks, 'cause Gary Floyd was this big fucking fat dude. There was a Dicks' song on the *P.E.A.C.E.* compilation that I really liked. There were skinheads and Jaks there.

Aaron Cometbus: It was a particularly ugly scene—some skinhead beat up an old homeless guy *and* his dog with a steel pipe. And Gary Floyd was there saying, "No, don't just blame the skinheads! They're not the enemy here." He always seemed to see the skinheads as these misunderstood, basically cool guys. I loved the Dicks and have total respect for Gary, but, man, what was he thinking?

Andrew Flurry: I was 13, so for me that show was mostly about the pit, and it was scary as hell 'cause I was tiny. The stage was in the park facing away from City Hall and there was a circle pit. Half the pit was on the concrete and half the pit was in the grass. But the lawn was sunken so there was a ledge and a gutter between the two. I remember this skate guy Zeke was in the pit doing handplants off the concrete into the grass. I thought it was the most badass thing I'd ever seen. The guy was like a fucking orangutan. I think he used to sell us acid.

Jeff Goldthorpe: A leaflet was distributed entitled *What Is Squatting?* which acknowledged that "we have to reach out to people in order to get support." But it was too little too late.

Hilary Binder: The squats started going one by one. We tried to squat a place south of Market and immediately got kicked out by the cops. They followed us in their squad car as we were wheeling our stuff down the street in our shopping carts, looking for the next place. It really got bad. It was one of the reasons I stopped squatting that town. I had spent too much time in jail and representing myself in court. I left for Europe to organize what I hoped would be the international Stop Business As Usual demo.

Gary Floyd: Hilary lives in the Czech Republic now.

Hilary Binder: HOLC was only open for six or seven months. It was a pretty short-lived revolutionary activity, but it was an important one.

Julie Generic: HOLC is a functioning laundry service again.

29

Fucked Up Ronnie

Sara Cohen: Reaganomics, the Iran-Contra affair. That's what Rock
Against Reagan was all about. We had a very clear understanding
about what the fuck was going on in our country, about what was
going on in the world.

Oran Canfield: I had a real fear that we were all gonna die. In Berkeley
and the Bay Area, Reagan was seriously the devil. I would see
him on the news and nothing he ever said contradicted the idea
that these fucking crazy egomaniacs were gonna end up destroying the world.

Al Schvitz: This was in the midst of Reagan's idiocy. MDC came back
to San Francisco from a tour in Europe and we got a copy of
Overthrow, the yippies' magazine. On the back cover was a review of our first album: "Album of the Year." We didn't really
know what the yippies were about, but they loved us. They were
doing a 50-city tour, and they wanted to know, could we do any
dates? Somehow this evolved into us pretty much doing all
50 dates, and bringing any bands we wanted. This was the Rock
Against Reagan tour.

It was a bunch of potheads. It was pot money. Okay, you weren't
gonna get Ian MacKaye to back you, but what the hell, it seemed
like a great opportunity. We wound up working with all our good
friends—the Dicks, Crucifucks, DRI, Toxic Reasons. We played
all these cool, cool venues that we never would have played.

Gary Floyd: We didn't have much money for food but we always had
cheap, disgusting beer, and we had hootenannies every night.
Glenn Taylor was the guitar player for the Dicks at the time and
he could play anything. He would yell out "Help Me, Rhonda"

by the Beach Boys and I would start making up filthy lyrics about dicks and titties.

Tammy Lundy: When we were in Madison, Wisconsin, the yippies actually got a couple of helicopters to fly over the gig and drop thousands of joints onto the crowd. We were onstage when that happened and it was raining joints from the sky. It was a miracle. It was like something Jesus would do.

Gary Floyd: But there were a lot of people who were really stoned making big decisions for the rest of us. The punks and the hippies really did not get along that well. MDC was sort of the go-between, trying to keep the peace. The Dicks and the Crucifucks became very good friends and saved each other from killing everyone else, including Dave and MDC for getting us on the fucking thing!

Tammy Lundy: We were out for maybe six or seven months. Sometimes we'd have these glorious moments where fishes and loaves fed the multitudes. And sometimes we'd go down this red-clay road in the middle of nowhere, and the vehicles would all get stuck. They didn't always have their shit together.

Gary Floyd: They guaranteed us at least one or two meals a day but it was always the same. They got a donation of 100,000 frozen turkey dogs, so we'd show up at some kid's house whose parents didn't know we were coming, and there'd be some huge, horrible pot bubbling on the stove. Of course, MDC had their 80-pound bag of carrots.

Tammy Lundy: If you were going to ride in the MDC van, that was your diet. No meat.

Al Schvitz: We played the Pot Parade going *up* Fifth Avenue, which is a downtown street in Manhattan—you can't drive up Fifth Avenue. We went from Washington Square Park to the United Nations building on a moving flatbed truck, with Dave yelling.

Tammy Lundy: We were staying just a couple blocks from CBGB's. We would go up to the editorial offices of the yippie magazine and sit with these '60s icons like Wavy Gravy and Abbie Hoffman. It was totally strange.

Gary Floyd: Central Park at the band shell. There were tons of cops and hippies and punks and it was a bright day. A bunch of Rasta people were playing onstage. And Crucifix, who had never even spoken to us in San Francisco, ran over to us with their huge foot-long spiked hair and they were really friendly. It was like, "We have arrived at last, Crucifix is being friendly to us."

We played a couple of songs and then they said the cops were thinking of turning it off. So we played "Dicks Hate the Police." In the middle of the song, I gave some drunken rant about freedom, and the cops pulled the plug. I could tell that it was going to become very, very chaotic so I turned into mist and blew away. I was drunk. I started a big bunch of shit and I left.

Al Schvitz: The culmination was this gig at the National all in front of the Lincoln Memorial on the 4th of July in 1983. We got Biafra to fly out with the Dead Kennedys for that one.

Tammy Lundy: There were a jillion people there, and it was really hot. Police helicopters were flying overhead, taking banking turns, and I remember someone asking, "Are those guns or cameras pointing out the door?" I was approached by a strange, heavily built man in shorts, sunburn, and Halloween mask looking for reefer. When I said I couldn't help him, he pulled a badge and threw me against our van. Biafra at one point gestured towards the Washington Monument, noting how much it looked like a KKK hood.

Al Schvitz: When we got back to San Francisco, we played Dolores Park with the Dead Kennedys. Whoopi Goldberg was emceeing it, and Dennis Peron, the weed activist.

Kriss X: There were thousands. It was exciting as hell! It was like us against the world. I felt like we were all saying a huge "fuck you" to the establishment and the Reagan administration. There was an overwhelming sense of camaraderie in the park that day. I was still young and green, and to be honest, politics were not at the top of my to-do list. But Feinstein was mayor and she had upped all the cops. I remember punks getting hassled almost daily for petty bullshit.

John Marr: If you were a minor, out on the street after 11 p.m., San Francisco P.D. would haul you in. *MRR* booked a series of curfew shows at the Mabuhay. I still have the flyer. It's a picture of this punk girl being hauled away by these two cops: "Tired of having your evenings end like this? Curfew shows at the Mab!"

Sheriff Mike Hennessey: There was no question there were conflicts with the police out on the streets. Punks lip off—let's face it, that's part of being a punk. And cops don't like being lipped off to. And there was drug use, there were kids getting drunk and passing out. The cops would attempt to try to control the group, and this is a type of group that doesn't like to be controlled. I filed a complaint against a cop one night for bashing a kid's head up against the grille of a car. But it was mostly, as we would say in law enforcement, mutual combat. We're here and we agree to fight, and then it's over with.

Andy Pollack: In 1984, around the time of the Democratic Convention, San Francisco tightened up. Never to be the same, actually.

Gordon Edgar: The *Chronicle* detailed the police dropping homeless people off at bus stations at the Nevada border.

Jeff Goldthorpe: Before the convention opened, 1,000 demonstrators noisily picketed across the street from the hotel where the Moral Majority was holding a "Family Forum" meeting. Across the street were a large number of police. Some demonstrators attempted to escape by circling a few blocks close by and trying to surge into the street. As the picketers moved toward Union Square for a planned rally, mounted police charged into the crowd, swinging clubs, trampling several people and arresting eight. Peace punks did a "die-in" in an intersection a block away, holding up traffic for 15 minutes. Others threw garbage cans into the street and set a dumpster afire.

Gordon Edgar: War Chest Tour was the '80s version of anti-corporate demonstrations, where a bunch of punks would rush into some

Photo © 2009 Keith Michael Holmes

If the Kids Are United: Rock Against Reagan

multinational's office and start screaming about their capitalist evils.

Mike Tsongas: The War Chest Tour was one of many predecessors to the Black Bloc. David Solnit hung around us a lot and was one of the primary people who organized the War Chest Tours during the convention.

Jeff Goldthorpe: On Monday, July 16, the WCT was ambushed by S.F. police. People were surrounded and charged with "conspiracy to trespass." A few demonstrators that escaped did a retaliatory "die-in" in a nearby intersection and were quickly tackled or dragged off by plainclothes police. It was all over very quickly, but was enough to get a headline in the next day's *Chronicle*: "Punk Rocker Protest—84 Arrests."

Mike Tsongas: It was really surreal. I remember walking down the street with my purple mohawk—Mr. Punk Rock with black eyeliner and studded belts. This white van pulled up beside me and the doors slid open. It was the news, and they were filming me. They followed me for almost an entire block before I ditched them.

Jeff Goldthorpe: "Punk rocker" was all the explanation needed by most media observers to explain the actions or the police response.

Gary Floyd: The Dicks played the Democratic Convention at Moscone Center. It was really historic. There were so many people there, not just punks.

Mike Tsongas: It was the pinnacle of the San Francisco punk scene. Punks from all over the country filtered in for this event.

Gavin MacArthur: By the time MDC played, it was pretty much a madhouse. There is no way that anything like that would fly now.

> There were around 5,000 people . . . the crowd was a curious mixture of punks, hippies, straights, gays, various minorities, and skins. As Dave MDC said from the stage, "We're all family. Let's take care of each other."
>
> —*Tim Yohannan,* Maximum RocknRoll *15, August 1984*

Hef: A bunch of us from Berkeley and Oakland came down. The cops were chasing people around with these motorcycles, riding down the sidewalk on dirt bikes trying to surround people.

Jeff Goldthorpe: Early in the show, 200 more marched off to Bank of America world headquarters. Demonstrators began to rap on windows as they chanted, and the TAC Squad suddenly moved between them and the building. Continuing down Kearny Street, they were suddenly surrounded again by police on horseback and 87 were arrested, charged with obstruction.

Mike Tsongas: We got surrounded by cops immediately, even though we weren't doing anything illegal. They said, "We order you to disperse. You are now under arrest for failing to disperse." Just like that.

Tammy Lundy: We got busted walking away from the Bank of America building. All of a sudden these policemen on horseback rode up on us—it felt like we were going to get trampled—and they pinned us up against the wall. It was really scary. I remember my brother saying, "Oh boy, mama's not gonna like this."

Courtenay Dennis: This really quiet, sweet, Filipino girl Joren got knocked over and kicked in the head by a policeman's horse. There was a lawsuit because of that. I got billy-clubbed. My arm was all black and blue. I got taken to 850 Bryant. As they walked us past the cells, people were yelling and chanting. A bunch of us were so young we didn't have IDs, and we wouldn't give our names or ages. I got to make a phone call. My mom came and was all pissed off. It was my 15th birthday. The police started to get freaked out so they brought three paddy wagons to bring us all over to juvy. On the way, I got a bunch of us to rock the paddy wagon back and forth, to try to get it to roll over. My mom followed the wagons to juvy. She said she could see one of them rockin' back and forth, and she knew I was in that one.

Jeff Goldthorpe: Those escaping the ambush got back to the Moscone Center concert and denounced the latest arrests. The Dead Kennedys played next.

East Bay Ray: We got sheets and made Ku Klux Klan hoods, with Reagan masks underneath.

Klaus Flouride: They were busting people left and right and dragging them off to jail. Biafra just kept saying, "Don't get busted! Don't get busted!"

Aaron Cometbus: David Solnit got onstage and gave this breathless speech. Moving, but sort of hysterical, too, which whipped the crowd into a frenzy. "The cops have just arrested . . . eighty of our brothers and sisters . . . for peacefully protesting against this fucked-up war machine. . . . We've got to do something. . . . We have to march on the Hall of Justice and get them out! Now!"

Mike Tsongas: We were watching the news, on the inside, and saw them marching down to the Hall of Justice. They did a big sit-in while we were in jail. It was an incredible feeling, to see that.

Hilary Binder: People were screaming and yelling for our release. It was really fun.

Mike Tsongas: People called the Hall of Justice pay phone, all the "stars" of the scene wanted to offer us encouragement. We passed the phone around. There were people from all over the country with us, people who had different experiences in their own scenes back home, but we were able to share this together.

Gordon Edgar: As we rallied outside, the police moved in. My weaselly brother made it through the police line at the last minute but I got stopped by a riot baton in my chest. I spent all night in jail before being sent to juvenile hall the next morning. Our protest became the biggest mass arrest in the Bay Area since the late '60s.

PART

III

30

White Trash, Two Heebs and a Bean

Fat Mike: I went to summer camp when I was 13, and Joe Escalante from the Vandals was a junior counselor there. At the school dance he was playing some punk rock. I didn't even know what it was. I went to a record store and asked the guy, "Have you heard a song that goes, 'Beat on the brat with a baseball bat'?" He gave me a Ramones cassette, and that was the first punk I ever heard.

Then I met our drummer Erik Sandin outside the Cathay de Grande, which was a punk club in Hollywood where I grew up. I had a Black Flag skateboard, and he was just, "Cool skateboard." We started talking.

We were all 16 and had no idea how to play musical instruments. Lucky for us we wanted to play punk, therefore we didn't need to know how to do anything. So Melvin, Smelly and I started writing songs and playing shows.

Mike LaVella: A lot of their success is just the fact that they never did a comeback tour. From '85 'til now, they never stopped. Not too many bands can say that. There's something to be said about the consistency. There's some kind of chemistry between those guys where they're like, "This is our job."

Fat Mike: No one ever liked us in L.A. It was a shitty town. So we just toured every summer and every vacation. We played places like CBGB's, Mabuhay Gardens, and the Anthrax. No one liked us, but that was okay 'cause we were having a hell of a good time.

Mike LaVella: I met him in '85, they played in Pittsburgh in my neighbor's basement. We just called our friends, "Some fuckin' band from L.A. is playing in Nick's basement." Maybe 20 people came, but it was packed. I had all these fat-chick magazines in my room. *Gent*, all that shit. Mike was like, "Oh, you like fat chicks, too?" He was probably the first guy who was open and excited about someone else having fat-chick magazines.

Fat Mike: The reason I moved to San Francisco—it sounds kind of corny or like I'm a loser. But I didn't want to give up punk rock, and L.A. was really dangerous. In the summer of '85, I went to a Dickies show in Santa Monica, and my friend got stabbed in the lung. For nothin'. He almost died. In San Francisco, skinheads were beating the shit out of everyone, too. But right when I moved here, they all left. So it was totally cool.

Noah Landis: I went to S.F. State with him and we had a lot of talks. He was another person who spoke truth to power. To this day, he does not have any qualms about saying exactly what he thinks.

Fat Mike: I studied social science. Minor in human sexuality. I was gonna be some kind of sex therapist.

Bucky Sinister: When we graduated I was like, "What are you gonna do now?" And he said, "I'm gonna be a professional punk rocker!" I was like, "Ha ha!" Joke's on us.

Fat Mike: I used to graffiti NOFX everywhere we went. I'd wipe off the back of the toilet and write my band's name there, 'cause everyone sees it, you know. I did that behind the toilet and in the urinal at the Farm. Of course, they got pissed at me. Most of our early shows were at the New Method Warehouse, but we'd played the Farm a couple times and we were trying to get a show. They said, "If you want to clean your graffiti off, then we'll let you play here again." And I fucking did. I went there, scrubbed the toilets, and got the NOFX name off of there. And then the Farm closed down. So we never got to play there again anyway.

In '86 we toured with a band called Subculture. That was my first year of college and I had a food card. I gained 30 pounds in a year. So a lot of cities we went to, people were like, "Oh, you put on some weight, huh? Got a little fat there, didn't ya?" They started calling me Fat Mike. Well, Mike—what kind of a name is Mike? There's gotta be something. Mike Suicidal, Mike Fuck-Up. So Fat Mike works.

Mike LaVella: People were really into Bad Religion, but I always liked NOFX more. They were more funny, more clever. Fat Mike is pretty charismatic.

Fat Mike: We had to have a sense of humor because, this is totally serious, we were the worst band of the '80s. The only thing we had going for us is maybe we were a little funny onstage. And we drank more than every other band. It was more of a fabulous disaster. That kept us going for awhile.

We kept on touring. In 1989 we wrote our first good song, "S&M Airlines." Brett Gurewitz from Bad Religion heard it and signed us to Epitaph Records. Then we made the *S&M Airlines* LP. It was weird, people actually started to like us. From there on, things got better.

I didn't really start the Fat Wreck label until '91. Even though I put out early NOFX records in the '80s, that wasn't a label. I just printed records and sold it to a few distributors and sold them on the road.

Mike LaVella: I was working at CD Presents. The world's worst record distributor. Mike needed a job, and I hired him. He did the mail order, I was the salesman.

Fat Mike: CD Presents, David Ferguson. He put out the Avengers record, and DOA record. The Institute for Unpopular Culture. That guy is the biggest piece of shit I've ever met. He burned Fat Wreck Chords for ten grand. Which, back then, was a lot of money.

Mike LaVella: CD Presents became Buried Treasure. Nobody worked there but me and Mike. And then we hired Spike Slawson. Spike was my friend, and I introduced those two. Then Mike left. He was like, "I'm starting a label." For his birthday, his wife made him business cards and stationery.

They reissued the *P.M.R.C.* 7-inch, that was their first, and I was the distributor for it. I remember thinking, Jesus Christ, it's easy to sell these NOFX records. People wanted them. In Germany, and wherever.

Jesse Luscious: Until really recently, if you put out a record on Fat you were guaranteed 50,000 sales.

Fat Mike: I don't know, we're fairly smart people. I mean, it's not that hard. The goal isn't how much you can get, it's how much fun you're having.

Spike Slawson: He wanted to do good shit for his friends. I think that was the main drive behind doing that label. And he is a pretty good businessman.

Fat Mike: We put out Tilt, Dance Hall Crashers, No Use for a Name from San Jose, Dieselboy from North Bay.

Mike LaVella: Most of the bands sounded vaguely like NOFX. He was like, "Well, if we can sell X amount, then I'll sign the bands." He was in a unique situation. He could do NOFX EPs or a live album on Fat, but he kept NOFX on Epitaph for a long time. Because by that time Epitaph had the Offspring, that sold 7 million. And they had Pennywise, and all that crap. And he knew they were solid. Like, this check is always gonna come in.

Davey Havok: The one independent label that no one has anything but good things to say about is Fat Wreck. Fat Mike does it from a place of pure love of music.

Dave Chavez: NOFX ruined punk rock, as far as I'm concerned.

Mike LaVella: They were not respected very much by the rock 'n' roll people here. Mike would go to Europe, and bring me back these posters for festivals they played. Hole and New Order had opened for them. I'm like, "New Order opened for you?!" And then they'd play the Bottom of the Hill for 75 people.

Fat Mike: Tim Yohannan always spoke highly of us. When people would bitch about us being jokes, he always said, "Yeah, but they're kind of a cool band. I don't really see what they're doing wrong." He was one of the reasons NOFX got credibility, and kept credibility.

> *You better watch out, you better not cry*
> *You better put out records DIY*
> *'Cause it's not what you've done, it's who you've been*
> *If you fuck up I'm telling Tim.*
>
> —*"I'm Telling Tim,"* NOFX

Fat Mike: Despite what people think, we have always been political in our records. Our very first 7-inch had a political song, but live, we didn't preach. We were funny live.

A. C. Thompson: There was actually a debate at Epicenter about a NOFX record called *Heavy Petting Zoo*, which had a cover of a person petting a sheep in a suggestive way. There was a sense that this was offensive to both women and sheep, and the vegans on staff were not going to stand for this.

My point was, there are no women in the picture, so how could this be offensive to women? If you can't make fun of sheep, then you really can't make fun of anything.

Fat Mike: We were actually banned from Gilman. For what?! The thing is we used to play Gilman and we've always taken a stand against major labels. There were four and a half months where we didn't know what the fuck to do. Green Day got really big and

Courtesy of Epitaph

Heavy Petting Zoo: NOFX's sixth full-length album

Offspring got big, and major labels wanted to sign us. We met with one major label and just felt so disgusted. So that was it.

MTV—Quit bugging us
Major Labels—Quit bugging us
Commercial Radio Stations—Quit playing us

We've been doin just fine all these years without you so
LEAVE US THE FUCK ALONE! Ass Holes
    —*Liner notes of* Heavy Petting Zoo, *1996*

Fraggle: NOFX always played sold-out shows at Gilman. Always. People would come from all over. There was a whole San Francisco crowd that would only come out for big shows.

Mike LaVella: They played well to kids.

Fat Mike: First time we headlined there, 80 people came. I got hit in the face with a basketball. Just when I came onstage. I was like, "Hi, we're NOFX, we're from L.A." *Bam!* Welcome to Gilman.

Mike LaVella: We once had this big fight because Mike liked Manhattan Transfer. I was like, "Dude, they're shit. You should listen to Lambert, Hendricks and Ross." I went out and bought the Lambert, Hendricks and Ross album, gave it to him. But he preferred Manhattan Transfer. Think about that. Gloss it up, take the soul out of it, take the jazz out of it. That's what he did with punk rock. I really thought those records were overproduced. There was no raw edge.

Blag Jesus: Most people don't look at music in a complete way, and that helps you market it better. A guy like Fat Mike loves punk rock, period. And he sold a couple million records doing just that. Try to be real expansive, you lose people 'cause they don't give a fuck.

Mike LaVella: When Me First and the Gimme Gimmes first started, Fat Mike came to my house and went through my record collection. He was like, "This would make a cover, this would make a cover." All those early Me First singles and the first album, they're just records from my collection. They would just put "Me First and the Gimme Gimmes" over the top of "Allan Sherman," or whatever.

Spike Slawson: I was the shipping manager at Fat Wreck. I wasn't very good at it.

Fat Mike: He was drunk a lot. I wrote the song "Go to Work Wasted," so what do I expect? My employees show up drunk!

Spike Slawson: I must have smelled like a distillery.

Fat Mike: My wife said, "We really have to get rid of this guy." It's because I wanted to fire him from Fat Wreck Chords, I put together this band and said, "Take it on the road."

Spike Slawson: I was doing karaoke at the time at the Mint, which is a gay bar in the Castro. I would sing in the warehouse while I was shipping. Mike said, a lot of the best songs on any record by a new punk band is the cover, so let's just do a whole record of them, a whole set of them.

Fat Mike: We started playing San Francisco. The whole idea was to put out 7-inches, no CDs. We were just going to play San Francisco. Just bars. It lasted for a couple years like that.

Spike Slawson: Cover bands are for bars.

Audra Angeli-Slawson: They did their first show at the Chameleon in early '97, which was tiny. Now it's just crazy. We recently came from Japan and the Gimmes played in front of 40,000 people. It was a festival, but still. It's a phenomenon. Spike always says, "I don't know why people like our cover band." It's because they are fucking hilarious and fun.

The first time I met Fat Mike, I was doing stage security. He said, "You're a badass!" We've had a mutual admiration society since then. I work with them, doing a lot of stuff. I do production and wardrobe. I tour-mom. If I don't feed them, they won't eat. They're my children. And all their wives are happier because they know the boys are taken care of.

And fuck if Fat Mike doesn't bail me out of trouble a lot. I've had Incredibly Strange Wrestling shows at the Fillmore where my headliner has canceled, and Fat Mike got NOFX to play, didn't even think twice about it. Sold out the room for me.

Noah Landis: Hats off to him. He's lucky enough to have had success with his music and his label, to have had the time and means to do things.

Jesse Michaels: Fat Mike took his power and put it to real, tangible use with Rock Against Bush. This tour went on for months, and planted seeds in the minds of an enormous mall-culture generation that wouldn't go anywhere near a protest march.

> Punkvoter is a coalition of punk bands, musicians and record labels, organized to educate and mobilize progressive voters. . . . Punkvoter aims to educate and energize the nation's youth about the political process, and inspire them to become involved in that process to change this society and shape the future of our nation.
>
> —*"Formation of Punkvoter," Fat Mike (Burkett), 2003*

Jello Biafra: I was involved in Punkvoter. Of course the more radical-than-thou got down on me. "What the hell are you doing getting involved with Fat Mike, that motherfucking sellout, blah blah blah." Then I thought, hey, wait a minute. He was born rich, is rich, but he's putting a lot of his own money into this because he gives a shit. He always did, if you look at his background closely.

I realized that Punkvoter with Fat Mike running the show would reach way more people than Punkvoter with Jello Biafra running the show. And if that meant working with people who were really into Howard Dean, or wanting a Democrat to win just so Bush wouldn't be in there—I don't agree with that, but

I'm willing to work with them. I'm willing to work with people more moderate than I am, to help achieve radical change.

Mike LaVella: I ran into him in Austin. He was like, "Mike, can we count on you? Will you get behind it?" It was like he was campaigning. He was really serious. And then I saw him at Stinky's Peepshow right after Bush got elected. I said, "Dude, sorry about the election." He said, "Oh, I don't care."

Fat Mike: I feel that we made it okay to talk about politics again in the music scene. A lot of bands were doing it. Bruce Springsteen. Dixie Chicks. But our music scene, which had always been political, hadn't been in the last ten years. Now Green Day is political. Blink 182, the most pop band ever, was stumping for John Kerry. A lot of bands were scared at first, but a lot of bands joined forces. That was the most important thing that we did. We got a few hundred punk bands to make the same stand against the Bush administration.

Jello Biafra: I respect Mike and what he did with Punkvoter publicly. But I really disagree with his decision to pull out. It had strong enough legs, he could have let it grow on its own, which in a way it has. The seeds for a large part of the Obama movement were planted by Punkvoter. In fact, one of the main Internet and text message organizers for Obama was the old political director of Punkvoter.

Fat Mike: We got the ball rolling and that's all I wanted to do in the first place. Organize all the bands I knew to take a stand. And now everybody is. So what's my job now?

31

A Chronology for Survival

Fat Mike: I lived in S.F. but I used to go to a lot of house parties in the East Bay in the '80s. Christ on Parade and Neurosis and Op Ivy—that was my generation. I knew all those guys. They always used to say, "Mike, you're out here again!" 'Cause the best parties were out in the East Bay. Half the best shows were in warehouses.

Adrienne Droogas: I was still in high school and living with my parents when I went to New Method, the warehouse started by Crucifix back in the '80s. By that time it was Christ on Parade, A State of Mind, Clown Alley.

Dave Ed: New Method was a bunch of really scruffy-looking punks, wearing dark clothing. Crass, dreadlocks, vegetarianism. It was pretty shocking, the size of the shows they got away with. The cops just didn't care. Emeryville was still no-man's-land back then.

Noah Landis: I spent a lot of time there. Those guys were several years older than me. They were living in a rotting warehouse, went on rent strike and took it over. That was the most empowering thing I had ever seen. These guys were living outside the grid 24/7. That was a mind-blowing revelation about what punk rock could be. I did a lot of growing up. I couldn't be a kid around them and spout off stuff that was overopinionated and underinformed. I had to pay attention.

Eric Ozenne: My first show was Christ on Parade, the Descendents and 7 Seconds. It was the coolest thing in the world, but I was scared shitless because I was 15 and I was from the Valley. Christ on Parade had a whole rainbow assortment of hairdos. Nohawks, twinhawks, mohawks. Everybody had ripped-up clothes and their music was really dark. I loved it.

Noah Landis: This super-tall guy with a big mohawk named Barrie Evans worked at Blondie's. He was in a band with some guys out in Hayward called Teenage Warning. The singer was Kevin Reed. He was amazing—just this screaming ball of sweat and hatred.

When their guitar player Jim Lyon quit, he asked me to come try out. I learned their songs—they were really fast and straightforward. Barrie picked me up from my mom's house on a motorcycle and drove me to BART. He showed me how to hop the gate by the elevator. We played at Ruthie's Inn. My very first show with Teenage Warning—Bill Collins, who taught me to play guitar, was front and center, heckling me the whole time.

When Teenage Warning dissolved, Barrie got together with the drummer and the bass player of Treason, and they brought me into the fold. Malcolm came up with the name Christ on Parade.

Kate Knox: Christ on Parade had this sound, along with their politics that hit your heart. It was how you felt about the world. They spoke to you.

Noah Landis: "Landlord Song" was about the guy who owned the New Method building. The idea of ownership of space was just ridiculous to us, so "End of the month, rent is due, tell your landlord, 'Fuck you,' " that came from real life. You can hear how young everybody was when they were writing these things, but the energy and the attitude was pretty fuckin' awesome.

Scott Kelly: I remember seeing Christ on Parade in San Jose, opening up for Social Distortion. The show was fucking amazing. There was so much tension in the room before they even played the first note. They had an intro tape going with news clips interspersed with explosions and all this shit, and they were kind of pacing around. And then they went right into it.

Martin Sorrondeguy: I was in Chicago and went to this crazy show at the Cabaret Metro—7 Seconds, Youth of Today, Christ on Parade and Indigesti from Italy. When Youth of Today played, I saw these guys in the pit I had never seen before. They looked super-ultra-punk. They had the spiked, dyed hair and they were in the pit dancing with smiles on their faces, puttin' their arms around people, pickin' people up when they fell, just goin' crazy and enjoying it. I remember thinking, "Who are these guys?" I had never seen anything like that. It was communal. I was used to kids at shows being pretty fuckin' nasty, and these guys were like into it and havin' fun. Then, all of a sudden, these kids jump up onstage. "Next up, Christ on Parade from the Bay Area!" It was in that moment I understood somethin' was different about the Bay Area scene.

Scott Kelly: The cornerstone of what they could do was their drummer Todd Kramer. He used a ride cymbal like nobody ever has. It would turn everything into this white-noise wash. When the mixture was good, they could just tear a place up. When the mixture was off—somebody was a little too loaded or it was just a bad night—it would just destruct.

Barrie Evans: I left COP at the start of 1987. It was just a difference of opinion. I got into rockabilly and psychobilly when I was living in Japan. It seemed so different and removed from the already fading punk scene in the U.S. It was nice to be part of a scene that had not yet gotten tainted and regimented. When I got back to the States I wanted to start a band that had the aggression of punk and the melodic structure of rockabilly. The Hellbillys continue to this day.

Noah Landis: Christ on Parade played all over Europe and the U.K. That trip really blew our minds. A couple of our members decided they actually wanted to move there. When we got back from Europe they said, "I think we're done." I was devastated. I felt really proud of all the things we had done. I didn't want it to break up at all. I still don't know how and why that fire peters out.

Scott Kelly: Neurosis practiced in the living room of New Method. I don't think I left Emeryville for an entire year. I worked in Emeryville, I lived at New Method, and I ate at the liquor store across the street. You didn't need to go anywhere else. We had our practice space, we had a gig space, we had our dealers, we had the liquor store, we had the food—it was done. It was a place filled with massive, mind-expanding nights, and a lot of really intelligent people were living there, putting out records, starting bands.

Jesse Michaels: Neurosis were my friends but they were just so *rad*, the word I would have used at the time, for having a band. They evolved from other bands like Violent Coercion and SFT, who I worshipped when I was a kid.

Scott Kelly: I remember being at Ruthie's when me and Dave and Jason first started conceptualizing our idea. We watched five bands in a row and they all sounded the same. It was that metal-core thing, a couple of longhairs and a couple of guys with mohawks, going back and forth between the chunky riff and the mosh part. We were not gonna do any of that shit.

Dave Ed: Things had been more stylistically open in the early '80s, even in the thrash and hardcore scene. We were in this quandary. Why should we even have to think about style? We should just play what was coming out of us. So we took some time to think about where this band was going to go.

Scott Kelly: It was basically a two-week conversation between me, Dave and Jason, where we X-ed out everything we didn't want to do. Then we isolated six bands, saying, "Okay, these are the real deal." Black Flag—that was a band that didn't give a fuck. Rudimentary Peni was a deep influence—that really introspective, dark, minor key, creepy stuff. Joy Division, which was just about as pure as it gets. The early Pink Floyd stuff with Syd Barrett and a little bit beyond. Amebix, which was this English Black Sabbath–influenced crustcore band. And everything from the Germs to bands like Voivod. Weird, experimental metal shit. We literally wrote these names on the wall. Our ideas to use visuals, keyboards—all that stuff was all established right at that point.

Dave Ed: We came up with a whole plan without even trying. And what we came to was, let's make this the band that we're going to be in for the rest of our lives.

Scott Kelly: We would do this until we were dead. And that remains the commitment. We will go until one or all of us is gone. And that will be the end of it. We were completely obsessed with leaving a mark. And also submitting ourselves to music, and letting music become us.

Dave Ed: I was about 16 when we started Neurosis.

Scott Kelly: I was possibly 18. Jason was 15.

Martin Brohm: Dave Ed's dad taught drafting in a math class in El Sobrante. He was a funny guy. He walked in one day and threw a cassette tape at me. It bounced off my head, landed on my desk. He said, "My son does this crap. It sounds like hell, but you might like it." It was the old Neurosis demo tape.

Noah Landis: I saw the very first Neurosis show back in 1986. I think Victim's Family played.

Sham Saenz: Man, the early days, the first shows. Neurosis was always a good band. Dave is a fuckin' amazing bass player. They

The Word as Law: Scott Kelly from Neurosis

got Steve Von Till in the band, and it was like the perfect key that they needed.

Kate Knox: Early Neurosis shows were absolutely amazing.

Anna Brown: People were writhing around on the floor. Not in like a Crash Worship–hippie kind of way, but in a "I can't contain myself this is so exciting!" kind of way. They had 20 totally epic songs that they would play, and people would just go fuckin' crazy. They played a lot, too. They were sort of an anchor.

Billie Joe Armstrong: There was an entire scene of people around them—this Oakland punk rock scene that included them and Christ on Parade. Neurosis were really scary.

Noah Landis: Scott and Dave both sang. Dave has within him the ultimate Cookie Monster voice. I don't know where it comes from. And Scott has a real intensity in his soul. Everything that comes out of him is real. He is not trying to do anything, it's just what is inside of him getting out.

Billie Joe Armstrong: One night Scott Kelly had a brand-new baby, and the mother and the baby were sitting onstage and the crowd was just going berserk. Someone did a stage dive and nearly kicked the baby. It was a brand-new baby, I don't even think it was six months old. Scott just lost it. He jumped into the crowd and just started beating this guy. Then he jumped back onstage and said, "That's my baby, man!" I remember thinking, there is a new life here. It was art and punk and children. There were kids from the suburbs, kids from Berkeley, and these old ex-hippie, Vietnam-era guys—all percolating in the same spot.

Adrienne Droogas: You'd get so swept up in the music and all the punks would be singing every single song. Before I was singing in Spitboy, I came up to Scott and said, "Hey, do you mind if I get up and sing part of 'Blister' with you?" And he said, "You see that microphone over there? That's your microphone whenever you want." I was all nervous but they started playing the song and I jumped up and started singing along, and then Noah from Christ on Parade jumped up and he started singing along, and then we did stage dives. They were just an awesome band.

Greg Valencia: At that time, Neurosis was the shit. They were the big Bay Area love.

Anna Brown: My dad thought it was funny that my favorite band was called Neurosis. He was the head of the psychiatric unit at the hospital. So Dave Ed gave him a Neurosis T-shirt and he wore it to the hospital Christmas party. He thought that was hilarious.

Noah Landis: Christ on Parade was intense, but we were fast and we had hooks. What Neurosis was doing was a lot darker, a lot deeper and a lot *meaner*. During that time, Neurosis was broadening its idea of what they were doing.

Jeff Ott: Both Christ on Parade and Neurosis started to head in a direction of intentionally doing dissonant music. But Neurosis was also about complicated songwriting and musicianship. The drive was, "Let's go further out than this." They were never going to find a formula and stick with it.

Scott Kelly: Christ on Parade's last show at Gilman never fucking happened because of us. The fuckin' fights were so bad that they had to shut down the show.

Ben Sizemore: It disintegrated into a big brawl. It seemed like every asshole skinhead in the Bay Area showed up. Econochrist played that show, and some skinhead girl with a fringe jumped up onstage while we were playing and tried to hit me. Neurosis was supposed to play right before Christ on Parade, and they couldn't get through a song without a fight breaking out. I remember Scott so famously saying, "Alright! Next fucking fight that breaks—" and of course a fight broke out. They stopped playing and then it spilled out onto the street, and before you knew it, the cops were there and the show was shut down. Christ on Parade never got to play their last show at Gilman. Later that night, they played at their house for 20 people instead of 600. By that point, most of them were living in a house by the Oakland Greyhound station.

Scott Kelly: These guys loved to fight to our music. It was a fucking disease that we just couldn't get rid of. We had to show up at gigs with our own security. We had a couple of guys that I worked with who were 'Nam vets, special ops guys.

Then we added keyboards. It wasn't a conscious move to eliminate the violence from the shows, but those guys didn't want anything to do with that. It was the funniest thing. Add keyboards, the fight's over. When we showed up with keyboards, people left before we'd even played a note.

Noah Landis: People were pissed. They were into Neurosis because it was the most intense hardcore band in the area. Then they put a keyboard out there and this new guy that nobody knew. People were just totally bummed. They were hurling insults, they were calling them Faith No More.

I stood there on the side of the stage watching this irate crowd. Unfortunately, it just took the guy forever to set up the keyboard. It felt like it was never gonna end, because he was building this whole contraption with little monkey bars. It was painful to witness.

Davey Havok: When Neurosis busted out the keyboard, it was like, "What are they, fuckin' Flock of Seagulls?" It confused people. It was no longer punk rock because—ignoring the Screamers or Suicide—punk rock didn't have keyboards. Neurosis was serious and brutal and dark and heavy and hard. And keyboards didn't fit into the perception people had of Neurosis. Which was a shame.

Noah Landis: For years there was a huge divide in the Neurosis fans. There were people who only listened to the first two albums, and everything after was crap. Anything with keyboards was crap.

Scott Kelly: Gilman was definitely our place for awhile. We played opening weekend and three of the first four benefits. Then, around '91, when *Souls at Zero* came out, they decided that we weren't punk enough to play there. They passed judgment on us the same time *Maximum RocknRoll* did. I remember calling up Tim, "Why won't you review us in your magazine anymore?"

"Well, you guys aren't punk rock. You guys are like fuckin' Yes. You play like ten-minute songs."

"What's the definition of punk rock?"

"Three chords and a cloud of dust, Scott."

It was so funny. I was like, man, you're a fuckin' hardheaded old bastard. But I respected that. In a way, it freed us from that entire dogmatic political scene. Which, in my opinion, never had anything to do with music.

Noah Landis: Simon, their keyboard player, wasn't involved in New Method or punk rock. He didn't share any of that history with the band. He was a guy with a keyboard that Steve knew from the South Bay. They couldn't hack it with him. When they came home from the tour, they kicked him out.

Scott Kelly: We quickly absorbed Noah. There were no walls.

Noah Landis: I said yes because it was bigger than any band I'd ever been in by that point, really powerful and unique. They were my best and oldest friends and I wanted to make music with them. But I was also on drugs. The early '90s were the darkest years in my life, as far as getting into speed and losing that ability to care about yourself or the person you're with. Everything becomes, "Fuck it!" Except your friends who are doing drugs with you.

I got a sampler and a keyboard and hung out with Scott, both of us just tweaked to the gills, pathetically pushing buttons. I felt like maybe I can't do this, maybe I've challenged myself beyond my ability. It was terrifying. Like being boiled in water or something. But I figured it out. Then things got really creative.

Kate Knox: Neurosis was one of the first bands that had that slower— what I call napcore.

Scott Kelly: We thought we can do whatever the fuck we want. Are we playing that too long? Well, it feels good to me, who gives a shit? Slow? Fast? It didn't matter. We fed off each other.

A. C. Thompson: I saw them in San Francisco. It was this totally mind-blowing, dark Bacchanalian event. You expected to see people killing one another or fucking each other in a mass orgy on the floor. You thought it might actually happen. They were so cinematic. It was like heavy soundtrack music.

Noah Landis: We've been doing this for so long, together through great times and hard times. Through children and divorces and marriages and serious losses.

Scott Kelly: And we're still doing our own thing. We put out our own records, we book our own shows. We learned to do that from the people who did it before us and showed us how. We're holding the torch for that.

Ben Saari: When I hear the name Neurosis, I get . . . It's sort of how I feel about my early girlfriends. Like every really important period of my life.

32

Sleep, What's That?

Andy Asp: Hardcore might have been really refreshing and exciting the first couple years, but nobody wanted to call themselves a punk band anymore. Punk became kind of this dirty word.

Jesse Michaels: In the early '80s there were fights at every show. People stood around and watched people kick the shit out of each other. You hear all these people talking about the hardcore days, how great it was. How great is watching five people beat one person up?

Then there was a dead period. This little pocket of weird kids were getting into punk, and it actually was a very creative and open thing happening.

Frank Portman: Crimpshrine was a strange marriage between Jeff Ott, who was the crazy voice and as close to a modern-day hippie as you could get, and Aaron Elliott, this really great writer who wrote the lyrics and was the drummer. Not really derived from anything. Destined for self-destruction, but this brilliance behind it.

Jeff Ott: Everything was very masculine then, and very angry and aggressive. What we did took punk rock into a very watered-down direction. People went, "Oh, that's melodic. It doesn't have to be all this angry, dissonant thing."

Anna Brown: Jeff Ott was like a messiah. A strong sense of justice. A born preacher. Very charismatic and very confident about the ways of the world, lots of ideas about things. Some of his ideas were just nuts, but compellingly crazy. Jeff took a *lot* of acid.

Jesse Michaels: Me and my friends followed Crimpshrine all over the place. They were a huge influence.

Photo by Murray Bowles

Quit Talkin' Claude: Jesse Michaels singing along with
Crimpshrine's Jeff Ott

Jeff Ott: I grew up in Berkeley. When I was 10 or 11, I met John Kiffmeyer and Aaron Cometbus. Dave Edwardson lived a few blocks away up in the Berkeley Hills with his parents. Arnie from my soccer team, his father was Wes Robinson, who ran Ruthie's Inn. We'd end up at soccer team functions at my house, and Wes would be checking me out, listening to Journey. He told me, "Dude, you should check out Motörhead."

John Fogerty's kids hung out with us. They're the reason I started getting high. After the band [Creedence] broke up, John Fogerty lived in between Dave Edwardson's house and my house. He had a band called Ruby, who played for my third-grade class. I thought they were great 'cause I had never seen live music before.

I was a straight-A student, and in between 13 and 15, I got

expelled. Did some back and forth in terms of living with my family. My parents were fairly checked out anyway. They were just interested in viticulture and drinking the by-products of it, namely.

Aaron Cometbus: A lot of us, like Noah Landis, Dave Ed, Jesse Michaels, Tim Armstrong and me, we'd grown up together and played in each other's bands. Most of the bands never even played shows, but they were still in the scene reports in early issues of *Cometbus* and they were on the compilation tapes I put out.

Ben Saari: I think it was Aaron Elliott, Jesse Michaels and Jeff Ott, they were called Trampled by Fish. And then Jesse went out to the East Coast, so it was just Aaron and Jeff, and they were shopping for a third wheel forever. It was Tim Armstrong for awhile.

Jeff Ott: We had this weird bassist guy who turned out to be in disguise. Had a wig that was like glued. And then he disappeared. Shortly after that we found Pete at Berkeley High, and it became Crimpshrine. The first show was at New Method. We'd all go across the street and get high, and there was this girl who crimped her hair all the time, I believe her name was Maya.

Lenny Filth: Crimped-out fuckin' blond hair that was just gorgeous. Aaron had a crush on her, but he never went up and talked to her.

Jeff Ott: Aaron was like, "We should call the band Crimpshrine." And basically named the band after her hair. This was like '84. I imagine by now somebody's told her there's this band named after her.

We played New Method, Own's Pizza, the Farm. We played shows with Soup at the Unitarian Universalist churches in Kensington and Albany. Always at Unitarian churches, though, 'cause they're all communists.

Ben Saari: They really personalized a lot of the songwriting. Until that point, people had been writing about the big outside world. They were more introverted and introspective.

Anna Brown: These incredibly impassioned lyrics that were about getting through life, about hope and despair at the same time. They were really catchy and raw. When you listen to them now, they're still great.

Jesse Michaels: And they were just fun to watch. The shows were really small. It was almost more like parties more than real shows.

Anna Brown: Jeff was really tall, thin, bald. You'd see him with this blood running down his head from shaving his head in the bathroom.

Rachel Rudnick: Jeff Ott would take a Bic lighter and burn the excess hair off so it'd be like an inch long. It smelled so bad. He also griped about his older brother, who was a football player. I remember being on the bus and Jeff bragging that he had found the life insurance papers his parents had taken out on their kids, and his was twice as much as his brother.

Aaron Cometbus: It was still a small town and you spent a lot of time just waiting for someone to arrive from out of town and make things more interesting. It was either runaways or people looking to buy large quantities of acid to bring back to wherever they were from. And the punks were involved in that, too. Acid was very much tied into the character and the economy of the scene. It was the main pastime and probably the main livelihood as well.

Billie Joe Armstrong: I lived in a house with Jeff Ott in Richmond. Tré lived there, too. There were a few college kids living there, but slowly the punks started to infiltrate. Everybody would be up all night on acid, and the students had to get up to go to school in the morning. Eventually, they moved out. I remember at one point we ran out of firewood, and Jeff starting chopping down the stairs outside the house. We just burned that.

James Washburn: The first time I ever saw Crimpshrine was in the basement at Jake Filth's house. That was a fuckin' awesome show. Aaron Elliott was just such a fuckin' unusual drummer. Zero drummer type skills but a badass drummer at the same time. The guy'd sit down with pots and pans and just go off. I thought he was an asshole. I don't remember why, but that was my impression. I always felt like, I'm from Pinole, and these guys are from Berkeley, so they're cooler than me. We became accepted later.

Ben Saari: At Berkeley High, by the end of the '85–'86 school year we had written "Crimpshrine" on every single locker, every single desktop. There was a reward for whoever was writing "Crimpshrine," so we got a bunch of those "Hello My Name Is" stickers and wrote "Crimpshrine" on 'em and started handing 'em out in the hallway. Some fucking dupe decided he wanted the 50 dollars. So he turned me and Jeff in, and we got suspended, and that led to me getting sent to the Oakland school system. Jeff ended up getting institutionalized shortly after that.

That was a fucked-up thing. There was this shrink in Albany who was getting kickbacks from an insurance company for institutionalizing kids. My parents and Jeff's parents were going to her. She locked up a whole slew of punk rock kids.

Noah Landis: Jeff Ott had horror stories about the way his parents reacted when they found out he was doing drugs. Piss tests and institutionalization and that kind of stuff. I remember going to shows way out in the city at Club Foot—hard place to get to when you're a kid—and his parents would show up to give kids rides home. So we'd all pile into this little minivan, and then they'd drive through the Berkeley Hills and drop people off at three o'clock in the morning. They just didn't know what the fuck to do. Their kid is on drugs and going out with other kids on drugs. You piss-test him, institutionalize him, and you drive his friends home.

Ben Saari: Then Jeff was going to some alternative school out in Concord. Nobody was in regular contact with him. He ended up back at Berkeley High.

Anna Brown: Jeff would take you up to campus where we would climb up the sides of these buildings. He had devised these weird ways to climb backwards up between two buildings, doing a crab walk.

Jeff Ott: I was up at Telegraph all day, when there wasn't a band function. Kids run away from somewhere else, and it was like, okay, here's a free breakfast, now what? Well, we could go climb buildings.

Anna Brown: He had memorized every inch of the campus before any of us had ever set foot in there. There is a network of tunnels underneath the campus, steam tunnels where people lived in the winter. We would steal marbles from the Earth Science building and roll them down the hills, or just take a bunch of acid and go into Wurster Hall.

Jeff Ott: We had a mural done with spray paint by Jesse and this white rapper kid, Josh. "Crimpshrine," like 30 feet long. Totally beautiful, New York subway style, across the top of Wurster Hall. Up there all night, just tripping on acid, watching them make this thing. You know, "Jesse, make us a mural!"

Ben Saari: We'd go to the top of the top floor of Eshleman, where all the student activist groups had their offices. We would go there and grab all the recycled paper, and go to the top of the student union and make paper airplanes, if we were coherent enough to do that, and just throw 'em all day. Or if we were too fucked up, we would just wad paper up and throw it down into the courtyard.

Jeff Ott: At the architecture building, there was a big grate that shot up air really fast. So you could pour water and it would come out and go up.

Anna Brown: Crimpshrine and Operation Ivy played a bunch of shows in laundromats for awhile. They would just show up at a laundromat and start playing.

Jeff Ott: Sweet Baby Jesus and some other bands started making little stickers that they put on matchbooks. It was this little cartoon guy and it said, "Crimpsoupocracy." So we had multi-band matchbooks.

Davey Havok: We were all so fascinated by "Summertime" by Crimpshrine because it referenced our county, Mendocino County. He was specifically referring to Mendocino the town, which was over the hill on the water.

Jeff Ott: When Crimpshrine did the first record, *Sleep, What's That?* was the obvious thing, because I was living outside and Aaron didn't sleep, except in the daytime a little bit. So then it was obvious to call the next record *Quit Talkin' Claude* because we were just saying it all the time.

Claude was Ben Owens, he hung out with Op Ivy and Crimpshrine and everybody else. He was from El Cerrito, this 14-year-old walking around with people who are just trying to get drunk or whatever.

Janelle Hessig: Claude was really crazy-eyed and talked constantly, and would always be twitching and fumbling all the time.

Jeff Ott: He would go on the most bizarre tangents. He would find out about this new drug DMSO that somebody just invented—"It makes this and this and this happen." Then he'd go, "Oh, I've been researching Aleister Crowley," and dadadadada. And then it would be like, "Oh, and this guy, he's trying to find the grand unified theory in quantum mechanics."

People were like, "Oh, shut up, Claude. I don't wanna hear about all that." So "quit talking Claude" became a phrase you'd use when somebody was talking about something too much. He became a figure of speech.

Cammie Toloui: Totally out of his mind. I thought he was doing too much acid. One time at the radio show, Claude was doing his best to get a piece of string to go in his mouth and out his nose. There was some point where he was arrested for walking naked down a median in the middle of Berkeley.

Jeff Ott: I hadn't seen him in eight years. And I went to pick up my older daughter in Berkeley, and here came Claude walking up the street. I ran over and said, "What's going on?" And that day he had passed the bar exam. Everyone was fuckin' telling him to shut up, and he's a lawyer now.

Mike K: I remember when Crimpshrine and Operation Ivy played their last shows before this tour. It was this crazy thing, like they were getting into a spaceship. We were thinking, this is part of our culture and what we were part of, and all this was going out and encountering weird alien life-forms along the way. And they would come back with great artifacts.

Andy Asp: Their legendary Pinto tour. Basically two guys, on Crimpshrine's first tour, said, "Fuck this! Fuck you! We're goin' home."

Ben Saari: When Jeff, Pete, Aaron and Idon got to Florida, Idon and Pete bailed. Paul Curran drove out, picked them up in a Pinto station wagon, and did the tour with 'em. In a Pinto—that wouldn't go any faster than 45 miles an hour. They finished the tour. This is how for real those guys were.

Aaron Cometbus: A station wagon? No way. It was a tiny-ass Pinto hatchback. In a station wagon we could have fit two bands.

Ben Saari: When Pete and Idon came back, nobody would talk to those guys. It was like, "You motherfuckers, you bailed. You did the one thing you're not supposed to do, you got homesick and you quit and you came home." That went on for months.

Andy Asp: That story had an impact on our work ethic. Don't put on any airs if the P.A. doesn't sound good, or you thought it was gonna be different. Doesn't matter. That's the show biz part of it, that you can't get too high and mighty about: "We didn't know this Nazi band was on the bill." Just play the fuckin' show. The Pinto tour was legendary.

Adam Pfahler: There was a certain amount of innocence in Crimpshrine. The songs were awesome. It was all very simple and there was something really innocent and raw about it. And there was a lot of strength in that. So when people started getting hooked on dope and stuff, it was depressing.

Sergie Loobkoff: I was never around Jeff Ott when he wasn't fucked up on some kind of acid, or really high, or drunk. He was a mumbler and would say non sequiturs to get a reaction out of you. Like people on acid often do.

I didn't realize that wasn't his personality as much as his state of mind at the time. He just went into drugs and that defined him. And when I met him as an adult he was really soft-spoken and totally sober. I was like, "Oh wow, this guy has a completely different personality that's nothing remotely like that." That's really trippy.

Jeff Ott: I stopped doing a band in '96. After being sober for a year, it dawned on me that for the first time in my life I didn't have to be in a band. Before that, that was all I ever did. I got high and I did bands. And all of a sudden I was sober. It was like one day I woke up and I was like, "I don't have to be in a band. Okay, I'm not."

33

Journey to the End of the East Bay

Frank Portman: The club was an East Bay idea. It involved a lot of the people who had put on random shows at various places. There was a pizza place on Shattuck called Own's Pizza. That was how the owner, who was Pakistani or something, spelled "Owen." One of my band's first shows was there. It was promoted by Kamala Parks.

Kamala Parks: When I started doing shows, this other guy named Victor Hayden and I combined forces. I'd book the shows and he'd find places for us to have shows. He was very supportive. He and I worked together well. I was probably about 17. It was a very unlikely combination.

Frank Portman: Victor was much like a lot of these eccentric older guys with pompadours who always gravitated towards these places. You just looked at him and you thought, "Wow, what is this weird Liberace guy doing at this pizza place?" I'm not making any kind of accusation. I'm sure he's a very nice man. But you know how Liberace could play a *Star Trek* villain? He was like that, to me. One minute he's talking about, "Oh, I really love your band's set." The next minute he's tying you to a giant chess piece. You were always a little bit wary of it.

Larry Livermore: Victor was extraterrestrial. A little bit spacey, like a hippie. But also very idealistic. He and Kamala were good buddies. Victor found Own's Pizza. I said, "I'll help out. Can our band play?" The show went off really well. It was Victim's Family, Nomeansno from Canada, Mr. T Experience, a really young thrash band from Marin County called Complete Disorder, and the Lookouts. Tré would have been 13. I'm pretty sure his parents came down. Afterwards Victor and I were sort of glowing about how great it was, and he said, "We've got to find a place where we could do this all the time."

Kamala Parks: Victor and I had done stuff at New Method, we had done stuff at Own's Pizza, we had done stuff at this practice place in San Francisco. But inevitably the show would get shut down by the fire department or the police department. It was incredibly frustrating, because these people would see big crowds of people, think it was a moneymaker and come to find that it wasn't a moneymaker, and so then they'd get angry and lose interest.

Victor and I started talking about finding a place. We knew *Maximum RocknRoll* was trying to find a place at the same time, but they were dead set on finding something in San Francisco. Victor and I were focusing on the East Bay.

Martin Sprouse: Nobody was at odds. We were all friends. I thought everybody was looking for the place together. Victor had been looking at other buildings.

Kamala Parks: Our plan was, we were going to be completely open with the owners about what our intentions were: "We're gonna have a punk club here because we're sick of getting kicked out by the owners, of the place freaking out wherever we were booked." We wanted it to be completely up to code, and aboveboard. Because it was obviously not working to do it as underground as we had been doing it.

Ruthie's Inn wasn't really part of the punk scene. The Mabuhay Gardens wasn't owned by anyone in the punk scene. You still felt like you were still under the whims and desires of people who didn't understand us. So when Victor and I were looking for a place, as well as *Maximum RocknRoll*, there was a sense of, let's be involved on every single level, including running the place.

Larry Livermore: About two, three weeks after the Own's Pizza show, Victor got in touch with the Caning Shop warehouse.

Kamala Parks: Victor actually tried to scare the owner, and told him, "We wanna do punk shows here." And the guy was like, "Oh! That would be great because I actually don't want anything going on here during the day, because we have our caning shop." Victor was like, "There's gonna be people with mohawks." And the guy said, "I *like* that idea." I went and looked at it, and it was the perfect space, the perfect size. At that time that area of Berkeley was really just warehouses. The closest neighbors were a block away.

The idea was that Victor and I would run it. But we didn't have the money. So that's when he contacted Tim, and just begged and pleaded and insisted on bringing him to see Gilman. Tim was like, "No, I wanna do something in San Francisco, I don't wanna do something in the East Bay."

Larry Livermore: I think Tim was kind of taken aback at having it actually presented to him. I didn't know them that well yet, but I know Tim put up a fair bit of resistance at first.

Kamala Parks: I think Victor actually drove over there and forced him into his car and took him there. And when Tim saw the place and met the owner, I think that's when the wheels really started turning for him.

Larry Livermore: We're looking at June of '86. Victor said, "I gotta talk Tim into getting behind it, 'cause he's the only one who's got the money to make it happen." We figured it would take at least 10,000.

Kamala Parks: Obviously Tim's vision really differed from what Victor and I had thought. It was very similar to *Maximum RocknRoll*, in the idea that Tim was really behind everything and really making the decisions. But modeled on the same principles, which was completely volunteer run. So it involved bringing in a lot more people than Victor and I had envisioned, and running it on these principles. Which Victor and I didn't necessarily agree with.

Martin Sprouse: A club, run by the people, for the people. That really didn't exist. Tim wanted to make it 100 percent independent and consistent. And on the up and up. You know, not a squat. Totally legal.

Larry Livermore: It took Victor a few weeks, but he finally got Tim to throw in *Maximum RocknRoll*'s fortunes with it.

Martin Sprouse: That guy who owns the building is the reason why Gilman's still there.

Jim Widess: I had a sign up. Tim Yohannan came by. He was personable. Obviously loved kids, had a huge heart. It was definitely a philanthropic idea for him. Clearly he wasn't going to make any money from it. But he was very dedicated.

He was going to have to get permits from the city. And we both knew there was going to be a problem getting the city to go along with it. As it turned out, it didn't seem to be that uphill. They presented a good proposal.

I was also hungry for a tenant. Definitely we didn't want another automobile repair place on Gilman. What Tim was proposing was a perfect use of the space. They would be there at night, we were here in the daytime. Our parking didn't conflict with each other. He could make all the noise he wanted and it wouldn't affect us. They were willing to pay the rent we needed. There certainly wasn't any downside for me as a landlord. Plus, I felt what he was doing was a really important thing for the community.

They were going to have to invest quite a bit into the space to bring it up to code for a club. There was one small bathroom in there which needed to be made into two—and both of them, obviously, wheelchair accessible. And wiring. The plumbing was the major expense for them. Tim carried insurance, in case there were any problems. Everything was very aboveboard. The kids did most of the work.

Frank Portman: My dad was a general contractor and had agreed to donate some materials. A lot of people's dads were involved.

Martin Sprouse: Frank's dad brought in the toilets, helped do the plumbing. The Guys In Black, these total punk rock anarchist guys, they built all the walls. Tommy Strange, who moved out here from Ohio, helped build the stage. People came in to help do the sound system, put the soundproofing all over. People came from everywhere. Men, women, everything. It was so diverse.

Dave Mello: Me and my brother dug the bathroom trenches. That was pretty fun.

Lenny Filth: Me, all the guys from Operation Ivy, all the guys from Isocracy, tons of other people. All the people from *Maximum Rock-nRoll*, Kamala, we all helped build that place. Put in the plumbing, put up the walls, built the stage, built the loft, all that stuff.

James Washburn: I made the Gilman safe in my shop class, and then bolted it into the soundboard. I painted it all primer black and put "924 Gilman" on it, "Keep Out." Welded a big ol' lock on it.

Larry Livermore: I almost electrocuted myself doing some wiring. It was 240 volts. Luckily I was in sneakers and up an aluminum ladder, so it only felt like a twinge.

Cammie Toloui: I took BART from Concord every weekend with my bike and rode over there. I did things like nail screws into the stage.

A. C. Thompson: I grew up in the suburbs outside of Washington D.C. When you read *Maximum RocknRoll* in '87 and heard about Gilman, how it was based on this utopian, DIY ethos that you could actually launch a project based on alternative principles and create an institution that isn't driven by the normal imperatives of capitalism—that was just crazy. There were photos of people working on it, and there was all this hype: It's run by the punks, for the punks, and it's cheap and it's gonna be so cool! And we were all so amazed because somehow this had never occurred to us before.

Matt Wobensmith: I read about Gilman through *Maximum* and it's like, oh my god, Gilman is a place you can go and people will be nice to you. In contrast to what I was used to in rural Pennsylvania, which was being beat up by and bullied by these fucking scary-ass Philly thug motherfuckers. And Gilman, they'll fucking give you a cupcake when you walk in the door. That's what you thought.

Orlando X: We volunteered to go around the neighborhood to let folks know that Gilman was opening up, to get their support. People invited us into their homes and asked us about the club, and we would tell them about it. I wore a hat. We didn't want to freak the people out.

Al Ennis: I was working at Down Home Music in El Cerrito and I met Tim down at Ashby Lumber. I was buying stuff to fix up my house and Tim was down there buying stuff for this club. He said, "Oh, Al, you have to come by, we're opening up this club, Gilman Street." That was my first inkling that that was going on. It was a real community effort, and all these kids were pitching together, and it was gonna be a club! And then he told me, "We're not even going to advertise the bands! It's just gonna be, you show up because it's Gilman Street, and whoever's there is gonna be a good punk band." They were gonna give everyone equal pay, it was all total equality. I thought it was very in keeping with what he wanted to do.

Sergie Loobkoff: I was a lazy little brat. I tell people, "Yeah, I helped build Gilman." But a couple of people were doing all the real work, and people like me were hanging around.

34

10 Seconds of Anarchy

Billie Joe Armstrong: Isocracy was like the house band.

Larry Livermore: They were like the kings of Gilman. They were *the* band until Op Ivy came along.

Martin Brohm: It was a group of us who didn't really know punk rock at all. A student named Mark Carroll was the local skater guy. The first record I got from him was Black Flag's *Damaged*. I was like, "Uh, this is kinda heavy." So he gave me a Go-Go's tape instead. I was like, well, this isn't *quite* enough, you know. I need something in the middle.

Back then, El Sobrante was maybe 10,000. It's very small townish. People who have never been to San Francisco because they would get AIDS. It's 15 miles from San Francisco, but a totally different world.

Jason Beebout: You walked down the street in El Sobrante and there's heshers, rednecks and douchebags. If you made eye contact with anybody, it was a fight. So I learned how not to look at people.

John Geek: Exodus, Possessed and Metallica all had members from West Contra Costa County. That was one of the birthplaces of thrash.

Jason Beebout: Everyone had a story: "I was walkin' down the street one time, garage door's open? It was fuckin' Metallica, practicin'—before the Black Album!"

Lenny, Martin and John had a band. A guy named Leroy was trying to sing for awhile. He wanted to play guitar and that made Lenny irritated, so Leroy was out of the band. And then John told them about me, said I would be the singer. I was 15. I literally didn't know what was the end or the beginning of a song. It just sounded like fuckin' noise to me. But I was like, "Yeah, that's great, man, I'm in." They had to step on my foot to tell me when to start singin' and step on it again to tell me when to stop.

Lenny Filth: Me and my bass player busted into the back of a couple arcade machines at the pizza place that we worked at. We stole all the quarters. That's how we bought our first instruments.

Martin Brohm: I'm not gonna say anything to incriminate myself. So no, I was not involved in that at all! We worked in a pizza place, there were a few goings-on there that maybe weren't legal but benefited us monetarily. Hey, when you're 18 years old, you're not floating in it.

Jason Beebout: We were Russian Anarchists On Dope before we were Isocracy. We practiced for three months in a garage before our first show. Lenny's stepdad would have a carcass of a deer he'd just slaughtered in the refrigerator next to the Fanta soda pops. It was really odd.

Martin Brohm: Later on, Larry Livermore interviewed us for *Maximum RocknRoll*. He was talking to Lenny about playing guitar, and

Photo by Murray Bowies

The Thing That Ate Floyd: Isocracy at Gilman

Lenny said, "Yeah, things really started coming together when I started playing chords." Larry said, "Chords?" "Yeah, you know, two strings." That tells you what we knew about music.

Jason Beebout: John was a really charismatic person and he found Victor Hayden from Alchemy Records, I don't know how. Victor came up to see us in Lenny's garage, in El Sobrante. He was like, "This is outrageous, you guys are fuckin' phenomenal!" We're like, "Really? Wow! Cool!"

Martin Brohm: I think a big part of the appeal about us was—

Jason Beebout: It was so bad.

Martin Brohm: Well, that, and just four fuckin' loser kids from this loser fuckin' town.

Jason Beebout: John changed the name to Operation Ivy. He had some code book of military operations, and I guess Operation Ivy was the one when they bombed the Bikini Islands. And then, according to John, he put his finger in a dictionary, blindly. When he hit "Isocracy" it was a political word, so that was perfect. I thought it sounded like '60s soft rock, like the Association or something.

We practiced at my grandma's dry cleaners, and we worked out a set. "Confederate Flags" was a big one. "Stabbed in the Groin" was always a plus because we'd switch instruments, and I'd play bass and Martin would sing, and Martin was a really amazing front man.

Martin Brohm: The lyrics went something like this: "Stabbed in the groin, stabbed in the groin." There's so many great songs that never got recorded . . .

As I remembered, it started off wearing pink suits, ruffled shirts, or dressing up as women. And then I think John went and got a bunch of fucked-up stuff.

Jason Beebout: Just before we played our first show at Gilman, John said, "We're gonna stop and grab some shit out of a dumpster." Everything he does, at least part of his mind has a little bit of theater behind it: "This is gonna be hilarious, people are gonna look at this."

Jesse Michaels: He was an instigator. John has a lot of energy and was always doing weird things. He had this thing where he would never drive over 55 miles an hour. Just, never, under any circumstances, no matter how late they were or how far they had to go. He also would park the van with one tire on the curb. That was just par for the course.

Martin Brohm: An Isocracy show would be 40 minutes long, with probably three songs played. The rest of the time, we were throwing shit out in the crowd.

Lenny Filth: Al would disappear for a couple hours. It was like, "Where the fuck is Al? Set up his drums, Jesus Christ."

Martin Brohm: It was mostly John and Jason driving around in John's VW van, finding crap. I remember they found these huge rolls of plastic wrap, four feet tall and three feet deep.

Jason Beebout: That was one of the worst. We stopped at a burrito processing plant, got giant rolls of this really thin cellophane. We started rollin' 'em out, and they became this bouncy blob that took over the floor of Gilman. It was great because you could dive off the stage onto it, like a trampoline. But then if you got tangled up it was horrible.

Lenny Filth: I was playing guitar and somebody wrapped one around my neck, and I got pulled off the stage by this giant roll of plastic.

Mike K: I remember being on the bottom of the plastic wrap and being smooshed by Dave MDC wearing an Elvis suit. He jumped off the stage. For a teenage kid, that's a pretty big guy to have smoosh you.

Martin Brohm: Matt Freeman went back to help clean up the next day, and this wad of shit was too big to pull out the door.

Matt Freeman: That was probably the show that pissed me off the most. There was shit everywhere. Obviously someone had tried to put it in bags and they just gave up. It was just like, "Oh man, you fuckin' people!" Finally I went to the Gilman meeting and I said, "Look, I think that I should get into one show free if I'm gonna do this. And when Isocracy plays I get two shows." They voted on it, "Okay."

I took that shit hella seriously. This little person, James the Crack Midget. He lived down the street, he would meet me down there and do this stuff. I was like 22 and he was my buddy. We got along fine.

Tim Armstrong: That sounds like a TV show. *Matt and the Crack Midget.*

Mike K: Al would roll his VW bus up to the side of Gilman. You never knew what was going to start pouring out of the side of the thing.

Jason Beebout: We'd pile everything inside the room, and then John set up his drums, and we started dragging our shit onstage. There was so much anticipation: "What's in *that* bag?"

Anna Brown: One time Isocracy threw like a hundred dictionaries off the stage.

Jeff Ott: Reams and reams and reams of recycled paper.

Christopher Appelgren: Little tiny scraps of paper with handwritten messages about the band, that would be flying amidst all this other trash and clothes and weird things: "Isocracy Rules."

Jeff Ott: Like, a hundred Big Wheels. But it was really good. Macho, scary-looking punk rockers riding around on Big Wheels.

Jason Beebout: Slither decided to help out one day by bringing a fuckin' 50-pound bag of kitty litter. He just whiffed it up in the air. Everyone was gasping for air and gagging. It sapped all the moisture out of your tongue. It was fucked.

Martin Brohm: It was horrible. In the middle of summer, 200 kids sweating, and then kitty litter coming down on them.

Dallas Denery: One show they brought hundreds of cigars and everybody started smoking them.

Martin Brohm: Cigar night. That was rough. The cheapest fuckin' cigars you could buy. All going at the same time.

Dallas Denery: They had to stop the show and open up the doors. And they banned cigars from the club.

Lenny Filth: We played this one show in Santa Rosa, it was just toilet paper flying everywhere. It was a fun, fun show. One of the biggest shows we ever played. There was like 400 people there.

Jason Beebout: People tell me, "Oh, I love Isocracy, I have that record!" You actually listened to the record? Going to the show I understand. It was fun to watch, but I'm not gonna sit there, tapping my toe.

Tim Armstrong: That Isocracy shit, that was it. Them guys came in with that vibe, it made them really fun. Just throwin' shit around, everyone jumping on each other. It was a celebration, man, it was fuckin' awesome.

Sergie Loobkoff: No one gave two shits about any of the music. It was all about, what are they gonna do? And what funny dorky shit are they gonna say? They barely knew how to play.

Frank Portman: No real club would have booked something like that. It was sophomoric, but kind of lovable. If you were in high school and there were some goofball drama people who decided to do a rock band stunt, it would be like that.

Mike K: The sense of humor was pretty sophisticated for teenage kids. Making fun of the ritualization of this tough-guy mosh pit stuff.

Jesse Michaels: The hardcore stuff got so ridiculous, you couldn't not make fun of it. Isocracy were especially funny because they were playing hardcore type music but they turned it into a big circus, and it was hilarious and it worked. They were like on acid without acid.

Jason Beebout: We realized that the only thing that was fun about it was throwing shit at people. Lenny really wanted to be in a band like Neurosis, and be serious, and play heavy shit. Martin and I didn't really ever care much about anything, we were just there to have fun.

We were all so naive. I had no clue. As far as I knew, punk rock was the guys on TV. *T. J. Hooker*, comb your sides back and spray-paint the top red. And then play, "Bang your head, bang it hard." I really didn't know. To just play, and realize you're nothing like what people were expecting to see, and be comfortable with that—fuck it, let's just throw shit at them, then.

35

Two Blocks Away

Mike Avilez: Back then, I didn't understand why there were a lot of rules at Gilman Street. Other clubs had no rules. A 12-year-old kid could drink beer. Anything goes at those underground venues. But they all get shut down. Gilman's been a club for over 20 years and it was all the rules that has actually kept it open.

Kamala Parks: This no-advertising policy was to me the stupidest thing in the world. In some ways I understood what they were doing, but the punk scene was so small at that point, why in the world would you want to make it even more obscure to go to this place?

Martin Sprouse: We were doing this secret thing. Meaning like, come to Gilman for Gilman's sake. We wanted people to come there, no matter who played. The clubhouse thing. It was all music based, but we didn't tell people what bands were playing there.

Chicken John: I was with Donny the Punk, in New York. We had heard about Gilman Street. Donny told the Alternative Press and Radio Council and the ABC No Rio people that it would be a good idea if they adopted Gilman's no-advertising policy. My first response was like everybody else's: "That's the stupidest thing I've ever heard." Donny was like, oh no, it would build community. It would make it so that people don't just come for the popular band. The idea is that it would be packed every night.

That was the "aha" moment. I learned more in that 30 seconds about the world than any other 30 seconds or 30 years. Not advertising bands, you're begging for failure. And you only know that you've given 100 percent of yourself when you fail. But it's in the failure that you really learn something, and it makes for a better person, a better human.

Kamala Parks: It was one of those things that just infuriated me. Especially as someone who booked bands on tour. I'd be pissed off if there was a place that was like, "Well, we don't advertise, we just expect people to show up." There was nothing. You were just supposed to go every weekend, Friday and Saturday, and whatever was there was there.

Martin Sprouse: We experimented with a lot of weird ideas. How bands would get paid, how the money was dealt with, the membership policy, what was on the membership card, why we had memberships, security, cleanup, booking. Sunday night or Sunday afternoons would be more art nights, benefits, everything.

There was some things that just didn't fly very well, like the keeping-the-bands-secret thing, and having the bands not talk about whether they were playing there. And no-flyer policies. It was worth a try. But bands fucking hated that shit.

We really tried to break it down. We didn't want any bands coming in there, thinking it was just for them. Where people just pay and watch a band very passively. We challenged that. In some ways it broke down some barriers that might have started building up between band and audience.

The Mindfuck Committee was another cool thing that I wish would have stuck around. Trying to make the shows interesting, trying to mess with things. One thing they did was talking about Apartheid in this really interesting way. Everyone got a South African passport, and people would randomly get arrested during shows. Kind of performance art, kind of political. A lot of great ideas but really hard to implement. Most people just wanted to watch Neurosis play.

Cammie Toloui: I got involved with the Mindfuck Committee. I remember this one. There was a pay phone inside Gilman and we'd pretend like someone was calling. I'd run into the pit and say, "There's a phone call for you." They'd come back and of course you couldn't hear a damn thing, and they'd stand there going, "Hello? Hello? Who is this?" It didn't serve any purpose.

Jesse Michaels: I thought it was really cool to have a great space, and there was a lot of good things about it. But I thought it was a little bit pretend, because it was so sterilized. Normally a punk club didn't have so many rules.

Mike Avilez: No drinking, no homophobia, no sexism. No, no, no. I remember years later, when we played with Dayglo Abortions, the singer said, "Where does it say 'No Canadians'?"

Marshall Stax: There was always a thing about no riders, no contracts, no backstage area. All the clubs you went to, the band would come in the special entrance, you wouldn't see them until they came onstage. Nothing like that at Gilman. The bands walked right offstage and you could walk right up to them. People could get up onstage and sing along with the band. That's something that doesn't go on in a normal club.

Blag Jesus: It breaks down the wall between the artist and the people, and in some ways I guess that's good. But if you've just done 30 shows in a row and you want to take a shit by yourself, it's not that great.

Martin Sprouse: The whole membership card thing was giving us a pass to kick people out who fucked up. If you started a fight, there would be no discussion about throwing you out. If you were a racist, there would be no discussion. You're out. You harassed somebody, you started a fight, "Look, you signed here—fuckin' out."

People didn't understand the membership thing. Like some drunk punk going, "What the fuck you mean, man, I'm not signing this." But if they wanted to get in they had to do it. And there was like some 15-year-old girl at the door, making people buy membership cards. It was fuckin' hilarious.

There were some tense times that first year, because we dealt with a lot of racist fuckin' assholes and skinheads. That whole S.F. Skins, early '80s thing was still going on in the city. After Gilman started, it was like East Bay rich white-kid skinheads, coming from the suburbs. Nobody could go in with Skrewdriver shirts or anything like that. That was a big deciding policy at the beginning of Gilman. It was like, how do we defend ourselves?

That was a really weird time. We had big talks: "Everyone's gonna get baseball bats. There'll be

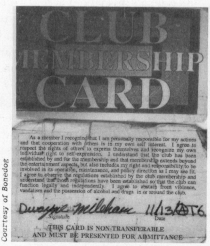

Gilman Street membership card

a hundred baseball bats upstairs." I think that was Tim's. It sounded great, but you just knew it wasn't gonna go down like that. It got shot down so quickly. Everyone said, "Okay, we're just gonna wing it." Just not let these people in. Let the front door be the main thing. Or push people out. And that's how it worked for awhile.

Fat Mike: Once you toured Europe, you saw clubs that are built on the idea of Gilman but a hundred times better. Because they have bars. The Ungdomshuset finally got shut down, but it was a squat in Denmark for—I don't know—20 years? There were clubs at the door. In case there was a brawl, everyone would grab a club and fight.

In Europe, punks fight cops. In Berkeley, everything's a vote. Once at Gilman Street, we were playing with RKL, and three skinheads came. They were big gnarly dudes, terrorized the whole club. There was a lot of volunteers there, and they tried to block the door. And the skinheads just start beating up people. You had 400 people here, against three people? And they wouldn't defend themselves. What the fuck is that?

Frank Portman: Gilman tried these experiments, which really took the idea of putting the bands in their place to a ridiculous degree. If you were gonna be a member, be involved in the club, you had to do work. It was like a co-op, a community. At first they didn't apply it to bands. Then they said, okay, you're not special just because you're in a band—you're part of the whole thing. So they introduced this rule where if you were a band, you had to clean the toilets. Just to show, like, Jesus washing the feet of—it's hard to keep a band together anyway. But there's no way in hell I was going to get my drummer to clean a toilet.

Kamala Parks: As a local band, whenever we would play Gilman we would always donate our money to the out-of-town band. That was generally what local bands did. It was the spirit of Gilman. I thought it was a great idea, personally. You brought everyone into the room and usually they would say, "There's 900 dollars, and we think that 400 of it should go to this band, and 300 to this band 'cause they're out of town."

Frank Portman: That meeting in the back room, where you have to reach a touchy-feely consensus on why you shouldn't be paid, remains one of the most perverse subversions of everything about human nature that you could possibly imagine. We did this big show with Bad Religion, there was a lot of money. The Bad

Religion dude had this awesome speech, about how they should get all the money. "If you add up all the hours we spend into creating our art, it works out to less than minimum wage. Is what we witnessed tonight worth more than minimum wage? I think we'll all agree that it is." I was like, this is awesome, I hope someone's recording it.

Blag Jesus: I always saw the money as chicken feed. I've had some stupid fights over the years about small amounts of money, but I always had a pretty good handle on the fact that we all were getting fucked. Another $10 or $20 wasn't going to make any fucking difference. So we never did much in the way of the haggle. I called it a free show, I just figured, fuck it. Anything we got from them was okay. Nobody was makin' a profit at Gilman.

Kurt Brecht: We were playing at the Omni and they'd pay us $4,000. You didn't wanna go back to Gilman Street and play for 200. These rules where every band gets paid the same. It doesn't matter if you're on tour from Sweden and the other band is just from right around the corner. Tim didn't care. Nobody's headlining. Everybody's name on the flyers should be the same size.

Blag Jesus: But there's a deeper way to look at it, which was that it was more egalitarian in their booking policy, which allowed some other people in. And most venues just weren't doing things that way.

Jason Beebout: Samiam played there one time and I asked for money back because they had Fugazi there. I was pissed because supposedly Fugazi was the be-all, end-all of that mind-set. And it wasn't that way at all. Ian MacKaye was a cock. He came in and stomped his feet and made everyone snap to. It was gross. I was like, "I see how it works. The popular band gets paid and the local band donates." I understand the mind-set of keeping the club going. But when it was a band making a lot of money on tour, it was like, "Why should I donate money to a band that's making plenty of money?"

Martin Sprouse: To us it wasn't about making rules, it was about keeping the place going and legit. We were dealing with the city, dealing with cops, dealing with neighbors, dealing with Nazis. All those rules weren't to tell people how to do it. But just to keep the club going and make it safe. Everyone made fun of that, but who cares? Gilman's still going.

Adrienne Droogas: After awhile Tim stepped back and said, "Okay, do this however you guys wanna do this." They would have people who were 18 or 19, setting up the shows.

I think that they saw it as a chance for punks in the scene to become active, instead of it being this thing where you're just coming and witnessing. It's like, why don't you come here and participate in making that show happen in whatever way you want? Go do whatever you wanna do, spray-paint on the walls, bring in a piece of art, nail it up, do whatever you want, but if you make a mess, just take care of it. If you fuck something up, fix it. That's what they were really trying to encourage.

Tom Jennings: For about a year and a half I was the main coordinator for shows. It was hard work—annoying, stupid and wonderful. I heard 30-plus bands a month for 18 months.

Kamala Parks: Having it be all-volunteer means that people get burned out. When you volunteer, you expect something back, and if you're not getting that something back, then it does make you bitter.

Maximum RocknRoll was a much easier project to run based on that principle. Tim had it down pat how to do things, and if someone flaked out, it was easier for him to pick up the pieces. Whereas it was much harder with Gilman, when you have shows every weekend.

Martin Sprouse: We had meetings on top of meetings on top of meetings. We got old Berkeley hippie people coming in, 'cause we were pushing it as an alternative community center to begin with. And the arty music scene. A lot of eccentric weird people coming in, a lot of local bands. We were trying to do this thing from scratch.

Matt Buenrostro: I remember having a moan about the rules. I said something like, "Can't we just say, 'No drugs, no alcohol. Let's rock and roll!'" Tim Yohannan just ignored me.

Jesse Michaels: People were talking about whether there's too much anti-feminist graffiti in the bathroom. "Should we paint over the graffiti?" "No, that's impinging on free speech!" Just incredibly trifling Berkeley bullshit.

Adrienne Droogas: Tim would say, "Well, we really need the manpower to do this." And someone would go, "Um, we need the people power."

Jason Beebout: "Two Blocks Away." That's one of the things we figured out at the meetings. If you wanted to drink at the club, it had to be at least two blocks away, so there wouldn't be any bottles littering the front of the club.

It was actually Tim Yohannan's idea. "We're gonna get this fuckin' place shut down if we don't explain to people that you have to go two blocks from this place or the cops are gonna bust us." And off the cuff, he said, "Isocracy should write a song about it—Two Blocks Away." We were like, "Done!"

Lenny Filth: That was the whole joke about the "talking bushes." You'd walk by and you'd hear people giggling and drinking and smoking, see smoke comin' outta the bushes. It was like, "Ah, the talking bushes are alive again tonight."

Jeff Ott: The policy on alcohol at the beginning really split everything in half. A lot of people who were into English bands and dressing up more really backed off from it. They would come to shows and drink outside in the car, and people who were volunteering security would be like, "You're in trouble." I think we could have just had a light that went on if the cops pulled up outside. We could have never even had the policy at all.

Maximum RocknRoll was like, "This is the prototype for a club in America." I think people really misinterpreted that. The people who started it thought that if we keep alcohol and drugs out of the place completely, we won't end up getting shut down by the police. In a way it was wise. But there was probably a less divisive way to have done that.

To this day I get e-mails from kids like, "Oh yeah, Gilman Street, you're all straightedge, right?" Hello, I was strung out and 105 pounds at this height. I think I had one crooked needle that I used for a year and a half because there wasn't a needle exchange yet.

Dallas Denery: We played with MDC once. They always brought glasses of orange juice onto the stage with them, and Gilman was always concerned that there were things mixed with the orange juice. Afterwards, whoever was cleaning the stage would be picking up all the cups and smelling them. Like, "Was this a screwdriver?"

Dave Chavez: We couldn't believe that you couldn't drink onstage. We were just such hardcore drinkers at the time. So we did anyway. They didn't have it together like they do now.

Kate Knox: Later on, after our friends Nando and Jerme weren't working security anymore, a girl and her friend got busted drinking at Gilman. And they were 86'd until they wrote a three-page essay, about why they shouldn't drink at Gilman. They came to a meeting, and read it. Their essay was like, "I will never ever ever ever ever ever ever ever ever ever ever ever ever drink at Gilman, because . . ." People were like, "We want you to read it onstage at the next show." And they were like, "No! This is fucking bullshit!"

But then there was a show with a gap in between bands, a problem with the equipment or something. And they were drunk, right? So they were like, "Fuck it, c'mon, let's go read it." They went up onstage and read it. "I will never ever ever . . ." One of the people that made her do this was Jesse Luscious.

Jesse Luscious: Branwyn was the only female head of Gilman for awhile. But she and some other people who should have known better were drinking alcohol inside. They put it in soda cups and mentioned it really offhanded to the wrong person. So we had this big thing. I let myself get overheated and I was like, "Yeah, they should have to write an essay and read it onstage." Which is a stupid fucking idea. I was totally caught up in the witch hunt.

Anna Brown: I never understood that as a young person. Why someone over 21 would not wanna go to an all-ages club where you couldn't drink? What was the big deal? Why did you have to drink? But now I feel like, "God, how could you go to a show and not drink?"

Andy Asp: I really feel for the cops that were around Gilman Street. We were just fuckin' dickheads.

Larry Boothroyd: I actually went to jail from Gilman one night. I got caught drinking. This woman cop tapped on my window, I was in the driver's seat. We had a bottle of Bacardi and a case of beer. We hadn't even gotten into it, and she poured the whole thing out. She carded us all, and one by one let us all go. Until it was me and my buddy. She asked him if he could drive my car home. I was like, "Yeah? Why?" It turned out I had an outstanding warrant from the Democratic Convention of '84, where I had a failure to appear. It was three days in jail. I was in with all these crack dealers, and I was completely freaked out. I had never been incarcerated. Did it scare me straight? You'd think so!

Jason Beebout: Trying to date girls. You'd go to Gilman, the last thing you're gonna do is go up and say, "Hey, I think you're really attractive, you wanna go out on a date?" You're being sexist or something. I didn't know how to be sexist. I was like, well, fuck, let's just avoid it.

Jesse Michaels: Gender roles were a lot less defined. At that time in my life I was just painfully, painfully shy. So my main experience was just complete shyness. Which is funny 'cause I was the singer for a band, and normally a singer for a band, at least with rock bands, is traditionally sort of a ladies' man, to a certain extent. I wasn't like that at all.

Anna Brown: I copped a giant attitude. Punk girls were allowed to be tough and to stick up for themselves. It's rough all over for teenage girls, but I think maybe you have a thicker skin as a punk. You let more things slide because you're in this kind of lawless world. But you also take less shit.

Coming of age as a punk, you are well versed in a lot of feminist thought and theory and lyrics, and a lot of ideas that many girls don't learn about until they take women's studies in college. I know a lot of young women who are like 22 before they become aware of the reality of discrimination. All that kind of shit is old hat to punks.

Blag Jesus: So the Dwarves made this record, *Blood, Guts and Pussy*. The cover is this great photo of two naked girls covered in blood. It's a takeoff of the Samhain record, obviously food dye, syrup. And we said, "Let's do that with chicks." So we got these two naked chicks with a dwarf guy that I used to buy weed off of in Brooklyn. To a lot of people it was objectifying women. Some even took it one step further, like it was advocating violence against women. If you actually look at the cover, it's much more like the women are in control and bold looking, and the dwarf is like a little guy yearning after them.

After that record came out, some people at Gilman said we shouldn't be allowed to play. Because of the artwork, and also we had songs like "Let's Get Pregnant" or "Free Cocaine." They thought we were advocating drug use, and hatred towards women. That was strange for me, because the Dwarves were very close with the girl bands during our era, like L7 and Hole, and Babes in Toyland and Lunachicks. We were not sexist type people. Sex is not necessarily sexist. Everybody likes it and we're all in this together, you know?

So they had us play at Gilman. This kid came up to me and said, "Yeah, violence against women is really funny, isn't it, man? Blood and pussy and all that shit is real funny, isn't it?" And I thought, this was a typical teenage guy, he hadn't gotten laid yet and he figured maybe this would win him some points with the feminist girls in Berkeley. I just laughed it off and said, "Yeah, man, you know, it's all in good fun."

This kid followed me, and started lighting into me again. I said, "Dude, do you really want to follow me around and give me shit?" I went outside and he walked up again, and was like, "Violence against women is real funny, isn't it man?" Blah blah. Obviously this guy was going to follow me around all night as his Gandhian protest against me and my music.

He wouldn't stop bothering me. I had a show that night. So I said, "Dude, just say one more word, man, I'm going to fucking plaster you in your mouth." Sure enough he opened his mouth and said, "Violence against women is fun—" I smacked him, he fell down.

The people running Gilman came over, "What the fuck are you doing? There's no violence here!" We were banned for many, many years. There's always a better way than violence to handle it, but at the time I wasn't really aware of what it might be.

Davey Havok: Lotta stuff you could do to get banned from Gilman Street. As a band, as a person. It could be going onstage and saying the word "bitch." Or saying the word "fag," just in passing. As long as you weren't Pansy Division. Pansy Division, of course, gets to. Ah, semantics.

Nick 13: The era when we started going to Gilman, political correctness had just gone too far. There was this unspoken thing that you had to appreciate this band because they were women, and what they're playing was just as important as what men are playing. To me that was more sexist, in a way. Why couldn't bands be judged on the merit if they're good or not good?

It was almost like women had been historically wronged in rock 'n' roll, and we need to right that wrong now. Regardless of whether or not it's any good. That was happening at Cal, that was happening in pop culture, that was happening everywhere at that time. There was just as much "You have to think exactly what I think or you're fucked" as you'd find at any Republican Convention.

Ben de la Torres: I did security for about six years. Was head coordinator, was executive director, was involved in booking. One of the best parts of working at Gilman is having the right to complain. There's this elitist mentality at Gilman. You get to complain about how no one else does the work. We're like old ladies getting their hair done in a salon. We just sit there and complain about everything. Everyone hates Gilman, and if you work there you get to hate everybody. They hate Gilman 'cause they can't drink.

Part of punk is hating rules and I understand that. Most of these people are going to places like Starbucks, but they want to come and harass people at Gilman. You're full of shit. You follow rules when you have to. You come to Gilman and you don't want to hear more rules, I understand. But it's bullshit. So they sit outside and complain about us, and we sit inside and complain about them.

36

Ever Fallen in Love

Dallas Denery: The Gilman thing had been swelling up for a long time. There were a bunch of bands that were all affiliated and knew each other, and it had been going on for two or three years before Gilman opened. And then Gilman crystallized it.

Dave Dictor: Let's face it, to get a gig at the On Broadway or Ruthie's you had to know Fang or MDC. It took a place like Gilman, that had five or six bands a night, two or three weekend nights a week, 52 weeks a year, for the cream to rise, for the Op Ivys to rise, for the Samiams to rise, for the people to come out of that world.

Dave Mello: There was definitely a core of people that really knew how to play their instruments. But then Gilman happened, and we had all these friends starting bands. It wasn't just people who knew how to play instruments. It was also the people who started bands and taught themselves how to play, therefore creating their own style. That happened a lot.

Ralph Spight: There weren't 8,000 bands that sounded exactly the same. Things were small, and there wasn't a bunch of media attention on it. There wasn't like, "We're all going to get big." There wasn't that kind of mind-set going on.

Sergie Loobkoff: We'd go to every show, Saturday and Friday, sometimes Sunday. What else are you going to do?

Dallas Denery: Other bands would show up from out of town, and they couldn't believe what they were seeing. Sometimes they liked it, and sometimes they would just make snide comments later. Gilman had a different vibe. And that whole vibe would catch people sort of by surprise.

If you went to the Mab it was just dire and depressing. The Chatterbox was a fine place to play, but those places were much more like, people go to the club, pay their money, see the show. Whereas at Gilman Street, there were all these people who sort of decided it was home. Or the center of their world. It was less an "East Bay–San Francisco" thing than a "Gilman Street and every other club in the Bay Area" thing.

New Year's Resolution: Gilman St. Project flyer

Mike K: Everybody was always completely out of tune. But you learned to feel this anthemic quality, even though things were totally a mess.

Scott Kelly: The whole El Sobrante thing came in, and they latched onto that super hard. That, to me, was when things started changing, when it started getting really fuckin' goofy. I remember we'd come out of the warehouse, we're on drugs and listening to Joy Division, and we'd go to Gilman and kids are playing leap-frog and shooting each other with Silly String. And we were like, "What the fuck?"

Aaron Cometbus: Tim had a vision of all these goofy, silly kids coming together to bring creativity and humor back into punk. A fine little vision, which very few people happened to share. Soon Tim is announcing, "Geekcore is born! Bring on the Big Wheels!" I wasn't the only one there who didn't consider themself a geek. But when the compilation of Gilman bands came out, there it was again: "File under Geekcore."

Scott Kelly: Tim and those guys loved those bands. Loved 'em. And really supported 'em. All these kids came in with a lot of energy. And, shit, basically they took it. I understand. That's how I live my life. If you want it, take it.

Spike Slawson: The energy was great and it was all—oh man, I fucking hate that I'm going to say this—it was all positive energy. It was. And there was this rhythm. The place was throbbing and everyone was soaking wet and it wasn't a bloodbath.

Dallas Denery: It's amazing if you think about the number of people who were in that area who had interesting musical ideas, and had this place to play. These shows would happen, and there would be the usual review of some dumb concert in the *Chronicle*. I would just think, "How can you not be paying attention to this?" It seemed like when Gilman was happening, essentially nobody else in the rest of the Bay Area knew it was happening.

37

You Put Your Chocolate in My Peanut Butter

Blag Jesus: I saw experimental things at Gilman, I saw weird things there. I saw a band there that played punk songs on turntables. Because it was a collective, you got crazy shit cropping up in there.

Larry Livermore: A band called Slapshot from Boston. The singer was called Choke. He used to play with a broken hockey stick in his hand, that he would wave at the audience, menacing them with it. There was a few hardcore fans that wanted to get right up there and be all macho with Mr. Choke. So a bunch of Gilman geeks started playing leapfrog, in what normally would have been the pit. Making goony faces, and acting really mock-horror and terror every time he would yell and growl. It was very hilarious.

The singer would just get madder and madder. "This ain't no punk show, this is fuckin' *Romper Room!*" He had another speech at the very end, where he was happy to play for anybody, anytime, but not for a bunch of fuckin' geeks. This was typical of the Gilman spirit. But Tim was really mad. He said we hadn't shown respect. He yelled at us afterwards, that they were a serious band.

Jeff Ott: The guy who's now called Michael Franti used to be in the Beatnigs. They would play Gilman sometimes.

Kareim McKnight: "They don't eat burritos in the White House!" I'm black, and it was amazing to see someone like Michael Franti onstage and pounding it out.

Jeff Ott: Beatnigs would accidentally light shit on fire, by having all these grinding wheels and sticking metal in them, all this crazy shit.

Kevin Carnes: One time we actually set up on the floor. The intention was to have people play along with us, put the music in the hands of the people, right? We set up all this stuff, and as people came in, they literally had to walk right up to this sculpture, and it was like pieces of metal hanging from it, that later on you might end up playing a little bit, at least touching it, because some guy shot sparks off of it with a circular saw, and another guy played it with mallets, and another guy burned a little piece of message that was attached to it.

Scott Kelly: Frank Moore. How's that for disturbing? At an all-ages club.

Jason Beebout: Frank was this quadriplegic performance artist who had a cable access show. He would sit there in his wheelchair, they'd play music in the background and he'd sing along. But he'd just make vocalizations. He had a little pointer on his head that went to a board with letters and phrases, so he could speak that way. He usually had women dancing naked with chicken blood.

Scott Kelly: Quadriplegic. Young, naked girl dancers. Fire. How do you do that? Shouldn't everybody who runs this club be in prison for doing that type of shit?

Zarah Manos: I remember Adjective Noun. Drummer got offstage, went into the bathroom, took somebody else's shit out of the toilet, ate it onstage and barfed! I'm not kidding. Adjective Noun, if a band could do more, be more, they were it. They were the worst and the most disgusting. I feel sick talking about it.

Christopher Appelgren: Juke were always an amazing band to see live. When nearly everyone was vegetarian and vegan, they set up a hibachi out in front of Gilman and cooked steaks before the shows. They also managed at one point to get a pig's head and have it on a stake onstage.

Nobody went to their shows. There might be 12 people strewn about Gilman. But Nick, the singer, would of course stand right in front of you and sing into a wireless microphone. He would start out with a trench coat, and then reveal underneath, his full-body nylon, nude body stocking with a little leaf over his crotch. Nick was pretty tone-deaf. He was an acquired taste. I think he's a professor in Utah.

Kate Knox: Boom and the Legion of Doom threw out fuckin' raw meat. Blast did that, too. That was pretty funny.

Sham Saenz: You'd see bands at Gilman like the Melvins, Neurosis,

Victim's Family. These bands pushed the envelope of creativity. They were creating new music and pushing it.

Noah Landis: Victim's Family were an amazing band. Their musicianship just blew me away.

Dave Mello: They had put a really groovy, jazzy twist on it, and made punk very musical and very harmonic and melodic and jazzy. With drums on the backbeat.

Tim Armstrong: I used to stand right at the edge of the stage in front of Ralph Spight and watch him play guitar. That guy was like my fucking hero.

Dale Flattum: Seeing Caroliner Rainbow for the first time and going, "Holy hell, these sets have taken this guy the last five years to paint." All these costumes. They'd be jumping on trampolines. Few other places would really want this. Or embrace it.

Sham Saenz: I had been kind of bummed out about punk rock by that point. I went through a low phase. Then Poison Idea played Gilman. Jerry A. came out and he was blowin' fuckin' fire.

The kids were going crazy, everybody was smashing each other, and picking each other up at the same time, and singing along. Once the show was over, everybody poured out onto the street, blocking traffic. This huge cloud of steam was coming out of the club and off of everybody's bodies, because everyone was so packed into each other. There was a little skirmish over here. People were covered in blood and laughing, drunk and wiping each other. That's why I loved this.

Dale Flattum: Schlong did all of Fleetwood Mac's *Rumours*. It wasn't just this half-baked idea. I think that's what was so great about Gilman. There was an outlet for it. That kind of inspires people to complete things.

Gavin MacArthur: We were listening to the *Rumours* album on tour a lot. We covered "Go Your Own Way." After that it was like, let's just do the whole thing as fast as we possibly can, and see if we can put the whole thing on a 7-inch. Somebody throws out a stupid idea, and everybody laughs and thinks that's the stupidest thing they've ever heard—and of course we're gonna do it.

Dave Mello: We tried to make it sound as garagy as we could. *Tumors*. One take. We recorded it in a couple hours.

Sergie Loobkoff: There's something really rad about watching a band that are doing it just because they love doing it. And they have no inkling of doing it for any other reason.

Gavin MacArthur: Pat Mello had a lot to drink, and I think he started singing "Maria." We were all closet fans of *West Side Story.* It's just something you can't deny from your childhood. Then Pat just said, "We're gonna record the whole *West Side Story* soundtrack!"

Dave Mello: Took maybe two weeks to learn all the songs. Got everybody to our practice space and had a dress rehearsal for a weekend, before we went in the studio.

Gavin MacArthur: People got paid in beer. It was really quick. One day for the music, one day for the vocals, and one day to mix it. We stayed up all night, finished mixing it at ten in the morning, went home, slept for a couple of hours. We went to Gilman Street while everybody was still in town and played the whole thing through. It wasn't any sort of stage production by any means, we just played all the songs, and the people who sang the songs came up and sang them. That's the only time that we actually did *Punk Side Story.*

Cammie Toloui: It was the 4th of July at Gilman Street. It was an all-day show with two million bands and people cooking burgers in the front. We were standing around, me and Joyce and Jane, looking at all of the boys. The punk scene was all about boys being up onstage and everyone giving them all the attention. There weren't a whole lot of women, especially not very many women onstage. The Beastie Boys had become very famous right at that time, which was 1987. So we were laughing, ha ha, we would be the Yeastie Girlz. Jane ran off, sat down and wrote this rap:

> *We're the Yeastie Girlz and we got yeast power*
> *we don't shave our armpits and we don't shower*
> *we don't say thank you we don't say please*
> *we put things in our vaginas that you wouldn't believe*
> *we're not your babies and we're not your dolls*
> *and we don't give a shit about your blue balls*
> *don't care about your biceps*
> *don't care about your dick*
> *and when you open up your mouth*
> *you make us all feel sick*

In between bands we jumped up onstage holding this piece of paper, shaking, terrified, and did this song. As would usually happen at Gilman, the boys booed. But it was something that really needed to be done at Gilman, because the boys ruled there.

We put out a demo tape that we advertised in *Maximum Rock-nRoll*. I think the name of our tape was "Suck Our Smelly Vaginas," which was Jane's idea. We had this ad that had a drawing of a woman giving herself a speculum exam. No one knew who we were.

We did a Prom Night show that was all girl bands. Everyone was wearing prom dresses. There's a main door, and then another door that leads into the main hall, and we changed that doorway into a huge vagina. Lots of red satiny material, I think the pubic hairs were some lacy stuff. People actually had to crawl through this vagina to get into the show.

Ruth Schwartz: That's what a hall like that is supposed to be about. You could be playing Turbonegro and have a vagina at the door at the same time. Something for everybody.

Mike LaVella: There was a lot of shit that was poignant. Youth of Today, their big thing was supposed to be like, "We have no ego." When they played, every kid in the audience held up a mirror. And all they saw was hundreds of reflections of themselves.

Hugh Swarts: They called Friday Alternative Night. Saturday was Punk Night. Sunday, sometimes they'd have plays, or art shows.

Dan Rathbun: We were always put into the non-punk nights with other bands that were viewed as appropriate underground entertainment, but didn't fit into punk rock.

Nils Frykdahl: We once did *The Rite of Spring* at Gilman, which was not so much theatrical as conceptual, with us playing Stravinsky. With music stands, and everyone sitting down on the floor like it was a concert. I don't know if we were doing clown outfits yet.

It really worked out. Everybody totally cooperated. Somebody even yelled out, "You're destroying music!" Which was the obligatory heckle from the original performance of *The Rite of Spring*.

Lynn Breedlove: You know who I saw at Gilman doing a play in the afternoon—what was her name? Just got the Cannes Film Festival brilliant genius award, dyke, filmmaker? Miranda July! She's huge now. She was like 18, and putting together these plays at Gilman in the middle of the afternoon. She was super artsy.

Miranda July: I was not a punk at this time, nor did I ever really become one. But in my own way I was anti-establishment and I really wanted to have total control over my production. I went to a meeting of Gilman volunteers, looking very clean and perky I'm sure, and nervous. But I was given a key to the building, which really meant a lot to me. The people in my play were pretty straight adults, but somehow they were game to spend time in this absolutely filthy, graffiti-covered space. I can still remember the smell.

The play opened during a three-day festival that Gilman had. I think Green Day played that night. I rented folding chairs from a church and set them up in rows. The regular Gilman punks were pretty confused by the chairs, but I think it was basically a success.

38

Ripped from the Headlines

Kamala Parks: It was the first year, '87. The first time the Feederz ever played Gilman.

Mike LaVella: I was out in front talking to Tim Yohannan and some kid from Isocracy. And here came Frank Discussion. He had a dead dog around his shoulders, wearing it like a mink stole. And around his neck he had a cat hanging from a noose. Wearing the cat like Run-DMC. Tim saw Frank Discussion before I did, and his cigarette fell out of his mouth and he went, "Oh my fucking god."

They hit the stage, and, man, it was insane. All these girls got onstage, and they were spitting on him the whole time he's playing. He had live cockroaches taped to his head. Which I guess was old hat. People had seen that.

He was surrounded by these punk girls, tough-looking hardcore chicks. They were lettin' him have it. Between the songs they'd take the mic off and they'd say, "We have an open mic policy here. This is bullshit." I remember Frank Discussion saying, "This is so typical of the bleeding left! You don't even know where these animals came from!"

Kamala Parks: He sang his first song, and then he said something like, "Well, I guess Lassie isn't coming home." He threw the dog off into the crowd, and it splashed all these people who were like serious vegetarians. That's what was so upsetting. Where the fuck did he get this dog, and why was blood still coming out of it?

Mike LaVella: These skins picked up the dead dog and were dancing with it, skankin' around with this German shepherd. They were swinging it, and now shit started coming out of the dog's mouth.

Photo by Murray Bowles

Happiness is a Warm Puppy: Irate Gilman girls protest the Feederz

Bile was coming out and splattering people. People were already fucking horrified as it was.

Jeff Ott: I just remember going, "Oh my god, that's fucking gross. I'm glad I'm way back here." On the other hand, all the vegetarian fanatics were getting really disturbed, so that was kinda cool.

Martin Sprouse: He paid somebody off to borrow the dog for the night. He said he was using it for a movie prop. But here's the most fucked-up thing—it still had its dog collar and tag on it. So it wasn't really a movie prop. That was some family's dog.

Anna Brown: I believe someone called the phone number on the dead dog's collar to tell the pet owners what was going on. They had put it to sleep, and Frank got it from the Humane Society garbage can. How fucked up is that? *Ever Feel Like Killing Your Boss?* is a great album, all the same.

Martin Sprouse: "Everyone's getting so mad about the dog, what about the beetles glued to my head?" That was classic Frank Discussion. He was there to fuck with people.

Jeff Ott: There were all these meetings about it, and Tim Yohannan kept going, "You know, he only did that so all you would be sitting here having this meeting, arguing about shit." And he was probably right.

Kamala Parks: A couple of days later, the *Weekly World News* listed this incident, and they had it factually really correct. It was amazing. I remember looking at it and going, "Oh my god, they really are clear about what they are talking about." So it's quite scary when you think, okay, they got this incident right. Are they getting the alien stuff right? Does the Bat Boy really exist?

Bucky Sinister: I was working at Kate Knox's school. She was telling me, "Poor Jerme, man. Jerme and a couple other guys were in Piedmont cemetery last night. Something happened." Like, real quiet. I didn't know where this story was going. Someone OD'd? Someone's in the hospital?

"In the cemetery. They went in this mausoleum, and Jerme found this baby's corpse, took it back to his house, and somebody saw him trying to cut the baby's head off, and freaked out. They called the cops on him, and he took the baby and split."

No one knew where he was. He was gone. That was how fresh the story was.

Jerme Spew: Not one of my smartest moves, no.

We went back to the house we were staying at. One of the guys was cleaning a skull with a toothbrush. I was examining this baby's body, going, "What the hell am I gonna do with this?" It was dry, and I was kind of picking at it. I was already starting to establish that this might be dumb.

Janelle Hessig: They were cleaning the skull in the living room. Heather Hahn lived there and she freaked out. Like, "You can't clean that skull here, what the fuck are you doing?"

Jerme Spew: I don't blame 'em. But some of the stuff that was said was amazing. One guy who got mad at us, he said, "I banish you and this evil from the house!" What was the great quote? "If you want to do these anti-authoritarian things, go have a fight with your father somewhere else!"

The hilarious thing to me was the assumption that this was something I've done to throw in the face of authority and society. When in fact it was just a really dumb prank.

I took my booty from the incident, and was like, okay, I gotta put this somewhere where it's secure. I had keys to Gilman. And

I thought, I'll go hide it in the sound loft. No one will ever find it. I went inside, I hid it, and went home. I woke up in the morning, and my roommates were still awake in the kitchen, debating how horrible and evil it was.

Janelle Hessig: One of his roommates called the cops. There's been a lot of speculation about who it was.

Jerme Spew: I went to do errands and came home, and the front door and the back door of the house were open. We were living in North Oakland, not so great a neighborhood. There was this guy out on the porch, friend of everybody in the house, and he was like, "Hey, Jerme, your neighbors say there was nine police cars here about half an hour ago." I said, "Oh, I know what that's about. I have to leave." Three people were arrested.

Tim Armstrong: It was at night, we were practicing at Gilman. There was a knocking, flashlights. It's Berkeley P.D. They told me they're looking for some bones and a dead baby that was taken from a crypt in Oakland, and did you know these guys' names? I played dumb, I didn't tell them much. The cops looked around and couldn't see nothing, so they left. But we know Gilman. If it was there, we were gonna find it. So up above the sound booth, we fuckin' found a Tower Records bag with a dead baby and a skull.

Janelle Hessig: Lint called the cops and was like, "I don't want to get the club in trouble, but we have this mummy baby we'd like to give back to you."

Andy Asp: The part I remember was that Rancid agreed to help the police if there was no mention of punk. They didn't want it to get out to the news about these cannibalistic baby-eating, grave-robbing punks. So it just became a grave-robbing incident and not a punk incident.

Jerme Spew: I was the last person to turn myself in, so I was the "ringleader." Even though, quite frankly, I still say it wasn't my idea. I had no money, no lawyer. And I ended up spending three weeks in Santa Rita.

Bucky Sinister: So he was like this skinny punk kid. Like, six-two and 160 pounds. Of course, everybody was like, "What're you in for, white boy?" And he wasn't sayin' anything. So they went to find out, and it all came back that he had felony counts. One for "malicious dismemberment of human remains," and "malicious removal of human remains."

So all they knew was, he'd been caught chopping up a body.

Nobody would go near him, except for this one dude, who came up and said, "When you kill a motherfucker you don't take him home with you later."

Tim Armstrong: Everything got fuckin' kinda hot after that happened. Oh my god, it was the punk rock scandal. It was like O.J. for punk.

Janelle Hessig: It was in all the papers. They had Jerme Spew quoting Nietzsche.

Frank Portman: I saw it on that Maury Povich show, *A Current Affair*. That, with the Feederz throwing a dead dog into the audience, yes, we made an impact in the world. With our ripping apart dead dogs, and mummified baby corpses, and so forth.

Greg Valencia: Grimple played with Insaints at Gilman, '92 or '93. The singer Marian Anderson had these two dominatrixes in the crowd. They had this live sex thing. I don't remember ever seeing anything like that.

Mike Avilez: They did this really long instrumental song while Marian got this banana shoved up her by dominatrix women onstage. She was naked and pissing onstage.

Kamala Parks: She'd do it all the time. It wasn't anything surprising, really.

Daniel DeLeon: I knew who Marian was for years before I met her. She was the freakiest punk in Modesto. She had a two-foot mohawk and liberty spikes, and crazy makeup and ripped clothes. She was looking for someone to jam with. And that was the beginning of the Insaints.

We moved to Oakland. It was better than living in Modesto. Marian got money from the government every month, 'cause mentally or legally she couldn't really do a real day job. She was a bit crazy. She started being a dominatrix in Oakland. So she decided to bring that into the band, for live performance. We'd invite other girls that she worked with to do sexual acts onstage with her. Fist-fucking and pissing, we had shows where dildos were involved. Bananas were going all weird different places. It was pretty wild. I just played guitar.

Marian ended up dating Tim Yo for awhile. Kind of a weird couple, her and this old gray-haired short guy. But Tim was great to talk to. I think the only reason why we even have an album was because Marian was dating him. *Maximum* paid for it all, which was cool. I don't know if he liked our music. I know he liked Marian.

Jerme Spew: The show got stopped. I went inside, most of the people had left by then.

Daniel DeLeon: This is what Marian told me. I forget the guy's name. He was from the Dead Kennedys. The hippie. The 90210 guy. He gave her a bouquet of flowers before we went on. Which probably meant he liked her a lot. She thought it was sweet. Thanked him, whatever.

Then as soon as he saw the performances—fist-fucking and pissing, and all this shit—he went to call the police. The cops showed up and she was covered in wet bodily fluids. And bananas. The cops handcuffed her and took her outside and wrote her up, for lewd acts in public. She was still naked. I mean, they didn't even let her put on a jacket. They cited her, and then let her go.

Jerme Spew: Kristen from Naked Aggression, and Mike Lymon, somebody else, told the Dead Kennedys guy, "Maybe you should come with us into the side room before you get the shit kicked out of you." I went in just 'cause I was curious what was going on.

It slowly came out that he had a crush on Kristen, and he also had a crush on Marian. So he would bring them flowers and stuff when they played. But it turned out he was a born-again Christian. He said that it was the lesbian love that was against God's word.

Klaus Flouride: This was crazy. "One of the Dead Kennedys members calls the police on Gilman Street!" We were all like, ah, for Christ's sakes. Talk about spin control. My phone was off the hook. Ray's phone was off the hook. It was before the Internet, or anything like that.

East Bay Ray: He's seriously—he's clinical.

Klaus Flouride: The walls talk to him.

East Bay Ray: It's not good to talk about this.

Klaus Flouride: We just let it go.

Daniel DeLeon: She went to court for a year off and on. The ACLU from the West Coast didn't want to have anything to do with us. So the ACLU from East Coast did. The charges were dropped. You know how you have to buy a membership card at Gilman? It was technically a private club. So it wasn't lewd acts in public. It was in a private club. And that's the only reason why she got off.

Ben Sizemore: I was working Gilman volunteer security, with Jerme Spew and Atom Thompson, aka A. C. Thompson.

Jerme Spew: It was a really small show, practically nobody was there. But it was a security nightmare. Seven or eight assholes kept fighting all over the club.

Jesse Luscious: Jello was there to see the Fixtures 'cause they were on his label. Or they were about to be. All of us regular workers were outside dealing with these douchebags.

Ben Sizemore: So we were in the process of throwing these guys out, and as we were chasing them off, someone ran out front yelling, "Jello's been attacked!!"

Jello Biafra: Basically I'd gone down to see the Fixtures and there was a group of crusties that I'd never seen before, and a lot of other people hadn't. For some reason they were allowed to do stuff that normally had been banned at Gilman by then. They were stage diving at will, shoving people around. They shoved me into a table several times, and finally one of 'em plowed into me and snapped my leg backwards. Plowed straight into the knee and snapped the whole leg. Kind of in half.

A. C. Thompson: I was right there inside the building when it happened. It was a guy who was dirty and drunk, who really wanted to skank it up, and he accidentally ran into Jello. Jello's knee buckled. It wasn't intentional, from what I could tell.

Jello Biafra: Not knowing what happened, I stood up on it, then really felt, "Oh my god, I'm really fucked up." I challenged one of 'em about it. And he said, "Oh, you're such a rich rock star, you fuckin' deserve it, don't you?" Or something to that effect.

A. C. Thompson: I remember Jello grabbing the guy and being like, "You just busted my leg. You need to tell me who you are because I'm going to make you pay for this." And the kid was like, "Get the fuck away from me, old man! Fuck you!" The next thing you know, Jello's going crazy and it's become this assault on him.

Jello Biafra: So then like a fool, on one leg, I took a swing at 'em. All his friends jumped me and split my head open with brass knuckles, and may have done more damage to the leg. I have no idea what. I also wound up with injury-induced glaucoma in one eye.

Jesse Luscious: The regulars at Gilman pulled people off of each other. And we called the cops.

Jerme Spew: Jello was trying to describe his assailants. He demanded one of their driver's licenses. I couldn't honestly tell you which one of them he was demanding. But it didn't matter, 'cause he was demanding the license of a man named either Cretin, Sphincter or Spider.

Jesse Luscious: These were like crusty squatter people with facial tattoos, from the Southwest. They were just traveling through, and they were there for the show. It wasn't like they were planning a crime. They were just assholes.

Ben Sizemore: I don't even know if they knew who he was. It's dark in there. I think they only realized it later that it was Jello Biafra of the Dead Kennedys whose leg they broke.

Jerme Spew: I saw none of it. The story I got from Jello was that they targeted him. Jello's version was that they started quoting *MRR* people, like Tim Yohannan. That they were quoting bad things that the columnists had said about Jello, as their ammo for reasoning why they were physically attacking him.

I believe they were attacking him because they were pretty antisocial and not so bright, and didn't know how to respond to an older punk rocker guy. Especially one who was Jello, demanding information from them, and so they kind of went, "Oh! Attack!"

A. C. Thompson: The kid ended up running out of the club.

Jesse Luscious: The cops came, the ambulance came. The police never really caught 'em. They went up north to the Northwest somewhere.

Jello Biafra: I could have sued the living shit out of Gilman and got the whole place closed down, but I thought that would be a terrible thing to do and it would be wrong. Many people urged me to do that, including the doctors who tried to fix up my knee. But I wasn't gonna do that. If anything, we need two or three Gilmans in every single town. I'd love it if they multiplied like Starbucks.

A. C. Thompson: Jello blew it up into this absolutely malicious attack on him, like it was some sort of beef between the new generation of punks and the old generation of punks. Jello had both messianic and persecution complexes.

Jello Biafra: I made the decision that I couldn't let this keep me away from Gilman. It was my place, too. I liked going there. I liked a lot of the bands that played there. I wasn't gonna stay away. Plus I had spoken-word shows booked there, two or three weeks or less after it happened. So against all advice I went ahead with the show. Some people in the audience made fun of me through the whole thing. But others were pretty angry at those people for doing it.

A. C. Thompson: He spoke for three hours, largely about himself. He needed to raise money because he felt he needed to go to a specialist who was *not* covered by his insurance. People were like, "Uhhhhhh, yeahhhh, whatever, dude."

Mike Avilez: He was sitting in a wheelchair onstage. Then I saw him a year later and he sang a couple songs with DOA in San Francisco. It looked like he had some metal thing on his leg.

Jerme Spew: I don't think there was a grand conspiracy, like things that have been said in *Maximum*.

Ruth Schwartz: Biafra got the shit kicked out of him, and he never forgave Tim for it. He held Tim responsible. Biafra wanted to say it was because of what happened at Gilman, but in fact it was something that had been building and building and building. But that's what was going on with him. It's all so ridiculous in some ways.

Tim wrote an article in *Maximum RocknRoll* about how Biafra had done something wrong. I don't even remember what it was. In Biafra's mind, it created an environment where skinheads could come into Gilman and beat the crap out of him.

Ginger Coyote: The fight between Tim and Jello Biafra was fun.

Dallas Denery: Oh my god. Here you had two 40-year-old men arguing for issue after issue of *Maximum RocknRoll*, about what real punk rock is. These endless debates. You were just thinking, come on.

Larry Livermore: I was very angry at the time about Biafra getting beat up. I always blamed that on Tim Yohannan. Not just exclusively. But he helped orchestrate that whole "Jello is selling out to be a rock star." He made one reference to Biafra living in this $650,000 mansion in the Mission. It was a fairly pricey house by San Francisco standards of those days. But not extraordinary. It's probably like a middle-class house.

Jello Biafra: I shouldn't have let it slide because this notion of me being the big bad evil rich rock star permeated the community. When all I was doing was supporting the same bands they were. And in some cases using my money to put out their records. That was the thanks I got from *MRR*.

I fingered *MRR* for creating the atmosphere that made it cool to violently attack somebody like this. Tim's response was to attack me personally, and eventually he accused me of faking the entire injury. In print. After two years of rehab and a badass knee surgery later—no, I didn't fake the fucking injury. I was very, very angry at him over that. It hurt all the more because it hadn't been very long before that, he was one of my dearest and closest friends.

Gavin MacArthur: A disagreement between punks? I mean, come on, man. What are you infighting for? Go beat up the CEO of Wal-Mart. Jello's got his own thing going, A.T. is its own thing, and he hasn't sold it to anybody huge. He's still maintaining a small business. That whole thing I thought was just completely fucking lame.

39

Rise Above

Mike LaVella: Gilman had so much to do with why I moved here. But literally, the week I moved here was the last week that Tim and Martin Sprouse booked Gilman: "Oh, this weekend are the last shows that we're doing."

Cinder Bischoff: When Gilman closed for a period because that kid broke his leg and sued Tim Yo, the name changed from Gilman Street Project to 924 Gilman. In the period of a few months when they were closed, the people started putting on shows in the back of Phoenix Ironworks. Rock Against Racism, GWAR. Oh my god, GWAR played my house on Halloween. That is so rad.

Anna Brown: The loss was felt acutely by us all. Tim decided he was gonna shut it down and chalk it up to a failed experiment in collectives. I think he ended up being disappointed by what he saw as a lack of dedication by most people.

Martin Sprouse: It was a lot of work. Everyone was working day jobs and doing this at the same time. And we were trying to figure out whether we were gonna shut it down. There weren't enough volunteers. It was the same old people doing it. It turned into, like, "You guys put on the show, we play the show." It was a very hard situation. It needed more time to grow, and it wasn't growing fast enough to keep it going.

Larry Livermore: As far as Tim was concerned, that meant it was finished. He'd put an awful lot of time and work, and $40,000, into the place. It ended up having a budget four times what they'd originally expected.

He wrote a eulogy to it. He announced that it had had a great run, but it hadn't really lived up to its potential. So he said, we shouldn't feel bad that it's closed. We accomplished a great deal. We can learn for the future. Let's say thanks for the memories. That kind of thing.

Bill Schneider: After *Maximum RocknRoll* backed out, a bunch of us got together and reopened it as the Alternative Music Foundation. I was right in the middle of that. Mike Kirsch was pretty active. Pat Wright, Jason Beebout, Tall Tim—there was a bunch of people. One guy, Jonathan, was the main guy, he was a grad student at Berkeley. He really was the one that organized everybody.

There was this creepy business guy named Lou, who we were all pretty sure had really shady intentions. But he was rich and had computers and knew people on the city council, so we were like, we're gonna use him for our own. And we really did. We wouldn't have been able to do it without this guy. He was a total creep, just trying to pick up on young girls.

Anna Brown: Lou was really weird, but there was always some earnest person to oversee what was happening in spite of all that.

Bill Schneider: *Maximum RocknRoll* was very against it reopening. They were offended: "How could these people try to continue what we decided is passé?" It was this funny East Bay–West Bay rift. Tim came in and yelled at us and told us that we were stupid. He was really pissed off that we would have the audacity to re-open Gilman because it's obviously not gonna work.

Martin Sprouse: We had meeting upon meeting upon meeting about this. The second group of people that took it over, that came out of the first. It's part of growing pains, I think, to get to the third or fourth stage, when things kinda changed. This second group kept a lot of the same policies, but were a lot more lax on other aspects.

Larry Livermore: Tim was genuinely surprised that it reopened. Once they got more reliable people involved, it actually ran better without Tim and his micromanaged style. I think he found that a bit annoying. He came to shows occasionally, but not that often. After that, he had nothing to do with it.

Bill Schneider: I'll be the dick to say it. A lot of the people who took credit for Gilman gave up on it. If you read that Gilman book, all the people that are in it, they gave up. It wasn't even a full two years. They gave it away. They shut it down. They hated the fact that we'd opened again. I'm not holding anybody to the grindstone. But they all saw later. They were able to step back and go,

"Oh, wait a second, it worked." The anarchy worked. It took over for itself.

Richard the Roadie: A second group opened it up as AMF. And it was really good. But a lot of those people peeled off. There was a huge shift at Gilman. They were just hemorrhaging money. It was just spiraling and going downhill. The shows were still good but it wasn't being run as an effective club. They were like three months behind on rent, the money wasn't being managed, bands had stopped playing there, 'cause they weren't being paid that well. It got nasty.

Larry Livermore: It was on the verge of closing. One thing I learned from Gilman, no matter how socialistic or cooperative the venture is, somebody always has to take ultimate responsibility. Gilman succeeded, with all of its faults, because Tim was able to step into that role.

I helped encourage this one young but very smart kid to be the new head coordinator. Basically I said to him, "Look, all this cooperative, collective stuff is great, but there has to be somebody that's willing to tell people to fuck off, and to say this is what has to be done. And I think you can do it."

His punk name was Mike Stand, but it's Mike Lymon. He later went on to found a very successful Internet company in Berkeley. He might have even been less than 18 when he took over Gilman, and completely saved it from bankruptcy. He was kind of an unsung hero.

Richard the Roadie: Mike Stand came through and just changed everything top to bottom. Made it run like a business. There was a big benefit weekend, and it was Green Day, Jawbreaker and Neurosis. All three bands were huge at the time. And they gave all the money back to Gilman. And it basically pulled Gilman out of debt. People say it's chaos now, but it's really well run.

Dave Chavez: Gilman's always gonna be there, 'til they burn it down or something.

40

All I Know Is What I Don't Know

Larry Livermore: I was up in Mendocino County, way up in the mountains. I was living with this girl who played drums, and we were forever trying to find a bass player who was into punk. Nobody trusted us because we had short hair. The neighbors thought we were narcs 'cause they were mostly pot growers.

I started a magazine, *Lookout!*, which was mostly about mountain stuff. The neighbors didn't like it because they didn't want the attention. They threatened to burn my house down. So I started writing about music instead. I did a lot of politics and environmental stuff.

Rebecca Gwyn Wilson: Livermore was a one-man *Maximum RocknRoll. Lookout!* was really funny. He would write about how he grew up in Michigan and how he was really bored and disenchanted.

Larry Livermore: I found some local kid to play bass, so I started looking for somebody else to play drums. The kid at the nearest house down the road, about a mile away, was crazy and full of energy. He was a showoff and a loudmouth, and I figured he'd be a good drummer. He was 12. That was the Lookouts.

We had a lot of offers to "Shut the fuck up!" from the neighbors. There was no electricity. Everything was either solar panels or generators, so it was very quiet up there. Our first attempt at a show was at a combination store and camping area down on the highway. It was the closest commercial establishment. It didn't go over very well. One of the old hippies unplugged us in the middle of our set and there was a confrontation about that.

I made up Lookout! Records basically to put out a record by my own band. I was at a temporary room in San Francisco, with

David Hayes and Dave MDC, and another guy called Joe. David was doing a tape label, and he did a compilation called *Bay Mud*. He got tracks from about 20 Bay Area bands.

Frank Portman: Mr. T Experience made our first record, called *Everyone's Entitled to Their Own Opinion*. It was like 1986. We didn't have a label, we got a loan from our parents. We went to the cheapest studio in the phone book, which was also how we found out about Kevin Army. Larry said, "Where did you get your record?" I said, "We recorded it with Kevin Army." So the Lookouts recorded *One Planet One People*, with songs like "Fuck Religion." That was Lookout! 001.

James Washburn: Livermore, he's not from Berkeley, he's from the hills. If you listen to the Lookouts' music, it ain't punk, it's weirdo stoner noise. He had a really open mind. Tim Yohannan had a very strict edge of what is punk and what isn't. And Livermore had a very different definition.

Frank Portman: *Maximum RocknRoll* had put out a 7-inch EP that was recorded by Kevin Army. The new sound of the East Bay, so it had all these bands. It was called *Turn It Around*. And it had a picture of this goofy dude Walter on the cover.

Dave Mello: They asked all the bands to be on it. That was the first time Op Ivy went into the studio to record something.

Billie Joe Armstrong: That was really great. That was amazing. That just summed everything up. I listened to that over and over and over and over again. It was like my favorite record.

Larry Livermore: I knew this kid Tim, we'd always talk and hang out. When I went to Gilman, Tim came running up and literally jumped into my arms. He said, "Larry, Larry, I'm in a new band, we're called Operation Ivy, we're gonna play." I saw my first Operation Ivy show and was so amazed. It was complete energy, everybody was singing along and jumping up onstage with them. They'd been together three months.

I said, "I want to make a record with you guys." I was thinking of putting out one by Isocracy anyway. I knew David was interested in Op Ivy, too. I said, "Why don't we join forces?" He had Corrupted Morals and Operation Ivy, and I picked Isocracy, and at the last minute we decided to do Crimpshrine, too, 'cause they already had a fully recorded tape.

Those came out in January of '88. David's first ad in *Maximum RocknRoll* was, "Nobody buys vinyl records anymore—so we're putting out four of them." All 7-inches. Five, six, seven songs, as much as we could squeeze on there. We sold out the whole first pressing of 1,000 each. At that time, that was a lot. Ruth Schwartz called up and said, "We'd like to distribute your records now." That made a huge difference. She instantly sold out our next pressing. I doubt the company would have survived without Mordam.

Martin Brohm: I used to live with David Hayes, we lived in this shitty little apartment. It's where Lookout! Records was run out of. They'd come over and have their big power meetings. There'd be piles of records in his bedroom.

Jason Beebout: We'd go to Marty's house just so we could check out all the different colored vinyls, to get the best vinyl. We had to stuff all the records ourselves. It was like splatter designs.

Jesse Michaels: Back then, no one ever expected to be actually on a record. We were thrilled. I didn't have anything to compare it to, because I had never met anyone who did a label and I didn't know anything about records. I just thought it was incredible that someone would actually do it.

Billie Joe Armstrong: I used to see Larry at different gigs. I was a little taken aback by how much older he was than everybody else. In

Photo by RD Deines

Mendocino Homeland: Larry Livermore

the scene, when they say "all-ages," they really mean it. 15 all the way up to 50.

Dave Mello: He was an older guy, but at the same time he made it feel like we weren't signing anything. Basically we were all just doing it ourselves. He made the record deal like it was an even-even deal: "Were not gonna be making money off you." We were all 18, 19, and not really knowing exactly what it entails, what a contract is, and what percentages are. We didn't really know the whole scope.

Jeff Ott: Larry had everybody record with Kevin Army out of this place, Dancing Dog—everything came out sounding very trebly. Pete Rypins from Crimpshrine, Matt Freeman from Operation Ivy, Dave Edwardson from Neurosis and Ron Nichols, who ended up being in Christ on Parade, are like four of the greatest bass players ever. And they're all on this label where the bass is turned way down. And everything's super trebly. It's like, how did that happen?

Aaron Cometbus: There's nothing like the feeling of putting the needle down on your very first record of your own band. It's a wonderful, wonderful feeling. But I also remember a different kind of good feeling, which is smashing your own record into a million pieces. I did that with copies of the Crimpshrine *Burning Bridges* EP on the way back from a show in Davis, tossing them out the car window and watching them splinter onto the highway. I was frustrated and sad. And angry, of course. But it wasn't just that. It felt good to destroy a little of what you'd worked so hard to create.

David Hayes from Lookout! Records did the same thing with copies of Op Ivy's album when it came out. To sort of christen it, and to express his frustration. That really bummed out the band, though. They were in the car right behind his.

There's a flipside to the joy of creation, this feeling of futility and loss that comes with it, and it was especially strong at that time because it felt like we were losing our whole scene just at the moment when other people were starting to discover it. That feeling was in the air—that just as we were getting out of the gate, we'd already lost something essential that couldn't be replaced.

There were more cynical, bitter ways of expressing the same thing. David Hayes would make another 20 Op Ivy records stamped "Number One" whenever he got drunk, just to fuck with the collectors.

Dallas Denery: To Lawrence's credit, I think he identified right away what was going on. More than anybody else. Sweet Baby and Op

Ivy and Isocracy and Mr. T were a bunch of really good bands that appeared all at once, in one place. And Lawrence understood what that meant.

Jesse Michaels: One thing that really separated our little scene from a lot of other people is we were really into the old melodic punk sound. The Clash, Stiff Little Fingers, the Buzzcocks, Crime, the Dils, all those old bands. Avengers, the Dangerhouse Records bands, Poshboy bands. And that influenced a lot of the so-called East Bay sound, if there is such a thing. Which is why stuff went back to mid-tempo, as opposed to breakneck hardcore tempo.

Andy Asp: When you saw what came out of Lookout!, compared to the darker San Francisco punk scene, it was that punk can be fun. It doesn't have to be so serious.

Christopher Appelgren: A punk friend at my school had become pen pals with Larry Livermore. He had a place outside of Laytonville. And of course his *Lookout!* magazine was distributed in southern Humboldt. She made me a tape that had the Lookouts' first album on one side, and on the other, all of the first Lookout! 7-inches—Operation Ivy, Crimpshrine, Corrupted Morals and Isocracy. And maybe the *Turn It Around* compilation, too.

I wrote to Lookout!, "I do this show at a local radio station. Can I get some records for my show?" Larry wrote me back suggesting that, instead, why doesn't he just come up and be a guest on my show? And he'd bring all the Lookout! records and maybe some new stuff.

Larry became my official co-host pretty quickly after. And we did the show for about three years. He must have been 40 or 41. I was pretty excited because I had the opportunity to meet somebody who was at the center of what was really interesting and important to me.

David Hayes had created the look of the label, done Lookout!'s art and design. And between the two of them, they picked the bands. But I think their partnership had soured pretty early on.

Larry Livermore: David was dissatisfied, he wanted to quit the label. It had become too much like a job, and there was too much money involved. I think we grossed sales of $20,000 that year.

David had been keeping all the records and the accounts on a couple pages of loose-leaf notebook. I was mostly hype. Meeting with bands, talking to people, getting attention. I was more like the spark plug, and he was the very solid engine.

Christopher Appelgren: Larry is a little difficult. I know David tried a couple of times to leave the label.

Larry Livermore: I was very petrified at the idea of him leaving. I was begging him not to. I said, you can stay under almost any terms. Part of the reason was that I couldn't do the finances, because at this time I was still on disability for crazy people. That was my income.

Jeff Ott: In the middle '60s Larry got caught pouring gasoline all over his school to burn it down. And rather than criminally prosecuting him, they put him on SSI.

Larry Livermore: I have a history of pyromania. It was the same thing that got me out of Vietnam. I had a series of years in the wilderness after that, where I spent a year hiding out from the police 'cause I had been involved in a big drug bust.

That's how I came to California in the first place. Living in squats, things were getting more and more desperate. By 1971 I was completely broke, and pulling up dandelion greens out of the backyard. I thought, I'll go down to the welfare office and turn my life over. Ironically the shrink that examined me was a hippie revolutionary, who basically said, "Look, I approve everybody because it's a way of subverting the system." The shrink later got arrested for pipe bombs.

I was on that for 20 years. If I had to start filing tax returns and financial reports, it meant I was working. And it was the end of my guaranteed money. Lookout! was making a small profit, but not enough to support the one person, let alone two.

So I told David, you can just be the front man, you just sign all the checks and file the sales tax reports and stuff like that, and you can still have half of whatever we make. And David was like, "No, I can't do it."

I was going to do a compilation, he was going to do a compilation. And both of them were going nowhere. But he had all the art. He finally shrugged and said, "Oh, well, let's just do it together then." His compilation was going to be called *Floyd*. So it became *The Thing That Ate Floyd*, a double record instead of a single record. It was meant to be a survey of everything that was going on in the Bay Area at that time.

Dale Flattum: It amazed me that they had the stick-to-itiveness, just the logistics of getting that many bands to get the recording done.

Davey Havok: The second compilation was *Can of Pork*. For us, that was, "Oh my god, this is the biggest band in the world—they're on the Lookout! Records compilation!"

Cammie Toloui: I moved into the *Maximum RocknRoll* house with Tim Yohannan and Lawrence Livermore and David Hayes. We were all there at one time. Lawrence hadn't figured out what he was going to be when he grew up. He just seemed really old to me 'cause I was 18.

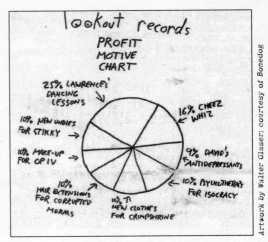

Between Friends:
Lookout! Records profit motive chart

Artwork by Walter Glaser; courtesy of Bonedog

Jesse Luscious: David Hayes was starting his new label, Very Small Records, and had just split off from Lookout! So that was kind of bitter and weird. Very Small Records was kind of a self-defeating thing. He would do really short runs or he would just do bands that he loved, that were tough for people to get a handle on, like Schlong or Elmer. He doesn't really care about selling records.

Christopher Appelgren: At this point Lookout! was Larry, myself, and Patrick Hynes, who Larry had met at KALX. Larry had started going back to school at Berkeley in late 1990, and had rented a room in a house. That actually was our Lookout! office for a number of years. He would fold up his futon and then we would do layout on the floor. Pat and I had this joke about a lot of pubic hairs getting in the layouts. There was no vacuum cleaner. There really were a lot of Larry's pubic hairs in the art. I know that's bad.

On the weekends, Pat and I would load up our skateboards with boxes of 7-inches, and go sell records. You'd stack them up on the front and you could stand on it like it was a little scooter. Our distributor was in San Francisco, so we'd take our skateboards, load up all the stuff and take BART with these big boxes. It was really bad through the turnstile, and going down the escalator. I remember thinking, I hope this is all for something. Especially since I'd flunked out of school.

Larry Livermore: After David had finally quit for good, I had to go to the Social Security and tell them I'm making money. I had to take this giant leap of faith that Lookout! was gonna start supporting me.

Andy Asp: Lawrence Livermore was a musician, and he was in a way the East Bay's Kim Fowley or Andrew Loog Oldham. "This eccentric older man is taking interest in my son's music!" Parents must have been like, "What the hell?" A lot of the early punk guys were music-centric older unmarried men. I didn't realize that 50-year-olds were going to punk shows. I remember meeting some of them on tour. Some guy would invite you to stay at his house, let's say in the Northeast. I'm sure there were different motivations.

Larry Livermore: Op Ivy and Green Day, the CDs were issued the same day, in spring of '91. We were kinda slow on doing CDs. A lot of punk labels were. It was a revelation when we finally did. Because our sales quadrupled overnight. That was probably the main thing that enabled me to get off welfare.

Mike LaVella: Lookout! was doing great. They had the Op Ivy record, they had the two Green Day records, which were selling. They were gold and platinum respectively, which is a lot. Imagine selling 500,000, a million of those three records. They had a lot of money coming in. They had some 60-40 split with the bands, where the bands got 60. I've never heard of that in my life. Lookout! actually gave more money to their artists than anybody else. And then they restructured it to 50-50, which is the standard.

Christopher Appelgren: Green Day had always been our bestselling band, and then suddenly, instead of a couple thousand CDs or albums at a time, we started ordering tens of thousands. We started selling a lot of records. A lot of everything else, too. There was a real wave of interest in all the bands on the label.

Davey Havok: Lookout! was very tastemaking within that scene, for the time. They were tastemakers. We wanted to be on Lookout! for sure, but they didn't care about AFI at all.

Christopher Appelgren: There was a crazy period of time, we were getting checks that were a million dollars a month. Writing checks to Green Day that were a million dollars. We always paid all of our bills in advance. But in order to be able to meet this need, we actually had to get terms from the manufacturer and the printer, because it was more money than we had.

Larry Livermore: It was growing very rapidly. We were selling probably 30, 40,000 Green Day records a year. And suddenly we were selling several hundred thousand a year. Once *Dookie* came out, we sold at least half a million of each of their records in a couple years. The first year Op Ivy came out, we sold 2,000 the whole year. And in '95 we were selling 2,000 a week. Of a band that had been broken up for six years.

I tried to rent an apartment down the street, 'cause it was getting too crazy, the phone ringing constantly. I said, "I run this company." They said, "Where's your office?" I pointed up the street, "That house, that room upstairs." The landlord called me back the next day and said, "No, I'm afraid we can't rent to you 'cause it sounds too implausible, you running a multi-million-dollar business out of that old slumhouse." So I got a suite of offices on University Avenue, and had about a dozen employees. Some of them I barely knew. It was a quick transition. Not a wholly comfortable one.

Some of the bands were saying, "You gotta spend a lot more money to promote us." I was like, "Look, why tamper with success? We've made this company grow very well." And they said, "Yeah, but you gotta get with the times." There was a lot of tension within the company as well.

It was getting a bit nerve-wracking. At Gilman you'd get chased around with people trying to give you demos. I started getting lax in my responsibilities. I'd also let the two guys who worked for me have half the company in profit shares, 'cause I couldn't pay them much in the early years. So they now had 49 percent of the company.

Christopher Appelgren: We had to make Lookout! into a business. Before, there was no paperwork. The company was just him doing business as Lookout! Records. In 1995, in the midst of all this stuff, we had a business lawyer help set an LLC in California.

Bill Michalski: I got this reputation, I guess, as the punk rock book-keeper. When I left AK Press I went to work at Lookout! Records for a couple years. They were just coming off the crest of when Green Day really hit it big. When I was working there, I think we were getting from Mordam probably in the neighborhood of like $250,000 a month. The bulk of that was Green Day and Op Ivy sales. There was 20 employees. And then, in the two years that I worked there, they just squandered it all to hell. That's basically why I had to leave. I was sick of telling people that we're not gonna pay you, or the check's in the mail or whatever kinda bullshit I had to feed them. I couldn't watch them flush the business down the toilet anymore.

I think their main downfall was that they lost track of where they came from. They basically abandoned being an advocate of the East Bay sound and scene. They really wanted to be Warner Brothers or EMI or something like that, instead of taking full advantage of being Lookout! They just didn't realize what a great thing they had.

Larry Livermore: I would appreciate making that kind of money today. So it's kinda hard to put yourself in that place of saying, "Oh, this is so wearisome, I've gotta get away from it all." But it was constant stress. A lot of people who had been friends were now either business associates or adversaries. I was getting really depressed. I was drinking a lot. I was near suicidal. It couldn't be helped. They don't ask you when they drive up the Brinks truck and dump out all the money. It just comes.

Deciding which bands to sign, and what approach to take, and how to promote them. That was the stuff I had always excelled at. And I was letting other people try their pet theories on it. I didn't like what they were doing, I didn't like the image it was giving the company.

You could say, look how democratic I am, look how willing I am to give everyone else a chance. Looking at it in a not so bright light, it's lazy, cowardly, not being able to stand up for what I was sure was the right way to do things. Not wanting to get people mad at me. It was costing horrendous amounts of money.

Christopher Appelgren: We started sending out more promos, booking more ads. We sent out CDs and posters when bands went on tour. Larry became less involved. He was traveling more. He had promised and threatened and warned that he wasn't into being a businessman.

Larry Livermore: I had 51 percent, so I could say, this is how it's gonna be. But because of my personality and my philosophy, it was difficult to do that. So when people would argue in favor of doing things a different way, like taking out an ad in *Spin*, or doing a video, more often than not I would say, "Yeah, I think it's a bad idea, but go ahead, try it. We can afford it. We've got plenty of extra money."

Christopher Appelgren: We had a dispute with Screeching Weasel, one of the first bands outside of the East Bay that we had signed. They disputed how we were calculating royalties. Weird faxes and letters. Larry filed suit against the band, to have a judge decide if we were upholding the contract.

Lookout! had this clause in our agreement about always treating each other with friendship and trust. And I felt like Larry was not doing that. He was not exhibiting friendship and trust. He was assuming that Ben Weasel was out for his own interests.

Larry Livermore: Two of us were on one side, Chris was on the other side. We couldn't reach agreement.

Christopher Appelgren: The conflict escalated, it was in *Maximum RocknRoll*. It was embarrassing, it was like a big part of local gossip, local shit-talking. It got to the point where I thought, well, maybe I'll quit. And then Larry escalated his plan he'd always promised, or threatened, that he was going to retire. He took Pat with him.

Larry Livermore: I'd been brooding about it. Part of my bitterness was that I was spending all of my time helping other people with their art, and I had no time left for mine. I was having virtually no fun. I went home, and somewhere during the night, I had one of those moments—"I know, Chris could take over." I withdrew my capital from the company. One of my other partners left at the same time, so it was left with Chris. I went around and saw the major bands, and explained to them what was going on.

Christopher Appelgren: I get a little bit angry because I don't know if I was Larry, 45 or 46 years old, if I would have felt it was the most responsible thing to leave a multi-million-dollar business in the hands of a 23-year-old high school graduate.

Larry was moderately involved for a time, but phased out pretty quickly because I made some pretty radical decisions that went against what he would have advised. Patrick became an employee, and worked for me. And gave up his vote.

At its peak in '96, we opened a record store. We had 18 people between the store and label. The store never made any money. It's hard to have a record store in the face of Amoeba and Rasputin's, all these great stores in Berkeley. It was more of our little clubhouse to have in-stores, and have cool artifacts. But it was a very expensive one.

Bill Michalski: After I left, I was still friends with a lot of people that worked there. One of the things that I heard they were trying to do was to have Lookout! bands on airline in-flight entertainment.

Like, you put in your fuckin' headphones in the airplane and you're gonna hear the Oranges Band or Gaza Strippers or some shitty band that they were promoting at the time. How crazy is that?

Another thing that was a real big mistake—they tried to get in on the Warped Tour too late. If they had done it when they had all the money and when the Warped Tour was first starting, it would have been cool. But when they finally decided to do something, I think it was '98.

Money was really tight at Lookout! All these other record labels like Epitaph had these free giveaways, goody bags and all this cool shit. Lookout! had a bunch of plastic bags printed up with Lookout! on it, maybe stick in an old Samiam cassette that they had laying around somewhere. So they were giving out basically empty bags. They looked like complete cheapskates. It was really pathetic. And it cost a ton of money.

Christopher Appelgren: It happened on my watch. I just really didn't know. We were also dealing with a more and more sophisticated underground and independent music industry, that was more competitive. It was harder. Green Day was proud of spending $900 to record their record. Then I was dealing with bands that wanted $50,000 to make records. That's a real different mentality. Lookout! ended our relationship with Green Day, because there was a long period of not paying royalties.

Larry Livermore: They stopped getting paid. You can't blame them. The bands weren't getting their checks regularly, and they were also complaining that Lookout! was signing all these bands they didn't like. They felt like the money that should be going to them was going to promote these new bands.

The Lookout! people would always say, oh, everything's alright, don't worry. I was on the other side of the ocean. So I didn't really know for a few years how bad things were getting. It's pretty much all gone now.

Christopher Appelgren: We basically renegotiated a settlement with Green Day, where now they are stakeholders in the business, in lieu of money that we owed them. We've gone out with our hat in our hands and admit some of our shortcomings, try to work things out. In some cases, it was successful. In other cases, it was too late.

It was really hard. It was in all honesty an overdue humiliation. Because a lot of those more desperate years, we were trying to

Photo by Andy Asp

Kerplunk: Chris Appelgren at Lookout! Records offices

prove to Larry that we were doing good things. We worked with some great bands. And made some great records. But ultimately, those good things didn't outweigh some of the bad things.

Our relationship with Operation Ivy ended pretty soon after.

With the same kind of situation. The one silver lining to the cloud for me is that the four of them have really come together in figuring out what should happen now with Operation Ivy. Jesse got up and performed with Rancid at the Warfield, those kinds of things.

Zarah Manos: I worked there after Livermore had left. The thing about Chris, he likes to have a good time and he likes everyone to be happy and to like him. You can't hate on somebody for that. It might have gone down really shitty, but I really think his intentions were right. He wanted people to have a place to work, he wanted to keep it DIY. He thought that more money was coming in, that he could employ more people. And it didn't go down like that.

Christopher Appelgren: Lookout!'s not putting out records anymore. We had to let our staff go at the end of the summer in 2005.

Larry Livermore: I don't even know the technical ownership. Someone runs sort of an office in San Francisco. They administer the Web site, answer the mail and phone. I don't know what else they do.

41

Unity

Dallas Denery: Something clicked around 1988. Op Ivy became very popular, more so than any other band at Gilman Street. There would be a line around the club.

Sergie Loobkoff: Who knows what would have happened, but it seems like Op Ivy would have been bigger than Green Day, bigger than Rancid. Because they stood out so far above every other local band that ever played there. They had that magic little pixie dust.

Matt Freeman: The first time me and Tim met, we both grew up in Albany and there was this thing called My Indian Guide. We were five years old. You'd do crafts or whatever, kids and fathers kind of stuff. I went over to his house and he had these two older brothers, Jeff and Greg, and they were just intimidating. I remember Greg was doing pull-ups.

Tim Armstrong: Albany was a mile square, 14,000 people. It's right next to the People's Republic of Berkeley, but in the '70s Albany was very working-class, not hippie. We grew up right across the street from the Golden Gate Fields racetrack. We would go there every day, me and the kids from the hill. We were 10, 11 years old. The first time I seen a pimp, all-purple suit. First time I saw a real knockdown, throw-down fight. It was exciting and it was just super shady.

My brother Jeff got into punk early on. I was 13, and we had a Radio Shack portable record player, and we listened to the Ramones' fuckin' *Rocket to Russia* record when it came out. Twenty times in a row, every day. I'd never heard anything as great as that. My older brother Greg liked more hardcore music, Black Sabbath. But the one thing that all three agreed on was the Ramones.

Matt Freeman: Jeff worked at 7-Eleven. Everyone hung out up there. He would play the Ramones constantly in the store. He had one of the biggest record collections I've ever fuckin' seen. A lot of roots bands out of L.A., like the Blasters, X, Los Lobos, that rockabilly band Red Devils.

Gavin MacArthur: We all went to Albany High. I was walking by one of the music practice rooms, going to class, and Tim and Matt were in there playing, just riffing out. I remember thinking, "Wow, that's cool—they're sitting there in the high school practice room, jamming." I stood out there and listened to them for awhile, it was kind of groovy. I never thought that you could actually go to the high school and rock out.

Tim Armstrong: My first band was called COD, which was Kevin Kechely and my brother Greg on drums, in '82 or '83. We were like Black Flag, Exploited. Kevin was a character, lived across the street from 7-Eleven. He had a mohawk, was at every show.

Aaron Cometbus: Tim had a ton of different bands one after the other, most of them with Matt. Surf Rats, Ratt Patrol, the Uncool, the Noise. Not punk bands, but they were good. Then came Basic Radio, which was a great mix of everything: surf, ska, a bit of punk, some Old World sounds, too, almost like Klezmer. And this wild rocker second guitarist doing blazing metal guitar solos over the whole thing.

Jeff Ott: Basic Radio was like, if they happened now we'd probably call it world music. They were kind of a punk band, kind of a ska band, kind of a reggae band, kind of a rock band. Dudes could play saxophones and all kinds of different instruments and shit.

Tim Armstrong: I loved Basic Radio, I still like it, I just think there was no real home in the mid-'80s for that kind of thing happening. We only played like 15 times in two years. Hotel Utah, house parties, Berkeley Square. A couple of recordings that didn't really come out well.

Jeff Ott: When I gravitated toward Telegraph Avenue as a homeless guy, Tim was an employee at one of the pizza places. He professionally hung out.

Tim Armstrong: I was working at Fat Slice Pizza on Telegraph. They did not want me playing the Dead on the P.A., 'cause you get the fucking Deadhead hippies coming in off Telegraph and dancing around.

When Basic Radio was falling apart, I didn't know what I was gonna do. I'm a fan of New York music, so I said, "I'm gonna take a Greyhound bus from Oakland to New York." In December of 1986. It took three days. My god, you talk about shady. And very regional, man. I heard accents I'd never heard before.

I ended up going to the Sunday matinee show at CB's, unbelievable scene happening. Murphy's Law had put out a record and it was coming out of the woodwork, everywhere you went, you heard that fuckin' record. New York was happenin' big-time. I was like, "I'm gonna move here." And then I went to a fanzine store and got a *Maximum RocknRoll*. There had been a lot of talkin' about the new club that was gonna go down—on Gilman Street! A punk rock club! I grew up right there. I had to go home. I wasn't fuckin' New York. I get chills thinkin' about it. I got back on the Greyhound, another three fuckin' days. No fuckin' money. I had crackers and water.

Matt Freeman: You actually brought me back a Rolling Rock beer. You carried it all the way. I'd never seen Rolling Rock beer before.

Tim Armstrong: We went to the first Gilman show, it was Christ on Parade, and a band called Soup with Tom Hammond. I knew Tom for a long time, his parents went to high school with my parents. So there it was, man—Tom Hammond's band, Christ on Parade, who I loved, new club, Gilman Street.

Jesse Michaels: I grew up in Berkeley. My first encounter with punk, a friend of the family had the B-52s record and I went crazy over that. I still love them. And then about a year later, when I was like 11, I heard other stuff like the Ramones and Devo.

I came from a very academic background. My father was a well-known writer and my mother was in grad school. My dad taught at Cal, and one of his students was Jennifer Blowdryer, who used to work for *Punk Globe*. She loaned him some records, which I got my hands on. And I got this book called *Punk*, which was about English punk bands. Before I ever really had much of the music, I had devoured the photos. I even decided I wanted to sing at some point, just from looking at the pictures of singers.

Aaron Cometbus: I met Jesse Michaels when we were eight or nine, maybe even earlier. Jesse and his brother were the kids who lived across the street from a friend of mine. One day me and Jesse are blowing up tubes of toothpaste on the schoolyard, then a few years later we're still little kids but now doing a fanzine.

Jesse Michaels: Aaron was a very, very obsessive kid. When he was into comic books he was obsessed with comic books. When he was into art he was obsessed with art. I think that's a characteristic of a lot of punk rock people. If it wasn't punk rock it would have been ghouls and goblins and role-playing games. It's that type of fringey, super-interested personality. And he definitely qualified as that. He already had fanzines and records and stuff. The walls of his room were covered with flyers.

We worked on a zine together. I was maybe 12 or 13. We changed the name every week, or every issue. It was mainly his thing, but I did my bit, too. And that eventually turned into *Cometbus*.

We did an interview with the Ramones. They were up at Lawrence Hall of Science for the *Rocket to Russia* tour, I think. We caught them at KALX, while they were walking from the studio down to their car. We pestered them through the glass window and held up signs saying we were Ramones fans. They humored us and did this very quick interview, and then they got us into the show, which was very sweet. It was Joey and Johnny, I think. That was a big deal for us.

Aaron Cometbus: A lanky, greasy-haired guy with a Ramones shirt worked at the corner 7-Eleven, where I bought comics and hung out playing video games. When he got married, I went to the wedding. Two kids there cornered me. "Is it true you interviewed the Ramones?" they said. One of the kids was Tom, who ended up playing guitar in Soup. The other was Tim, the little brother of the 7-Eleven guy.

Jason Lockwood: Tim used to play pinball with us on Durant. There was a period when he decided everybody had to call him Lint. You never give yourself a fuckin' nickname! Someone gives it to you and you resist it like mad. I told that to everybody I knew, and they were like, "Dude, you've got Tim in your belly button."

Tim Armstrong: We were drinking beer one night, one of those little parks in Berkeley. Lint, it just stuck. People called me Lint for awhile, but then people would be like, "Check it out—I know your real name. It's Tim Armstrong!" Like, yeah, yeah, that's my name. So I got tired of the nickname. Some people still call me Lint, though.

Jesse Michaels: Tim is quite a go-getter. He just goes for it. He just makes bands whenever he wants to. I met him at a Crimpshrine band practice, and he talked about wanting to do a band, and to do something more like Crimpshrine, something more punk.

Tim Armstrong: Jesse went away to Pittsburgh to live with his mom, and he reappeared at the end of '86, early '87. We had played video games a few times over at Universal Records. We never knew each other really well. We were hanging out and I was like, "Yo, me and Matt Freeman want to start a band. I heard you played drums, I want you to play drums for us."

He was 17 and I was 21. And he said, "I want to sing." I was like, "Okay, I was gonna sing, that's fine, I don't really care." That was it.

Jesse Michaels: I was into it. I don't know how he picked me out. Well, I shouldn't say he picked me out, 'cause I kinda wanted to do something, too. We sorta found each other.

Jason Beebout: Jesse asked us if he could use the name Operation Ivy. I think that was after we'd already switched to Isocracy. And Jesse said, "Oh, that's cool, can I take that?" We didn't care. It was more fun to name your band than to stick with it.

Jesse Michaels: We were doing this sort of semi-ska thing, and I thought it sounded a little bit mod-like. Operation, the whole spy thing, in the two-tone ska sense. I thought it might work.

Bonedog: One time Jesse was painting a big huge mural at Gilman. I went up to him and said, "What are you painting?" "Oh, it's my new band, Operation Ivy." It was this big huge thing. They hadn't even played a show yet.

Jesse Michaels: By the time we had four songs, we had a show booked. It's just one of those things. We got Dave, and Matt and Tim put him through drumming boot camp and he became a drummer.

Dave Mello: I went to Albany High School. Matt and Tim graduated in '84, when I was a freshman. The speed metal scene was really big. Fifteen-year-old kids were taking lessons from Joe Satriani in Berkeley, and they could really play their instruments. But that doesn't mean they knew what they were doing, or why they were doing it.

I started playing in a punk band with my brother Pat. He was a 14-year-old kid with a really high voice. We gave him a mohawk. He sang or yelled, and I was playing drums. My mom used to let us throw afternoon shows in my garage across the street from high school. Basic Radio played two shows, and that's when I really met Tim and Matt. Tim liked the way I played, so when that band broke up I was the first person they asked.

They'd been out of high school for a couple years. I knew that Matt could probably buy alcohol by now. So when they asked me to play I was really excited. Just from meeting Tim, there was something about the guy. If I joined his band I was gonna have fun, and my world was gonna open up.

Tim was just a character. He has a very slow personality at first, where he just speaks really slow, kinda slang, like he's trying to be ghetto. But then you realize that he's always like that. It's just his personality. He looked like a punk rocker. Because of what I thought at the time a punk rocker was. He always liked to have droopy pants, belts and things falling off of him.

Matt always talked like he was in his 30s, like he'd experienced life way more than everybody else. He had a way of talking like he was a stand-up comedian. Telling you how life is hard and how he's experienced a lot. He was maybe 21 at the time. But he had confidence about him, and that I was really drawn to. I was an alright drummer, but he taught me a couple tricks on how to play with a bass player. And that's what I needed.

I met Jesse a couple weeks later. He was a really good guy, but a little more withdrawn. I didn't really know what to think of him. Honest and sometimes hard to deal with, but very creative. We all got together, and I knew that was gonna be a creative band. At the time I was extremely shy. I really felt that driving force of Tim and Jesse, and wanted to see where that was gonna go.

Matt Freeman: We played our first show in Dave's garage.

Tim Armstrong: Then the next one was with MDC at Gilman Street. It took us two months to get a set together.

Dave Mello: We all liked catchy songs. We all liked the Clash. We were really young, and all four of us liked to go crazy onstage. I was really shy at first, but the energy that they had—especially Tim, who loves to run around with his guitar onstage and still stay on time. I really dug that. I would do the same thing.

Jeff Ott: Jesse, cute guy, Tim, cute guy. That was a lot of the immediacy of success. I don't want to sound derogatory about either Rancid or about Jesse's bands. But for me personally, the thing about that band was Tim and Matt writing the music, and Jesse writing the lyrics. Each half was perfect in its own right.

Dave Mello: It was a lot about playing weekend parties. At such and such house, Eggplant's house, my garage. It was all these people from Gilman becoming friends and saying, why don't we just have shows every weekend? If it's not a show here, it could be a barbeque or picnic here or a party. We played with Crimpshrine all the time.

Jesse Michaels: A lot of young kids were doing very spontaneous obscure little things in backyards and basements. So it was a perfect time to have a real sneaky little underground thing going.

Gavin MacArthur: My band in high school opened for Op Ivy at the Albany Rec Center, across the street from both the Mellos' and my parents' house. As soon as Op Ivy showed up, the place just filled up with all these punks. The place went totally crazy. It was super energetic. I'd listened to a few ska things, and of course I listened to punk. That was the first band I heard that combined the two.

Jesse Michaels: We played all over the place. Berkeley, Oakland, El Cerrito, Alameda, San Jose, Santa Rosa, Sebastopol, Pinole, Benicia. If you took a map and drew a 50-mile perimeter around Berkeley, we played within that.

Matt Freeman: We'd go wherever. "Oh, you're having a party up in Lake County near Healdsburg?" We'd go up there.

Tim Armstrong: We also played the Albany Laundromat. Wherever we could.

Matt Freeman: Gilman Street would have all these bands, and Operation Ivy would be at the bottom, always. They'd say, "You gotta play last," because they didn't want people to leave.

Jesse Michaels: I think we wore the place out a little bit. We'd play there like twice a month. Less than a year into it, we recorded some songs for the *Turn It Around* compilation. I wondered if we were ready. But Matt and Tim are just a machine, they never stop. And of course they were right, you have to strike while the iron's hot. So we recorded two songs. And did a 7-inch I think within six months after that. We were playing constantly.

Tim Armstrong: Lookout! wasn't even a label yet. Then '88, *Hectic* came out. I was skeptical we were gonna sell out the first pressing. But Larry always knew that the shit was important. He would tell us that, and we would be like, "Oh, dude, shut up."

Murray Bowles: It was a really phenomenal scene. When Op Ivy first started playing there would be 20 or 30 people, and all of a sudden the shows would be packed. Nobody had heard of speed ska before.

Billie Joe Armstrong: People from Danville started flocking over to come see 'em play. I loved 'em, I thought they were the best.

Jason Lockwood: They were playing at Gilman, I got there and saw my friends up there making great music. In between sets I climbed over all the kids and got up in Tim's face and was like, "This is fantastic! I thought you guys were gonna suck so bad, and you're great!"

Larry Livermore: They were very good musicians. Matt's one of the most amazing bass players in the world. Tim's a very interesting guy, and a very intelligent guy. But he's also got a persona that some people find it hard to get through. I don't have any great difficulty talking with him. But some people do. I think he puts it up as a little bit of a barrier. 'Cause he's very much a self-made man. I don't know what Jesse's like now. But in his heyday, he had the room in the palm of his hand.

Anna Brown: The first time you saw them it was just really clear that they were totally special. There were whole groups of people dancing to really good lyrics about things. Deep but catchy. They weren't ever sappy.

Sham Saenz: Gilman had this battle of the bands one time and it was Green Day, El Vez, Crimpshrine, Operation Ivy. Operation Ivy got up and did a cover of Journey's "When the Lights Go Down in the City" and it was the most amazing thing on earth. It was funny and clever and executed super well and I was like, "Okay, these Gilman guys are doing their own fuckin' thing."

Jesse Michaels: It's hard to talk about because we were very lucky. I don't want to sound like I'm blowing our horn or anything. But we generally won crowds over because we really brought a lot of energy. Every night, no matter how small the crowd was. People dug that. Also a lot of people had never heard the ska thing. We hit 'em with a gimmick right away and they liked that, too.

Tim Armstrong: After we made our first CD, Christmastime 1988, in our house on Pierce Street, my whole family was there. My uncle from Florida, who's just this bombastic character, in front of everybody, he was like, "Tim!" Room got quiet. "So Tim, when you gonna find your niche in life? Everyone in here has a niche. What's your niche? You need a niche." And my poor mom, "Oh, no, here he goes." I said, "If anybody in this family has a fuckin' niche"—the room got dead quiet, I was lookin' at everybody—"it's fuckin' me. I'm in Operation Ivy, I made a record. All I want to do is make a record and be in a band and be a part of somethin', and I did it! So if anybody in this family has a fuckin' niche, it's me!"

That's almost 20 years ago. I was in Operation Ivy at the right time. It's weird, I can't even intellectualize—maybe it doesn't come across—but I always felt like I made it back then. I tried to

Bombshell: Lint and Jesse Michaels of Op Ivy

Photo by Murray Bowles

tell my uncle that. He don't really want to talk to me too much about anything, really.

Jesse Michaels: Before I was in a band, I was into stuff like the Bad Brains, Crucifix, Jerry's Kids, and Minor Threat and MDC and BGK and Marginal Man. Generally with hardcore, it was all political back then. It was even political when it probably shouldn't have been. Some people had no idea what they were talking about. But I was in that consciousness and did what I knew. The world was an extremely fucked-up place, and you should talk about it with music. That was a natural thing to communicate, especially punk music because it takes basically a rebel standpoint. If you're gonna be rebellious, what are you thinking? Do you have ideas, or is it just a fashion?

Sham Saenz: We all knew something big was going to happen when Operation Ivy played the anti-Apartheid riots. There was a huge sit-in at Sproul Plaza up on Telegraph. Everybody was up there protesting, and they had this day show. I sat on this balcony not really giving too much of a shit about Operation Ivy. I had dreadlocks but I was more peace-punky. I looked down and they started to play, and the crowd accumulated, and then it kept accumulating. And then it seemed like as far as you could look there was people watching them and knew the words. I was just going, wow, people like these guys.

Noah Landis: Back then, things like the Specials were what everyone played at high school parties. They tapped into a little bit of that energy and incorporated it with the new punk rock East Bay thing that was happening.

Jesse Michaels: Part of what we were trying to do was the positive energy thing. To bring a hardcore intensity with less negativity. It was still dark but it wasn't like Condemned to Death or Flipper. It had a couple more colors in the spectrum.

Anna Brown: Jesse was a great front person. He just would bounce off the walls the whole time.

Billie Joe Armstrong: I really looked up to him. He was like a hero because he wrote amazing lyrics and was a great artist and had this great punk sensibility. But he was also an incredibly kind person, just really sweet. He took real interest in what people had to say. In what I had to say.

Martin Brohm: Everybody knew the words. Seven people wrapped around the mic with Jesse. Everybody was singing except for us. We were telling them to fuck off. We had a bit of banter going back and forth, with Isocracy and Op Ivy. Some people liked it and some people didn't. We would have fake fights where we'd jump onstage and fight with 'em. It went over good with Jesse. Matt was good with it. Tim didn't like it at all. Lenny didn't like it at all. But in between songs we would be screamin' and yellin': "You guys fuckin' suck! Fuck you!"

Jason Beebout: "You're breakin' my heart! You should kick your own ass for suckin' so bad!"

Martin Brohm: That was great fun. A lot of people would come to those shows who wouldn't go to other Gilman shows. So you'd be out in the crowd going, "You guys are fuckin' shit!" And these 14-year-old girls would be going, "Dude, what the fuck is your problem?"

Tim Armstrong: That was a part of the whole Isocracy humor. Heckling, garbage, I never took it personal. People probably did, though. All that shit was cool. That was just part of the territory.

Matt Freeman: They were fucking kooks. So when we got back from tour we did that Isocracy song "Rodeo," as ska. That was funny, they were watching and—"Ah hah!"

Jeff Ott: People would go out after shows and jump in people's bushes all over the place, in the middle of the night. With the object being to destroy them. Literally. We'd get kids coming from the suburbs to see Op Ivy, to go out and jump in hedges.

Jesse Michaels: It was sort of an extension of skating.

Jason Beebout: It was a cop's nightmare, just a bunch of fuckin' 16-year-old douchebags running around the streets, with nothin' to do at four in the morning. You'd go up into the Berkeley Hills where all the professors lived. They had these really expensive houses and nice cars. You'd find a really beautifully manicured hedge. Some were really good, some were really forgiving, others were soft and downy, and some were horrible.

Martin Brohm: Your best bush was a finely manicured juniper. Because the juniper had good spring-back. You'd get in there and it'd pop you out. A lot of times, if they're too soft, you'd jump in and go straight through it, and you'd land on whatever's on the other side. Or you'd get stuck with one of the strong branches underneath. You'd get a juniper in the rib cage.

Jeff Ott: Aaron Cometbus opened his head up.

Spike Slawson: I landed on a stump that was cut at an angle.

Lenny Filth: I landed on a sprinkler head in front of the Ford place on San Pablo. I thought I broke my back.

Jesse Michaels: The person who invented it, to me, was Noah from Christ on Parade. And he probably doesn't get credit for it. But I remember hanging out with some people and he was doing it. We made a song about it. Maybe not the most well-advised song, but, yeah.

> *What happened to your bush*
> *It's not the same*
> *Something in your hedge*

Made a violent change
We come we see
We dive and destroy
And annihilating shrubs is what we enjoy
Hedgecore hedgedive hedgecore
We're doin' hedges to stay alive
It's anarchy night every night of the year
With chaotic mayhem
We keep your bush in fear
Terrorist assassins of creative gardening
Fucking up your hedge here's what we sing

—"Hedgecore," Operation Ivy

Jesse Michaels: Upon reflection I regret in any way popularizing fucking with people's yards. Some things aren't meant to go beyond the handful of idiots who do them. This is one of them.

Noah Landis: Watching Op Ivy get more and more popular was pretty exciting. Not only were they really great, they were really great personalities. To watch Dave play the drums was like, "Heck, yeah!" You couldn't even take your eyes off him.

Martin Brohm: They called him Animal. 'Cause that's how he played drums, like Animal from the Muppets. He had this big goofy hair, this little scrawny kid, he was everywhere. He was so fun to watch. It went from top to bottom in that band.

Fat Mike: The first time I heard them I was on tour and someone had their 7-inch. It just blew my mind how great it was. I got back here and started hanging out with Lint a little bit, and we starting doing some shows together.

Frank Portman: People just really, really loved them. They really had some star quality. They were a great band in the ways that great rock 'n' roll bands are great. They evoked a spirit. I would maybe prefer the Fall to the Clash. I was touched more deeply inside by Crimpshrine than I was by Operation Ivy. But the world is big enough for every version of show business.

Anna Brown: Their first and only tour was in Matt's car. They built a crate on the roof, put their amps in it, and put all the rest of their shit in the trunk. All the way across the country in a four-door passenger car.

Matt Freeman: A '69 Chrysler Newport, green with a 383. It's actually one of the longest production cars ever made. I bought it for 900 bucks from my fuckin' neighbor Mrs. Cogden, who was blind in her right eye so the whole right side was all bashed up. You'd look at the driver's side, "Oh, what a nice car." You'd look at the other side and there was like dents, the mirror's hanging off.

Tim Armstrong: We were the first Gilman Street band to tour. Crimpshrine, Fang had toured, obviously. But they weren't Gilman acts.

Matt Freeman: Us four and David Hayes. Kamala Parks booked it. That was a shoestring budget. We would go to supermarkets and get cheese sandwiches and eat on the hood of the car.

Jesse Michaels: Driving around in a car with five people for a month and a half is absurd. Absolutely absurd.

Dave Mello: If anyone had heard us at that time, especially on the East Coast and Midwest, it was because of the *Turn It Around* comp and *Maximum RocknRoll*. In Delaware we played a house party and their parents made the kids sit down. So they had pits where they were just crawling around on their butts. We played a show in Lexington, Kentucky, for four people.

Jesse Michaels: There was all these little places. Some of them were actually clubs, some were basements, community centers, punk houses. Invariably every place had terrible sound. We played this show where kids in this punk house put on the movie *The Decline of Western Civilization* and had a pit going in the house, while they watched the movie.

Tim Armstrong: Kenosha, Wisconsin. David Hayes slept in the car that night, and so did Dave Mello. I slept upstairs by this fuckin' door. I felt like it was raining. I woke up, "Where am I? I'm in Kenosha, a punk house, it's raining?" It's not raining. The door was open and this burly-assed skinhead was pissing out to the backyard, but it was coming in and I was getting sprayed by piss.

Martin Sorrondeguy: I remember when Op Ivy came to Chicago. That was an amazing show. They grabbed the mic and started talking about, "This is about you, this is about everybody, it's about punks, skins, this, that." There was this real sense of inclusivity. This new wave of the early Lookout! stuff was a whole new scene developing. It was a reclamation of what a lot of the old people were slowly and surely killing. These new kids were coming in and goin', "Forget all that, this is what it's about right now." We all took to it. Everybody sensed it.

Larry Livermore: They were the first Lookout! band to go out to the rest of the U.S.A. They called back from their first show and said, "The kids already know all the words to all the songs." Which was weird, because the record had been out maybe a few weeks at most.

Jesse Michaels: Larry's a great guy but you have to take what he says with a grain of salt. Did the audience know all our words? No, a couple people in the audience sometimes knew a chorus. That being said, it still was pretty impressive, because how did they find this shit out?

Dave Mello: After the tour we were getting more popular. Touring bands were coming in and they wanted to play with us. We were trying to record an album for Lookout!. We weren't really thinking of anything else. It felt like this could be something. We didn't know what it could be. Something scary, even.

Noah Landis: They couldn't play where they were supposed to play anymore, because too many people would show up.

Dave Mello: On one hand you have Matt and Tim who are really excited about this, and Lookout! says we can go to Europe. It was a little bit too much for Jesse. He didn't want it to go that fast. He didn't want to have a whole bunch of people liking him, being his fans, and him having to live up to something. He was the front man. It was his lyrics, his message. He was still very young, not really sure of what he wanted to do with the band. We just got off a tour. He didn't have that great of a time.

So he didn't want to go on another tour. Both Matt and Tim were gung ho for Europe. That was a big conflict. When he told us over the phone, it was a big argument for a couple days. And then Jesse decided that it wasn't gonna happen.

Tim Armstrong: It wasn't brutal. It wasn't like, "Fuck you, dick!" It was a premeditated breakup.

Dave Mello: When it all came down to it, all four of us had to admit that we had a hell of a time. It's easier to celebrate those two years. It wasn't just our band, it was all our friends and all those other bands, all those people who were at the picnics.

Frank Portman: That last Op Ivy show at Gilman was a spectacle. And they were all very excited and emotional. It was like a real show. Like few of those shows were, that I remember.

Dallas Denery: I had never seen the place so crowded. I was looking around and I was thinking, "Who are all these people?" I didn't even recognize any of them. Because they had gotten outside of Gilman and the Gilman devotees.

Dave Mello: Green Day played, and also Crimpshrine—I think that was their last show. It was kinda poetic. Because even though they started a year before, we both ended on that night. They just let everybody in. There was at least 600 people. My mom was packed up against the front of the stage. It was crazy. We had a great time. Played every song.

Anna Brown: People were literally hanging on to the walls trying to catch a glimpse.

Martin Sprouse: They broke up a week after their record came out on Lookout! People that just get into punk now can still put on that record, and that record has power. It's timeless. It still fucking kicks ass on a lot of punk.

Matt Wobensmith: By breaking up as they put out this masterpiece record, the signature record, it only made people want them more.

Andy Asp: What a great punk outfit it was. They only played 100 shows or something like that. They didn't do a reunion. One single album with a couple EPs. That's more punk than Sex Pistols or Fugazi.

Anna Brown: We all felt a sense of real loss because they were just getting really big. Some people were like, "Thank god, they'll be ours forever." And other people were like, "It was a shame."

Dave Mello: I was sad. I wanted it to go on for a little longer. I was still only 20 years old. At the same time, I felt like I had a new awakening. I wanted to go in a different direction. The same adrenaline kicks I had when Operation Ivy was starting, I also had that when it was ending. I had never been in a band that was that popular. It definitely opened avenues for me.

Jesse Michaels: I was a lot different from all of my friends, even in the punk scene. I worried more, I thought too much. So a lot of this shit for me was pretty dark. For them it was fun, for me it was escapism because I was just so fucking unhappy. That's what went into the intensity of the lyrics. As much as making political statements about society, I was kind of lashing out against my own inner problems and fucked-up nature. It was very internal. I don't even know what I was so bummed out about, probably just weird family shit, who knows.

James Washburn: It's just like the Rancid song, you know, "Too much attention unavoidably destroyed us." That's what happened.

Anna Brown: Jesse went through this whole thing for awhile. He dropped out and was soul-searching, going on Buddhist retreats, and he moved away.

Jesse Michaels: I went to Nicaragua. I just wanted to do something really different. I did have a social consciousness, and wanted to see if I could be of service. It turns out I was completely lazy when I was there. Spent most of the time drinking. It didn't really work out. But I had good intentions.

I just had a rough time in my 20s. I'm a lot happier now. But then again, you know, we're talking about punk rock. I don't want to turn into Sigmund Freud about it, but a lot of those kids were just fuckin' miserable beat-up kids. Some came from really dysfunctional families and were trying to find a family in punk, often doing it in really dysfunctional ways. We don't talk about that. We talk about how great it was to see Marginal Man.

Eric Ozenne: I ended up joining the Marines. I was in Okinawa, Japan. It was just really lame. I needed to get back to who I was, mentally. This kid from Benicia, California, had an Operation Ivy tape on him. I was like, "You've got to be kidding me! You have an Operation Ivy tape? Let me borrow it." I played this thing over and over again for like a week. And the lyrics and everything about it just snapped me back into a place where I felt comfortable as myself.

I tried to get out of the Marines, which didn't work. But during that process, I ended up running into all of the degenerate military guys—a lot of them were punks. Some from Chicago, some from Southern California, some from Wyoming. We started hanging out almost every night in a vacant barracks filled with these broken fans, so we called it the Fan Club. We'd sit in there and listen to the Operation Ivy stuff, Gorilla Biscuits, the new Rancid record. I cooked for everybody on a hot plate, so we'd sit around and eat vegan food, and listen to punk and hardcore and mosh around the barracks, throwing fans at each other, just go crazy. We did this for months. It was really cool. I wouldn't go back into the Marines to do it again, though.

Dallas Denery: I'm now a 42-year-old college professor in Maine, and I can walk down a street in Portland and see some kid on a skateboard with an Op Ivy shirt. There's this temptation: "You know, I saw those guys 30 times." You don't want to be the old guy trying to relate to the kids, 'cause that's pathetic. But it's kind of remarkable, this stuff is 20 years old.

Jesse Michaels: I don't know why or exactly what it did. But I feel grateful that it did something.

Tim Armstrong: My decline with alcohol and drugs started to get really bad. It turned into a sad spiral, but it had to go there. At the end of Operation Ivy, I was already fuckin' up shows.

Fat Mike: I'd bring people from the city, "Man you've gotta see this band Op Ivy, they're so amazing." And they were so fucking bad. Lint broke a string once at Ruthie's and it took him, it had to be ten minutes. 'Cause he was wasted.

Tim Armstrong: Everyone seemed to know. I'd never think about anything but right now. We played Covered Wagon with Mr. T and I was so fucked up, I couldn't play my guitar.

Mike LaVella: Their famous worst show ever. Where Lint was too drunk to play.

Tim Armstrong: I felt bad about that shit. It was that show that Larry took me aside and he said, "Look, I come from Ann Arbor, man. I was at Woodstock and I've seen a lot of friends of mine go down from drugs and alcohol and never come back. Don't go down that road." It was a seed that was planted.

Matt Freeman: We'd been friends for years, and we'd talk every day. But he'd disappear for a couple days, and I knew by the end of day two, like, okay, he's drinkin' again. He wasn't hard to find. He was up on Telegraph doing some fucked-up thing. There were these places in Richmond that had a detox, and I took him there, like, four times. He'd go and dry out for awhile, and then he'd slip.

Tim Armstrong: It got bad. Olde English. And then I liked Cisco a little later. My brother Jeff found me on Telegraph, took me to the hospital, my blood-alcohol level was .39, almost .40. Legally drunk is .08 or something. So I was like, dead. They asked my brother, "Is Tim trying to kill himself?"

I was hospitalized three times. By '91 I had nowhere to live. I had no job, I was just fucking nothing. My mom wouldn't let me sleep in the basement anymore. I'd go into the Salvation Army program in downtown Oakland. You got a bed. I did that for a couple weeks. I was doin' drugs, too. But that wasn't my main thing. I loved to drink so much, I'd just be drunk nonstop.

Matt Freeman: I never saw anyone drink as hard as him. No fuckin' joke. It was a learning experience for me, too. He'd say, "Oh, I need some money for food," and I'd say, "Okay, here's money," and he'd go buy beer. I'm like, okay, can't pull that trick on me again. So I'd say, "Well, let's go eat, I'll buy you groceries." After awhile we couldn't possibly play music together, because of this. He was too unreliable.

Christopher Appelgren: There had been Downfall, right after Operation Ivy had broken up, which was an attempt to continue.

Ben Sizemore: Then Lint was in this band called Generator that was a little more metal. He played with Dance Hall Crashers and he quit them.

Christopher Appelgren: I saw Generator at Gilman. There was lots of excitement and anticipation for their first few shows. They had rewritten this Downfall song that went, "Are you gonna be there when the storm comes?" And Generator had rewritten the lyrics: "Are you gonna be there for the inner-city holocaust?" I remember being really bummed out. Inner-city holocaust? I hope I'm not there for that.

Tim Armstrong: Downfall never really released anything officially. Generator never recorded a thing. Those two projects fell apart. I couldn't keep these two bands together.

Matt Freeman: It was a weird scene. You talk about how great Operation Ivy was, and we were cleaning Gilman bathrooms three years later, just to fuckin' practice.

Tim Armstrong: Cleaning the sick-ass fuckin' toilets. But we got to practice for free. That was the way it should be, man.

42

White Picket Fence

Ben Sizemore: There was this whole culture of punk houses in West Oakland.

Jesse Luscious: Dementia House, 1640 House, which had a ton of parties. Maxi Pad, Little Arkansas, Fifth Street House.

Anna Brown: The Madonna Inn, the Ashtray, the Pill Hill House, Fairview Upper and Lower. Punks would move in, and eventually the landlords would have had enough and evict the punks.

A. C. Thompson: There was a push to do shows in houses because clubs, even all-ages clubs, were too formal. Because keeping people a foot away from the band was just too much.

Anna Brown: I probably spent every weekend of high school at the Ashtray, smoking cigarettes and listening to records. The house was a complete disaster. There was a giant hole that went from the kitchen all the way down to the basement, like the wood floor had rotted away. All the windows were smashed out.

Jesse Michaels: I lived at the Ashtray with Jake from Filth and Lenny from Isocracy.

Martin Sprouse: They were total smart-asses. They created this whole fake dirt punk thing. I think the Filth logo had two crossed hypodermic needles or something.

Jesse Michaels: We would exaggerate it. We would cut ourselves in a semi-joking way. But at the same time we were really, really into it. So it was ironic and yet not ironic at all. It was ridiculous to spray-paint "Big fat lines of meth" on your wall. But we were into it anyway.

Anna Brown: There was graffiti on all the walls. This guy Joe Pestilence lived there for awhile. When they wanted him to leave they didn't ask him. They just started writing on the walls, "Joe Be Gone." Eventually he left.

Jason Beebout: The house was so close to another house that there was a window that opened up to a brick wall. These rats took it over and filled it full of hay and made a nest. We played a party at the Ashtray. It turned into a fight, and James Washburn grabbed a skinhead and threw his head through the fuckin' window. The rats went flying everywhere. That was exciting.

Lenny Filth: We had our own little rat zoo. You gotta remember, at the time I was a heavy drinker, too. I think I was blacked out during the whole fuckin' Reagan administration.

Kate Knox: The Maxi Pad was this two-story, three-bedroom house. It was me, and Adrienne and Todd, who started Spitboy. An all-women punk house. By then I was over my thing about only being friends with guys.

Wendy-O Matik: Maxi Pad was a big part of my life. I knew all the women in that house and all the women who came and went out of that house. I met people from all over the world there.

Kate Knox: We tried to make it an open, European-style squat punk rock home. Anybody was welcome. There was one bathroom—the "myn's room"—and there were usually seven or eight people living there. We had bands staying in the living room. We had people tattooing out of the closet. At one point, I had 13 Germans staying in the attic.

They showed up three days after an old man, who was getting head from a prostitute, gunned his car through our living room. The old man picked the prostitute up at McDonald's at 11 in the morning and, for some reason, decided that our driveway was a good place to get head.

Lenny Filth: It wasn't a bad place to take a hooker, really. Down this little alley. Maxi Pad was all the way in the back. None of them would have cared. The man just needed to learn how to drive correctly.

Kate Knox: He had one of those old Lincoln Continentals with the bench seats from the '70s—pure steel. Engine's running and she was all, "Pay me first," so he pulled out his wallet, she grabbed it, and took off. So he reached across the door, stepped on the gas by accident, flew down the driveway and we got a fuckin' Lincoln Continental in our living room.

Lenny Filth: It was a good thing nobody was sitting on the couch.

Kate Knox: When we finally got the guy's daughter on the phone, she said, "Again?!" It was the second time he'd gotten busted with a prostitute. We ended up getting an insurance settlement from it and we paid our rent for months.

Richard the Roadie: Kate is an absolute international production. She started the B.O.B. Fest, this whole German and European thing, with punks coming over here as tourists.

Kate Knox: It became an international punk rock festival. B.O.B. is based in three punk rock sister cities: Bremen, Germany; Bath, England; and Oakland. In the late '80s, I went over to Europe with Fang and we ended up in Bremen. Immediately, there was this amazing affinity. Like Oakland, Bremen's a smaller city. Something just clicked. So this traveling circuit started. People would come from Germany and go through customs and say, "We're going to Oakland." And the officials would be like, "Why are you going there?" In the '80s, Oakland was so not the tourist destination.

Adrienne Droogas: Econochrist had this house on Arlington called Little Arkansas. That was the big party house that everyone would go to and hang out after the shows, party 'til six in the morning.

Bucky Sinister: Oh god, it was just a little piece of old Arkansas to me. The first time I met the Econochrist guys, I was trekking through this party and I heard those accents. I just about started to cry 'cause I still had a bad drawl back then, and I didn't feel like I fit in. I just really loved being around those guys.

Jason White: Little Arkansas made it easier for me to come out here. Because as soon as I met someone and they asked, "Oh, where you from?" I'd say Arkansas. And it would just be, "Oh, another one."

Lenny Filth: We all lived within a five-block radius of each other. So you'd see everybody just about every day.

Anna Brown: After the Ashtray shut down, everybody moved over to Little Arkansas. They had epic drunken throw-downs all the time.

Ben Sizemore: There was a party every night. I was one of the few people that was straightedge. Basically, you could do any drug you wanted, except heroin was frowned upon. But you could snort pounds of speed and drink as much as you want.

When I moved out of Little Arkansas, I moved in with Lint. He lived in this boardinghouse in South Berkeley, at Harmon and Adeline. It was him and another younger dude, and an Arab kid that worked in the store, and a couple of old men.

Tim Armstrong: A lot of people went in and out of that place. The

Adeline House was like the Middle East, 'cause downstairs the owners were Arabs, and Stanley was this old Jewish cat, 70 or some shit. He hated the owners, and the owners hated him. They would talk shit about each other, just racial slurs. They were hard on each other.

Zarah Manos: I called it the Rock Star House because that was where the Rancid guys lived. Ben Sizemore lived there, then some of the Dead and Gone guys moved in. I got to live there for a month.

Ben Sizemore: It was fucking dirt cheap. Slowly we took it all over, except for Stanley, the old man down at the end of the hall. Poor guy.

A. C. Thompson: Everyone tightened the lids on all his food so he'd have to exert effort and hopefully do himself in. They'd put their penis in his mayo. People took his door off the hinges and peed in his room. Once, some people came looking for him and they said, "We know he lives here because it says 'Fuck Stan' on your front door." He was so mistreated there.

Fraggle: I started Dementia House. It was a little rickety house with a white picket fence and trees in the front. It had a basement that wasn't attached to the foundation. So it was like sitting on the ground. You could walk up the stairs and the house would shake.

Richard the Roadie: Fraggle always ran a household. He was a teeny bit older. I wouldn't say more responsible. But he was able to deal with renting a big house, having this revolving cast of characters.

Fraggle: The first party was December of '89. We put out flyers. The turnout was insane! The bands played in my backyard— Econochrist, Blatz, maybe Downfall, maybe Filth. I remember looking out our front door and the entire street was nothing but people. And the cops were just standing out there.

Jesse Luscious: Then Fraggle ran a house called Pill Hill Zoo Haus, which was on Pill Hill. It's literally a hill covered with hospitals and old-age homes and dentist offices. And there was this huge three-story house built into the hill. They had shows inside, they had shows outside, they had barbecues.

Fraggle: Right across the street was the convalescent old-age home. To the right was the Berkeley Clinic. And down the end of the street was the hospice where you go to die.

Hef: Fraggle would buy a keg of beer and charge you a few dollars for as much beer as you could drink. On Sunday afternoons.

Fraggle: As long as you had the cup, you could come back for more.

The great thing about punk shows is, people go dance, get drunk and fall down. The cup gets crushed. But we never made a profit. We always just bought more beer.

Richard the Roadie: It was wall-to-wall apeshit. Sometimes you'd go to those parties in Oakland and it was kinda creepy or weird. But Fraggle, you'd go to his house and it'd be fun.

Fraggle: One of the last shows we had, the cops came by at noon. I think it was Screw 32, AFI, Dead and Gone. We never had problems with cops before, so we didn't think anything of it. They were like, "How come you didn't invite us? Next time, you have to invite us," and then they left.

Then somebody got in a fight in my backyard. There was this guy full-throttle kicking this other guy while he was on the ground. And the entire party piled into the backyard and kicked the guy out. A couple hours passed, everybody was having a good time, then someone came in and said Nando got arrested. The cops said, "This party's over! Anyone on the street is gonna get arrested." I was trying to get everybody in our house. A cop tried to come in, so we locked the door. Then he called for backup.

Soon, there were 19 squad cars outside—it was like a 1960s L.A. riot scene. Orlando was upstairs trying to call the news media. Marcus was up there shooting cops out the window with a *Star Trek* phaser. I walked outside and said, "Okay, the party's over." And he said, "Okay, good, you're under arrest."

I don't have my finger on the pulse anymore, because all the shows I work now are 21-and-over so all I see is the old fogies. But I think punk is very cyclic. Things will die down, then there's a whole new batch of kids to pick it up again.

Janelle Hessig: Fraggle looks almost exactly the same today. I'm sure his spine is just fucked up because he wore 30 gold chains around his neck. Every novelty punk accoutrement—tons of skull rings on all his fingers, multi-colored bi-hawk, little ax earrings.

Fraggle: Metal should be worn, not heard.

43

Up the Punks!

Ben Sizemore: There were riots. There were earthquakes. The East Bay hills were on fire. There were blackouts. The first Gulf War and the Rodney King trial. There were huge fucking protests in San Francisco with people burning cop cars down by the Transbay Terminal. It was a crazy time. Being a young, idealistic punker from Arkansas with real leftist political views, I thought it was great. The revolution was just around the corner, man! And I was gonna be there!

Kareim McKnight: I just assumed the whole punk movement was political. At every event, there were punks. The music that everyone was playing was protest music.

Jesse Luscious: I came out for the 1989 Anarchist Gathering in San Francisco. I definitely didn't expect to stay out here.

Oran Canfield: They swarmed in from all over America.

Bucky Sinister: I don't know how much of this was going on in other parts of the country, but I'd never seen it before. We all knew the anarchy sign, but we didn't really know what it was. There were people out here who knew the history of anarchism.

Ben Sizemore: We went to a picnic in Dolores Park and there were 2,000 punks in the park. It was so exciting.

Antonio López: The anarchist conference was held in the Mission, at some elementary school that was leased out over the summer. My most memorable workshop was an anti-TV one. One of the students wanted to videotape it. And the guy teaching the workshop—long blond hair, very muscular, with Levi's shorts cut so high his balls are practically hanging out—was furious. The student who was taping said, "There's a bunch of people in Canada who can't be here and they want to see this." And the guy said, "If you go to my house you can play guitar or make love or read a book, but you'll never watch TV. I will never let anyone do anything that has anything to do with TV. And if you don't like it, get the hell out of my workshop! And if anyone else doesn't like it, get out!" I actually joined about half the people and left.

This conference was like an alternative university. People took it very seriously, and in retrospect, I appreciate that a lot. There were the pacifists, the anarchists, the thinkers, the artists, and the poets. And then there were the direct action people.

Tom Jennings: I was one of the organizers in San Francisco, and published the gathering's handbook. It was the last in a series that had started in 1986, with the Haymarket Gathering.

Patrick Hughes: These agitator types showed up, demanding street action. And when we demurred, they started calling us wimps and shit.

Jennifer Rose Emick: They called it the Day of Action.

Liz Highleyman: There was a great deal of debate about whether such days should be a part of conventions. In fact, this Day of Action was scheduled after the gathering proper. Because the gathering organizers didn't want to be associated with the riot.

Tom Jennings: I took no part in the Day of Action stuff. It seemed at the time to be mostly people looking for excuses to throw rocks, political coloring mixed with a lot of naivete.

Patrick Hughes: We didn't want the cops to come bust up what turned out to be over 3,000 attendees from all around the world. Who were fed two meals a day and housed, by the way—all for free.

Antonio López: They had their own secret meetings. Everyone knew basically what they were planning. But it felt kind of exclusive, like if you weren't part of that, then you weren't really an anarchist. I chose not to be involved.

Patrick Hughes: Their Day of Rage, as it was also known, was to be held in Berkeley on the third day of the convention.

Antonio López: The plan was to occupy this burned-out hotel in Berkeley on the corner of Haste and Telegraph, and make it housing for homeless. The first wave was to occupy it and the second wave was to defend it.

Liz Highleyman: Unfortunately, the police got word of the planned takeover. They knocked out the building's stairwells to make it impossible to access past the first floor, and completely surrounded the building.

Antonio López: It was a ludicrous plan. Everyone in the first wave got arrested. The support group had nothing to do. This is where it got comical, because there was this roaming mob in Berkeley.

Oran Canfield: I walked alongside them from Bancroft up to Telegraph. Someone started burning a flag. They were all wearing the black bandanas. It was a motley group of people, for sure—kind of a Mad Max scene, but way more extreme and violent.

Kareim McKnight: Black Bloc is anarchist. They all wear black clothes and black bandanas to cover their faces. They link arms and form this mobile fighting force. It's a very intense spectacle. They still play a big role in demonstrations.

Jennifer Rose Emick: It was three-quarters punk, if you counted the anarchists. It was a parade. Everybody was walking and yelling slogans, the usual kind of thing. And then we noticed people behind us were stringing ropes between stop signs, disrupting traffic. I bent over to pick up something I'd dropped and some girl's bookbag hit me in the head and it was full of bricks. They came prepared. They were the reason it went ugly.

Antonio López: I lived about five blocks from People's Park so I could see everybody from my front porch.

Oran Canfield: When they turned down the one-way street, the panic on people's faces in the cars was fuckin' unbelievable. Those that could, backed the fuck up and got the hell out of there.

Antonio López: They were all dressed in black, chanting and yelling, but there was nothing to do. They marched right by my house. I walked out on to the street to watch. Just then, coming around the corner off of Telegraph was a Coca-Cola truck.

Oran Canfield: That's when shit hit the fan.

Antonio López: They ran towards it like locusts on corn and surrounded it. The driver was totally horrified. I was close enough to see his face. He thought he was going to get killed.

Jennifer Rose Emick: He looked out the window and said, "Aww shit!" and hopped out of the truck. Nobody said a word to him. So of course, people opened up the truck, pulled out crates of soda.

Antonio López: They tore this truck apart. They spray-painted it, they rocked it back and forth, and stripped everything they could. There was just so much anger and excitement. After it was over, it was like they had all had sex or something.

Oran Canfield: Some people ran back up to Telegraph and were throwing Coke bottles through the windows. They were somewhat selective. They got the Gap, which had opened up recently.

Liz Highleyman: I get off on the adrenaline rush of running wild in the streets ahead of maddened cops as much as the next person. Unfortunately quite a few homes, cars and small shops were trashed, too, which certainly doesn't help.

Oran Canfield: The cops had a police line across Telegraph and everyone was going nuts. Then a Coke bottle came flying out of the crowd and the cops came at us. It seemed like they were focusing on the people with bandanas, but they beat the shit out of whoever was in their way. It was just insane.

Jennifer Rose Emick: They sure beat the crap out of me. I was 17 and I got separated from the group.

Oran Canfield: There were riots on Telegraph all the time during the rush week of frat parties, but this was pretty exciting.

Gordon Edgar: At the same time, a whole 'nother group of people were creating a community garden, planting trees and organic plants, and building an irrigation system. It was definitely a big divide within the movement itself.

Patrick Hughes: Nothing was ever heard of the agitators after that. Makes you think that the whole enterprise was designed to discredit what we were doing and portray the convention as a bunch of childish morons. The Coke truck incident is all that anyone ever talks about.

44

Going to Pasalacqua

Janelle Hessig: Rodeo is a podunk town. A small town where no one expects anything of you.

Billie Joe Armstrong: Everybody knew each other. It was like small-town Americana in a lot of ways, but there was a problem with methamphetamine. It was a refinery town. A lot of people worked at the C&H sugar factory. There were no record stores or anything. Rodeo was a cool place to grow up, but a good place to get the hell out of at the same time.

Everybody went through the John Swett school district. That's where I met Mike and my friend Sean. I met Mike in the fifth grade and we were playing music together. We were all best friends. Those guys ended up at Pinole High, and kind of left me in the dust at John Swett. Everything was happening in Pinole, which is a strange thing to say, but there were a lot of bands.

James Washburn: When I got to high school in Pinole, all the early punks were graduating. Ninth grade is when I met Mike Dirnt. I was totally talkin' shit about him, talkin' about how he fucks cows. And it got back to him. He approached me and was like, "Dude, why you tellin' people I fuck cows?"

He was one of the most ridiculous-looking persons I'd ever seen in my life. Beret sideways, really long hair, like almost to his ass, horrible acne, brown trench coat, moccasins laced up to his knees. He looked like an absolute fuckin' clown. He had all these bands written in Sharpie goin' down one side of his coat, like Dead Kennedys, Corrupted Morals, Isocracy. After we settled the cow-fucking thing, we immediately became friends.

Jennifer Rose Emick: I went to high school there. Mike was a monkey.

Just skinny and goofy, always real hyper. He seems so serious now, but he was just the opposite back then. We used to have this tree over our lunch table, and most of the time he was hangin' from it upside down.

James Washburn: Billie Joe wasn't going to Pinole at that time. He came a year later. There wasn't a whole lotta shows going on. There were a couple punks with big mohawks, but they seemed totally unapproachable. They're three years older. You don't feel like you know them, because you're not *that* fuckin' weird. Yet.

Billie Joe Armstrong: Tenth grade is when I really started getting curious about other styles of music. I had a really cool older sister that got me into different kinds of stuff that wasn't, you know, Van Halen. Mike and Sean Hughes kept coming back home, 'cause they both lived in Rodeo still. Everybody congregated at Sean's house.

James Washburn: I started hangin' out with Eggplant and Mike, and it became like a little family. Janelle and Heather and Billie Joe. Sean Hughes was a weirdo, and he always had food at his house, so we'd always go over when his parents weren't home and eat all the food.

Billie Joe Armstrong: There were a lot of honestly great bands happening in such a weird small place. And they all knew their history. There was Corrupted Morals, there was Isocracy and No Dogs. One of the guys from No Dogs had hair that made him look like a chemo patient that someone had thrown up on.

James Washburn: Todd Pond was so gnarly. He was a skater and the singer of No Dogs. He was the most full-throttle son of a bitch I'd ever known. He was completely nuts, so totally unapproachable, because he'd tear your head off and shit down your throat. Just out of his fuckin' mind. The guy that would fight to fight. It was like, who the fuck wants to go meet that dude?

Billie Joe Armstrong: Then there was Possessed and Sacrilege, they all played at Ruthie's Inn. They were a few years older and were kind of scary.

James Washburn: Isocracy was good. Billie was in Corrupted Morals for a short time. Corrupted Morals just kicked your ass, their early music was just great. I don't think they ever really got known outside of the East Bay.

Billie Joe Armstrong: I got introduced to more people through Eggplant. People like Jesse Michaels, and Aaron, and Jeff Ott and Jake

Sayles. There were already bands that were playing together that were from Pinole, Berkeley and Oakland.

In a lot of ways, the punk scene was already over. The Dead Kennedys were gone, Social Unrest was breaking up, the Farm was gone, there were no Avengers. We didn't really have these heroes. So maybe, even reluctantly, some of the people we hung out with and their bands—like Crimpshrine, Operation Ivy, Corrupted Morals—they were the people we looked up to.

We got harassed because we smoked so much pot at the time. I used to sell joints at school for two bucks apiece, so people called me "Two Dollar Bill." The Berkeley people were a bit over it because of the whole hippie thing. But we were dope-smoking suburban kids. Eggplant, James Washburn, Joey Perales, who ended up playing drums in Blatz—we used to go across the street to my brother's house and smoke weed, raid his fridge, and go back to class.

Janelle Hessig: Billie Joe was really funny. He was a hesher. He smoked a lot of weed and had long hair. He'd wear flannels and a backwards baseball hat and was just kind of a burnout.

Billie Joe Armstrong: I didn't end up meeting Janelle until I think I was a senior. I knew her friend Rachel really well. I went to the prom with her.

Janelle Hessig: *Absolutely Zippo* was the first zine I ever saw. A lot of inside jokes and stupid comics. Eggplant had a lot of contributors. Billie Joe got suspended from school one time because he was selling *Zippo* on the campus.

Billie Joe Armstrong: Robert would come to school with a bunch of copies of his zine and he'd say, "Billie, take ten and go around. They're a quarter apiece." It was filled with profanity, and the trendier kids in 11th and 12th grade, of course, thought it was the coolest thing ever. My teacher came up and grabbed one, "What are you selling there?" and I said, "It's my friend's magazine. It's a quarter. Do you want one?" The cover said, "Legalize Crack!" I got suspended for five days, something like that.

I tried out for one of Lucky Dog's bands and didn't get the gig, but we became really good friends. We were both at one of Robert's parties, when Robert lived across the street from Pinole Junior High School. So me and Lucky and this guy Mark Moreno decided to go up and play a song or two. Lawrence Livermore was there. I had been going to Gilman quite a lot but I didn't really know anybody. I was still on the outside, surrounded by all these interesting people.

Lawrence asked what the name of our band was. I said, "We're Sweet Children." The next thing I knew, Lawrence was doing a mock scene report in *Absolutely Zippo*, about who played in Eggplant's backyard that day. Maybe he figured out something was happening in Pinole and El Sobrante. He called us Sweet and Sour Children. It wasn't a mistake. He was mocking us. That nickname kind of stuck with us. Robert would always say, "So, how's Sweet and Sour Children?"

James Washburn: Billie and Mike would play with Raj Punjabi as Sweet Children. Billie taught Mike how to play bass. Mike didn't know how to play instruments. Billie was incredibly talented, musically. He cut his first record at five years old. He'd already been playing guitar for years and taught Mike how to play. I actually have a recording of them playing and switching instruments back and forth, and they're playing Crimpshrine songs, Sweet Baby Jesus songs, Isocracy songs.

Billie Joe Armstrong: Mike was like part of my family. It's the most natural thing to play music with someone you grew up with. We went to school together, we went through puberty. We're just sort of in synch.

Jeff Ott: I stopped doing Crimpshrine then, Op Ivy ceased being a band, Sweet Children started playing shows. It was like a lot of pages all on the same page.

Bill Schneider: We all knew each other 'cause we'd all go to parties at Eggplant's mom's house and play in the backyard. They had their whole other little Rodeo scene.

Photo by Murray Bowles

Slappy: Mike Dirnt at Gilman

Jason Beebout: It was really obvious from the very first time you saw them play. I remember being totally jealous, like, "Fuck, they're totally playing guitars, in time."

Richard the Roadie: I'd seen Sweet Children play in Davis and all these other places. As flowery as the music was, they were as political as Econochrist and other bands. As far as their show ethics. All ages, really low door price.

Billie Joe Armstrong: We really didn't know if we were going to be a band anymore. John Kiffmeyer from Isocracy came up and said, "I heard you guys were looking for a drummer. My band's breaking up and I really want to be in your band."

Jason Beebout: John just decided this one day to join 'em. And that kind of broke up Isocracy. John and I had gone up to Willits to hang out with Larry and Kain and Tré, and got to know them pretty well. We came back and suddenly John had gotten hooked up with Billie and Mike. I remember him telling me, "I got this great new band." I was like, "Really?" "Yeah we're gonna be huge. The singer's a genius." It was like, okay, whatever. John was always really full of shit about stuff. But then he started playing with them.

Larry Livermore: Nothing had jelled until John came into the band. He gave a lot more than just the drumming to the band. He also was the organizer and babysitter, 'cause they were very young. I think he was about two years older, maybe three. He was definitely more mature and serious. And he had a car.

Frank Portman: Their first show was either with us or Sweet Baby. I do remember seeing them and thinking, okay, these guys know how to write good songs, which is this incredible anomaly among most rock bands.

Billie Joe Armstrong: We could never get a gig at Gilman while Tim Yohannan was running the place. I gave him a demo, and then I called him. "No, I haven't listened to it yet." I called him again. "It's a bit too pop." I remember saying, "We don't care, we'll play with anybody. You can put us anywhere. What about Sweet Baby Jesus? I mean, they have the 'sweet' in their name, too!" And he said, "No." He probably had enough bands from Pinole. I was about 15.

James Washburn: That was very defined, that they weren't allowed to play there. But when you listen to their first stuff, it really is just sappy, pop happy, and it doesn't fit the lines of punk at all.

Larry Livermore: They'd been a band a couple months. John called me up and said, "I'm in a new band with these two really cool dudes. Know of any shows where we could play? We're having trouble getting shows."

I said, "Tré wants us to play at some high school party." He was at this point going to Willits High School, in Mendocino County. "It's way up in the mountains, it's on a dirt road. The weather's bad, it might snow. I don't know if anybody's gonna come. And there's definitely no money involved." And John said, "We'll be there."

Billie Joe Armstrong: On a mountaintop in Garberville, with the Lookouts. It took us forever to get there, and when we pulled up, Tré said we had to go way up in the woods to this house where this girl was throwing a party. There was no roof, no electricity.

Larry Livermore: Five kids showed up. Not even the kid whose house it was. It was like his parents' cabin up in the hills. We actually had to break into the place and find a generator. Most of the places up there are pretty easy to break into, because there's not a lot of crime. You don't want to make it so somebody has to chainsaw the side of the house open to get in. The generator was only enough for the band, so we had candlelight. Sweet Children played for five high school kids who'd never been to a punk show before.

Billie Joe Armstrong: These kids from Willits and Garberville holding candles and sitting on the floor. We had played maybe four songs, and some guy came up and asked us to move our van so he could get out. John said, "You are gonna sit down and you are gonna listen to every song that we play, because I am not going to move the van." So we played. Larry just loved it. He thought it was great.

Larry Livermore: Billie was very gentlemanly. Had this kind of arrogance and aloofness at the same time. "Thanks for coming, I really appreciate you being here." It was like, "Yes, I know I'm a star." I've always said, although it was these five kids by candlelight, it was like the Beatles playing at Shea Stadium.

Afterwards, he came to me and he said, "What did you think of our band?" Very shy, and 16-year-old like. I said, "I wanna put out your record." I had no doubt. They were like the Beatles to me. They had the potential to be that big.

Billie Joe Armstrong: We just loved those first 7-inches by Crimpshrine, Operation Ivy, Isocracy and Corrupted Morals. And now Lookout! wanted to do a record with us. So we had to meet David

Hayes, too. The day we were supposed to meet, we went over to the Ashtray. I had never been there before and it had these really flimsy stairs. My feet flew out from under me and I went *boom, boom, boom* all the way down the stairs on my tailbone.

So I was in total agony when we met up with Larry and David Hayes. I couldn't sit on my butt. We were talking about doing some 7-inch, and John was arguing with Larry. John had a little napkin, and he had pieces of his eyebrows sitting in this napkin. It was just this nervous habit. Larry said, "Are you picking your eyebrows and putting them in a napkin?" And John said, "Yes, I am." And Larry said, "That's fucking disgusting."

David and Larry were at each other's throats, too. Mike and I were really young and we couldn't figure out what everybody was arguing about. When Larry went to the bathroom, David said, "Forget everything he just said." We were like, "Oh my gosh."

Larry Livermore: We put out a 7-inch the next spring, in '89. They changed their name to Green Day, basically a few weeks before the 7-inch came out. We had a big argument, had to change the covers and everything.

James Washburn: Actually, I think John came up with the name Green Day.

Ralph Spight: We played this show with them, Halloween 1989 in Santa Rosa. Victim's Family and Green Day. It was a benefit. And people wouldn't give Green Day ten bucks for gas to get home in their fucking VW van. This alleged benefit, and people fucking left them stranded with their van.

Nick 13: I remember seeing Green Day in 1989. Billie Joe still had long hair, and their only release was their first 7-inch. They were opening at the River Theater in Guerneville. MDC was headlining. That was a really cool show. It was the original lineup of MDC from 1980. That was definitely more of an old-school punk crowd.

Noah Landis: Green Day opened up for Christ on Parade at Klub Kommotion, which was in the Mission on 16th Street, a great funky place with a bunch of old sofas. They played with such exciting energy. So tight and with so many hooks. All these riffs that just go *bam!* and get you. People were just jumpin' up and down. They were all about having a good time. You can't knock that. We all wanna have some fun.

Adam Pfahler: Jawbreaker moved here and we were like 24 years old. Green Day were probably just getting out of high school or something. Their first record had tons of hooks all over it. And I was like, "Wow, this is just like a pop record." We were still listening to the Pixies and Nirvana and Government Issue.

Martin Sprouse: They were geeky kids. I remember seeing Green Day, and someone came up to me, and I said, "What's up with this band?" And he said, "We call 'em cotton-candy punk." 'Cause he had seen 'em a lot and it was like, oh, they really write catchy-ass songs. They played one New Year's Eve at Gilman and they tore it up. Everyone had fun. Tim Yo was dancing around. This was way before they were even remotely popular.

Bill Schneider: Billie did windmills on his guitar, and Mike always sang harmony.

Gavin MacArthur: The first time I saw them it was in a backyard in Pinole. I asked Dave Mello, "Who's this band?" Dave says, "It's Green Day. You've never heard them? They kind of make you bob your head like this"—he bobs his head—"for about five minutes, and then, you know, that's about it." And that was exactly what it was. They came on and they started playing, and I went, "Wow, this is great!" And then I got bored. But for five or ten minutes, it sounded really fantastic!

James Washburn: Green Day played my 16th birthday party. About four songs into it, Billie's mom called. He didn't do his chores. So he had to get a ride back to his house so he could feed the dogs. 'Cause his mom would whup his ass. She was a redheaded firecracker. Billie's dad passed away when he was ten, so mom, as a waitress— she had to deal with all these kids. Billie's the last of six, so she had her ass-whuppin' tactics down. He had to get a ride home, feed the dogs, come back, and then they finished their set.

John Geek: My friend Talia used to date Mike when she was in junior high, and he was a sophomore or junior. She gave me a demo, with the stuff that was on *39/Smooth.* I was about to go into ninth grade, and remember listening to it on a trip with my parents. They just thought it sounded like the Beach Boys. They were like, "Oh, this is really nice."

Fraggle: In late '89, early '90, people weren't going to shows anymore in the East Bay. Gilman had peaked in '88. The bands didn't draw people in. Ten or twenty people would show up. And you can't pay rent on that. Once Green Day hit, late 1990, things started picking up again. More and more stuff started happening. A new generation of kids showed up.

Christopher Appelgren: One of the biggest shows I remember, in 1990, was the record release show for Green Day's first album, and Neurosis's album *The Word As Law*. And also the first 7-inch Lookout! put out by the Mr. T Experience—and Samiam, their first 7-inch. So it was this big release show for basically all of our records.

Billie Joe Armstrong: We were putting out an album, so we were expected to play last. We were like, "This is bullshit." Mr. T Experience was a bigger band—they were playing Berkeley Square and in San Francisco clubs.

Christopher Appelgren: Billie Joe was really nervous. Larry had to talk him into agreeing to play after the Mr. T Experience. The show was amazing, all these bands. They sounded beautiful and incredible and giant.

Larry Livermore: If it hadn't been for John, they probably never would have come to Gilman. He got them their first shows there.

James Washburn: John Kiffmeyer was very important to Green Day. Too bad he wasn't a better drummer, but he was an excellent *person* to come in. Because he completely embraced Mike and Bill as Green Day.

Bill Schneider: John was the leader of the band. They were little kids and John was like the puppet master. It was like, "They're mine, my precious."

James Washburn: He had already been completely versed in being a punker, where Mike and Billie weren't. They weren't in other bands, they didn't really consider themselves a punk band. They didn't really have the skill of booking shows. John was very connected because of Isocracy, and so he knew people and places.

Oran Canfield: I met Tré when I was 13. I ended up living with an ex-Sufi clown who started Camp Winnarainbow with Wavy Gravy. I went to Winnarainbow every year for a number of years. It was a theater and circus camp. Awesome but totally insane. Members of the Grateful Dead were counselors, all their kids went there. Country Joe's kid went there. There was sweat lodges. We sang the national anthem but we had to do it standing on our heads. Really bizarre stuff.

I was a junior counselor there and so was Tré. I was kind of the camp's poster child. I joined the circus, and won the international juggling competition. But I was really shy and timid. I didn't have a whole lot of interaction with the other kids. The counselors, on the other hand, would get me high.

When I met Tré, I could kind of relate to him. The camp was in Laytonville and he was from Willits. Lawrence Livermore took him under his wing, and that's how he got into the punk stuff. I was very impressed 'cause he could play the drum solo to "Burning Down the House" at 13.

Noah Landis: I remember seeing Tré Cool play with the Lookouts. He was the worst drummer I'd ever seen. We played with them at the Bandshell in San Francisco at a Food Not Bombs rally and he was really young and really small. I was like, that kid is horrible! Man, he sure turned that around. He can play the shit out of those drums now.

Billie Joe Armstrong: The first time I ever saw the Lookouts, Tré was onstage wearing an old woman's shower cap.

Larry Livermore: The Lookouts got back together and did some recording. I asked Billie to come in and do some lead guitars and sing some backup vocals. That would have been the first time that Billie and Tré actually played together. And then in 1990, Green Day went on their first national tour.

Billie Joe Armstrong: I met a lot of my best friends on that tour. I met Adrienne, who is my wife. I met Jason White, who now plays second guitar with me.

On that tour, John didn't speak for about a week and a half. And he put on this weird hat and carried a bongo drum. It was basically once for yes, twice for no. He became Mute Man. He was a weird guy. I loved him. He was so smart. He's one of the guys that I really looked up to. I learned a lot from him. He may have been dealing with some depression, too. I think he had some inner demons that he may have needed some extra help with.

Larry Livermore: Somewhere in that tour, John let it be known that he wanted to go away to college, get the full-on college experience. He was gonna go to Humboldt State in Arcata.

Billie Joe Armstrong: It was such a terrible thing, when I found out John was leaving. It was the beginning of summer and we were in Benicia—me, Aaron and this girl from Arkansas—and she was saying, "God, everybody's leaving. So-and-so is going to this place. And John is going up north to college." Aaron kind of looked at me and said, "He didn't tell you that? Oh. That sucks." I thought it was the end of my band.

Larry Livermore: They heard about it from other people. John's reaction was, "Well, we're not breaking up the band, we're just gonna

39/Smooth: Early Green Day flyer

go on hiatus for awhile. We can still play shows, like vacations, stuff like that." To him, it was more just something you do. There would always be opportunities.

Billie told me he was just beside himself. He left school, just a few weeks before graduation. Figured all he was ever gonna do was play music, he didn't know anything else. And suddenly the band was falling apart. They debated for a long time over whether it was right to replace him.

Billie Joe Armstrong: John told us about Tré. At the time, we were like, okay, we'll give it a try. This will be a temporary thing. I talked to Larry about it and he thought we should think about it as a permanent thing. And I was like, "No, John's our guy."

Larry Livermore: Around November they said they were gonna do a show with Tré playing. I went to it, and it just jelled really well. I said, I guess that's the end of the Lookouts.

It dragged on for a few months. John said, "Oh, it's alright if Tré replaces me for a couple shows. But I'm still the drummer." A couple times he showed up at shows at the last minute, when Tré was expecting to play, and said, "No, I'm playing."

Billie Joe Armstrong: It was rough at first. John ended up playing one more gig with us in Petaluma. Larry was really pushing for Tré. Mike was really pushing. And I started to realize what a great drummer Tré was. I think Tré had even taught John a couple things.

Larry Livermore: One in particular was a Bad Religion show, one of the bigger shows they'd played at that time. It was very upsetting for Tré. John showed up at the last minute, and Billie let John play. But then afterwards, he said, "That was so fucked. That's never gonna happen again. Tré's our drummer."

Jason Beebout: Samiam played a show with Jawbreaker at the Women's Building in San Francisco. I think John had just quit, and was planning to go to school. We showed up and John was parked right in front of the front door. I hadn't seen him in probably a year. He was out front and was talking with a megaphone, "Fuck this show, fuck Samiam, fuck these poseur sellouts!"

Sergie Loobkoff: I was friends with John, but he was a strange guy. He was dead serious: "You guys suck!" What? What are you talking about?

Martin Sprouse: It caught Samiam off guard. It even took me by surprise. He did what he thought was the important thing to do.

Jason Beebout: He made T-shirts that said "GREED" and "SAMIAM" and was selling them for ten bucks a pop. I couldn't tell if he was being serious or if he was just enjoying being a nut. He was like, "Fuck you guys, you're just the wrong thing, you're ruining the scene right now!"

Martin Sprouse: Jason was like, "Do you hate us, John? What's going on here?"

Sergie Loobkoff: I never had a beef with him or anything. But that was really weird. I'd like to talk to him now, because now he's like an old man like me, and it would be interesting to see what he was thinking.

Martin Sprouse: It was a big change that we all noticed. You used to know him as this goofy John. When he left Green Day, he became very strong in his beliefs. He didn't cash his royalty checks from them. It just wasn't his thing.

Christopher Appelgren: They did try to cut him into publishing. He just might have not responded, and ultimately they just said forget it. We're not gonna give you any publishing, any writing credit for these songs. He really holds true to what being a punk meant to him.

Larry Livermore: John had made a lot of money off the first Green Day record, too. He was getting paid for one-third of the record. I ran into him a few years ago. Some bad blood occurred between us a long time ago, so I tried to work things out, apologize for whatever I'd done. We had a nice chat. He's very happy and content with his life.

Christopher Appelgren: When Lookout! negotiated a new deal with Green Day, I was like, "John, we still have some outstanding monies due to you, and here's what we did with the other guys in the band, and we can do the same with you." I haven't heard back from him.

Billie Joe Armstrong: Tré and I kept getting closer and closer as friends. But he was really obnoxious. To the point where I didn't even know if I really thought the guy was that cool. We wanted to be more conscious people. We carried the ethics of Gilman into our lives. Those codes were sort of intact. Tré was not even close. Didn't care what anybody thought, didn't care what anybody did. He did anything he wanted all the time. And that was really hard.

Bill Schneider: Tré had a way of being able to offend anybody. He could walk up to anyone, and within 15 minutes, he'd know how to pull their strings. He drove everyone crazy. That was his game back then.

Carol DMR: Tré was always a smart-ass, and now he's a smart-ass with a lot of money.

Bill Schneider: Once Tré started playing with them, it was like, oh yeah, that's the rest of the package. John was a good drummer, but Tré would just beat the crap out of the drums. He would be sweating from head to toe.

Billie Joe Armstrong: A lot of our songs were about girls. It was one thing with someone like Dr. Frank singing love songs. But when it comes from a 17-year-old kid, the songs are just gushing. It drew a lot of girls. It was weird. We got a lot of shit from other bands because we had love songs. But I wanted to sing about truth and where I'm at, my relationships with people. Or lack thereof.

James Washburn: The girls dancin' in the front. They'd put their hands down at their sides and kinda flop around, just like if you're fishin' and you pull the trout outta the water and it flops around on the ground. My friend Richard called it the Trout Dance.

Fat Mike: NOFX played with Green Day in Petaluma, and they went on before us, and the whole front was full of girls. We were like, "Cool!" And then we came out and were like, "Where did they go?"

Billie Joe Armstrong: We would play Santa Rosa or Petaluma, and tons of girls would show up. Then they started showing up at Gilman, it would be 75 percent women. It almost feels funny to say, but we never took liberties or anything like that.

Bill Schneider: All the cheerleader girls from the suburbs would put on their heavy mascara and their funny clothes and come to Gilman. And you'd be all, "Whoa, this is a whole different place."

Jason Beebout: You know every 14-year-old girl was creaming her jeans, every time Billie said the word "love" in one of his songs.

Bucky Sinister: They would squeal just like they were on the fucking *Ed Sullivan Show*. They were losing their shit.

James Washburn: I think everyone was jealous. I mean, who doesn't want chicks? Chicks want chicks. Everybody wants chicks. Chicks are cool. And I was hangin' out with them, so I thought it was cool as hell.

Billie Joe Armstrong: There were a lot of really strong women in the scene who could beat up the guys, like Todd and Kamala and Adrienne. So there were as many girls as guys in our immediate crowd who might have thought, "Fuck Green Day! They write stupid, fuckin' sappy love songs."

Nick 13: In sixth grade, we'd go to a party and put on our music, and it would be Black Flag, the Misfits or the Ramones or whatever. People would immediately bum out and want us to take it off, or want us to leave. And when people started putting on Green Day, the girls and jocks that would have bummed out didn't try to get us to change the music.

Anna Brown: We used to make fun of Green Day because they were *so* poppy. Which is funny because they kind of became punker as they went on.

Ben Sizemore: Billie, he sang. He didn't scream.

James Washburn: I did a Green Day van trip with Lucky Dog. That motherfucker, he was so impossible to tour with. But I'm sure I was impossible half the time, too. It's a community effort. Bein' an asshole sometimes takes more than one person. So we went on this van tour. It was more a trip for Billie to go see Adrienne. Billie's heart went pitter-patter. So we drove for 36 hours straight to Minnesota. Played only two or three shows, and parties that sprung up while we were there. But these shows were completely sold out.

A few times it was really trippy. I remember this one guy that hunted deer a lot. He had venison salami, and he was like, "Fuck, man, welcome to the Midwest! Bay Area boys are outta their element here!"

On this trip, Lookout! Records was still very small and they had just released *Kerplunk*, their second album. We were at a show that was absolutely shoulder to shoulder packed. I remember Bill stopping in the middle of a song, and the entire audience knew every single word. I was thinking, I'm in the fuckin' middle of Minnesota! I knew what was coming, what we know today as Green Day. That was '91.

Jason White: When they played in Memphis and Little Rock, people showed up in droves. I don't even know how they knew about 'em.

Bucky Sinister: Almost every other band just sounded like shit. They wouldn't practice or they'd show up fucked up. Green Day always sounded good. Like 'em or not, they fucking sounded great. Every time. They worked hard and they looked good. That's a combination right there.

Matt Wobensmith: The best show I saw of Green Day was at a punk picnic in Golden Gate Park. This was maybe in '91 or '92. There was this tradition of having these punk picnics. So we were in this meadow, a Sunday afternoon and everyone was waiting for the beer to show up. There was like 20 million crusty punks there and a who's who of East Bay bands: Blatz, Filth, Econochrist, 23 More Minutes, like everyone. And Green Day.

Finally the keg arrived. These two dudes carrying it across the field. And it was the most comical thing, because a whole fucking mess of crusty punks ran after them. With their dogs and everything, like, "Beer! Beer!" They were just pathetic. You could make a sitcom about crusty punks. We've talked about it.

The bands played, and Green Day went on, and they were maybe into their second song. And suddenly here came a whole bunch of cop cars, sirens, making their way over to the meadow, and you knew they were gonna unplug us. Green Day didn't miss a beat. They played harder and they played faster and they played better than ever. The whole crowd was watching the cops. But Green Day had their backs to them, didn't care, didn't know, or whatever, playing their heart out. I've never enjoyed a band more.

Jeff Ott: Lucky Dog, who was in Crummy Musicians, East Bay Mud, Fifteen, some other bands, he would roadie for them. I specifically remember a night before he was going to go roadie with them. Probably '91 or '92. We were sitting around drinking, and for the first time, I got it. I was like, "This is the last time they're gonna be in this sort of a thing." It was sort of odd. Green Day is gonna make a giant record and it's probably gonna sell a lot.

I have lots of thoughts about Green Day as a band and everything that they've done. But I have very different thoughts about Bill and Mike as the people who would split their last Top Ramen with me. So while I politically didn't like what was happening, some part of me felt just good for them.

Jesse Luscious: I always thought that Green Day musically was whatever, but live they were just a force to be reckoned with. What a great show.

Jason White: The night after I moved here, we went to Gilman and saw Econochrist, DOA and Rancid. Billie Joe was playing second guitar with Rancid that night. Todd, my girlfriend at the time, said, "The word around town is that a major wants to sign them." People were talking about it.

Noah Landis: They were being courted by IRS. But they weren't born from the same world as bands like Christ on Parade or Crucifix or Conflict. That was our thing, but that wasn't their thing. They were coming down from Rodeo and discovering Gilman and writing some catchy rockin' tunes.

Billie Joe Armstrong: We talked about it for about a year. Larry had people calling him every once in awhile, and I think he kind of shooed them off. After *Kerplunk* we started to become our own thing. We still played Gilman and we still considered ourselves a Gilman band. But we would draw lines out the door at Berkeley Square. So we started to wonder, where do we go after this?

Bill Schneider: They had grown to the size where they were kind of too big for the scene. They were too big for Lookout! They could play any club across the country. Green Day would go on tour opening for Bad Religion, and then half the crowd would leave after Green Day played.

Billie Joe Armstrong: This guy Dave was a paralegal, who worked for Cahn and Saltzman, this management and legal firm. He asked if we had thought about being on a major label. We were petrified. We loved Larry. He was like a father figure to us, and he gave us a lot of great guidance. But we ended up meeting with these lawyers and making a demo tape. We did it without saying anything to anybody. But because this scene is so incestuous, it started to leak out.

Larry Livermore: I found out about it by rumor, and confronted Tré about it, and he said, "We're talking to a management agency." I said, "Get the band in here, we gotta talk about this." During the course of the conversation it became obvious that they were already determined to go on.

Billie Joe Armstrong: Larry called us over to his house. He said, "Wow, so you guys really want to do this thing?" And when we said yes, he said, "We can offer you something." I looked at Lookout! as the ultimate independent label. For that era, it was perfect. But I didn't want to be with an independent that was subsidized by a major. And I didn't want to be somewhere in between. I just wanted to go for it.

Larry Livermore: We'd sold about 55,000 of those records by then. That was pretty big for an indie label in those days. I thought there was a pretty good chance they'd go on to a major label. But I felt really strongly they should do one more indie record. They needed to be in a better position for contract terms. 'Cause I'd seen bands already get dropped if they didn't do well right away. Sweet Baby was one of the examples I was using.

Billie Joe Armstrong: He said, "You gotta know what these people are like. Some of them aren't going to care about you. And there's going to be a huge backlash around here."

Larry Livermore: I thought they were making a mistake. I said, "The chances of you guys doing well right away are fairly marginal." They said, "No, we want to try it."

Billie Joe Armstrong: There was just this heavy feeling of sadness. But I didn't want to have that huge what-if hanging over me all my life. We walked outside Larry's house, we were standing on the front steps, and I remember looking at him, saying, "That was a bleak conversation. Maybe we are making a mistake." And he said, "I think you could be the biggest band in the whole fucking world."

Larry Livermore: We were still running Lookout! out of my room, 12 × 12 with no kitchen, when Green Day's management firm came to meet with us. Elliot Cahn. Cahn Management. He was the one who was in Sha Na Na. All seven or eight of us had to crowd into this little room. There was only three chairs. My bedding was rolled up in a corner.

I didn't completely trust their management, but they seemed to know what they were doing. As time went on, it seemed like they were getting the hype going, and things were working out. So I thought, "Ah, it'll probably be alright."

John Geek: They were packing Gilman. They were packing Berkeley Square. They were already one of the largest indie bands in America. Everybody knew they were gonna get huge. They knew they were gonna get huge. They never had any qualms about it. They never said they were gonna do anything else. It's not like they were pretending to be anything they weren't.

Bill Schneider: They were still the same people. They were living with ten people in a punk rock house. Mike was the only one that could hold down a job. He worked as a cook. Billie and Tré just lived off the T-shirt money.

Adrienne Droogas: I was in a different punk scene. These punk scenes coincide, all at the same time, but are very separate from each other. I remember hanging out with Billie Joe, I was dating his roommate Greg. This was before *Dookie* came out. I said, "Billie, I've never heard Green Day. I don't know what you guys sound like." He was like, "Really? Can I play you something?"

He grabbed a record and put it on, and he was so excited. He was like, "Wow, someone who's never heard Green Day!" It must have been like *39/Smooth* or one of those earlier ones.

I was like, "This is great, Billie. I just—it's really poppy, it's not my musical style." He was sweet about it. He played us the very first Green Day video. He said, "It's not out yet. Do you wanna see it?"

It was filmed in that apartment. At the very end of the video he's stabbing a couch, and feathers are flying. We were sitting on that couch. I said, "So, Billie, was it a fake knife? Like those ones that retract or something?" He lifted up the cushion and underneath were all the stab marks. He had just taken the cushions and flipped 'em.

Ben Saari: Word got out. The last show before they signed the contract was in Petaluma at the Phoenix Theater. There were tons of people. Everybody knew the next day they were signing the deal with the devil and everything would suck. They would be sellouts, nobody could be friends with them, they would be on tour forever, they would blow up. Things would get really good for them. And people were aware that this was also gonna bring in a whole new level of attention to what we had been doing.

Jason Beebout: After they moved out of that house, Mike and I moved in together. And then Bill and I lived together after that. It was a weird time. Me and Billie lived together for like a year, and I probably saw him four times.

Bucky Sinister: I was at BFD [Live 105's concert] the year they were playing, and they played first. It was an awkward thing. The single had come out a week or two before, and it was shooting up the charts. The next band started, and everyone went out to the concession vendors. It was easy to tell even by the first single they were gonna be a hit.

Jerme Spew: They sold ten million records their first major-label release—their first shot at a major label. Nobody knew. They didn't even know. When they hit a million records, I remember hearing how Billie Joe was like, "A million? Who in the hell is buying this shit?"

Martin Sprouse: Green Day sent Tim Yohannan a gold record of their first record. That was fucking funny. They put either Tim's name or *Maximum RocknRoll*'s name on the little plaque. That was pretty great. That was those guys being smart-asses.

Howie Klein: It went gigantically fast. Billie is an amazing songwriter. Yes, they play well, they're a tight unit. He's a great performer, they have great stage shtick. But it's all about the songs.

Anna Brown: It's weird when you hear your local band on the radio. It's even weirder when they get famous enough to play the Super Bowl halftime show.

Jesse Luscious: The first show I saw them on was Conan O'Brien. I was in southern California with these Germans, we were at somebody's house. I was like, "Holy shit, it's Green Day. That's insane."

Janelle Hessig: I was watching *Saturday Night Live* at my parents' house, and at the end Rip Taylor was throwing confetti, and there's Roseanne Barr, and then Billie Joe was in the middle of them. That was the first time it really struck me how surreal things were.

Jason White: I remember taping every bit of it off MTV. I don't know how long this is gonna last and this is gonna be so funny, I'll look back years later, "Look, Green Day was on TV. Can you believe that?"

Jesse Luscious: After Green Day signed, they were really good about keeping Gilman out of *Rolling Stone*. They were very protective. But kids dug and reporters dug and they found out what Gilman was. And so we literally had tour buses driving by saying, "That's where Green Day started." Fucking insane.

Martin Sprouse: They still give Gilman credit for everything. They've always been pretty honest about their roots.

Frank Portman: When Green Day made it big, my reaction was, okay, our side won. Because out of all the things that everybody was trying to do, pop songs won over the hardcore. Pop songs about things that you really think about, or care about, that have verses and choruses, and justify their existence by being real songs. On the other side, the Offspring became big, so their side won, too.

Aaron Cometbus: After *Dookie* came out, Billie came over and said, "Hey, have you got any records by the Buzzcocks, or 999?" I put them on and we sat around nodding our heads. He said, "Wow, these are great. What a compliment." All the reviews were saying he ripped them off. He'd never even heard those bands before. He got turned on to a lot of great bands that way. It's one way to discover new music, I guess, but kind of harsh. Anyway, the press couldn't have been further off the mark. His influences were mostly the records of his depressed-poet older sister: Replacements and Hüsker Dü, with the Who and a bit of East Bay stuff.

Jeffrey Bischoff: We had probably played 50 shows together. Anytime it was possible, Green Day, Rancid, Tilt played together. Jawbreaker also, and Samiam. When the *Dookie* record came out, they asked Tilt to come out. It was eight or nine weeks in the States. It started at Slim's in San Francisco. You could see the buzz progressing as we traveled. It was like watching the world decide they were cool. Venues got pushed up from 600 to 1,500, so we were playing 1,000-seaters and maybe some 1,500s on that tour. We came back and the next U.S. tour started going to even bigger venues.

Bill Schneider: The '94 Woodstock on TV, they kinda stole the show with the big mud-fightin' thing. Every article and every news thing about Woodstock was all about Green Day. It was kinda like, "Oh, okay. This is gonna be something different than just selling some records."

Jeffrey Bischoff: Tilt went to Europe in the fall. We were watching the stuff about Green Day on TV and getting the occasional phone call. At the end of '94 I got a call from Billie Joe and he said, "We're having our end-of-tour party." It happened to be the same day we got back from our European tour. And it happened to be at the Oakland Coliseum. We went directly to the Coliseum from the airport, and I saw Green Day just as they were at Gilman. It was just these three kids, up there working the crowd, just doing their thing. For 15,000 people.

Hank Rank: The first time I heard a Green Day record: I was at Sundance, and their record label was giving *Dookie* away in a pile of other junk. I brought it home and put it on, and I just laughed. I thought, "This is preposterous. I can't believe there's a band doing this today."

Howie Klein: I was working at Warner Brothers at the time. The CDs were going around the building, and I had heard snatches. But it wasn't until the record was finished that I got to hear it, and it floored me. This was *Dookie*. I went back and listened to the earlier records, and I thought, "Oh my god, this band is amazing."

Eventually I became the president of Reprise. The first thing I did when I became president was go to England. Because the Europeans didn't understand Green Day. It was already double platinum in this country, and not selling anything in Europe. I went to the head of our U.K. company, who was very respected all through Europe, and I said, "Rob, we've known each other for a really long time." He had bankrolled my publishing company, when I was at 415. I said, "Rob, you gotta believe me. This is gonna be the biggest band in the history of Warner Brothers. Don't blow this thing. We need you."

He said, "Fuck you. This band is corporate rock."

We fought about this. I was the president of Reprise, but I couldn't force him to do anything. So I went to the head of our German company and said, "Look, this is the biggest band that we have. This is a fucking great band, and the English aren't helping us with it. You do it. Don't wait for them."

Within months, they had green carpets in front of every major record store in Germany. It went platinum. And they forced the English into taking it seriously. It was the biggest no-no you could ever do. It was so not allowed inside of the Warner system, and I did it anyway.

I used to live in England, I knew they were gonna love Green Day. I went to one of the big festivals, in the middle of fucking nowhere, and Green Day was playing, and they were the biggest band in England that day. And I was so happy, thinking, alright, it worked.

Zarah Manos: I remember kicking Billie Joe out of Gilman. Like, "I know who you are, you need to leave."

Billie Joe Armstrong: I personally got 86'd after the fact.

Zarah Manos: I had to fuckin' work at the Gilman worker party, which I'm still bitter about, my own fuckin' party for us. And they were all drinking in the bathroom.

Jesse Luscious: Aaron Elliott, Billie Joe, Janelle, Robin, people from a bunch of different bands who all knew better. They were having a party in there, kinda drunk, throwing cans of beer.

Billie Joe Armstrong: I think about three years later, Aaron said, "I went to a meeting and you're not 86'd anymore."

Orlando X: The sad thing is that Billie Joe liked to go out to shows, and it got harder for him to go out. There were times you would see him and he'd be trying to disguise himself. He used to be a normal person, have a good time, but then he started getting mobbed by people.

Zarah Manos: Billie Joe always was rockin' the wigs. A black curly wig. There was a blond one, too, like a mullet. He was just doing it to get attention, I think, like fuckin' with us. It wasn't malicious at all.

Billie Joe Armstrong: I wore a pair of glasses and a hat. No wig. I went to see Dead and Gone play with AFI. I wasn't sneaking in. Green Day had just gotten really big and it got really uncomfortable. I just wanted to kick it with my friends and see the show.

James Washburn: Billie actually told me once—and it kind of stopped me in my tracks—he said that a lot of the inspiration for the things he writes comes from stuff that I say. I'm like, "What the fuck are you talking about?"

Billie Joe Armstrong: James is our buddy and he comes out on tour with us sometimes, just to hang out. He's one of those permanent fixtures in my life. He's become the subject of folklore because he's kind of this indestructible person. He got shot in the back of the head. The bullet shattered on his skull. He's got a big scar. He got the name Brain Stew because he wrote for *Absolutely Zippo*.

James Washburn: I have a lot of respect for Billie. He's been very successful just as a person. He's very bighearted, very generous. And I'll love him to death forever. Being where he is, in the eyes of society, in the music world—they're like a fuckin' supergroup

Photo by Murray Bowles; courtesy of Jesse Luscious

Sweet Child: Billie Joe Armstrong at Gilman

now. But to hear those things now, I guess it sets me back a little bit and I'm just like—I guess it completely embarrasses me.

He has given back a lot, and he respects the scene and respects the people that are here and in it. I think he feels proud that Gilman's still alive. Billie does a lot of things in helping the scene. Whether it's through donations, or whether it's still making punk rock known.

Kate Knox: The things that Green Day has done in the scene—in terms of keeping their money in the East Bay and still working with T-shirt companies and hiring friends and that kind of thing—I think is fantastic.

Bill Schneider: They're a rock band. They're not politicians. They don't want people to think they're trying to save the world. But in their own way, of course, they want to contribute and make things better. I think it goes back to the Gilman scene in general. We were all young and impressionable when we got into punk rock. That scene helped shape who we became later in life.

Winston Smith: People figure they're just a band of loony punks doing their own thing. Which they certainly are. But they also have a deeper side to them. After some horrible earthquakes in Nicaragua, they were fortunately in a position to make a contribution that was significant to people.

Ben Sizemore: I remember they played a benefit at Henry J. Kaiser for Food Not Bombs, and raised thousands of dollars.

Penelope Houston: When I was on Warner Brothers, Howie Klein said, "You should write with some people who have had hits. What about Billie Joe Armstrong, from Green Day?"

So pretty soon I got the phone call. "It's Billie Joe, I'm a big fan of the Avengers, blah blah blah. Come on over, we'll write something together." I was like, okay.

Billie Joe Armstrong: She came over to my house and we talked. I was just blown away.

Penelope Houston: Brought over some lyrics, he looked through them. Pulled one out. Said, "I could do this." He did it as a demo. Then he said, "You can come over and we'll record it with these guys I know, Joel Reader from the Mr. T Experience, and Danny Panic from Screeching Weasel." I was like, cool.

Billie Joe Armstrong: We put it together and got Kevin Army to engineer. She wanted to rerecord the Avengers' "Corpus Christie," which was awesome because it is one of the best songs ever written. The Avengers should have gotten more credit than they did.

Penelope Houston: We had a couple rehearsals. He had a recording studio in his house. The living room wall, all the way up to the 20-foot ceiling, was just covered in Gilman flyers.

We gave the recording to Howie, and Howie's like, "I wanna get this on a soundtrack." They were gonna put it on the soundtrack for *Lois and Clark*. But it died. So then they put it on the soundtrack of *Friends*, which was even better. Every time that show gets rerun, it's like my BMI check. It's decent, I'm not living

off it, but it's nice. And then I put the version of "Corpus Christie" on one of my best-of records.

Billie Joe Armstrong: It was a great experience and then she ended up
putting her band together, which is really cool.

Oran Canfield: I didn't want to be seen at a Green Day concert. One
day I got a call from my mom. She was like, "You gotta get over
to Laney, I'm playing with Pharoah Sanders." I drove over to the
community college and went down to the music rooms, and my
mom, Pharoah Sanders and Tré Cool were playing in this inter-
mediate jazz combo trio together. It was like, what the fuck?
Green Day was huge at this point. Tré was fucking great.

Larry Livermore: We used to see Winston Smith at various cultural
events up there. He lived about 50, 60 miles south. Tré met him
when he was 12 or 13 and always got a kick out of him: "Man,
that old hippie's crazy." That's how he ended up doing the *Insomniac* record cover for Green Day many years later.

Winston Smith: I got a call from Tré, "Hey, can we come over and
check out your stuff?" He and Bill came over, and Rob Cavallo,
who was their producer at the time. We looked through a bunch
of pictures. I thought they were still gigging around at garage
sales in the East Bay. I asked Tré how things are going. "Do you
have a day job?" And he said, "Oh, our last record sold nine million records." Shit, I nearly fell down.

Billie Joe Armstrong: He stayed up all night doing the album cover. I
think that's why we ended up calling the record *Insomniac*.

Winston Smith: Billie Joe noticed the title I had on it: "God Told Me
to Skin You Alive." They all recognized immediately that that
was a line from the Dead Kennedys' first record. I think they
liked that it had gone full circle.

Billie Joe Armstrong: On the cover, there was a guy sleeping in a ham-
mock and a blonde woman holding a gun to his head and my
guitar. When it came out, people were saying it was some kind
of metaphor for Kurt and Courtney. Like, what the fuck are you
talking about?

Winston Smith: I wasn't going to get any royalties or residuals, and I
had been through that with Dead Kennedys and other bands. So
I thought I'd just take the highest that anyone had been paid for
artwork, and double it. I said, what about $25,000? They were
cool with it.

Quite awhile afterwards, I was sitting having a pizza in Berkeley. This guy came up to me and gave me a big kiss. I was like,

"Hey, man, back off." Didn't know who it was. It was Tré, they'd just gotten back from Japan. Somehow the subject got brought up about payment for the artwork. I made some remark like, "Oh, be glad that you guys were with this major label, that was able to foot the bill." And he said, "No no, you don't understand. *We* paid that."

Bill Schneider: The *Insomniac* tour was kind of a total disaster. They still wanted friends to work for 'em, but they needed to find people that actually knew how to tune a guitar and fix stuff. Billie came to me right when he came home and was like, "Hey. You need to work with us. Come out with us, be a guitar tech, be a bass tech. Just come on out and it'll be fun." That was in '95.

At the time I was a partner in a music store called Black Market, which turned into Univibe. I was already the guy that was fixing all their stuff anyway. So we just went headfirst in and started doing all kinds of festivals, and then years of touring. I've worked for 'em for about 12 years. Started guitar teching and then doing all their day-to-day management. If you're gonna have somebody that's gonna drive you around the world and do press and make you show up at the lobby in time to get to the gigs, it may as well be me, I guess. I'm the one that wakes everybody up every day when we're on tour. And makes sure they're on the bus at the end of the night.

Jason Beebout: Jason's allowed to be in videos now, and he's allowed to be seen onstage. He's been playing with them for a long time.

Jason White: The first show I did with them was Shoreline in front of 20,000, and that was huge. Billie and I, we had been friends for years at that point. I lived on his couch for a long time. It was '99, one of the Neil Young Bridge show benefits. He said, "We're doing this acoustic thing. We kinda want to get another guitar player so it'll beef up the sound. You think you can handle it? Are you gonna get nervous and freak out?" And I said, "Yeah, I can do it." I was ecstatic.

It was definitely shocking. There's a huge crowd, the P.A.'s a lot bigger, the stage is a lot bigger, but you look beside you and it's the same guys you've been sitting in the living room practicing the show with for a month. That's what made it comfortable.

Adeline Records was a label started by Billie Joe and his wife Adrienne, and Jim Thiebaud, who had been a pro skater, and his wife Lynn. Doug Sangalang was around when they first started it. They just wanted to start a local label. It's named after Adeline, the street that runs through the East Bay.

I worked for 'em right after they started it in '98. Jim had a warehouse on Adeline where he had a ramp, and it became the de facto location of the label. It grew and grew. Lookout! helped us out quite a bit. AFI, the Criminals, a lot of Minneapolis bands like the Crush, and the Soviettes. We put together a package tour, the Adeline Showcase. We did shows in L.A. and San Diego, and at Gilman. It was a cool label. In its East Bay incarnation, it was 1998 through 2004.

Jesse Luscious: Green Day played Gilman during a set at some Adeline showcase. I wasn't there. I would have been like, "Oh, they shouldn't be on that stage." But people who were working were like, "We grew up on Green Day, we're not gonna fucking stop that." They just jumped up on the end of that set 'cause they were all there.

Jason White: The feeling in the air was very strange. It was like four days after September 11th. We had this thing booked, and we're like, "Well, I guess we're gonna go ahead and do it." Everybody was just feeling a little crazy and weird, and why not? Green Day got up and played and blew off some steam. That was the only time they'd played Gilman since *Dookie*.

Jesse Luscious: I think the people who were there were just so happy. A lot of them had never seen Green Day in such a small place.

Fat Mike: Green Day got big 'cause they were better than everybody else. And all the bands that weren't very good faded away. I always thought Bad Religion should get bigger. But it shows you how much charisma plays into it. Green Day had a lot more charisma than Bad Religion. And Greg Graffin is not Billie Joe.

Ben Sizemore: It's just weird that people you used to hang out with, and that your band would play with, are now millionaires. Green Day are like literally one of the biggest bands in the world. Personally I could never really generate that much animosity towards them. They're all perfectly nice guys. They're millionaires, and I'm a social worker, working with crazy people in the city, and really don't make any money at all. Who's to say I did the right thing and they didn't? More power to them.

Noah Landis: I always felt proud. Here's some guys I know who've always been nothing but nice to me, actually finding some success in this world. Before that happened, nobody who played in a punk rock band ever even thought about success. It wasn't even on the menu. We were making anti-music, we were making music that was not going to ever be that.

And to see the world finally catch up, desperate for music that makes you feel something, music with emotion, honesty, truth and aggression. These feelings that are undeniably in every young person born on the planet, especially people who have had to—god forbid—live through hard shit. The world finally caught up to that and wanted some. They wanted their Green Day songs about teenage alienation and masturbation.

Scott Kelly: Billie Joe's just as real as we are. The stuff he writes is the same shit that he wrote when he was 14 years old, sitting in a fuckin' party in Oakland. He's true blue. He's one of those artists who is able to tap into a larger sort of general feeling.

Noah Landis: Music is for anybody who feels it and wants it. The angst and the darkness in Kurt Cobain's songs—they reached people. And you think about the youthful energy and freedom you feel listening to Green Day—that's for anybody who feels it. It's not just for those who were there in 1977, or like me in 1982. It's bigger than that, and that's the beautiful thing about music.

Sham Saenz: I consider punk music art. It's not pop music, it's art. It's being creative. There's punk bands that reference other things like reggae, ska. That to me is what makes art. When you take something as a reference, and you make it contemporary by putting your own twist on it. Green Day isn't a punk band. They're a rock 'n' roll band that references punk. A lot of these bands today that call themselves this or that are actually rock bands or pop bands referencing punk, instead of punk bands referencing something else.

Billie Joe Armstrong: I could never live in Los Angeles or move into the [Hollywood] Hills. I grew up in the East Bay. That's where I'm from and that's what I'm used to. I think it's got a lot to offer.

Bill Schneider: It's always in retrospect that things seem huge. When you're on tour you do the exact same thing every day with the same people, the same faces. It's all the same. All that changes is the building you're doing it in. It's still the same jokes, the same dumb movie that you watch every day. It's the same food that you get served at catering.

You go to a Gilman gig, the band walks off the stage and they're standing there with their best friends and patting each other on the back. Everybody's sweaty, hugging each other, yelling, screaming, running down to go do whatever it is after the show, get a beer, hang out, have a party, whatever the plan is that night. Or it's Green Day coming off the stage at a stadium, and you go to a room backstage where it's all your best friends and the same people you've known for 20 years, and drink a beer and have a party and go off to do something. It's the same. It doesn't change for the people involved.

Anna Brown: It makes a lot of sense, now. Why wouldn't you get paid to play music and travel the world? There was some anxiety and animosity from some people about people getting rich and famous, but you can't deny that it is kind of thrilling to see your friends turn into humongous rock stars.

Bill Schneider: When you first join a band you think the biggest thing in the world is gonna be, "We're gonna write a song." And then after you write a song you say, "Well, we're gonna play a show." And you play that show and you say, "Well, we played that show. Let's try to do a 7-inch." And then you record a 7-inch and you're all, "Well, that's pretty cool. Let's try to do a tour." Then you go on tour and you're like, "Well, touring's pretty cool but how 'bout we try to put out a CD or an LP—put a full record out." Then you put the full record out and you're all, "Wow, that was pretty cool. But you know what would be really cool . . ."

It's just these steps that lead to steps—and then at this point, standing on the side of the stage when Green Day's playing to the stadium shows at the end of *American Idiot*, 60, 70,000 people. And you're just sittin' there going, "Okay, this is pretty crazy. But you know what's gonna be *really* crazy . . ." It's funny, it really is, watching your friends do really well. But being along for the ride, it all becomes incredibly normal.

Dallas Denery: I remember there was a documentary on Green Day— it might have been *Behind the Music* or whatever. I was watching it with my wife and I was just thinking, "God, I'm so proud of them." Because you do sort of feel like, that was our thing. It's really great that out of that little room in the Berkeley industrial wasteland comes these great bands.

Ralph Spight: I never really resented Green Day for getting huge. Because they're a hot band. Nobody fucking cared. Now they're international. I make my living teaching guitar and I teach Green Day songs all day long. So whatever, it pays good.

Dennis Kernohan: I was at this Oakland warehouse party in the late '80s. They were hilarious. Just little snots, hassling everybody. I had long hair then, so they were calling me an old hippie. I didn't even know they were Green Day. Later on I saw their picture and recognized them as those kids that were giving me so much grief that night. It made me laugh so hard. I was all for 'em, you know? I think it's great that they've adopted the same makeup artist as the Damned. I think that's genius.

Danny Furious: I love Green Day. I love Rancid, too. It ain't 1977 anymore, and obviously punk is here to stay. I prefer to think positive about it. And I'm glad the Avengers and others can be cited as influences.

Bruce Loose: To me, that's not a Bay Area punk band. They weren't there in '77, they weren't there in '78, they weren't there in '79. If you weren't there in the '70s, you weren't a punk band. You were an aftereffect in the punk movement. But I think Flipper was an aftereffect in the punk movement. We've been able to emulate it. I may be only speaking for myself.

Dave Chavez: I really wish the Buzzcocks would have never formed. Then we would have never had Green Day and all this garbage.

Hank Rank: I definitely felt that the groundwork had been laid, but that's usually the way things work. The popularizers are not the innovators. They're the people who just fine-tune it and put the elements together. They're all young and cute, and the singer definitely had a very dynamic, recognizable style. And they played great, and they wrote songs with plenty of hooks, and more power to 'em.

Aaron Cometbus: All the old washed-up punks from '77 came crying for royalties, wanting credit for creating Green Day. Fuck them. We kept the scene going for 30 years that they abandoned after two. Just like deadbeat dads.

Ruth Schwartz: When my kids' favorite band is Green Day, I'm kind of grateful. It could be Britney Spears. I took the whole family to see Green Day. There's just a whole dynamic with this generation. They're not like us. I've had a lot more time to reflect on it, but the fact of the matter is that everything that we stood for in 1980, they don't give a crap about.

45

No Sleep 'Til Hammersmith

Lenny Filth: Kamala was my first girlfriend. I used to have to sit there and listen to her booking bands, while I was watching TV, waiting to hang out with her. The women in this scene played as much a part of the scene as the men did, without any shadow of a doubt.

Adrienne Droogas: Kamala was on top, in terms of shows. Kamala had her fingers right on the pulse of every single venue, house, garage, somebody's basement in their parents' house. She had this list, she had phone numbers, she had addresses, she had directions. You would go to Kamala's house, open up a map, and go, "We wanna do this." And she'd go, "Okay, here's the numbers, here's everyone you'd call." You'd call one person and they'd go, "My parents won't let me do shows anymore, but Joey's doing shows, or Susan's doing shows, so here's their number." And you'd call that Susan and Susan would be like, "Yeah, when do you wanna play? Cool."

Ben Sizemore: Kamala gave me numbers of places all over the country, and so I would book the tour. Econochrist even went to Europe twice.

Kamala Parks: I had booked Clown Alley on tour, and so that led to people calling me and wondering if there was a place to play in the Bay Area. There were always different people doing things, so it wasn't just me, it was a bunch of people. DMR was booking shows at this time, *Maximum RocknRoll* would sometimes organize a show.

Bill Schneider: All the bands shared. Phone numbers of people who didn't have a club or anything, you'd call them and go, "We need somewhere to play." And they'd go, "Oh, lemme go check the pizza place." Or, "Let me go check the VFW hall."

Chicken John: People like me and George Tabb made a network in North America. A touring network that later became the *MRR* book *Book Your Own Fucking Life.* I had these different colored notebooks, four regions in four different colored notebooks. I was calling everybody and collecting numbers.

There was a guy Ted, from Shreveport, Louisiana, and he set up shows in his toolshed. He called it Theodore's Shed. Which is funny, 'cause you'd want to call it Ted's Shed. But if I wanted to play a show in Shreveport, I'd have to find the fucking show. So I'd call up Peaches, which is a major-label record store. I'd say, "Hello, is there anybody there with dyed hair?" "Uh, yeah, Brian's got dyed—" "Can I talk to him?" "Hold on . . . Brian! Some guy wants to talk to someone with dyed hair." "Hello?" "Yeah, hi, I'm from New York and we're in a band and we're traveling through. Who's having punk shows?" And Brian with the dyed hair is like, "Oh, well, this guy Theodore . . ." There it is.

Davey Havok: *Book Your Own Fucking Life* came out I think once a year. It was invaluable, because there was no Internet. There was no way that a band like us at that time was gonna get booked at regular clubs. It was getting booked at the Pill Hills and the garages and the Gilman Streets around the world. Basically it was a compilation of: here are the bands in this area, here are the labels in this area, and here are the promoters in this area, and here are the places to play.

Chicken John: *Book Your Own Fucking Life* outlived its usefulness the instant it was published. It fucked all of us. Now this is a bold statement—the reason why punk rock became Top 40 is because of *Book Your Own Fucking Life.* It was the first step. Ted in Shreveport went from talking to me and four other people to getting like 50 tapes a week. Professional, glossy fucking press kits. And he was like, "I can't let all these people play." So people became club owners, started graphic design businesses, booking businesses. And it's like, bleh. Is that what all this is for?

Bill Schneider: Everybody in the East Bay scene had stolen military exchange calling card numbers. Every single band used the same numbers. You'd dial this number, and then from there it was another beep and then you could dial a number. They worked I'd say up until '93.

Fat Mike: Book all the tours from a public phone booth, 'cause you couldn't do it from your house.

Chicken John: Booking a tour would cost like 800 green dollars. So if you couldn't freak the phone, then it wasn't going to work out. People can't even imagine it 'cause everybody has cell phones now.

Ryan Mattos: Me and Eric Ozenne did booking. He had a job—I later had the same job—installing phone and data lines in office buildings. So he would spend a lot of time up in the ceilings of office buildings, using their phones, calling people to try to get shows.

Bill Schneider: In my band it was me. In Green Day it was Tré. Every band had the one guy in the band who did it. Everybody else was trying to pick up on chicks or get food, or meet people. You'd be sitting there in a phone booth next to the van with your notebook, calling—I'm not even joking—100 people. Every evening, trying to get these people to answer the phone, and leaving messages. You'd hopefully have somebody at home who would take messages for you, because there was no voice mail.

Richard the Roadie: Kamala changed it for a lot of people. And she's never given credit. She was the most organized person at the time. Everybody else was just chaos. She absolutely paved the way for East Bay bands to tour. A few of them did before, but as far as networking before the Internet, she was absolutely the person to go to. Amazing resource. She was the first one to grow up.

Chicken John: I remember Kamala Parks. Oh yeah. Fucking bitch, fucking wouldn't share. Not one fucking ounce of information, nothing. I used to fucking mail her fucking lists, mimeographs, where I used to have to write in marker, big, so that it would mimeograph, 'cause if you wrote in pencil too small it couldn't copy. Fucking bitch, man! Fucking wouldn't share! I was just like, you cannot be serious. You're gonna try to profit off this? It was just disgusting.

Ben Sizemore: You'd meet people who would put you on a pedestal because you were from the Bay. We would say, "Yeah, come visit, man, come stay with us." One time when we came back from tour there were a couple kids already on our couch. We had met 'em in Michigan.

Bill Schneider: People were so excited to have people from out of town, especially from California. They were drooling, waiting for us so they could show us all of the fun stuff to do in their town. You'd pull into somewhere and they were like, "Okay, first we're taking you to the place where we do the rope swing down into the creek, then later we're gonna go cut down as many Wall Drug signs as we can and throw 'em in the back of the truck, with an ax." They kept you so busy that you couldn't even sleep. There was always something fun to do.

Adrienne Droogas: "We're gonna go dumpster-dive, we're gonna go to underground lakes and ride in a boat."

Dale Flattum: You're suddenly on acid and on the bayou in Louisiana: "How did we get here?"

Bill Schneider: Someone took us mud-bogging at Three Mile Island. You could jump off cliffs into this weird mud pit, and you'd slide like 50 yards. Or you'd be in Seattle and they'd take you to the unfinished freeway that went halfway out on Lake Washington, then ended. And you could jump off, and you had to climb a ladder back up. Every city you went to had something weird like that. In Lincoln, Nebraska, they were like, "Hey, you guys wanna go where all the weed they planted during World War II to grow hemp is?" And you're all, "What?!" There's fields and fields and fields of marijuana growing. They would bring everybody from out of town there and watch people smoke tons of it, and then laugh their asses off when you're puking and have a headache. 'Cause it's like ditch weed.

Mike K: Relying on the people you meet to save your ass, and help you out and give you a place to stay. Getting to experience that was definitely eye-opening.

Davey Havok: We showed up to this kid's house in I don't know what city in the middle of nowhere. We were playing in his basement. But his basement had a carpeted stage and a sound system, and his parents were letting us stay there, and all the kids from this town were showing up and Mom was cooking us food. Amazing. Moms across the country have taken care of punk rockers for years. You know, taking care of their boys.

Fat Mike: We were on tour with East Bay Mud, or Fifteen, in Columbus, Ohio, in '88. Some member passed out with his shoes on. Usually he gets written on. But luckily we were at a girl's house, and she was an artist, and she had a lot of plaster of Paris. So we cast his leg up. He was very disoriented when he woke up.

Aaron Cometbus: NOFX duct-taped someone to the ceiling.

Billie Joe Armstrong: We played in Rhode Island at this skate ramp. I think one of the kids who ran it, his father was in the mob, because there were all these kids drinking 40s outside, and the cops drove by without saying a word.

We had a few days off, so this girl said she would have a party at her house. Her dad had a massive collection of antique bottles in the living room. We knew they would come crashing down, so Aaron, Mike, Sean, John and I put duct tape across all the bottles. John was missing a cymbal stand so this girl who was hosting us took a piece of rope, and people took turns just holding it up. As soon as we started playing, the house just got completely wrecked. That was the first time I ever saw Aaron get really drunk.

I urinated from the top of the stairs on this young couple that was getting together for the first time. People were throwing everything out of the refrigerator onto John. So John got naked and wrapped his whole body in Saran Wrap, running around being Saran Man.

John was trying to get together with this girl but he couldn't remember her name, so he got a bunch of eggs and walked around to each person going, "Say your name." When you said it, he would smash an egg over his head. Nobody really had any etiquette when it came to dating at the time. There was all kinds of stupid shit. I remember waking up the next day, and someone was running through the house with a chain saw. And there were chickens all over the floor.

Lenny Filth: There was a couple of summers where there'd be four or five Bay Area bands all on tour, crisscrossing the country, just missing each other. One year I remember we were two days behind Neurosis. We'd show up to this barnhouse in middle-of-nowhere Kansas—nearest neighbor had to be a mile away—see Neurosis stickers and flyers still up. They had played there two nights before.

Andy Asp: Nuisance rode to Little Rock. We had the day off. Somebody asked us, "Do you wanna play at the governor's mansion?" Bill Clinton had just left Little Rock to go to Washington, and the next guy, Jim Guy Tucker, had taken over. In order to make his daughter feel at home and make friends—she was a punk kid— her dad agreed that they could do this all-ages punk show out on the back lawn. She was probably 15. Several bands played from Little Rock. And us. They built a little stage and had a P.A.

The neighbors all called, but it was outside the city jurisdiction. They had no say. Troopers were guarding the gate. They were letting tons of kids in. It made all the press: "Something of a Nuisance at the governor's mansion in Little Rock." We made all the newswires for that reason.

Davey Havok: A lot of times the place you were supposed to play didn't exist anymore. Or some guy puts you in this weird little bar and you're playing in front of four or five barflies in Missoula, Montana, and the flyer is a cocktail napkin with "Swingin' Utters and AFI" written on it, pinned to a corkboard.

Andy Asp: A tour that normally would've lasted 25 days might stretch to 45 days. Because you had days off, the booking was sloppy. The kid's dad pulled the little garage show. It was definitely spotty.

Fat Mike: We siphoned gas, sold acid to pay the bills.

Mike K: You have these weird fantasies of the road trip, and then, like, okay, I think our next show is in Florida. Then we're going to have a show in Chicago. And we're broken down in a desert and it's 115 degrees at ten in the morning. And Bill is getting heatstroke because he slept in his truck, and now he's throwing up. And all we have to eat is olive oil and falafel balls.

Dallas Denery: It is the most boring thing in the world, except for two hours every other day. It's real obvious why entertainers end up being drunks. It's just tedious.

Greg Valencia: I slept between the rug and the equipment. For three months. I still, to this day, sleep like this.

Richard the Roadie: Most roadies then were just fucking slackers. A lot of them would just go along as your loser friend that wouldn't leave the living room. I've roadied with probably between 25 and 35 different bands. There's some bands like Citizen Fish, I've done like 17 tours with them. I liked crowds up to about a thousand people. After that it really goes into this other world. If you're a musician, it's everything you wanted. But it gets kinda boring if you're not a musician.

Janelle Hessig: When Richard first started hanging out and lived in Sacramento, he was pretty quiet and sweet. Then all of a sudden he started being "Richard the Roadie" and started hanging out more.

Richard the Roadie: I got into a mechanic trade school and realized there was this amazing opportunity. Nobody knew shit about cars. Then I got this job at Vantastic, this hoopty-ass van service that transported disabled people, run by this woman Vicky. She had 17 punks working for her. It was pretty fucking amazing. Jesse, Jake, Joey, everybody had a job there. And she paid so little that punks would work for her and that's about it.

So for five years, if you were disabled or needed transport with a lift van, there was a punk showing up at your door. But you'd go to a show somewhere, and you'd see a Vantastic van. That's how the band got there. Somebody once got caught in Pinole stealing building materials, and he was dressed up in this white party dress, drunk, in a company van.

A. C. Thompson: Richard the Roadie was an amazing, amazing guy. He didn't take his boots off for a year. He was on tour with Paxston and they all had scabies. He apparently hadn't been afflicted, but his feet were kind of hurting and so, after a year of sleeping in his boots, he took them off at the hospital. His feet had grown into his socks—they were fusing in an unholy alliance—and the medical personnel said, "Wow, it's really good that you came in today because you're about to get gangrene."

Richard the Roadie: The problem was, my feet smelled so bad I couldn't take my shoes off. 'Cause any time I did, it would make people sick. I've made people throw up. I went to Europe with Avail. We were in a van. I farted, and made the bass player throw up, which was so awesome. Then I changed shirts and left my shirt in the van. He went in the van after a show, thought it was his shirt, wiped his face with it. It smelled so bad that he actually threw up again.

I never thought I was crusty. I just never showered. We had a tour with Paxston Quiggley and the first or second night I got drunk and peed myself. I wore those same shorts for the six-week tour. I didn't really think about it. I had an Asbestos Death shirt I wore the entire time. This was a summer tour, hot as shit. Which is probably why I never had a girlfriend for years and years and years.

Janelle Hessig: Richard moved into this abandoned house I had lived in. The landlord eventually came and shut it down. So when Richard was leaving, he booby-trapped the door with a bucket of rancid piss. One of those big-ass plastic buckets.

One night I had a date and I didn't want to take my date back to where I was staying. I was like, "I know, let's go back to my old house!" I was taking him on this little adventure. So I took him to the house. I knew that something was amiss because there was a little door in the fence, and it was nailed shut. I wrenched it open and we went in.

You had to go through a trap door to get into the actual house. It was dark in there and you couldn't actually see. I climbed up the plank and was at the top of the trap door, and it was stuck. I was like, great, they nailed this shut, too? I pushed and pushed and gave it one great big shove and it gave. And it somehow went behind me, and tipped over and my date was standing below me. You could hear the sound. Gallons and gallons. Everything was quiet as the last trickles were coming down. He was like, "I hate you." It was the worst date ever.

46

Runnin' Riot

Richard the Roadie: When I was 16 or 17, I started to hang out with metalheads in Sacramento. They were speed freaks. I just went through this string of crazy houses. Always doing speed, speed, speed, speed, speed. You couldn't tell, 'cause it didn't make me social. It didn't make me wanna have sex. It made me not eat and pick up bugs.

I was buying from these bikers who couldn't even get colors. And they didn't even have motorcycles. They were just fucking losers out in this abandoned mobile home. There was some huge Air Force base out there. The cooks were right up in the hills.

It got to this point where we were all getting followed. There was a gunfight at the trailer. The guy I was buying from, he and his dealer went down. The writing was on the wall. I was in a house where everybody was slamming. I was having nosebleeds, throwing up blood, struggling to get sober. I didn't know anything. My best friend Paul had a room on Capp Street. I went up to visit and spent ten days reading with the window open. That was it. I decided to move to a new city and reinvent myself.

At that point I was reading *Maximum* religiously, going to Gilman. And really saw that I might be able to be a participant. I was helping with shows. So right before I moved, I did a show in Sacramento.

Rented a hall, did everything I was supposed to. Rented a P.A. from a hippie. He never showed up, so we used a bass amp. Typical thing, never trust a hippie. It was my first show. Mostly East Bay bands. And it ended up in a mini-riot.

Al Sobrante basically gave me everybody's number. The show

set itself up, except for the weird crappy industrial band who drove everybody away. That of course I did. It was an amazing show. Green Day, Samiam, Econochrist, Corrupted Morals. I paid 'em all 20 bucks. Probably 120 people showed up, 70 or 80 from the East Bay. The East Bay sort of invaded Sacramento.

Sham Saenz: Me and Ron Nichols from Christ on Parade met Econochrist at Your Place Too, this blues bar that had 25-cent beers and let anybody in. There was some punks sitting there, and we just walked up to them and said, "Hey, what are you doing here?" "Oh, we're from Arkansas." "Oh cool, you want a beer?"

We ended up driving in their van to Sacramento, ten people laying on the top of amps. Everybody was laughing and drinking in the back. We get there, and the guys from Green Day were already loading their equipment in. They had this nice VW bus.

James Washburn: Econochrist, Green Day, Filth, Anger Means—a lot of good bands.

Richard the Roadie: Skinheads showed up. There was only like five or six or seven of them. But from what I remember they were huge, just absolute monsters.

Sham Saenz: They were some trippy skinheads to me because these motherfuckers wore overalls. I had never seen this before. Like, are they skinheads or just rednecks?

Richard the Roadie: In Sacramento I never peed at a show. 'Cause you went in the bathroom and you didn't know what's gonna happen. The small scrappy guy would just start fucking with you, and then there's like eight on you. You'd go to the parking lot, there was a row of skinheads just knocking people down.

So these guys came to our show. In my head, these guys were like eight feet tall with swastikas on their foreheads. They stood onstage and fucked with the bands. They just had the run of the show.

Sergie Loobkoff: Basically everyone wanted the show to get over, so everyone wouldn't get their ass kicked. Green Day and Samiam switched off, we played two songs, and they played two songs.

James Washburn: The skins, in a classic skinhead maneuver, went the wrong way in the pit, swingin' their fists. Most people didn't want to start a fight over that.

Ben Sizemore: A Nazi skinhead from Sacramento, Iron Mike Ortiz, had stabbed a ska guy and killed him, and went to prison. We knew that had happened. So there was some real fear.

Billie Joe Armstrong: We didn't know if they were good skinheads or bad skinheads—Nazi or SHARP. But in the middle of the second song, I saw Lenny push this guy. The thing about Lenny was, sure, he was in this artistic punk rock scene, but Lenny's from El Sobrante. You can take the kid outta El Sob but you can't take El Sob outta the kid. They started pushing each other, and I remember him screaming, "Come on!"

Ben Sizemore: One of them punched Lenny from Filth, and then it was on.

James Washburn: The lights came on and within seconds it turned into a huge fucking brawl. Everybody was just swingin'. It was like holy shit, every single skinhead was fighting one or two punks. There was not even 10 or 15 feet in between fights that had nothing to do with each other. I'd never seen anything like that before.

Sergie Loobkoff: They were really tough, mean skinheads, and most of us were nerdy guys, never-been-in-fights type of guys.

Martin Brohm: It was typical Sacramento. The reason they came is 'cause it was a bunch of Gilman bands. Goofy, faggy bands, going up there to play.

James Washburn: Mike Dirnt punched a skinhead with everything he had, every ounce of his being, every bit of his body weight, and the guy just shook it off like it was a bug. I think Mike thought he was gonna fuckin' die.

Richard the Roadie: It just totally escalated. Ben from Econochrist was fighting one of 'em. Todd from Spitboy was trying to hit somebody over the head with a 40.

Martin Brohm: It was a war zone. I remember seeing a knife come in. Some guy picked up one of those metal pamphlet things, and slammed some guy in the head with it.

Ben Sizemore: We were throwing chairs and stuff.

Billie Joe Armstrong: I was standing there like a deer caught in the headlights, and these two girls came up to me in the middle of the mayhem and asked, "Do you have any records for sale?" Like, are you kidding me?

James Washburn: Everybody was going full blast. The punks were like, "Skinheads out! Skinheads out!" We got 'em through into this lobby, and there was the front door after the lobby. Everybody was yellin' back and forth, and once we got to the front door, they stopped. I was like, "Fuck this, they are goin' out the door!" and I just started pushing my way through people, and there was a big skinhead, staring me right in the face. I reached back to punch him and saw out of my peripheral vision another skinhead, his arm cocked back to punch me. So I kept my eyes focused on the biggest skinhead, crossed my punch sideways and hit the other guy, knocked him out. That got the attention of the skinhead I'd locked eyes on. That made him stutter for a second, so then I just started whaling on him.

Billie Joe Armstrong: James Washburn threw one guy to the ground, turned around, punched another guy in the face, turned around again and threw a chair over this one guy's head. It was like a scene out of a Chuck Norris movie. James Washburn fighting all these skinheads single-handedly. This was one of our guys from Pinole.

Aaron Cometbus: You've got to give credit where credit is due. It was Econochrist that made the difference. Those guys knew how to fight! A well-oiled machine. Tighter offstage brawling than they'd been onstage playing.

James Washburn: Eggplant threw a garbage can and hit a skinhead girl in the face and knocked her out. We got 'em out the front door, and then they took off. We knew they weren't gonna take a beating and just leave. They were gonna fuckin' come back.

Ben Sizemore: And then we're like, "Let's get out of town, this is their town." So we all packed our shit up and tried to get out of there as quick as possible.

Billie Joe Armstrong: When the cops showed up, we said, "You have to stay because these guys are gonna come back again." And the cops were like, "Well, you all look fine." And they left us there.

Richard the Roadie: We started breaking the show down, everybody was loading out. I was talking to somebody, and I saw these little things, like way out in the field, coming towards us.

Billie Joe Armstrong: Everybody had left, but for some reason we were lagging, loading out our equipment. So it was just us and a car of people from Pinole.

James Washburn: John Kiffmeyer was going super slow loadin' his shit. Like, "Dude, c'mon, they're gonna come back!" We heard this *clump clump clump clump!* The sound of boots. We looked over and probably 15 skinheads were running down the street with chains, bats, knives, everything.

Billie Joe Armstrong: Oh fuck, it was one of the scariest things I've seen. These guys were monster big.

James Washburn: I remember Mike just yelling "Run!" and I started running. Man, I musta been outta shape or something because I was running as fast as I could, full adrenaline pumping, and

Mike Dirnt was running in front of me. By the time I was out of breath and couldn't run anymore, he was out of sight. I have never seen him move that fast in my entire life. Mike was running so fast because he heard *my* boots and he thought I was the skinhead. He was fuckin' gone. I ran up onto somebody's porch.

Richard the Roadie: We locked the hall down. Billie Joe got stuck outside. One of 'em got inside Al's Volkswagen van and took the keys. The skinhead got in the van with a knife, and I remember seeing Billie jump out the side window, like he got shot out of a cannon.

Billie Joe Armstrong: I got into the driver's side and one of these guys was grabbing my shirt through the passenger's side. I thought I was gonna die so I dove out of the window, and he ripped my shirt right off my back.

Sergie Loobkoff: He opened his driver's door to get in the car, and then opened the passenger door, and he ran through his car. And the other guy was chasing him through his car. It was like this cartoon.

Billie Joe Armstrong: I just started running, and I could see silhouettes of all these punk rock kids running as fast as they could. The skinheads slashed our tires.

Martin Brohm: Some girl got beat the fuck down. Like five-on-one kind of thing.

Richard the Roadie: This woman Sophie, who knew some of 'em, just got the shit beat out of her with a baseball bat.

James Washburn: After things had calmed down and we went back, every single window was smashed out of Joey Perales' station wagon. Joey had to drive home very cold.

Billie Joe Armstrong: Coming home, I think there was some sort of solidarity that came out of that. The scene had been a little disconnected, but everybody knew each other a little better after that, and became a little bit tighter.

47

Outpunk

Jello Biafra: In the very early Mabuhay scene, many people were openly gay and it wasn't a big deal. Theater was part of what you did. You weren't supposed to cop a rock star attitude, but when you were onstage you better be a fucking star. And offstage you were just a regular person in the community like everybody else. That was the way it worked.

When punk morphed into hardcore, and *MRR* got really doctrinaire and Gilman Street became very anti–rock star, people became more strict about what music they wanted and how they wanted people to look. It took away some of the flash. People were less likely to be outrageous for the sake of being outrageous. Theater kinda got stamped out.

Matt Wobensmith: AIDS took its toll, and a lot of people were dying, and it really affected the San Francisco artistic landscape. But there were still little pockets of stuff going on. One of the things that was interesting in San Francisco was actually right down the street from my apartment.

I had just turned 19 and I couldn't go to bars. The only place that would let me in was this place called the Crystal Pistol. It was called Klubstitute, and it was the home for this drag-punk-weird art-performance-literary-cabaret spoken-word thing, run by the Popstitutes. Diet Popstitute, Reemix Popstitute, the whole bunch. It was a freak show. I could watch weird performance art and see a punk band. All kinds of drag, just crazy shit.

Jello Biafra: In a way *Homocore* and Diet Popstitute and Klubstitute helped rebuild some of that sense of fun that had been missing from punk and hardcore. It even challenged a newer generation's attitudes towards different sexual orientations and practices.

Shawn Ford: Tom Jennings started up *Homocore* towards the end of my time at the first Shred of Dignity warehouse.

Richard the Roadie: Tom was a punk and he was gay, but at that point those worlds didn't really intersect.

Matt Wobensmith: *Homocore* was one of the original big gay punk zines from the late '80s.

Tom Jennings: I was the editor, along with Deke Motif Nihilson, from 1988 to 1991. We kinda messed with a queer/punk hybrid thing, based upon anarchist principles, discordian silliness, distaste for de facto separatist gay culture, and a burning desire to get laid. We also put on a bunch of *Homocore* shows. It was sort of a big deal for awhile, now no one remembers it.

Shawn Ford: Tom got really involved with the Radical Faeries movement, and a lot of Faeries started coming through the warehouse. With the Radical Faeries and *Homocore*, the gay punk identity became a lot more solid and recognizable as a distinct part of the punk community.

Ian MacKaye: Fugazi did a lot of shows with *Homocore*. These people were deeply creative, deeply visionary.

Tom Jennings: We used the "stone soup" method of organizing events. We worked with absolutely minimal tools and components, silk-screening T-shirts with cardboard stencils and spray paint. We have the honor of having the last actual punk show at the original Deaf Club.

Lynn Breedlove: The whole thing about San Francisco—with there being dykes and fags in punk—is we all felt this void. We'd go to straight punk shows and we'd be the only queers there. All of the other queers would be down at Amelia's having just finished playin' softball, rockin' out to "Push it! Push it real good!" We'd be listening to KALX on the way to the bars, and then we'd have to listen to disco to hang out with other queers. It was terrible. Matt Wobensmith is a big fag and he's a punk. He's all tatted up. He felt that alienation.

Matt Wobensmith: In 1991 I started working for *Maximum Rockn-Roll*. I was also helping with the last issue of *Homocore*. And I met this crazy punker kid named Jux at Gilman. Bisexual, according to him. Really fun-loving and filled with grand ideas. I made a fast friend.

At the time, there were all these dudes moshing at shows, this little macho thing going on. So Jux and I came up with this idea to subvert it by square-dancing in the pit. Or by doing ballet, or interpretive dance, or same-sex dancing. We would do that at Gilman.

If someone got really really aggro and violent, we would go hug them. We called ourselves the Huggy Crew for awhile. It wasn't just us, lots of people started doing it. Then one time, when Jux and I were dancing or doing something really silly, this kid ran out of the pit screaming, "There's a faggot in the pit! There's a faggot in the pit!" We thought that was the funniest thing, so we made a record about it.

There's a Faggot in the Pit was an exploration of gender roles in punk. Most of the bands on it were not gay bands, but they were supportive East Bay bands. That spawned me doing gay punk records with Outpunk, from 1992 onwards.

Tom Jennings: *There's a Faggot in the Pit* was the first local queer punk 7-inch I remember seeing in San Fran.

Matt Wobensmith: Outpunk put out 15 or so records, and seven issues of a zine. The first Outpunk record I did was *There's a Dyke in the Pit*, 'cause I figured we ought to have a companion record.

I did a queer issue of *Maximum* in early '92. Tim let me be a guest editor. I did this whole thing with articles on Tribe 8 and Pansy Division, etc., etc. And the *Maximum RocknRoll*–Epicenter world were very supportive of me doing my label and doing gay punk stuff. As I got older and a little bit more evolved, I got hugely into the riot grrl movement that was happening in the early '90s. Bikini Kill was a fucking life-changing event for me.

Davey Havok: The whole riot grrl movement was the Rosie the Riveter version of punk rock. It's something a lot of people don't know about. If you weren't there to see it, it kind of disappeared. But people talked about it a lot back then. I remember being frightened to go to Bikini Kill shows as a young, small, frail boy. 'Cause the girls were scary. Kathleen Hannah saying, "You boys, get the fuck back! This isn't for you." The Bay Area scene was very pro-female and anti-misogynistic. They went very far left in that scene.

Dave Dictor: It was really the natural flow of things. You know, 75 different scenes came out of the punk hardcore scene—everything from dykecore and homocore to eventually riot grrl and everything that came out of that.

Matt Wobensmith: I noticed that Tim and *MRR* was really bristling under this whole new wave of feminism. They weren't covering it. I started writing a little bit about it in my fanzine. I challenged the machinations of the punk scene. In some cases, I was just trying to unearth the hidden history of homosexuality in punk and hardcore. You find out about Gary Floyd from the Dicks, and Biscuit from the Big Boys, and Karen Allman from the Arizona band Conflict. Little factoids here and there. It seems inconsequential, but it was a big deal when you found out that the lyrics were gay.

Gary Floyd: I got interviewed one time by this big gay journalist and he said, "You're openly gay but your songs are not openly gay." My songs are gender-free. Why would I let anyone dictate my art?

Matt Wobensmith: There was a lot of animosity because I was young, bushy-tailed and occasionally naive. Which worked to my benefit sometimes, but you're dealing with a lot of people who are jaded and older and who want to kill your enthusiasm. So I got a reputation of being somebody who was too PC and humorless. But I felt Tim was trying to control the punk scene. I believed in what I wrote and I stood by it. There were a lot of hard things that needed to be said. Tim was spotted at Epicenter hiding my magazines behind the racks so no one could find them.

When riot grrl started getting media press, so did queer punk. I was often asked by reporters, "Can you send us pictures of gay punk clubs and gay punk mosh pits?" I explained, "You don't really understand. *Outpunk* is literally just me sitting at home listening to a record, writing a zine, and putting it in the mail."

Michael Hoffman: My first Gilman show was Friday, March 25th, 1994. It was Tribe 8, Pansy Division, Mukiliteo Fairies from Olympia. It was an Outpunk Records showcase, all queer bands. It was really amazing. And at the end of the show the lead singer of Tribe 8 pulled out her bloody tampon and flung it into the crowd. I was 13. That was the most incredible thing I'd ever seen.

Lynn Breedlove: I like to skeev people out and make 'em twitchy, so I just whipped it out and kind of twirled it around my head a couple of times and *whip!* It did seem to me like it skipped over people's heads—*thwp, thwp, thwp*—like a stone skippin' on the beach. It was a good solid tampon, though, probably o.b. It wasn't going to splash around.

Gary Floyd: I really, really loved Tribe 8.

Lynn Breedlove: I was in San Leandro, the most racist town in California, and I knew that I was queer from the moment I fell in love with my kindergarten teacher. As I became a teenager, my pals used to pick me up in their pickup truck and take me to Cloverdale. At the time, I was still listening to Fleetwood Mac and Journey and all that crap. As soon as I opened the door, they'd crank Black Flag and I'd be like, "Turn that shit down!"

Then I got totally addicted. It was hilarious! "Six Pack," "T.V. Party," "Gimme Gimme Gimme" . . . Oh my god! Funny funny funny. Those guys were like stand-up comics set to music and it was all about getting rage out, which—guess what?—I had a lot of, being a queer.

In the '80s I mostly hung out in San Francisco and went to a lot of straight punk shows. I went to see Tragic Mulatto a lot 'cause they had a dyke drummer. I was like, "Ooh! There's a dyke, there's a dyke! Oh my god!"

In the meantime, I was at home goin' to Cal State Hayward and running around the house, fuckin' yelling into a beer can to Black Flag CDs, doing the punk rock face. I really wanted to be Henry Rollins, but that was a boy thing, a straight-guy thing.

After I got clean and sober, somehow the ten years of speed rage and the Henry Rollins and the fact I actually heard some lesbionic folk songs, where they used the female pronoun—all that came together. I thought, I can do this! Alright, punk rock love songs about sex. I'll channel Henry and Jim Morrison and Patti Smith, I'll get all of my pals to come and throw panties. We'll do this our way. Tribe 8 was the first all-dyke punk band that was singin' about being dykes. There were bands that had dykes in them, but they were singin' "you" instead of "she." And that's just cheatin'.

Tribe 8. Tribade was the original word for lesbians back in the turn of the century. A tribade practices tribadism—tribbin', flat crackers, rubbin' your flat parts together. Flat Crackers—that should've been our name.

Matt Wobensmith saw us playing at Klubstitute with Diet Popstitute's band. Outpunk put out our first record, us and Pansy Division.

Jon Ginoli: I started playing under the name Pansy Division by myself, just me and my guitar in '91. I got a few go-go dancers to dance behind me at Klubstitute. Tribe 8, it was their second show. I remember thinking, "Wow! They've got a whole band! And they're all dykes! Man, this is great!" I loved it. I thought, "I wanna do this with guys!" Seeing them, actually, made me want to go out and get a whole band.

Lynn Breedlove: We meshed the two cultures for the first time. There were no gay bands going, "We're fags! We're dykes!" There was only us and Pansy Division. Matt put a lot of energy into publicizing us. He was super organized. He got the *Advocate* to come do a photo shoot with me and Gary Floyd and some other guy that was in a hot queer band. Then Jello gave me a blow job onstage at Klubstitute, proving his dedication.

Jello Biafra: I didn't realize how dirt covered it was until it was already in my mouth. Where did they store this thing, the Humane Society?

Wendy-O Matik: I went to my first Tribe 8 show at Klub Kommotion in San Francisco. Most women at the show took off their shirts. Lynn Breedlove put on a cop outfit and pulled her cock out and got a gay guy to suck her cock, then eventually castrated herself and flung the cock out into the audience. We all went crazy. It totally changed my life.

Lynn Breedlove: Good Vibrations donated some dicks to us. They have a rejects box 'cause if you order a rubber dick, and you're in Idaho, and then the dick comes and you're like, "Ooh, that has too many veins, it's too realistic, I wanted the Porpoise," you send it back. The law is that you can't sell a rubber dick that has already been sold, because god knows where they put that thing. Mere soap and water will never get that cunt juice off.

So I'd just go to Good Vibes and grab a box. I like 'em big and realistic. Because it has to hurt the rapist out there in the crowd watching. When he sees the knife going through the dick, he has to feel it in his own dick. That's my idea of aversion therapy.

I kept needing to amp it up. Everybody had seen a rubber dick, everybody had seen the blow jobs. The knife was big. Then it got bigger—like 13 inches long with jagged edges. Now what? I got a chain saw.

During all this, I started Lickety Split. It was the first and only all-girl bike messenger company in America. Babes would call from all over the world, and say, "I'm comin' to San Francisco and I need a job. Can I work at Lickety?" We had about 100 women working for us over the ten-year period.

Kegger: I grew up down in L.A., where the SST boys ruled the scene, always talking shit about women. I had gone to all these hardcore shows in L.A. but it was all dudes. I was so stoked when I got here. I had never seen chicks going crazy.

Bucky Sinister: Kegger was in the Hags. Oh man, the Hags were fuckin' scary, man. Jesus Christ. At the time, S.F. butch was flannel shirts and the Indigo Girls, right? The Hags were these crazy metal punk girls and they were all gacked out of their mind with speed. They rode dirt bikes and skateboards.

Matt Wobensmith: Basically a bunch of tattooed, rough, hard-living San Francisco fucking rock 'n' roll dykes. I loved the idea that there were roving girl gangs.

Kegger: Hags SF were a sisterhood of crazy rocker dykes that weren't going to back down to dudes who gave us shit. There was Stacy Quijas, Car Crash, Mona, Head Hopper, Julian, Fiver, Alice B. Brave (I think she was a Hag), Becky Slane, Boomer and Joan of Anarchy—she was crazy. That was my crew. Wendy-O Matik and Noah from Neurosis were our buddies so we'd go to their house in the East Bay.

We had vests and we spray-painted "Hags SF" on everything. We'd go to Oakland and we'd say, "We've come to fuck your women and drink your beer!" We were just obnoxious fuckers. I guess we were trying to outcore everyone. We just fought everywhere. We'd fight on buses.

Bucky Sinister: The Hags all went out with strippers, these beautiful high femme girls. You would see them hanging out at the Market Street Cinema and some of the nastier strip clubs in the Tenderloin, waiting to pick up their girlfriend after work. They all packed dildos in their pants, visible like in Spinal Tap. The strapon was still a little taboo at the time—it was before the whole tranny-boy scene. And they would pop up their skateboard and hit you in the face with it.

One night, I was in the Lower Haight and I was on acid, and I start hearing skateboard sounds outside my window. And these nasty, nasty conversations—like Redd Foxx nasty—about some girl they both fucked. I looked outside and it was a couple of the Hags. They were saying the basest things I had ever heard. It was really frightening on acid.

Lynn Breedlove: Feminism in San Francisco has always been like 15 years ahead of everybody else.

I actually wrote a song called "Menstrual Revolutionary" which never made it onto a recording, thank god, because it was ridiculous. We had friends who would just wear their bleeding pants. Just skanky, you know, the same pants every month.

Jibz Cameron: I thought Lynn was gross. I didn't have any reference for what was going on. I was just like, "That gross lesbian, eew!" I have this weird thing with feminism. It felt like hippieism to me. It was whiny and dorky. I didn't buy it.

Wendy-O Matik: Lynn didn't take any shit. If someone was fucking shit up, she'd stop the song, grab the fucking guy by the neck, and toss him outside. You felt really protected.

Lynn Breedlove: After awhile people would say, "My boyfriend's scared to come, everybody says that boys'll get killed." So then, there were no more boys at the Tribe 8 shows, and the only mixed shows were at Gilman. Tribe 8 shows were always packed, like 500 people.

So what's the point of this whole story? Oh yeah, Miranda July got her start at Gilman and so did Green Day. And they're millionaires, billionaires. They're huge! They're gonna be president. And Rancid, they got their start at Gilman, too, and they're on the radio. What happened to me? Why am I not president? Everyone keeps sayin', "It's 'cause you're a dyke and you're a dick-chopper and people don't want a dyke dick-chopper for president." If I had it all to do over again, I would've just sang sappy love songs in a major key.

Jon Ginoli: The first time Pansy Division played as a full band was at Klubstitute. We were nervous. It's not that we were a gay band, but the fact that we were really in your face about it. We thought, this is gonna piss people off! If we form a band like this, we are just going to be *hated*.

Jesse Luscious: They are probably some of the most fearless people I know. "He Whipped My Ass in Tennis (Then I Fucked His Ass in Bed)"—incredible song.

Jon Ginoli: There's our song "Curvature" about curved dicks. There was "The Cocksucker Club" about somebody trying to figure out his sexuality. Our most popular song is called "Bunnies," which describes the early part of a relationship, where you just fuck like bunnies.

At the time, there was a shitty, sludgy, non-melodic style of S.F. punk at the Chatterbox and later the Chameleon. Bands were sort of like biker punk and I just thought, god, this music is just so fucking stupid. That's what people like around here? I had never gone to Gilman Street before we played there. I'd never heard of Operation Ivy and Green Day and Isocracy and Blatz.

Matt Wobensmith: Jon came by Epicenter with a demo and I thought it was okay. It had promise. Jon was a little bit older than I was, coming at it from a different angle, but I saw the whole thing as connected. I definitely saw a place for Pansy Division and I was really shocked when Larry Livermore signed them. That was really ballsy for Larry to take that chance.

Jon Ginoli: The "Homo Christmas" single came out in November. We identified with the pop punk sound, the more melodic stuff. Suddenly it seemed like we were in the right place at the right time. After we'd finally gotten a record deal set up, we played at Gilman. And lo and behold, we were opening for Tribe 8 and Bikini Kill.

What was sad about the night was that even in enlightened Berkeley, enlightened Bay Area, the sexist shit from the crowd, the catcalls—it was so stupid. If you were writing a movie about this and you wrote down that dialogue, it would seem unbelievable. I could imagine this back in the Midwest, but I thought people would be smarter here.

By the middle of '93, our record was coming out and we did a three-week tour around the country. People came out of the woodwork. The audiences were a lot more straight than gay. This has been true generally—we play a style of music that most gay people don't care about. But we made money, everything went really well.

I was on my way to Lookout! on BART and I ran into Chris Applegren. We were changing trains at MacArthur station, and there was Tré from Green Day. Chris introduced us. We got on our train and Chris said that Green Day liked our album. I was like, "Wow, I'd love to open for them." So he gave me Tré's phone number. When I called, Tré was watching TV and he didn't sound very interested in talking. He just said, "So, you guys have a van?" I said yeah, and he said, "Oh, alright. Well, I'll let you go." I thought, that was a pretty offhand dismissal.

Then six weeks later, he called me up and said, "We're doing a tour this summer for about a month. Do you want to come open for us?" We were like, "Yeeeeeeaaaaw!"

I talked to Green Day about it. I said, "We're really glad you picked us. But what were you thinking?" And they said, "We've got all these mainstream fans all of a sudden, and we really want to do something to show that we're not just your average, typical mainstream band."

Jason Beebout: They could have done anything, and they were like, "Okay, fuck it—let's go on tour with a gay band."

Matt Wobensmith: I got to be a roadie for parts of that. Pansy Division, the most obnoxiously gay band in the world. Not only was it a great strategic move, and it was great for Pansy Division, I think it helped sort of insulate them a little bit. Maybe helped their psyche.

Billie Joe Armstrong: We wanted to bring a band that was a good band but had some shock value to it, that was for real. It wasn't necessarily Marilyn Manson being spooky or something like that. We thought of it as being sort of educational. It was like, yeah, this is something that we come from. This is a place where there's that freedom and that open-mindedness.

It was great. I remember one show, people were sitting there and watching them play, kids would just be rocking out, not really understanding, and then slowly they would be, "What's going on?" And then Chris came out on the microphone and said, "Has anybody figured out we're a bunch of fags yet?"

Jon Ginoli: The first show, in Calgary, Alberta, was actually one of the worst. There were people flipping off Chris, who's more flamboyant than I am, and throwing stuff at him.

Green Day's manager called us about a month later and said, "Look, they're going to play arenas. And they want you to open for them." We were just like, "Oh my god!" We started our band with really modest ambitions. We never thought it was going to go over with a general audience.

San Diego Sports Arena with 11,000 people. I'll never forget that. It was just so disorienting 'cause we're used to playing to 100 people. I was stuck at the microphone singing. I really wanted to be floating in the air above it, just looking around and taking it all in. Groups of people yelling at us and flipping us off and throwing drinks at us. People moshing and cheering.

I had the most conversations with Tré. So before the show I asked him, "Are you nervous?" and he said, "Fuck, yeah!" That

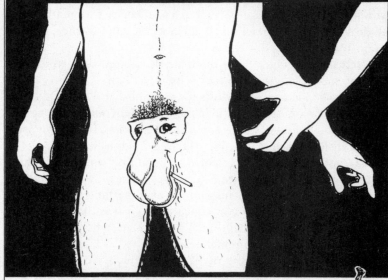

PANSY DIVISION

Touch My Joe Camel

Courtesy of Lookout! and Pansy Division; artwork by Anonymous Boy

Homosapiens: Pansy Division 7" 1993

might have been the last time Tré Cool was nervous about anything.

Billie Joe Armstrong: We were playing a show in Madison Square Garden, and we found out that Bon Jovi was playing. And we were like, "No way, we're not playing the show. Not with Bon Jovi. We're not gonna do it." They were like, "Come on, you guys gotta do it. You guys gotta do it." It was funny 'cause Weezer and Hole were playing on that gig, too, and they decided not to play. Then Courtney told the people, "If Green Day plays, we'll play." And then Weezer was like, "Well, if they play, then we'll play." And we said, "Well, if Pansy Division plays, we'll play." So we got Pansy Division to play with us, at Madison Square Garden. In front of this almost prestigious kind of crowd, 12,000, 15,000 people, Jon singing "Cocksucker Club." Okay, now that's cool.

Ray Farrell: Maybe parents wouldn't understand it, but then Pansy Division becomes something that these kids could relate to. They may not come out of it convinced that they should be gay, but you have to really appreciate the humor that band had, in the way they did it.

Jon Ginoli: Our songs are kind of cute. We were just not punk enough for a number of people at *Maximum RocknRoll*, but our songs are never about conquest. They were all about mutual desire. It's not like, I'm going to do this to you, I'm gonna give it to you, baby. It's like, you're hot, we're going to do this together.

Kids get so much anti-gay propaganda and so much anti-gay peer pressure. Here is a gay band in your midst, being as blunt and outspoken as possible. And people responded to that. So having access to the younger ears, we had to be as uncompromised as possible and do our thing and be honest and not condescending. If some parents were upset, well, whoop-de-do. We're countering propaganda just by being ourselves. And to me that's punk rock.

48

My Boyfriend's a Pinhead

Aaron Cometbus: A bunch of us in Berkeley were professors' kids. Professors' kids who never went to college ourselves. A few of the professors were pretty high profile. Not mine, though. He taught economics at the crappy state school in Hayward. My mom was famous in her field, which was basketry and textile art. But it was a very small field.

The slightly older kids in my neighborhood started burning disco records in the schoolyard. I followed them into this wonderful new thing they had found, which was a somewhat confusing mix of Alice Cooper, Jimi Hendrix, Devo and the Dead Boys. Confusing but cool.

Of that crew, one went down in punk history by getting his head split open by the Misfits. Another went on to play in bands, but nowadays his father is probably more well known in punk circles: Ronald Takaki, the Asian-American historian. It's pretty sad for a punk when your dad is more popular than your band. But this wasn't the only case of it happening.

Noah Landis: Aaron was around when I was 12 and first finding punk. He had his greasy hair and his little journalist notebook. He would interview me about the band I had with the kid next door. This was before it was called *Cometbus*. He would make these things out of paper, like a 16th of a sheet of paper, and it was called *Still Too Small*. You'd flip through this little thing and it would have scene reports of bands and things that people were doing. It was annoying that it was so small. But he just found his path and kept at it.

Ben Sizemore: Aaron played drums in Crimpshrine and was just a real character. Type of guy who knew every nook and cranny of the East Bay. Where to get coffee at three in the morning in East Oakland. Knew the good dumpsters to dive in, stuff like that.

Janelle Hessig: Aaron was exactly the same as he is now. Maybe a little less disappointed or something back then. He was a big, Lurch-y guy and he smelled really bad.

Robert Eggplant: Aaron used to be known for convincing people to go on adventures in the middle of shows and missing all the bands.

Ben Saari: He was two or three years older than me, which when you're 15 is hugely older. He really looked out for me, showed me around, stuck up for me. I was the new kid from the suburbs, I didn't know fucking anything, I was an easy target. Aaron always made sure that I was invited to everything, and introduced me to the idea that I could do stuff on my own. I could book shows, I could be in a band, I could write. He was sort of an intellectual scholar, while a lot of people just wanted to get high.

Bucky Sinister: He had this way of living when he was 18, and he hasn't changed his mind about it. He's still living now the way he lived then. He lives a very ascetic, minimal existence. He can move easily. He can go from one place to another. If you want your geographic freedom you can't have a lot of stuff. And I think that was always a motivating factor.

It's like, how much do you want to work for your stuff? So why don't you work less and do more? Aaron got a lot done. It's not like he was just a slacker, or a drug addict or whatever. That's why people would let him crash at their place, because he was providing, he was giving some kind of entertainment back. And chronicling a lot of it.

Ben Sizemore: Aaron put out *Cometbus* pretty religiously, since the early '80s or so. Great writer. He was always around selling zines.

Bucky Sinister: It was very personal. As far as zines go, it was definitely autobiographical, but he'd reach out, he'd interview people.

Fat Mike: *Cometbus* was interesting—all the tour diary stuff.

Bucky Sinister: People wanted him to do signings and readings for *Cometbus*, and he was like, "No, never." He still has never done one. People wanted to put him on TV, interview him, all that kind of shit—no. He won't do it. Doesn't want to. He sticks by it.

Anna Joy Springer: Aaron was my friend, and I saw one of his *Cometbus* zines and I was just like, "Oh, so you have pictures of women in here, and then an article written by one woman, but everything else is written by guys. That seems really fucked up." He was just livid, and called me a bitch. But that was a moment when I was feeling like the scene had nothing to do with me. We actually became lovers later. And he now knows more about dyke and feminist literature than I do.

Bucky Sinister: Almost every other zine at the time was about either politics or music. *Cometbus* and *Absolutely Zippo* weren't. They were about personal stuff. Stories, or traveling, or where to get the cheapest burrito, anything. It was like how to live your life, and people would get ideas from them. Now there's a bunch of that autobiographical kind of memoir punk shit, but those were the first two. Everybody goes back to them.

Aaron Cometbus: I was living in a little warehouse on the waterfront. It was wonderful and cheap. Paul Curran and I each paid 50 bucks, and the bands that rehearsed there split the other 50.

Bill Schneider: It was called the House of Toast. I was never quite clear on whether it was a practice space or Aaron's house. Aaron slept in a closet. He was the guy in the other room that we woke up at four in the afternoon, when we started playing music.

Mike K: He just seemed like a serious, deep guy. The other people were more goofy. He was the weird grumpy older guy that we knew we were bugging.

Aaron Cometbus: A couple guys from one of the bands, the Skin Flutes, suggested we play some music together.

Bill Schneider: The Skin Flutes was our high school punk rock band in Walnut Creek. It was me, Mike Kirsch, some different drummers and Scott Meyer singing. Scott was very much the crazy guy of our group. He was six foot seven, blue hair, dressed completely out there.

Aaron Cometbus: These guys were in like four bands each, rehearsing all day long, and yet at the end of the day they still wanted to do more, to try more. I liked that. And so, we played together all that spring, Bill, Mike and I. Without a band name, or any plan to take it further.

Bill Schneider: After band practice, me and Mike would stay and hang out with Aaron. We started jammin' and writin' songs.

Aaron Cometbus: Then I left on tour. I was Green Day's roadie on their first few tours. Late at night when the rest of the band was sleeping or partying or whatever, Billie and I started collaborating on songs.

Billie Joe Armstrong: Those early tours were like Green Day–*Cometbus* tours. You couldn't tell who was headlining. Was it Green Day supporting *Cometbus* or was it *Cometbus* supporting Green Day? Aaron always had a shitload of magazines to sell on the road. It was great.

We started writing songs together on a ferry, going from Victoria to Vancouver. I think I whined to him a lot about girls. Aaron had a very romantic vision of the world, and of the ethics and culture of punk rock. Punk rock is like a bible to him. There is deep, deep meaning to him that goes beyond waving the flag. Almost the spiritual aspect of punk rock. I learned a lot from Aaron. Those songs ended up being some of the songs we used for Pinhead Gunpowder.

Bill Schneider: Aaron said, "We should all play together." And that's how we started Pinhead.

Aaron Cometbus: Organically, even accidentally. Which is why it was so annoying later when people called us a "supergroup" or thought of the band as something fabricated. It was just a matter of bringing together the natural elements that were already there.

Mike K: Aaron had gone to Olympia, Arcata, he had moved to some different places. "Pinhead Gunpowder" was a bulk tea at the Arcata co-op.

Aaron Cometbus: Pinhead was also a conscious effort on my part to cast my lot in with the younger kids, the second generation at Gilman. Already among the original Gilman folks there was a lot of cynicism. There were ambitious people just dying to use the scene as a stepping-stone. There were bloated alcoholics playing fake metal. There were people talking about how the old days were better. It was just like any scene anywhere, except that we had Blatz. We had this tremendous new wave of fresh energy that had arrived to kick our ass. Forming Pinhead Gunpowder was a way to take part in that. For me, it was really a matter of life or death. Do something new and exciting or get stuck with the dinosaurs. Besides, having a band that not only all went to shows but who all danced at shows was for me a dream come true.

Bill Schneider: We did a couple 7-inches with Mike, and then he moved to the city and we didn't see him as much.

Mike K: At some point, we played a benefit for war resisters. Everybody there was really into that old-style punk thing, spitting and throwing cigarettes. Nobody talked about what was happening in the world. It was this total apolitical event that just happened to have something positive attached to it. Meanwhile, people were getting killed.

The question became, is it important to maintain this image, this punk caricature that was created almost to be funny? Or are we going to deal with the facts that have allowed this horrible situation to unfold? I started getting more comfortable with the idea that it was okay to do different things. I didn't have to turn Gilman into my vision of what it should be. It was okay for me to go in a different direction and pursue the part of punk that I was interested in.

Bill Schneider: I think that he told us he wanted to quit the band because Green Day was signing to a major label, or something stupid like that.

Mike K: When the major-label feeding frenzy started, that drove a wedge between a lot of people. But even though Green Day was getting bigger, they hadn't really gotten to a level where it was really noticeably different. That wasn't the primary thing. It wasn't like, "Oh my god, he's this fuckin' movie star and I don't want to be in a band with them."

Bill Schneider: Mike was always way more political than the rest of us. He was tighter with the *Maximum RocknRoll* people. So he quit Pinhead Gunpowder, and Jason started playing with us.

Two weeks after Jason joined Pinhead Gunpowder, we took my mom's station wagon on a two-week tour of the Northwest. Aaron gave us all scabies and I met my wife on that tour. That's the first thing I ever gave her.

49

Shield Your Eyes

Andy Asp: I remember playing an afternoon show with Jawbreaker and this band Jolt at a warehouse somewhere in Oakland with four people there. It's amazing that Jawbreaker has had this wonderful afterlife, that people are still so appreciative. But I remember playing some shows with them where there was *nobody* there.

Davey Havok: There was the white-belt Spock rockers wearing their backpacks on the dance floor, just bobbing around. That crossed over into Jawbreaker, who were fantastic, combining a little bit of Oscar Wilde with some seriousness. And some great pop.

Adam Pfahler: When we first had a really good Gilman show where we were the headlining band and packed it out, that was such a great feeling. It was so awesome. Because half the people there were either in other bands or people that were friends. That's a really exciting thing that happens when you're in a band. It's just a big party that happens to be in a venue.

A. C. Thompson: Everyone loved Jawbreaker. Except that Blake couldn't sing, he had a terrible voice.

Bill Schneider: It's funny, it took an L.A. band to move up and bring the East and West Bay together. Blake moved out to the East Bay and bridged the gap. I lived with him in a house on 41st.

Jason White: Jawbreaker lived in the city but they were kind of an East Bay band.

Fat Mike: Were Jawbreaker East Bay or West Bay? I was gonna name them as one really good band from San Francisco. But I guess they moved here, too.

Bucky Sinister: They were like a prototypical emo band. What we now know as emo.

Adam Pfahler: If you were in L.A. in the mid-'80s, some of those hardcore shows, there were a lot of meatheads and it was very guy energy, jock energy. So we were grateful that women were into our band. It was all by design. Something about the way Blake was writing words that appealed to women specifically. In the stories that he told, he wasn't objectifying women like in so many rock bands. It was more like he was just telling short stories where everyone's playing an equal part.

People don't talk about it, but at a certain time in a band's life, if they get too popular or stick around too long, your friends stop coming to the shows, and you're playing to strangers. It gets a little bit weird. But we never did a tour in a bus. We were always just in our van.

Econochrist, we met those guys on tour and did a good long chunk with Fifteen and Econochrist and Filth in the summer of 1990. Just the gnarliest, hottest summer, no air-conditioning in the van. Those bands were totally fucking insane. They would just walk right into your van and sit down and light an M-80 and walk away. Or you'd go back to your van and the inside would be covered in Filth graffiti.

Mike Filth: I wasn't *that* mean! It was probably Jake or our roadie. That's more likely.

Adam Pfahler: The very first time we played in front of a lot of people was when we played with Nirvana.

Bill Schneider: We were touring with four guys in a '78 Dodge van. Nirvana had ten buses, and our van was parked next to the ten buses at a loading dock.

Adam Pfahler: We started the tour in Albuquerque. The place was filled up with a bunch of kids that wanted to see Nirvana. It was more people than I'd ever seen. It wasn't a rock star moment. It was one of those, "Oh, Jesus Christ, what have we gotten ourselves into?"

Bill Schneider: They got a really good response. Then it was like, "This huge band really likes our band. Maybe it won't be all bad. Maybe we should do this."

Adam Pfahler: We were doing just fine on our little indie label, selling 30,000 records or whatever, and touring a good amount of the year. We were making a living. We didn't see any reason why we had to sign. And we were loudmouths about that.

Bill Schneider: Jawbreaker resisted and resisted and resisted. They had a hard time with it. They had people beatin' down their doors to sign them because everybody was looking for the next East Bay thing.

Adam Pfahler: We met Nirvana's A&R guy, and he started calling up. And then it was like, "Oh shit. Okay, people are starting to call us. How do we do this?" We didn't even know how it was done.

So we called Dave, who was then working for Cahn Management, who managed Green Day. We said, "We're getting a lot of calls. How does this work? What do you do?"

We went back and forth. We labored on it, and we knew that a lot of the kids that were on our side were gonna be pissed off if we did this. We knew that *Maximum RocknRoll* was gonna come out fuckin' two barrels blazing. And well they should. 'Cause that was their thing. Politically, we knew that was gonna happen.

Billie Joe Armstrong: Jawbreaker got it worse than we did. What happened to them was brutal. It was bullshit.

Adam Pfahler: There was huge backlash. Because we were loudmouths. When we 180'd and changed our mind and jumped ship, we took a lot of shit for that. And that was the main story of our band. We were hypocrites, and whatever was gonna become of our band, we probably deserved it.

Bill Schneider: They're good at beatin' themselves up about it, but it made more sense than you'd think. They had seen Green Day do it with complete success.

When they decided to do a major-label record, Blake had to have surgery. He had to completely change the way he sang, or wasn't going to be able to sing for the rest of his life. All these sorta things all lined up at the same time, so that Jawbreaker changed just enough, when their major-label record came out.

Adam Pfahler: When we signed to the bigger label, we went on a couple of tours with the Foo Fighters. We would play those radio station shows where they get a shitload of bands together, like the Christmas show for Live 105. We did a couple of those up and down the coast. We were playing with Oasis and Radiohead and No Doubt. We really had no business being there.

They would do these promotional things, where kids would wait and you'd sign your posters promoting your record. I remember feeling really embarrassed about that. It was just weird. Because we were coming from the punk rock thing, where anyone in the crowd could walk up onstage at any moment and take your guitar away from you, and you'd be fine with that. Or you could fall into the crowd, and that would be cool.

Jason White: It didn't work out for Samiam. It didn't work out for Jawbreaker. The fact that *24 Hour Revenge Therapy* sold more than their major-label release was telling.

Adam Pfahler: We did Europe a couple of times. We got on good tours with Sonic Youth and the Beastie Boys. And Pavement and Beck and Rancid and Bikini Kill. But I don't even think we even played that many shows. We never went to Japan. The only big festival we ever did was the one in Australia. Other than that it was us on our own, just kind of grinding it out.

The only show I remember we all agreed that we would do was the *Jon Stewart Show*. But that never happened. We didn't get huge. We didn't sell any records. And no one knows our band. It's just that we have this great following of this very small group of people who just love our band. And a lot of those people started bands themselves and got popular. That's why our name is still out there, because these younger bands loved our band.

50

. . . And Out Come the Wolves

Dallas Denery: I would bump into Matt Freeman every once in awhile. He was always telling me about the new band they were trying to get going.

Sergie Loobkoff: All the bands right after Op Ivy that Tim and Matt were in didn't do well. People didn't like them.

Tim Armstrong: Ian in Fugazi had said something to me that really stuck: "It's always good to start a band with your friends." That was the idea for me and Matt. But it took a year for Matt to start Rancid with me. He wouldn't do it.

Matt Freeman: He managed to stay sober during the MDC tour. It was fun playin' MDC songs, but it wasn't my band, I worked for them. Five dollars a day or whatever it was.

Dave Dictor: Matt played, and Tim was our roadie. Lived in a van with them for three months. I think they're good souls.

Matt Freeman: I learned a lot bein' in that band. But unless it was with Tim, I'm never going to jump in full steam. I don't really wanna play with anybody else.

Tim Armstrong: I got sober at the end of '91 and ended up moving into the punk rock house on Adeline Street. I didn't have a job. Operation Ivy started selling some records. A little royalties were coming in.

Ben Sizemore: This kid Brett moved into where we were living.

Tim Armstrong: Brett Reed would always hang out on Telegraph. He was a skater, punk rock kid, just learning how to play drums. So he was perfect.

Janelle Hessig: Me and Hollie ran into Tim on Telegraph when he was first putting Rancid together. He was trying to come up with a name for it, and he was like, "It's either gonna be called Rancid or Base Head. I kind of like Base Head because it's like a double meaning. Like a crackhead, or like a bass head, like a cabinet." We were like, "Definitely Base Head. Go with Base Head."

Ben Sizemore: I remember giving Lint shit, like, "Rancid? That's kind of a cheesy name." And he got all pissed off at me.

Tim Armstrong: So we started up the band. We made a single on Lookout! But Lookout! had changed to me, it didn't feel the same. David Hayes was gone.

Matt Freeman: We wanted to make that 7-inch, and we had to guarantee the loss they might take with our Operation Ivy royalties. And also, we didn't sound like Operation Ivy.

Christopher Appelgren: Lookout! did their first 7-inch. There was a plan that we would put out a series of 7-inches, and then an album or CD. But there wasn't a lot of enthusiasm.

Larry Livermore: I was not being very open-minded. Although I had told them I would put out any record that they did, post–Op Ivy, I was not very forthcoming about it.

Tim Armstrong: It was different. It was the sound that we were around, our environment. I was living with Ben Econochrist. It was a different vibe. It wasn't '87 anymore.

Christopher Appelgren: At the time they were just this scrappy, metallic punk. They hadn't embraced some of the more melodic elements. The conversations we had at the time, it was almost a backlash to Operation Ivy. They wanted to be tougher, so as not to get called ska boys.

Larry Livermore: I had some arguments with Tim. I think they wanted to put a gun, a pistol on the cover. In the style of NWA or something. I was like, "That's just not a good message to send." He was like, "Oh, you don't know what it's like, living down in south Berkeley, you live in north Berkeley." I was one block north of University, basically downtown Berkeley, which is no paradise either. That was the kind of back-and-forth going on. I was like, it's okay, I'll put the record out. But I felt used in a way, to put out that 7-inch first, to promote them.

Christopher Appelgren: Tim and Matt came by the office and said, "We're gonna do a record on Epitaph. Mr. Brett really likes us. He's offered us a great deal, but basically he's just really into the band, and really excited about it."

Larry Livermore: Tim and I had a big shouting match out in front of the house, which was the closest to bad blood we'd ever had. But

Photo by Cathy Bauer

Let's Go: Matt Freeman and Tim Armstrong of Rancid

it worked out well for them. Epitaph probably did better for them than I could have done anyway.

Tim Armstrong: We got along with Gurewitz from the very beginning. He always loved Op Ivy. I loved Epitaph. The records they were making, and NOFX, Pennywise, Bad Religion, the Offspring. The new thing that was happening. And we were the only band from Northern California.

Sergie Loobkoff: People were sort of laughing, like, "What are these guys doing? These guys aren't punk rockers. Op Ivy wasn't punk. Tim and Matt's bands in high school, that wasn't punk." And then they came out like gangbusters. Like, really punk. It took a little while before everyone realized what a great band Rancid was.

Fraggle: They grew really fast. They went from opening at Gilman to being second only to NOFX shows two months later.

Jibz Cameron: Tim was like, "Yeah, I want to make money." He didn't have any bones about it. That was cool. I think he was kinda bummed about Operation Ivy. And he's such a rock star. He's like a natural that way.

Tim Armstrong: Listen to me, that's a misconception, that we had this hunger to get back on it. I'm living my life. We had a drummer that could barely play. We were playing Fraggle's house, playin' Nando's house, playin' Gilman Street for a year before we got $100. I just wanted to do it, man. It wasn't until Lars actually joined that this shit started to get crazy. When we started getting really big again.

Billie Joe came and played a set with us, played guitar. And that worked out, but obviously he's in another band. That's when we decided to get Lars.

Lars Frederiksen: I already knew who Tim was. There was an instant connection. He came up to me and he said, "Hey, how you doing, I'm Tim. I really like your guitar." Just the coolest guy. The way I grew up, you kinda sniff people out. "Hmm, not too sure about that one." But instantly, *boom*.

Tim Armstrong: I knew he was the right cat, the guy who really belonged in there with us.

Matt Freeman: Lars is a very talented guy, he knew those songs really well.

Lars Frederiksen: I got up there for my first or second band practice. Freeman took me to this Mexican joint around the corner from Gilman. He ordered a pitcher of beer. This was like 10:30 in the morning. Matt, the responsible guy. I basically drank the whole thing. I think that was his first clue that there might be something awry.

Matt Freeman: I brought Lars to Jesse's house, a block down from Gilman, and was like, "Hey, this is my buddy, I'm gonna introduce you." We got a 12-pack. Lars drank about half of it. Most of it. And just talked shit, just "Rah rah rah rah!"—insulted everybody in the room at least twice, myself included. I was just getting angrier and angrier.

Lars Frederiksen: I guess I offended some people. Green Day and Tilt were playing at the Berkeley Square later that night.

Matt Freeman: I knew Tim and Brett were at the frickin' show. Lars said, "Let's go." I didn't really care at this point. I literally kicked him out of the van: "Okay, Berkeley Square's right over there." I locked him out. I was so pissed. I drove back to Jesse's house and they were like, "That guy's a fuckin' dick!"

Tim Armstrong: I introduced him to my friends, and he was just saying stupid shit. He was getting' progressively worse, drunker and drunker. He put his arm around my pal Joe. They kind of grew up around the same area. I looked at Joe's face, I've known him for a long time, and he was scared.

Lars Frederiksen: I guess I threatened to beat up Joe Sibb if he didn't buy me a shot of Jack Daniels, and so he did. And a beer. I think I squeezed that out of him, too.

Tim Armstrong: He ended up going pee in front of everybody, as the show was ending. He was on the street, University Avenue, cock out. Genius, right?

Lars Frederiksen: Pants around my ankles, peeing on people. It wasn't a very Green Day thing to do.

Tim Armstrong: Fuck, I'm an idiot. I took him back to my house. He slept on the floor. Next morning I heard some rumbling, it was him leaving the house.

Lars Frederiksen: This was like six in the morning, and I was trying to get to Ashby BART. I had no money, I figured I'd just panhandle for it. All of a sudden he's chasing me down the street, "Hey!" He gave me ten bucks.

Matt Freeman: I called Tim the next morning, "That guy's a fuckin' nightmare." I told him what happened, and Tim was like, "Oh yeah? Guess what he did to me?" And he told me about the pissing. I said, "Well, fuck him. I just went through this bullshit with you, I don't want to go through it with some guy I don't fuckin' know."

Tim Armstrong: I said, "He's got a problem. If he doesn't drink anymore—or do heroin, PCP—maybe it'll work."

We put him up at our place for a couple weeks. For awhile, Cinder was like, "I can't believe you've got that guy in your band, he's a dick!" I had to deal with that. But I believed in the dude. I could see that he wanted a better life.

Lars Frederiksen: He found me a place to live and gave me 100 bucks and said, "Here's your first month's rent." He really looked out after me. I think because of my antics at the Green Day show, they saw that that might be every night, you know. But I was already looking for that. I lived there at the Derby Street house for about a summer. And I got a job on Telegraph, making salads.

I know I was probably a little bit more wild than those guys. But I found where I needed to be. I was just stoked to be playing punk with two guys from one of my favorite bands. Cool. I'm not copping on Mission.

My first gig was at fucking Cloyne Court. The pit was crazy. The naked Berkeley guy was in the pit with his fuckin' little doinker, his backpack on. And I remember just going, "Fuck, bro, put some clothes on. This is a punk show."

We played Gilman pretty steadily. Any time a band would cancel they'd call us up and we'd be there. We were playing local gigs here and there, driving up to Petaluma. We played down in L.A. at the Hong Kong Ballroom. That was my third show with the band, in front of Brett Gurewitz. Which was kinda nerve-wracking. Richard was with us at the time.

Richard the Roadie: I was doing shows with them before, and suddenly there was this new guy in the band, Lars. Which was awesome. It totally changed the sound, and made 'em a lot better band.

Lars Frederiksen: Richard was one of the stinkiest people. But the motherfucker could work. He wouldn't let you carry your amp into the gig. He'd be like, "No, no no, that's my job." And then he'd put it on his shoulders and carry it in.

Richard the Roadie: In the beginning when I started, we were just playing a lot of house parties, small shows. People up here fucking thought they sucked. If you listen to the first 7-inch, I thought they sucked, too. It was so different from Op Ivy and any of the other stuff they'd done.

Then I saw them play an acoustic show at the Occidental House on 61st. All of a sudden I got it. And I have fucking absolutely loved them since then. At that point in '93, I thought they were probably one of the best punk bands in the U.S.

Lars Frederiksen: There was no other band like Rancid going off at that time. It was all the pop punk shit like Green Day. Or like Econochrist, Grimple, that kinda shit. There was nothing like Rancid, that was like fast, melodic, Discharge-y, GBH shit. Mixed with the Ramones and the Clash.

Mike Avilez: When I first moved up I did a zine called *Piece of Shit* and Lars was one of the first people I interviewed. They were totally nice to me. I asked Rancid if they had done much touring and they said, "We've been up and down the coast like no one's business but we haven't done any major tour." Their first album on Epitaph was just about to come out.

Lars Frederiksen: I didn't go outside the state of California until I joined Rancid. On Rancid's first tour, on the visor, it said "States

Lars has never seen." So each time we'd go through a state I'd give it one to five X's, on what I thought of the state. Matt would always be giving me the Sharpie at seven in the morning. I think Texas got a 5X. I liked Texas for some reason.

Richard the Roadie: Rancid was no bullshit. It was five dollars, all-ages, or they wouldn't play. They had a booker, Stormy Shepherd, which was really unusual at the time. She was awesome. She's not nice when you try and screw her, which I've seen. She really opened up doors for them.

Stormy Shepherd: Tim and Matt had been booking their own tours for years. Rancid are still self-managed. That band divides up everything between the four members and they do everything themselves. They are extremely hands-on, which is just unheard of for a band of that size.

Richard the Roadie: We were basically all sober. And we were all really young, or relatively young. It felt as close as what I read about Black Flag. We were just going for it. We were all in this tiny windowless van, and every single night they played as hard as they fucking could. Once they started they would just go full on until they stopped. They wouldn't fuck around and talk. They were on fucking fire, those first two years.

Lars Frederiksen: We took the Swingin' Utters to Europe with us, took them out on tour. It was really fun. I think we paid for them to come out there.

Johnny Bonnel: Opening up for Rancid was crazy. It was packed. They still had the buzz from Op Ivy. Lars was helping us out big-time. He got us these shows and eventually went on to produce *Streets of San Francisco*. Always said great things about us.

Lars Frederiksen: It just snowballed. Green Day was blowing up, Offspring was blowing up. We were playing fuckin' Vino's Pizzeria in Arkansas when we found out that somebody was playing "Salvation" on the radio.

Martin Sprouse: Not that they should be compared, but there was something that organically, naturally happened with Op Ivy. I think Rancid was preconceived. They're very real guys. But they were trying to set out to do something.

Lars Frederiksen: Although it's two totally different animals, people were curious.

Anna Brown: Jesse was sort of the soul of Operation Ivy, but Lint was the one who became the star. It became very clear early on when Rancid started doing videos, that they were going to be big. They had this tough thing going on that was really different from the peaceful Op Ivy thing.

A. C. Thompson: People didn't think they were as smart as Op Ivy. Their songs weren't as immediately catchy.

Matt Wobensmith: Tim is a sweet guy. But then you go see Rancid and it's, like, überpunk. Who do they think they are? Affecting like they're from the streets. There was this tough gang sort of aesthetic, which is totally not them at all. They're from Berkeley and from around, and they're just soft guys. The greater public ate it up.

A. C. Thompson: They went from playing house parties to being on MTV in six months. It was really quick.

Ben Sizemore: One day I came home and Rancid was filming a video in our apartment. I knew it was going to be happening. There was a camera crew there. I was like, "This is fuckin' nuts." They had catered some Chinese food, so I got a free plate of food out of it. I went in my room and shut the door. It was a little cheesy, you know. Lip-synching a song on MTV.

A. C. Thompson: Tim came over to my house and showed me their first video. I thought it was kind of bullshit. This cartoony stereotype of punk rock, where he's carrying around a baseball bat and acting macho. I told him what I thought, and I remember him being kind of bummed about that. When I look back on it, the song is really excellent.

Lars Frederiksen: I always looked at videos as a way to just document shit. You can see me by the loft, kinda hanging out, rockin' out. I'm not really in the band yet. There was always a joke that when Rancid plays songs off the first record—that a loft is gonna come out and I'm just gonna put the guitar down, and hang out in the loft and watch.

Janelle Hessig: It's so funny. After they started getting big, in one of the videos there's a picture of them looking all thugged out in this graffiti-covered tunnel. But it's this tunnel that goes along Solano Avenue in the most affluent area of town.

Richard the Roadie: Most hardcore East Bay punks thought Green Day were stupid, but nonetheless they were able to find a local following. Rancid never did. That was always the joke. We'd go to Seattle or L.A., and it was absolutely fucking amazing. And come back to Gilman and get treated like shit.

Sergie Loobkoff: That kind of punk, with mohawks and leather and spikes and stuff, that wasn't really what Gilman was about. Just as much as what Samiam was doing wasn't really what Gilman was about.

Richard the Roadie: It was a weird time in the East Bay. Green Day was signed. Samiam signed. Jawbreaker. Screw 32 and AFI were slowly building up at the same time. If your band was doing well, because Green Day and all these other bands signed to majors and were getting bigger, you got the same venom as everybody else. A lot of it was misplaced.

Jesse Luscious: When Rancid were talking to Sony, I was like, "Matt, that's a shitty idea." But they didn't jump. Fuck no, they didn't.

Richard the Roadie: Rancid, Jawbreaker, Green Day, we're all scumbags, but everybody had their little niche. But Rancid, it was almost worse for them. It just got out of control. It was a really bad environment. Tim, walking down Telegraph, would be threatened by people.

A. C. Thompson: Part of it was that people felt resentful. These guys were going to make money and live comfortable lives, and our lives were all fucked up and janky. People who were subcultural purists didn't want their subculture being disseminated to the masses. Even though they said they had a political message that everyone should hear. So there was this cognitive dissonance.

John Geek: I liked Rancid a lot when they were peppier and more angular, weird punk. But then they got really big. I remember going to the show and the line was around the block, and I was like, "Ah, this is just not my thing anymore." It just didn't feel like home so much. Me and a bunch of other people were feeling the same way.

Eric Ozenne: I remember Tim riding his bike down to Gilman. All those Rancid guys were going to shows a lot. It was starting to get hard for them, because people were constantly giving them shit. But they still were going to shows pretty consistently. I got to see it from their perspective. My wife and I and Lars all moved into a house in Berkeley. I watched them go through the process of making . . . *And Out Come the Wolves*. I realized these guys are totally passionate about what they do, and they're not trying to screw anybody. And they're also giving back to the scene. It was a really interesting time, for sure.

Greg Valencia: I remember being in the Rancid guys' shit. I was younger and I didn't really get it. I don't have any problem with those guys these days. I still have respect for them. At that time, I think it just sucked more 'cause their heads got giant.

Kate Knox: I used to know Lint. He used to lie about his age to get with the younger girls. I remember him being at a party and being like, "Look, I got Madonna's phone number!"

Orlando X: Some people did treat those guys bad, when they started getting big. Especially Tim. Which was kind of fucked up.

A. C. Thompson: I saw Tim in South Berkeley and he said that he felt really out of place, people were hassling him and yelling at him on the streets. Overnight, he had gone from being a celeb in that DIY world, to being someone who was cast out. So he moved to L.A. He took the fuck off. I think it was a scarring experience.

Jeff Ott: Sober people don't do well with celebrity. Part of me was like, "Okay, they're totally the same punk band as they ever were, sober, doing big stuff." But a lot of people who got into the aesthetic of punk, and were more on the English band side of stuff, they were more severe about, "Oh, they sold out. They're not a punk band." I would look at that person's life and go, "Well, you're not a punk in the first place, so who are you to go around saying anything anyway? You're a fucking idiot in a costume who's acting all day."

Lars Frederiksen: Every manager we've ever had doesn't want to work with us, because we've always done whatever the fuck we wanted to do from day one. Whether it was record labels or whatever, if they said, "Do this," we're like, "Fuck you, we're not gonna." You want us to do press? We're not gonna do press for five years.

You can't just walk around blindly and let somebody else handle your shit, because they're not always gonna have your best interests. So all that did was made us more insular. It's hard to kinda break in, to get to us. It's like, I don't fuckin' know you. At that time that's what it kinda was.

Dallas Denery: It's hard to imagine it got to a point where they're selling more records than the Buzzcocks. I mean, they're really great. But when you go back and think the Buzzcocks were really great, and the Ramones were really great. And they didn't even get close to that. That is really surprising.

Lochlan McHale: I heard Rancid in San Diego through Taylor Steel surf videos. I believe it was off the *Let's Go* album. Every day we'd drive to school and listen to that album. I went to their shows and met the guys, hung out. Lars and I hit it off. He showed me producing, how to play guitar, the business side, the fun side. Through that I met Tim, and they kinda took me under their wing and it was like, okay, what do you want to learn? Rancid stuff is a history book. It's real story oriented. It's a little bit more hooky than New York hardcore.

Eric Ozenne: Lars and Tim have helped so many bands by getting them shows. Doing record labels that help other bands. They'd take young bands out there on the fringes under their wing, and bring them back in and help them out. People have actually seen money come from Rancid, put back into businesses for the scene. To help them do things, like, say, screen printing. Rancid put a lot of stuff back out there.

Lochlan McHale: If you look at it, for punk to be good you gotta have something to say. Majority of the people with things politically to say are the immigrants, or people who are facing struggles from the government. So what's Tim doing right now? Echo Park, a huge Latino community. Those kids have a lot to say right now. The stuff that's going down with them trying to kick out people who don't have green cards. Tim's supporting all sorts of those bands.

Orlando X: You see Lars out all the time. He still goes out. They didn't all of a sudden get big and just leave, they've all contributed something back. They haven't forgotten where it got started. So that's really cool.

Nick 13: Steve List introduced me and Tim. I was wearing a Crimpshrine shirt. Tim was a big Crimpshrine fan. He gave me his number and said to give him a call, "Maybe we can put your band in a show." Which he also told every other band about the same slot on the same show.

Stormy Shepherd: When they tour, every single night they handpick a local opener to play their shows. They do a syndicated radio show online, and they start talking months in advance, saying, "Hey, we're going to be touring, send us your demos." Tim and Lars listen to everything, and then they send me a list, by city, of every band that they want to have open.

Martin Sprouse: They're still going. They could not put out a record for 20 years, and sell out shows everywhere. People love what they're about. It's different than what I'm about. Even though I still have a lot of love and respect for those guys.

Dallas Denery: If you want to put it in perspective, the Rolling Stones put out a record in 1966 that has "19th Nervous Breakdown" on it. Twenty years later, they're putting out stuff nobody wants to hear. So in 1987, Op Ivy records its first record. And in 2007, Rancid is still a viable band.

Adam Pfahler: It's a pretty amazing story. There's a handful of things that are still going, that were going back then. It's pretty inspiring.

Anna Brown: Now Lint's this punk institution. He's like Joe Strummer to a generation of people that are in high school.

51

I Wanna Get a Mohawk
(But My Mom Won't Let Me Get One)

Davey Havok: I was surrounded by music since I was very, very young. At family functions, I would get paid a dollar to sing into a wooden spoon. I'm sure everyone thought it was very adorable, that the little boy was singing "Mister Moon" and "The Darktown Strutters Ball." Going to the malls in Sacramento, I was always enamored of all the punks and death rockers. I told my mom, "Oh, I want a mohawk, and I wanna get tattooed," and she was like, "I'll put my head in the oven if you do." When I was 12 years old I moved to Ukiah.

Nick 13: Ukiah is about two hours north of both San Francisco and the East Bay. There were a lot of hardcore communes, mixed with this more conservative redneck hillbilly mentality. It's definitely a strange place. Ukiah was the final staging ground for Jonestown. Charles Manson spent time in Mendocino County. Those two serial killers, Leonard Lake and Charles Ng. The guy who killed Polly Klaas, they caught him in Ukiah.

It was a place where people came to hide out. These weird punkers or kids from group homes, you knew that they were either running from some drug deal or group home, or someone wanted to kill them. They would show up in Ukiah for a week, and we would always dub whatever punk tapes they had in their backpacks, and then you'd never see them again.

Davey Havok: I predated Trenchcoat Mafia, but that's pretty much where I was at. Combat boots, black jeans, silver chains, Madonna silver bracelets, dyed black hair, black T-shirts, black jackets.

Nick 13: The first few seasons of *90210*—everybody looked like that. You had to have a mullet, you had to wear spandex biking shorts and Oakley shades, you had to drive a mini-truck, you had to listen to Vanilla Ice and Paula Abdul. People looked at you like there was something wrong, because you listened to the Ramones and wore creepers. In a school of approximately 2,000 kids, there were a dozen people that had any interest in punk.

Davey Havok: We had to leave to get anything, whether it was *Maximum RocknRoll*, music, Manic Panic, pyramid studs, anything. Villains in San Francisco had the Christian Death shirt with Jesus shooting up on it. Daljeet's had the Doc Martens. Back then, the girls who were wearing the two-toned Wayfarers and the Guess jeans also had them draped over some oxblood Doc Martens. Which was weird.

Nick 13: I met Dave in high school when he was a freshman and I was a sophomore. He had a Misfits shirt on. He seemed really happy and that kind of annoyed me. My first instinct was to hit him. But he was so personable, and well liked and popular. We've been friends ever since.

Davey Havok: Because we were really secluded, our influences came from all over the place. I was listening to everything from Black Flag and Descendents and Negative Approach and Dag Nasty and Minor Threat, to you know, Bauhaus and the Cure and Joy Division, Duran Duran. Most of what I listened to predated me.

Nick 13: The only punk show that ever happened in Ukiah was the Lookouts, Lawrence Livermore's band. Before we got our own bands and started playing our own shows.

Davey Havok: As soon as any of us was able to drive, we started driving down to see shows at Gilman Street and the Phoenix Theater. I'd go see Dead and Gone all the time, and Neurosis. Those are fantastic bands.

Nick 13: I went to shows in S.F., because they'd be advertised in the *Chronicle*. Fifteen of us would pile into a van and go to see the Circle Jerks in the city. Like '89, 90.

Davey Havok: We started the band AFI when I was 15 years old. We called dibs on instruments. I was the musical theater choir boy so I got dibs on singing, and the rest came together. We named AFI to have an acronym. Because it was such a facet of punk rock and hardcore and thrash. TSOL and MOD and DI and RKL, DRI. So we wanted an acronym band. That allowed us to play with a lot of things. Our publishing company would be Anthems For Insubordinates one year, and then we'd change it to something else. We'd say, "If you want a free patch or sticker, send a self-addressed envelope to 'Asking For It,' at P.O. Box . . ."

In the scene back then, everyone had such glorious stage names. Unfortunately, I'm Davey Havok. I have such a horrible name compared to Darby Crash, or Dinah Cancer, or C. C. DeVille. They're far more ingenious. One of my favorites from the rock 'n' roll scene, Nikki Sixx, I think that's hot. Iggy Pop, probably one of the best names.

Influence 13 was the first real punk rock band in Ukiah. They were fantastic, and it was comprised of Nick 13, who is now from Tiger Army, and Jade, who is now in AFI, Geoff Kresge, who was in AFI in its almost original lineup. They were really the first punk band from Ukiah that could write songs.

Nick 13: Influence 13 were together for two years. We played gigs whenever we could. Gilman Street was not very cool about putting on out-of-town bands that weren't touring bands. Dave and I both had this experience. There would be a certain time you would call, say it was five p.m. Wednesday. We would call and they'd say, send us a demo. We'd send them a demo. They'd say call us back at this time—and no one would answer the phone.

Davey Havok: AFI would play house parties in Ukiah. The first time we played live we had probably seven songs, so we played them all twice, terribly. Half of which were our own, and the other half were like, Black Flag and Descendents covers. We might have thrown in [Green Day's] "Going to Pasalacqua," as well.

There were shows in Lake County. Lakeport was the city. It really made Ukiah look like San Francisco. Tilt would come and play. The Wynona Riders, Juke, Fifteen would play a lot. We tried to get Green Day once. I think Geoff was on the phone with Billie, and Tré was there, and Billie was like, "No. Tré says Ukiah sucks. Tré says there's no scene in Ukiah." We were like, "Fuck, he's right!"

AFI played its first show at Gilman Street technically when we jumped onstage at a Rancid show that we all came down to see. Then Rancid put us on first of a five-band bill at Gilman Street, and from that point on, we played Gilman a lot. Basically, us, the Swingin' Utters and Screw 32 during the early '90s were constantly playing together everywhere.

Lars Frederiksen: Davey was a little skinny kid. Always had a skateboard. Davey would always go, "Here's a tape of my band." He was a wicked front man, even though he's talking about his balls or whatever. But you kinda knew that something would happen. "I don't wanna fuck you, so fuck you." Cool shit.

Bill Schneider: Davey was straightedge and had X's on his hands and a Youth of Today sweatshirt. Even today, he's just the same guy.

Fraggle: This little frantic punk who always wore pants with no shirt, with one suspender up and one suspender down.

Davey Havok: I had a mohawk. Not a lot of mohawks in '93. We looked ridiculous. I don't look back at pictures with the mohawk and go, "Yeah, we had it right!"

Billie Joe Armstrong: I used to ask Jesse Michaels what was going on, and he told me he thought AFI was really good. I remember really liking them. Davey was not the Prince of Darkness that he is now. He was wearing suspenders and he had this Danzig-style devil lock.

Davey Havok: What we were playing was different than what a lot of people were playing. We weren't political. And we were accepted. Gilman Street supported us, we played tons of shows around here. But there were a lot of people who totally hated us.

Zarah Manos: Love AFI, they had great shows. When I was at Gilman, we counted on them for money. An AFI show would be 800 people. There were bands that helped us get the bills paid. You had to have one major show a month that was gonna pull your bank because we had high bills. Once they hit, it was really sad.

Ryan Mattos: I went to an AFI show at Gilman and went straight to the merch table, and was like, "Hey, can I get that T-shirt?" It said "I Hate Punk Rock" on it. Which I thought was kind of weird. I bought a shirt, put it on, and as I started to walk away, the guy was like, "Hey, is this your first show?" and I was like, "Yeah, how'd you know?" He was like, "Oh, I don't know, just haven't seen you before. Hi, I'm Dave." He was totally friendly to me and nice.

Later I saw him right before they played, checkin' the microphone, and I was like, "Oh yeah, that makes sense, that's like their crew or roadie guy." Then they started playing. And I was like, "That's weird, why's the singer selling their merch?" I still wasn't in the mind-set that punk bands are just people.

Tiger Lily: Davey Havok contributed to my zine for a period. He had a leather jacket with the blue Germs circle painted on the back. Sweetest guy ever. Sometime in 1994, AFI came on my show at

KALX. Most of AFI was in school, and Dave went to Cal, maybe Adam did, too. They did not like it when I asked if they had to go to class after the show. Funny how going to school is so uncool.

Ryan Mattos: All the AFI guys lived in this big frat house by UC Berkeley. It was a frat house that had lost its charter and started renting out rooms to people. Adam had gotten in, and got someone else in, and slowly started taking the house over.

Nick 13: It was most of the guys from AFI and a few other friends. I wound up crashing on Dave's floor for awhile, then I was able to get a room there. That house was basically where I worked until Tiger Army really got going.

Ryan Mattos: There were 17 rooms, at one point we had 12 of them. There were a couple students, some random voodoo doctor guy. It was two blocks from campus and two blocks from Telegraph. When Cal had a football game, they basically shut down the streets so people can just walk around. We'd sit on our porch,

This is Berkeley: Davey Havok of AFI at Gilman

and thousands of people would walk past the Acacia frat, and then they'd get to our frat, and it'd be a whole bunch of dudes dressed in black with black hair and tattoos, and they'd all be like, "What frat is that?"

Davey Havok: I think AFI played our last show at Gilman in 1997.

Bill Schneider: AFI have changed so much over the years. Instead of breaking up and changing their name, they have just kind of evolved into what they are today.

Ryan Mattos: I have an AFI tattoo that says, "I don't grasp your values," which is from one of their songs. I think it pretty much fits. I never got why my friends just wanted to talk about getting wasted, and then would get wasted. I cared about launching a water balloon more than I cared about getting wasted.

Lars Frederiksen: AFI actually played with us on our Canadian tour after we did *Saturday Night Live*. We took 'em through Canada with us. Good dudes.

Ryan Mattos: We thought they blew up like five times before they did. The first time I saw them headline at Gilman there was like 250 kids there. But the girl in back of me in line was talking about Davey—"I wonder if his hair's gonna have that little curl?" It didn't matter if it was 200 kids or 20,000, they've always had that charisma.

They did a big video shoot at Berkeley Square. And then it was like, oh, they're on Nitro [Records], that's so crazy. And it was like, Offspring covered one of their songs, now it's on Live 105, they're huge. And then it's like, "Oh, you guys sold out a 12,000-capacity venue in eight minutes?" So I stopped getting as excited.

Eric Ozenne: Knowing Adam and Dave for a long time, it was incredible to watch them go through these musical changes. There's no sellout about those guys. They straight up were doing what they wanted to do the whole time. And they were very much, very real punk rock people. They hold a lot of that stuff as their values and morals.

Ryan Mattos: I don't think those bands start out like, "Oh, let's play this kind of music and then we can catapult to something else." There's no way that when AFI started in their living room they were like, "Okay, let's play shitty punk rock shows for eight years, and then we can start making mainstream accessible music." I think it just happened.

Dave Chavez: Every once in awhile I'll hear an AFI song and I'll go, "That's kinda cool." I actually thought they were a decent hardcore band 'cause they had a lot of energy. A lot of people really like 'em. I'm not really a big fan of theirs, but I think they're more progressive and original than all their other Bay Area cohorts.

Jeff Ott: I go to a gym in the morning because I'm getting to be an old guy. There's four TVs up on the wall at Sonoma State, and I'll see AFI and I'll just go like, "Oh, I can't even believe—this is ridiculous." But I'll put in headphones, I'll listen to them, I'll be like, "This is another song about nothing. What the fuck is this?" They probably spent a million dollars to make that, probably spent hundreds of millions of dollars on manufacturing it all and selling it to people, and it says nothing at all. And I feel slightly responsible. I think in the beginning, a lot of people thought so long as the music is very dissonant and not melodic, it will never end up there. Well, no, you can do all that. Sometimes I go, "It sure would be nice if the whole thing never went to that at all."

Davey Havok: We were sitting in the back of a Town Car driving through New York, having just won the Best Rock Video award for MTV, and it's one of those moments where it's like, "We're so lucky." Later that night at a party I found myself talking to Axl Rose for the first time. I didn't want to bother him, but I am a big fan of Guns N' Roses. Which is certainly not a punk rock thing to admit to, but I am not much of a punk rocker these days, and have no problem admitting to it.

It was furthermore a surreal moment to not only be talking to him, but after I stammered out something about *Appetite for Destruction* being one of the best rock 'n' roll records of all time, and Day on the Green with Metallica in San Francisco, and I was in seventh grade, and this and that. And thinking, "Oh man, he is so bored, I wish I wasn't saying this to him." He's standing there just kind of nodding and smiling. After I get all that out I think, "Oh, I bummed him out." And he said, "Yeah, when I'm doing my warm-ups on my iPod, right after my warm-ups come on, your record comes on." And I was like, "Oh my god. This is out of control."

And later, Hunter and I were standing on the other side of the room at the party, and I was like, "That was amazing!" And Hunter said, "But really, think about this. Think about when we were in junior high, think about someone coming up and telling us that we were simply going to be in the same room as Axl Rose."

It's not simply celebrity moments like that. I really, really appreciate everything we have. We started doing this band out of the love of music, and coming from a scene where we were encouraged to play music that we liked, with complete disregard for whether or not anybody else liked it. And with no concern as to whether any of us could play our instruments. I just feel very lucky that at this point in my career, I'm continuing to be able to do what I love.

Mike Avilez: AFI, they were once a hardcore punk band, and now they're just mainstream bullshit. I like Davey and more power to him. If he can do it, then that's fine. It's just strange.

Davey Havok: The Bay Area really provided a scene for my life to grow out of. This is where we were drawn. Seeing Crimpshrine and Green Day and Operation Ivy and Wynona Riders and Samiam and Monsula and Jawbreaker and bands like that coming out of the scene, who were all great bands, drew us here. And the community that was centered around Gilman Street and centered around the Bay Area scene was something that really appealed to us.

Playing with Screw 32 and Dead and Gone and the Swingin' Utters, and going to see Rancid and Green Day at the tiny clubs, all those bands, the Gr'ups, and Blatz, and Filth, was just a part of it all. It was inspiring to be a part of that. It was a very supportive scene, a very unique scene.

52

(I'm Not Your) Stepping Stone

Jeff Ott: You were the kid that everyone shit upon. You were the one with pimples and glasses in high school, and everyone discarded you. And that was your place. So when these bands started to get popular, we felt like we were used as a stepping-stone. Who would care about this group of fucked-up kids? Why would any of these bands ever be popular?

Orlando X: It's the progression of music. Fans make the music.

Jello Biafra: Every underground rebel art culture, if any good, is always gonna get co-opted. It was bound to happen.

Blag Jesus: Youth movements take off in the most egalitarian and idealistic way, but ultimately people come in and profit off them. That's what happened with punk rock in England, that's what happened with punk rock in New York, and that's what happened with punk rock in the East Bay.

Lars Frederiksen: You could see it coming, from Nirvana first putting the stamp on everybody. But I never could see that we would be doing it. Whatever happened with Offspring or Green Day and us—I would have told you you were out of your fuckin' mind.

Adam Pfahler: Blake and I were at Jabberjaw in L.A. While Nirvana was recording *Nevermind*, they played an unannounced show at Jabberjaw and it was packed out. We looked at each other and were like, "This is gonna be fuckin' out of control."

Billie Joe Armstrong: We went to Europe, just playing squats. We booked it ourselves. When we were on tour, Nirvana started getting really popular and I remember thinking, they made a great record. And they're on a major. And they still have this consciousness about them. It wasn't something that was made up or fabricated or contrived. It was real.

Noah Landis: When *Nevermind* got all that attention, for the first time it was something that somehow everybody *got*. Everybody understood the intensity and the emotion of those songs.

Jesse Luscious: I was listening to rock radio and I heard "Aqualung" into "Smells Like Teen Spirit." I almost crashed the car.

Dave Chavez: I thought Nirvana was a half-ass kinda thing. I thought he wrote really good words but thought the music was just—he was trying to be like Flipper and Negative Trend, but he didn't have the balls to do it all the way.

Noah Landis: Punk rockers hated it because it was bringing this punk rock to MTV. But there were a lot of punk rockers who were like, "This is undeniably really good, this is really powerful, and it makes you feel something when you listen to it."

Jello Biafra: Once Nirvana got that big, the major labels took the ball and ran with it.

Adam Pfahler: Then two years later, Green Day sold eight million records or whatever, and then the whole Bay Area got gobbled up. It blew up completely. And then it blew up in everyone's faces.

Lars Frederiksen: A&R guys would find out what hotels we were staying at, and stay at the same hotels. "Oh, hey, guys! You're Jim from Rancid, aren't you?" People wouldn't even know our names. "What label you with? Blah blah blah." It was that bizarre.

Adam Pfahler: Jawbreaker would get those lame form letters in the mail: "I am blah blah blah from Columbia Records. Please send me a copy of your blah blah blah and we'll have lunch."

Kamala Parks: That to me is the antithesis of punk. It was supposed to be DIY. You're not supposed to take your popularity and benefit some high-ranking mucky-muck. You're supposed to keep things local and in your scene. And not buy into this fame bullshit that they were feeding bands.

Lenny Filth: Back then, it was a no-no. You were supposed to live in poverty your whole damn life. And just play because you wanna play.

Andy Asp: Green Day's first shows after they'd signed with Warner Brothers, you could see that there was a line drawn. There were protesters, picketing 'cause they had signed to a major label. That was the end of the innocence.

Jibz Cameron: All of these younger, more trendyish kids started coming around, and it pissed everybody off.

Andy Asp: You could see our world changing. Here it was, being spoon-fed to people via television and major magazines.

Jason Beebout: There's a lot of passionate people who really believe in that Oakland hardcore sound. It means something to them. You ride your bicycle everywhere, and you're wearing everything black for the past 20 years because you're so to-the-fucking-core. And all of a sudden you're looking at Clear Channel, and it's loaded with images that are looking a lot like you. You start to feel like you have no identity anymore.

Adrienne Droogas: The people I knew who were heavily into the politics wanted it to be very separate. If you wanna be on MTV and you wanna sign to a major label and go do these things, that's great. That's awesome. But you're not a part of the punk scene anymore. The punk scene I know and that I was a part of, and that meant everything to me, had nothing to do with that world.

Kamala Parks: You have the talent here, and you should use that locally, rather than selling yourself across America. To become someone who encourages other bands to do the same things, and represent your values if they want to. To not make yourself a generic punk rocker.

Jesse Luscious: Major labels may be the nicest people. They might love kittens and bunny rabbits, but at the end of the day their corporate owners make guns, missiles, they pay lobbyists to destroy the environment. And by choosing to put your art into the maw of that planetary machine, I think that's ethically suspect.

Winston Smith: It's kind of a black-and-white way of looking at things. I could never understand that kind of logic. General Electric, they make all kinds of guided missiles and other bad juju. But I can look up and count five little incandescent bulbs with "GE" on it. So I've given GE money, which means I've contributed to the death machine. I'm helping their CEO keep his golden parachute. If you're playing a record, with the electricity from a little string that goes into the wall, that's created by a giant power plant, PG&E, which is Profit, Greed and Exploitation. Every time you pay your electric bill, you're giving them money to pour into Diablo Canyon, building a nuclear power plant on the San Andreas Fault, which is insane. For thousands and thousands of years it will be radioactive and carcinogenic, and so every time you play a record, or pay your bill, or anything, you're contributing to this machine. You can take that, and reduce it down to any argument, and everyone is guilty, all the time, everywhere, all at once.

Nick 13: I still don't understand the major-label debate. The Ramones' first record was on Sire, the Sex Pistols were on a major label, the Clash were on a major label. And those three bands, along with the Damned, who were also on a major label, they all started punk. You can go back to the Dolls and the MC5 and all that, who were also on majors. It wasn't that I didn't appreciate the ethic. Because I certainly never thought a major label would be interested in putting out my music.

Kamala Parks: Having your image splattered across the TV—it's not like you're actually saying something. It's like every other fucking video on TV. I do believe that there's a certain element, for punk at least, that has to be struggle. And the struggle can't come from having a multi-million-dollar record contract.

Adrienne Droogas: A lot of people would sit there and say stuff like, "Well, we can get our message out to a lot more people this way." But you lose the message. Because the second there's a Pepsi ad, and then George Michael's ass shaking in some video, and then you guys, your message has gotten lost in all of that.

Cammie Toloui: One of the last shows I went to was a Green Day show. Gilman was packed full. The regular Gilman people were wearing T-shirts that said "Down with Green Day" or "Kill Green Day."

Jibz Cameron: There was a huge "Green Day Sucks" graffiti right above the stage, like, two feet tall and ten feet long.

Frank Portman: One famous Green Day show at Gilman, everybody was gonna turn their backs and walk out when they started playing.

Jesse Luscious: People who knew them for years were just like, "You've made that jump. I can't support you." If you're in this comparatively tiny scene, and you have these agreed-on guidelines that you exist within that scene by, well, it makes all the sense in the world.

Billie Joe Armstrong: There was almost a socialist aspect to it. It was like, "This label is part of the bigger system that kept Noam Chomsky from printing a book," or something. It was taken very, very seriously. There was this feeling that if you did this, you could expect to leave your friends behind. All of your relationships with people were over and there was no turning back. It was really hard, but I took responsibility and did it. You know, people need to have their beliefs. That's what keeps Gilman so strong. It was tough. I carried that baggage around with me for about five years.

Davey Havok: They recorded an amazing record. Clearly that translated, because the same people that were saying "Fuck them" were at their shows when they played.

James Washburn: There's been anti–Green Day from the beginning. It's about punks thinking, "Punk is ours, and you're not, so you're not gonna come and change it for us, because punk is *this*." Which is fuckin' absurd.

Bill Schneider: There was some jealousy, 'cause everybody was in a band.

Billie Joe Armstrong: It was sort of this culture shock. I was still the guy with the garbage bag full of clothes and a band that was getting big. It was like being caught between two worlds. The punk world was like, "You're not allowed here anymore. We told you." And I didn't want to be part of this other world, so I was just floating in the middle. It took me a long time to say, "Fuck it. This is where my life went and I've got to be proud of it."

Marshall Stax: After Green Day got big, reporters wanted to come in the club and film.

Jesse Luscious: TV news shows were calling, "Can we come down and film outside?" We were like, "No. Fuck off." *Rolling Stone*, *Spin*, whatever—we were like, "Go away. We don't want to talk to you."

Marshall Stax: No one at Gilman liked the idea of this becoming another Seattle scene, where it just turned into some circus. People became very defensive about the media.

Jesse Luscious: I helped write the No Major Label policy at Gilman. We didn't want Gilman to be a minor-league grooming place for bands. We didn't want to be the Roxy in 1979, or the Whisky, whatever. First of all, I don't think we could have handled it. Second of all, that was completely against everything we were about.

Jason Beebout: One of the things was, "We don't wanna have any more sellout bands play in our club." 'Til they started losing money. And then they started asking some of those bands to come and play.

Howie Klein: When the record companies saw Green Day break, so gigantically and so fast, all of the record companies thought, "Well, we can do that. All these punk bands are the same anyway. My kid has a friend who's in a punk band. I could get them and they'll be our Green Day." Some record executives honestly thought Green Day was the first punk band.

Jason Beebout: *Maximum RocknRoll* didn't like Samiam. We got banned from playing Gilman. The kids voted us out, along with Jawbreaker and other bands. People like Jake Sayles wouldn't go to any shows that I'd play. Jake was the person who called us sellouts. I couldn't tell if he was joking, because we were friends. We started growing apart. I felt hurt.

Lars Frederiksen: We played with Jawbreaker at Gilman. I remember one time watching them and they said, "We'll never sign to a major label," from the stage. And then they signed to a major label. I just never got why would you say that.

Adam Pfahler: It wasn't just the indies and the little zines, the mainstream press jumped on that story, too. So whenever we got a review, it was like, "This is the band that sold out and shame on them. This is gonna be the undoing of this band." And sure enough, it was.

Fat Mike: It's silly. When I was a kid, we all called X sellouts! That's just what kids say. They don't even know what they're talking about. Taking some company's money, I don't see anything wrong with that.

Sergie Loobkoff: So it wasn't like all these Berkeley bands were becoming big or anything. Gilman was still going on, and little bands were still playing. At that point it seemed like there was still a neat little scene going on. To me the thing that changed everything was Warped Tour and Hot Topic, and indie labels that had a lot of money.

Dale Flattum: On tour, you'd show up at these clubs and there'd be some brand-new Econoline van parked in front of the club. Some band you'd never heard of. They would have all this nice equipment, this little flurry of people around them always talking on the phone. Then they'd play, and it just sounded like a bunch of nice equipment.

Jason Beebout: Lotta new guitars, lotta new vans, everyone had new tennis shoes. There was a big conveyor belt, like, "Get 'em in, get 'em in, take their photo and then scoot 'em out, scoot 'em out, scoot 'em out!"

Frank Portman: You thought, how can it possibly be that they suck so bad and get so much money?

Dale Flattum: I always thought that Ford should have made an indie rock model of the Econoline. Their sales must have just spiked in this way they probably never understood. "Why did all those vans sell in the '90s? We couldn't make enough of those things."

Jesse Michaels: The punk that did get big was unrecognizable to me as punk. It's the common complaint: Punk stopped when I stopped going to shows. I don't mean to hit you with that old saw.

Blag Jesus: You'd see NOFX, and four bands that were exactly like NOFX. A lot of it was the booking agents, and the way they wanted to do things.

Jesse Michaels: A lot of the stuff, like on Fat, sounded so unbelievably cookie-cutter to me. I just thought of it as something completely different and alien, that I didn't have much relationship to. I'm sure lots of people before me would have thought of Op Ivy that way. Like, this is nursery school stuff. Compared to the Fuck-Ups, or whatever they listened to, it was probably a joke to them.

Fat Mike: What's hard is fighting your ego. When everyone tells you you could be bigger, that was the hardest thing. Green Day used to open shows for us all the time. Offspring paid us to go on a tour with us in Europe. These bands that were smaller than us, they all got big. To a lot of bands, that makes them feel really insecure. "All these other bands that opened for us are getting bigger than us. What are we doing wrong?"

Sergie Loobkoff: Besides Green Day, which bands signed to major labels actually did anything with it? I can't think of one. The only other bands to get sort of big like that were Offspring and Rancid. But they didn't even take the same route.

Lars Frederiksen: We were never in competition with Offspring or Green Day. We figured if we could be like Bad Religion then we were cool. The only time that we thought about majors, I was like, "Well, maybe if I get some dough I can get my mom out of the projects." My brother had gone to jail and all this bullshit. When we realized it wasn't right for us, we just stayed with Epitaph. But everybody had opinions. It was just like, Jesus fucking Christ!

Fat Mike: Hollywood Records, the guy was telling us what he could do for us. He was like, "Oh, you guys are so great, we can make you this big." We were like, well, we have all that. We have a big fan base, we have money. We sell lots of records. And he said, "Well, if you guys want to be second fiddle to the Offspring your whole career . . ."

I was like, wow. So that's what you do. You make people feel unsure about themselves. That's how they get bands. We just told our lawyer, there's no fucking way we're doing this. I think we made the right choice. We don't answer to anybody. We just do everything ourselves.

Adrienne Droogas: It was hard for Green Day because they were just so wildly popular. I don't think that any of them could go anywhere without people freaking out. Grocery shopping, anywhere. They were in a tough position.

Lars Frederiksen: You didn't know what was going on, you knew there was some crazy shit happening with your life. You're playing *Saturday Night Live*, you're on MTV, you're playing gigs, your records are selling pretty damn good. But at the same time you wanna keep your feet on the ground, because it's not gonna last forever.

I remember being at my mom's house, the "Salvation" video came on. And she said, "I hate this song." My mom's got the silver tongue, likes to bust my balls a little bit. I said, "Really? Well, it's paying your fuckin' rent, isn't it?" I got her back.

A lot more people wanted to talk to you. I was at a Walgreens once, looking for a halogen bulb. And this girl came up to me and said, "Hey, you're Lars Frederiksen, right? What are you doing here?" I was like, "Buying a halogen bulb. What are you doing here?" She said, "Don't you have somebody to do that for you?" Like I got my halogen bulb guy. Joe. "Yeah, Joe, check it out, the bulb burnt out again. Can you go down to Walgreens and get me one?"

Adrienne Droogas: It takes it from something that you know, family and support, to this place that's so far removed. It happened with Lars. I came over to the warehouse that he lived in, and I remember him going, "Hey, I just got this note from Madonna."

Lars Frederiksen: We were on tour with the Offspring, late '94, early '95. We were at the Roseland Ballroom. She was there. And she wanted to say hi to us.

I was trying to get my shoes on, I had these creepers. I didn't tie 'em, for some reason. We went and met her. There was like 100 people in the hallway. Offspring was pretty big at the time. Madonna was at this end of this room. We met her, she bummed a cigarette and asked if we want any food. She said, "I really like you guys's band. I like 'Harry Bridges.'" She was knowledgeable about our stuff. We're just like, "Fuck, Madonna. Like a Virgin's here." She was just really cool. I got tripped out a little bit by it. I ran out of the room, and I lost my shoe on the way.

She said, "Oh, Lars . . ." In front of 100 people. And I said something like, "Don't be a stranger." Or something stupid. It's fucking Madonna! The next day we played in Baltimore. And of course Noodles, the guitar player for the Offspring, was going, "Oh, Lars, you forgot something!"

So there was this basket with some fruit and a bottle of hand lotion, weird stuff. Champagne and shit. We gave the booze to the Offspring. And there was the card. It said, "It was really nice to meet you guys." It was on Madonna stationery, sealed with a kiss. And there was a photo in there, from her *Sex* book. A Polaroid of her bending over this stool, kinda doing the Marilyn Monroe trip. It was like a frontal shot, but you couldn't see anything. You couldn't see any ass. It had a caption out of her mouth that said, "Sign with Maverick," which was her record label. And a copy of her record, *Bedtime Stories*.

Everybody made a big deal out of it. They all fucking came after us, man.

Jeff Ott: I think you can make a living off of music, I just don't think you have to go this well-trodden path to do it. My feeling is if you have moral issues you feel are important, that's more important to follow than to take the path that's easy. My problem with Green Day and Rancid and Offspring is that I felt like they took the well-trodden path, and didn't really reflect too much on the path they were taking. And they got really pissed off at you if you criticized. They just felt like they were being attacked. But what do you expect?

Ben Sizemore: The most self-righteous people are only into it for a couple of years, so those of us who have been into it since, like, 13, we see these people come and go. A lot of people who were calling Green Day sellouts in 1994 are probably like stockbrokers now, sellouts themselves. Looking back, it seems silly to hold such animosity.

Dave Dictor: It's a big joke. At Gilman they had a big calendar board, what's going on for November and December, and they had this big thing, "Upcoming shows: Green Day, Rancid."

Davey Havok: When we signed to Nitro Records, a big independent label out of Orange County, someone made the mistake of sending a stack of those little promotional posters to Gilman Street. I could have told them not to bother. We walked into Gilman one day, where we rehearsed, and up on the wall facing the stage, they had made a big dollar sign out of our AFI posters.

We were all living in the same room in a frat house with two other people, and four other people that would kind of wander in and out. And volunteering at Gilman Street. We were really raking in the bucks. We would take our jet to Gilman Street. I mean, it was a Lear. But the Gulfstreams are so unreliable these days.

Ryan Mattos: I never felt that way about any band. Because if Rancid wasn't on MTV, if I hadn't seen people with mohawks in 1995, '96, I wouldn't be here. I thought nothing happened after 1980. If Green Day hadn't been on the radio and trickled down to all those other bands, I wouldn't know shit.

John Geek: I hate to set myself up as a spokesperson on something like this, but looking at the history of it, I don't think ideas about anti-commodification, the stridently underground ideas about punk, were part of the original thought in 1975. That was something that came around with Crass and bands like that a little later on. The rest of it was like, "Let's get as big as possible and thumb our noses at as many people as possible on the way."

Which is kinda awesome, too. I can see that that's punk, in its own weird way. But the kind of punk I've always felt more a kinship with—the stuff that can't be commodified—that doesn't work on commercial radio. Stuff like Econochrist, Rorschach, Blatz, Filth—dirty and underground, forcing its way into the field of vision like an ugly sore.

Davey Havok: Major labels are straight up. They're like, "We're not your friend. We're trying to sell records. This is what's going to happen, and this is what's not gonna happen." Whereas most experiences that I've had with independent labels, it's all buddy-buddy. "We're friends. This is all art, this is all artistic." Until it comes time to make a business move that can really improve the business matters of the label, and then your friendships change. Which is fine if that's the basis of your relationship. But when it's veiled, when it's cloaked in a pseudo-friendship, it's really nasty.

Howie Klein: I loved turning people on to Green Day. But it was really more about the fact that I was an executive at a record company and Green Day was bringing in a lot of money. On a personal level, yeah, the music is wonderful. But on a business level, I had a responsibility to my employees and to my shareholders and to the company. And Green Day was a huge part of that.

Blag Jesus: There used to be a corporate-label stigma. But there really isn't anymore because kids can't really conceive of another thing. They grew up with their favorite bands being on corporate labels, for the most part.

Davey Havok: We got zero flack for our album on a major label. Because the notion had become obsolete at that point. The culture changed so much. A major shift moved from caring about what labels people were on to just caring about what music they were making. Music has been in such a downward spiral that people no longer can focus on such trivial things as who's putting out the record, when you have to really search to find bands that are worthwhile.

Jello Biafra: My attitude towards that was, you're wasting way too much energy on a bunch of bullshit at this point. We all knew how good this music was when we got into it. There were always great classic songs, if only the masses could hear them. And now the masses hear them, and everybody's yelling at Green Day, the Offspring and Rancid for being so damn big. It was good music, it was bound to happen. You could either waste your energy freaking out about that, or you could support people you like who need your help deep down underground.

Blag Jesus: You'll always have people who are "underground people," those people in the tipping point who are the connectors, or who grab things and make it cool for other people.

Andy Asp: The real thing is still the real thing. It hasn't diminished.

Jason Beebout: It was an education. I'm happy about it. I got to tour, I got a bunch of money up front, that went to my managers! And I can tell anyone else, that's exactly what's gonna happen to you.

53

Longview

Frank Portman: It is weird to think about. You're there at Gilman, this disastrous show. "Wow, my father donated these grab bars. The plumbing materials." The toilets I refused to clean.

Sergie Loobkoff: I feel sorry for people that didn't have something like Gilman. It doesn't have to be music. It could be anything. It could be a Christian youth center in Mississippi. It could be a Satanist cult in Vancouver, or whatever. Just something outside of high school.

Ben Saari: Gilman couldn't happen anywhere other than Berkeley. It took advantage of the triple threat of liberal Berkeley, a fucked-up industrial neighborhood, and the social privilege of the kids who were going there. If it had been a bunch of black kids doing that in North Berkeley, it would've got shut the fuck down right away.

Billie Joe Armstrong: The way I look at it, you can't just go there. To go to Gilman is to be involved with Gilman.

Spike Slawson: It's sort of a free exchange of ideas through music. That was the impression I got. Of what was possible.

Jim Widess: I take it as a little hidden badge of pride that we can do this. As a landlord, I'm very happy with the arrangement. They're good tenants, they take care of it, and they pay the rent on time. I don't want another nail salon in the front. I think we're also providing something that the community needs, and that does something for my ego, of course. I'm not that fond of the music. But that's okay.

Jeff Ott: If I ended up with a ton of money I would absolutely take it and go to other places and start a place just like Gilman, so that other kids could have their own thing. I would be obliged to do that.

Mike Avilez: You go to the Warped Tour and walk around and you'll hear 100 bands that try to sound like Green Day or NOFX. It's just disgusting. They're missing the angst. To me, punk rock is supposed to be angry and pissed off. Some of this other shit nowadays is college rock. It has a whole 'nother meaning.

Jimmy Crucifix: I had a punk band come in to Lennon Studios the other day—one of the new ones. They'd never heard of bands like Fang and Crucifix. They've heard of Blink 182, Green Day, AFI and all that stuff. They were talking business plan. Songs and structure. They made it so serious. I would go out there either naked or dressed in drag.

Aaron Cometbus: Everyone acts like in the old days it was pure and now it's totally different. But look at the early S.F. bands—they all broke up because no one would sign them. Flipper jumped at the chance to be on Def Jam. And Jimmy from Crucifix, he tried out for UFO. It would be hard to get more corporate rock than that.

Mike Avilez: The new kids do their research on the Internet. There's a whole group of new bands out there in the Bay Area that are '87 punk rock. There's Second Opinion, Instant Asshole, Nightstick Justice, Warkrime and Throat Oyster. The kids are learning and they take that early style and try to play like it. A lot of them are trying to be like Minor Threat.

Davey Havok: Ceremony seem to be quite the buzz band in the hardcore scene right now. They have 40-second songs that sound like a cross between Negative Approach and maybe early DRI. It's very interesting. That's the jam right now. And the look— flipped-up baseball hats, the bandana-tied wrists and head and legs, it's very interesting. That thrash hardcore is in.

Martin Sorrondeguy: Punk dies for people at different periods. Somebody from 82's gonna complain about somebody from '78 because they said it died that year. It's an endless cycle. Every kid growin' up is gonna have their own unique experience. No matter if somebody wrote a song similar to that 25 years ago, they're living it right now.

Lochlan McHale: I enjoy hearing punk music everywhere I go. I love seeing kids walk down the street with a Rancid back patch or Green Day or Op Ivy back patch. I'm all for it. For a punk to say shitty things about the community, it's like, why? It's one of the raddest things ever.

Chicken John: Punk wasn't a kind of music that a couple people played. Punk rock was a fucking movement. If you'd asked me in 1984 how many punk rockers are there in America, I would say, "I don't know. Hundreds." If you had asked me in 1988 how many punk rockers are there in America, I would've said tens of thousands. How many people have been exposed to the punk movement now? Tens of millions! I mean, just because no one's given fucking Ian MacKaye a gold record doesn't mean that Fugazi's first record didn't go quadruple platinum.

Jello Biafra: Punk and hardcore always drew people of all extremes because it's an extreme form of music. There were people from the extreme left, from the extreme right. There were people who are extreme in their militant party-animal apathy. People say, "Oh, there's a punk philosophy." Really? Which one?

Punk was never a movement, it was a sound. It was an inspiration, entertainment. More than entertainment to many of us, in a spiritual way. But it is not a movement. A movement has its eye on the prize. What would the prize be here? More punk? It's something else. Something that drew all types of people, who got all kinds of different things back from it.

Anna Brown: I gave up trying to be someone else. You can't do it. Every time I travel, I say, this time I'm gonna go to museums and do cultural stuff. But the best times are still when I end up finding the punks, because those people know what's going on. We have a certain way of seeing the world. You can travel the world as a punk and people come to see you and you go to see them. That's what you have in common and that's actually a lot. It's radically transformative. I am grateful. True 'til death! Just not death at 25.

Larry Boothroyd: Don't wait for permission.

54

He Who Laughs Last

Tim Yohannan, editor of *Maximum RocknRoll*, passed away today, April 3, 1998 at home with his friends by his side. Love him or hate him, Tim had a huge influence on punk rock. He will be missed.

—*A Tim Yohannan Memorial*

Martin Sprouse: Tim smoked a lot. Two packs a day. Benson & Hedges Lights. Gold pack.

Mike LaVella: He could smoke a whole cigarette in about three drags. Really hit that fuckin' thing.

Martin Sprouse: But the day he found out he had cancer, he quit. He had a pack of cigarettes sitting on his desk, he just stopped cold turkey. Even though it wasn't related to his cancer. That's that weird kind of brain that guy had.

Cammie Toloui: In the end, when he was dying, I wrote him a letter to just say everything that I had been feeling about what happened between us. A week before he died he wrote me back, telling me how much he loved me and that I was okay, and all this good stuff.

Martin Sprouse: We had people lined up to take things over. Things were in place. He was sick two years, three years. In the process of bringing new people in, he was there. He was such a control freak. He helped select the people, and helped talk about it, and the debate of whether *Maximum* should go on.

Martin Sorrondeguy: I knew it was progressively getting worse. I was in Chicago, but everybody knew. It was word of mouth.

Martin Sprouse: They had tried everything. When he got diagnosed, supposedly it was already in the fourth stage. Non-Hodgkin's lymphoma.

Martin Sorrondeguy: I remember one day deciding to call *Maximum* because a friend had said, he's not getting out of bed much. I was told that he was already losing memory.

Timojhen answered and I said, "Hey, is Tim around?" And he said, "Well, yeah, but he might not know who you are." But I guess they said, "Hey, Tim, it's Martin from Chicago." He took the phone and he said, "Cómo estás?" I knew he knew. So I said, "Hey, Tim, how are you?" And he was like, "Don't stop sending us your records."

Martin Sprouse: There was about four of us there, throughout the whole night. His ex-girlfriend, me, Timojhen and Jerry Booth, an old friend of Tim's who did the accounting for *Maximum*.

When he couldn't really talk anymore, he started humming and moving his head a little bit. His eyes were closed. You could barely hear it. We all got up close and realized he was humming a Flipper song: "Isn't life a blast, it's just like living in the past."

Martin Sorrondeguy: I got a call the day after. It was a really weird moment for me, and really sad.

Martin Sprouse: We made hundreds of phone calls.

Jeff Bale: I was teaching at Columbia at the time. I had just talked to him on the phone a couple of weeks before, and he didn't sound good, but he didn't tell me how critical his condition was. The next thing you know I fuckin' hear he's dead. I felt such a loss.

Jello Biafra: Ruth called me. I was surprised how upset I was. I quickly found myself focusing on the good times we had, when we were good friends. All the positive things and hard work he did for the community vastly outweighs all the crap he pulled when he went off the deep end.

Martin Sprouse: He definitely didn't want any recognition or memorial service. He made that clear to me. At the time, we were juggling a lot of things. I said, "Okay, I'll make that promise to you." And I made sure there was no memorial for Tim.

In hindsight, that was Tim's controlling factor. But a wake has nothing to do with the dead person. It's how people grieve, get over it, celebrate this person's life. And deal with each other. It made everything a little bit isolated. All of us were kind of in our own heads. No one was really hanging out. It was really fucked up. Not that those were Tim's intentions.

I don't know if the magazine mentioned it, I don't even remember. This comment Web site came up, and everyone told their stories. That was kinda cool. A lot of people, some from around the world.

Jeff Bale: I posted something on that. Some of Tim's enemies posted some nasty comments.

Martin Sprouse: The mainstream press gave Tim more recognition than the people who were close with him, who shared his ideas. *Rolling Stone* paid their tribute to Tim Yo, when he had nothing to do with *Rolling Stone*. The *San Francisco Chronicle* had a one-liner, where they spelled his name wrong.

Tim Yo didn't want anyone to deal with his body when he died. He had this naive idea that if no one claimed his body, the city would just come pick up his body and process him as a John Doe. In theory it sounded good, but it's like something out of a Humphrey Bogart movie.

The hospice nurse asked us, "Have you made arrangements?" We hadn't really thought about it. I just reiterated Tim's plan. And they said, "Uh, that's ridiculous. You do it that way, the homicide squad's gonna come out there and yellow-tape the whole place, and check for suspicious death." So the hospice people hooked us up with a funeral service.

The very next day, I had to go meet with these people and tell them we didn't want the ashes. They could not understand that. We had to give them extra money. We didn't want a plaque, we didn't want to know anything about it. I sat there for an hour, trying to explain this to some funeral director. He thought we were crazy. But I knew this is what Tim would have wanted.

They dumped his ashes out in the bay, with a bunch of other people's. I told his brother this whole thing, and his brother said, "Wow, that's so ironic. Because the bastard couldn't swim."

55

Rock 'n' Roll High School

Jello Biafra: Tim once explained to me why he was a socialist and not an anarchist. He felt there needed to be some kind of government entity, to transfer the wealth from people who had too much to people who have too little. And I think he's right.

Jeff Bale: I wish he was still around, so we could argue and listen to records. But he isn't.

Dave Dictor: I loved him. I wrote a song for him called "Timmy Yo."

Jeff Ott: He was very Marxist. It took quite awhile to realize how much he had going on. Never been in a band, fairly soft-spoken guy. He'd get angry and argue or whatever, but for the most part, his method of having power in the world was talking with other people, or writing, and handing it over.

Dave Mello: Tim Yohannan was always that older guy, smoking cigarettes in the corner. He was a quiet guy, but he was very much the guy that organized Gilman—with 14-, 15-, 16-year-olds. It wasn't like we were really scared of him, but he could chew your face off if he started to yell at you.

Ben Saari: Tim was kind of an asshole at meetings, but he really had a concrete vision. About kids creating their own culture and running things themselves.

Blag Jesus: The hippie generation of people were the first to turn around and become the worst kind of capitalists. So the fact that a guy like Tim Yohannan held on and always stayed true to his ideals, that's a beautiful thing. He deserves to be commended for that.

You can make fun of him for it, and I did, but he had a sense of humor. If you got rich from an East Bay punk band, you owe everything to Tim Yohannan. He was making a world-renowned magazine. If you had a bumfuck band in Milwaukee, only some people in Milwaukee knew about it. If you had a bumfuck band in the East Bay, everyone all over the world knew about it.

So Tim, in an indirect way, is responsible for making bands like Green Day and Rancid very wealthy. They should fuckin' have a permanent memorial to the guy. The East Bay punk scene owes everything to him, and a lot of the California punk scene does.

Mike LaVella: There was a lot of mystery around Tim. He had a daughter. A lot of people didn't know about that.

Kurt Brecht: A friend of ours lived up near Haight-Ashbury. MDC turned us on to this cool lady, said she was punk-friendly. So every now and then I'd ask her if I could take a shower.

Her and Tim Yohannan had a baby. They weren't married. He didn't ever acknowledge the child. He didn't want to have children. The girl's grown up, probably 20 years old, 21, 22.

Martin Sprouse: Jello called me maybe three years ago, and told me he had met Tim's daughter in Texas. She wrote me once or twice. I guess she had a lot of anger towards him. She'd never met him.

Bill Schneider: I really wonder what Tim Yohannan's take on Gilman was, later in life. He seemed to rail against everything the East Bay scene became. He hated that all the bands got popular. I wonder if he was ever able to step back from being bitter to see what really came out of Gilman. He had more foresight than he ever knew.

Mike LaVella: He was the machine that drove *MRR*. I can't believe it's still going. Now they have *Punk Rock Confidential* to tell them who got married. When that thing came out, I was like, Tim Yohannan is rolling over in his grave. "Blink 182 on the golf course," or whatever. Oh my god, that would make him sick.

Kevin Carnes: Anybody that's ever been in Gilman, onstage or through the doors, was blessed because of that guy. If he walked in this room, I would run over and kiss him and hug him and say, "Thank you for doing what you do." Between that space and *Maximum RocknRoll*, that guy left a huge thing.

Chicken John: The man was unbeatable. It doesn't matter how wrong he was, the guy had an idea and he was gonna stick to it. That is the greatest lesson in life, stick with it. Don't think about how unfair he was, think about how much *more* unfair someone else would have been.

Think of the contribution he made to our lives. What if he

didn't do it? What if he became an interior decorator instead? What if people like Tim didn't rise to the occasion? History as we know it would be seriously altered if three people like Tim chose different paths. I'm glad I knew him.

Steve Tupper: I've seen a whole lot of labels come and go over the years, distributors, record stores, radio shows, DJs, fanzines. *Maximum* just keeps going as an institution.

Jello Biafra: I open up an issue now and it's almost like reading an issue from 20 years ago. In one way that's good 'cause there's still the same energies and concerns, reviews of lots of unknown bands. But reading the letters section, in particular, also reveals the same hang-ups and the same *nya nya nya*, gossip, gossip, gossip. Two demerits for this person for being politically incorrect, three demerits for this one.

Martin Sprouse: I stayed involved until a year after he died. Just to make sure the transition happened well. I look at it from time to time. I talk to those guys. But you know what? They're fine. They're doing it right.

Martin Sorrondeguy: It's continually being flooded with the newest punk music from everywhere. Things are really similar in the look of the magazine, it's been pretty linear in that sense. Same paper, still on newsprint. Everyone talks about having the ink on the fingers, so you still get that experience.

Jeff Bale: Tim created such an organizational machine that even after his death it continued functioning like a zombie without a brain that kept stumbling. Frankly that's kind of the way I see *Maximum RocknRoll*.

Martin Sprouse: Much like Gilman, it's on its tenth generation of organizers. They're not sticking by these rules because the elders told 'em to. But because it's the way it should be done, and they agree with it.

Martin Sorrondeguy: *Maximum RocknRoll*, for me, has always been the pinnacle of what is punk culture, and putting that out there. The radio show still happens in the house weekly. They don't let too many bands stay there, because people started stealing from the collection. They put some of the really rare records on lockdown. Basically you can sign it out, like an archive or a library. The collection is anywhere between 45 to 60,000 records, something like that.

I've heard a lot of young people say, "Fuck *Maximum Rockn-*

Roll." You don't even realize how important that magazine was. That was like your *news*. That was what linked you to the rest of the punk goin' on outside of you and your friends. That's how you tape-traded with people, that's how you got zines from people. That's how you got in touch with bands. You couldn't click on your computer back then.

Jeff Bale: There's always gonna be underground bands that release their stuff on underground labels, and I say thank god for that. Because that's where all the fresh good stuff's gonna come from. People are gonna buy those records and go see those bands. That's just the way it's gonna be. Whether the corporate world takes notice or not is pretty much irrelevant.

Martin Sprouse: When I was involved, the whole world was different. The economy was different, punk rock was different. *Maximum* had money. But *Maximum* doesn't make that much money. *Maximum* gets by.

Martin Sorrondeguy: It's still connected with Gilman. They aren't there all the time, but a lot of the same people that work on Gilman stuff help out with *Maximum*, and vice versa. The magazine's still coming out, and the magazine still features or covers a band

Photo by Cammie Toloui

Tim Yo Mama: Yohannan at Epicenter

that no one knows. Because it still sticks to that basic thing of Right Now. And that's really the true essence of punk.

I saw a dude sittin' at the bar with his old punk shirt on, slammin' beers, goin', "I saw Discharge in '81." And a kid said to him, "Yeah, who've you seen since then?" It's like fuckin' nobody, man. Who cares?

WHO'S WHO

A. C. Thompson: Former 924 Gilman and Epicenter volunteer. Now toils as an investigative reporter.

Aaron Cometbus: Publisher of *Cometbus* fanzine since 1981. He lives with Anna Joy and their three children on a ranch just outside of Laramie, where he is developing alternative energy methods through the use of wind turbines.

Adam Pfahler: Drummer for Jawbreaker. Currently lives with his wife and two daughters in S.F., where he owns Lost Weekend Video and Blackball Records.

Adrienne Melanie Droogas: Spitboy and Aus Rotten singer. *Profane Existence*, *Maximum RocknRoll*, and *Slug & Lettuce* columnist, and self-proclaimed punk rock goddess. Currently adventuring in the land down under with the man of her dreams.

Al Ennis: Co-founder of *Maximum RocknRoll* Radio. Still crazy about music. Works as an accountant.

Al Schvitz: Drummer for MDC.

Andrew Flurry aka Frog: S.F. native. Member of Team 'O Fools.

Andy Asp: Singer/guitarist for Nuisance. Currently an "aesthetic pilgrim" based in Oakland. "Once a bum, always a bum."

Andy Pollack: Director of the Farm, 1983–1986. Continues as a tax-preparing, musically inclined, San Francisco/Northern California hippie.

Anna Brown: Berkeley native. What she does is secret.

Anna Joy Springer: Onetime member of Blatz, Cypher in the Snow, and the Gr'ups. Now an ex-punk Buddhist dyke writer of cross-genre works about the complicated intersections of love and grief. She teaches writing at UC San Diego.

Antonio López: Co-founder of L.A. punk zine *Ink Disease* and the international zine distributor Desert Moon Periodicals. He is a product of Peace and Conflict Studies at UC Berkeley. Creator of a multicultural media literacy curriculum, Merchants of Culture. Author of *Mediacology*, a book on media education and sustainability. He resides in Rome, Italy, with his partner and daughter.

Audra Angeli-Slawson: Onetime peace punk and skinhead. Longtime booker. Creator of Stinky's Peepshow. Director of Incredibly Strange Wrestling. Den mother.

B. A. Lush: San Francisco punk. Co-founder of Team Lush. Now holds a master's of science in psychology and has become an authority figure to be rebelled against.

Barrie Evans: Lead singer of Christ on Parade. Now fronts the Hellbillies.

Ben de la Torres aka Crimson Baboon: Gilman volunteer since '96. Spoken-word artist, singer/drummer for Clan of the Bleeding Eye and Super Happy 9/11 Dance Party. Got clean. Still a punk, still in the pit.

Ben Saari aka A-Head: Moved to the East Bay in 1985, just in time for everything to start sucking. Moved back to the North Bay in 1988, just as everything was becoming awesome. Any greatness he has is purely by association.

Ben Sizemore: Singer for Econochrist. Currently living in Oakland and doing social work in San Francisco. Still punk, vegetarian, and straightedge.

Bill "Halen" McCracken: Jak's Team since '82. Ran the Valencia Tool & Die. Onetime owner of Government Records. Stage manager at the Mabuhay Gardens, Elite Club, and On Broadway. Bass player with Unstrung Heroes. Manager of Verbal Abuse. Currently bass player for the Wrong Impressions and a manufacturing/machining professor who books shows when he's inspired.

Bill Michalski: Former punk rocker. He lives in San Francisco and misses New Orleans.

Bill Schneider: Onetime bassist for Monsula and Skin Flutes. Bass player in Pinhead Gunpowder.

Billie Joe Armstrong: Lead vocalist, guitarist, and lyricist for Green Day. Guitarist and vocalist for Pinhead Gunpowder. Singer for Foxboro Hot Tubs. Still lives in the East Bay.

Blag Jesus: Rock legend. ("Eat a dick!")

Bob Noxious: Singer for the Fuck-Ups.

Bonedog aka Dwayne Mileham: Bay Area punk. Onetime Gilman shitworker and member of planning committee. Still has a complete collection of *Maximum RocknRoll* and over 10,000 records.

Bruce Loose: Vocalist for Flipper and Not Flipper.

Bucky Sinister: Has released one CD and written four books, the latest of which is *Get Up*, a recovery book for the punk crowd.

Buzzsaw Bill: Singer of Naked Lady Wrestlers. ("It's not so easy being a billionaire playboy.")

Cammie Toloui: Gilman shitworker and founding member of the Yeastie Girlz. Living happily in Portland, Oregon. Still taking pictures and singing loud in the car.

Carol DMR: Former gangsta and concert promoter 'round the Bay. Currently easing tension with therapeutic massage and making music/drama videos.

Chester Simpson: Freelance photographer who captured the early San Francisco punk scene. Now lives in the D.C. area and shoots it all, from Civil War reenactors to rock stars.

Chicken John: Showman and contrarian living in S.F. Still putting on free shows and pulling off unrealistic stunts. His life remains a punk rock disaster movie.

Chip Kinman: Vocalist and guitarist for the Dils.

Christopher Appelgren: Owner and former president of Lookout! Records. Album cover artist and member of Bumblescrump, the PeeChees, and the Pattern. Now general manager of the Noise Pop music festival in San Francisco.

Cinder Bischoff: Singer of Tilt and Retching Red. Co-founder of Cinder Block.

Courtenay Dennis: Former San Francisco/Berkeley loudmouth. Now an L.A. smartmouth and gets paid for it. On a radio or screen near you.

Creetin K-oS: Lead singer for Social Unrest. Owner of Proudflesh piercing studio.

Dale Flattum: Bass and vocals for Steel Pole Bathtub. No longer sleeps in a van, and enjoys spending his time playing with scissors and his son.

Dallas Denery: Managed to scream more or less in tune for three years with the Sweet Baby (Jesus) and now teaches medieval history somewhere in New England.

Dan Rathbun: Came to the Bay Area to attend UCB engineering school but chose a life of music. Member of Acid Rain, Idiot Flesh, Charming Hostess, and Sleepytime Gorilla Museum. Owner of Polymorph recording studio in Oakland.

Daniel DeLeon: Guitarist for the Insaints.

Danny Furious: Co-founder of the Avengers. The angriest, sweatiest, hardworkin'est, and arguably best and most beautiful drummer that ever smashed up his kit.

Danny "Radio Shack" Norwood: Founding member and longtime guitarist of Social Unrest.

Dave Chavez: Jak's Team since 1985. Former bass player for Sick Pleasure, Code of Honor, and Hot Rod Shopping Cart. Lives with son Ivan and wife Rachel, and still plays with Verbal Abuse.

Dave Dictor: Singer/songwriter for MDC.

Dave Edwardson aka Dave Ed: Born and bred in Berkeley. Bassist for Neurosis. Member of Jesus Fucking Christ and Tribes of Neurot.

Dave Mello: Former drummer for Schlong and Operation Ivy. Now guitar player for Jewdriver and full-time father, living in the East Bay.

Davey Havok: Lead singer for AFI. He created the clothing line Paden. Still straightedge and vegan.

David Solnit: Editor of *Globalize Liberation: How to Uproot the System and Build a Better World*, co-author of *An Army of None: Strategies to Counter Military Recruitment, End War and Build a Better World*. Key organizer of the direct action shutdown of the World Trade Organization meeting in Seattle in 1999 and the shutdown of San Francisco the day after Iraq was invaded in 2003. He is a puppeteer and still a punk.

Dean Washington: Founding member of EBU. Skater for life, still grinding and going to shows. He lives in Oakland.

Dennis Kernohan: Singer for the Liars/Sudden Fun.

Dirk Dirksen: Booker of Mabuhay Gardens.

East Bay Ray: Guitarist for Dead Kennedys and Jumbo Shrimp.

Edwin Heaven: Manager of the Nuns.

Eric Ozenne aka Sheric D: Unit Pride, 1985–1989, Redemption 87, 1995–1997, the Nerve Agents, 1998–2001. Currently in Said Radio. Grace's dad and student of social work.

Fat Mike: Lead singer and bassist for NOFX. Bass player for Me First and the Gimme Gimmes. Owner of Motor Studios. Founder of Fat Wreck Chords and *Punk Rock Confidential* quarterly. Founder and organizer of Punkvoter and Rock Against Bush. Still lives in S.F. with wife Erin and daughter Darla.

Floyd: Epicenter and Blacklist worker, ISW worker, Fat Wreck Chords employee, *MRR* shitworker, and occasional advice columnist.

Fraggle: Longtime doorman at Gilman. Co-founder of Dementia House and Pill Hill. Drunk for life.

Frank Portman aka Dr. Frank: Best known as the singer/songwriter of the

Bay Area punk band the Mr. T Experience. His bestselling young adult novel, *King Dork*, was published in 2006, so now he goes around calling himself a "famous author." His second novel is called *Andromeda Klein*.

Fritz Fox: Singer of the Mutants.

Gary Floyd: Ex-hippie, punk, commie, Hindu redneck queer next door. Fronted the Dicks, Sister Double Happiness, Black Kali Ma, and Gary Floyd Band.

Gavin MacArthur: Guitarist for Schlong and mastermind behind *Punk Side Story*. Now lives in New Orleans and is currently on a quest for the ultimate gravy biscuit.

Ginger Coyote: Singer for the White Trash Debutantes. Founder and editor of *Punk Globe*.

Gordon Edgar: Bay Area punk. Cheesemonger at Rainbow Grocery Cooperative since 1994. Writing a book on cheese, food politics, and punk.

Greg Oropeza: Founding member and guitarist of Ribzy and early '80s promoter.

Greg Valencia: Guitarist and vocalist for Grimple and El Dopa. Currently playing with Watch Them Die.

Hank Rank: Drummer of Crime. Film producer.

Hef aka Jeff Hoffman: Former and sometimes background singer with Fang and Special Forces. Resident at Madonna Inn (Fang house). Now environmental attorney, but still a punk!

Hilary Binder: Founder of HOLC. Co-founder of Studio 4. Currently living in the Czech Republic and running CESTA, an international not-for-profit center established to foster cultural understanding and tolerance through the arts. Still playing in Sabot with Chris Rankin.

Howie Klein: Founder of 415 Records, former president of Reprise Records. Currently a political blogger.

Hugh Swarts: Vocalist and guitarist for Thinking Fellers Union Local 282.

Ian MacKaye: From Washington D.C. Co-founder and co-owner of Dischord Records. Has played in a number of bands, including the Teen Idles, Minor Threat, Embrace, Fugazi, and the Evens.

Insane Jane aka Jane Weems: San Francisco punk drummer and artist, 1978–2003. Now retired and living in Northern California.

James Angus Black: Onetime roadie for Verbal Abuse, Urban Assault, Fuck-Ups, DRI, and Boss Hoss. Currently planning a one-man show and staying out of trouble.

James Stark: One of the photo and graphic artists instrumental in the beginning of the San Francisco punk rock scene.

James Sullivan: Former *San Francisco Chronicle* music critic. Author of *The Hardest Working Man: How James Brown Saved the Soul of America.*

James Washburn: Gilman, 1987–1992. Backyard Believers since 1994. Automotive mastermind, cop hater, East Bay Creep, and a bulletproof ass kicker. ("Fuck yo mama.")

Janelle Hessig: Bay Area animator, writer, drummer, and comic artist who continues to publish her zine *Tales of Blarg.* She was the inspiration for a number of songs, including Bratmobile's "The Real Janelle."

Jason Beebout: Ambidextrous chanteuse for Samiam and Isocracy. Is into earth tones and spends much of his time in the water.

Jason Lockwood: Young punk rock fart turned BASH Boy turned old punk rock jerk. Now mild-mannered father and East Bay Rat.

Jason White: Onetime guitarist for Monsula. Guitarist for Pinhead Gunpowder, Green Day, and Foxboro Hot Tubs.

Jeff Bale: Inveterate countercultural libertine, contrarian, and rebel. Cofounder of *Maximum RocknRoll* magazine, former singer in two garage bands, and ex-editor of *Hit List* magazine who is now pretending to be respectable in his capacity as a college professor.

Jeff Goldthorpe: Fifteen years of "No" led to *Intoxicated Culture: A Political History of California Punk*, which sold 20 copies. Fifteen years of "Yes" led to a partner, two kids, a house, and a teaching job. Currently writing political memoir, where "Yes" and "No" meet.

Jeff Ott: Singer for Crimpshrine and Fifteen. Author of *My World: Ramblings of an Aging Gutter Punk* and *Weapons of Mass Destruction and the Real War on Terror.*

Jeffery Bischoff: Guitar player for Tilt and co-founder of Cinder Block, a merchandise company that designs, manufactures, and distributes band merchandise for tour and wholesale worldwide. Now a painter, country songwriter, and chef.

Jello Biafra: Lead singer of Dead Kennedys. Owner of Alternative Tentacles.

Jennifer Blowdryer: Singer for the Blowdryers. Author of *Modern English: A Photo Illustrated Trendy Slang Dictionary.* Founder of Smut Fest.

Jennifer Miro: Singer for the Nuns. Fetish model.

Jennifer Rose Emick: Gilman volunteer and Klingon from '87 to '92. Now a nonfiction writer, blogger, and PTA mom.

Jerme Spew: Former bouncer, bike messenger, and spoken-word artist. Now a Brazilian jiujitsu practitioner and husband.

Jesse Luscious aka Jesse Townley: Longtime 924 Gilman and KALX volunteer. Alternative Tentacles and Lookout! employee. Band member of

Blatz, Gr'ups, Criminals, and Frisk. Green Party politician. And all-around rabble-rouser.

Jesse Michaels: Singer of Operation Ivy and Common Rider. Currently writing, painting, and songwriting as always.

Jibz Cameron: Now a wealthy performance artist going under the moniker Dynasty Handbag.

Jim Jocoy: Photographer at the Mab. Now a physical therapist.

Jim Lyon: Guitarist and songwriter for Teenage Warning, 1981–1994. EBU for life.

Jim Widess: Gilman landlord. Owner of the Caning Shop. Authority on gourd craft, gourd carving, and gourd musical instruments.

Jimmy Crucifix aka Francis Schmith: Played in Pretty Killer, the Next, the Rave, Crime, Chaintown, TVH, Crucifix, Fang, Resistoleros, and Proudflesh. Currently solo artist and operations manager of Lennon Rehearsal & Music Services in San Francisco.

Joe Rees: Video documentarian and mastermind of Target Video.

Joey Shithead: Singer for DOA.

John Borruso: Founding member and visual artist behind early '80s peace-punk band Trial.

John Geek: Formerly a pseudo-revolutionary suburban East Bay acid-punk dirtbag kid. Also fronted the Fleshies. Currently sings with Triclops!, and is an overeducated Berkeley wingnut doing archaeology and cultural heritage preservation.

John Marr: Uses the lessons learned from three years of *Maximum RocknRoll* shitwork on his own zine *Murder Can Be Fun.*

Johnnie Walker: British pirate radio legend and DJ for the Deaf Club.

Johnny Bartlett: Guitarist for the Phantom Surfers, 1988–1996, Saturn V, 1996–2002, Barbary Coasters, 2002–present. Currently creative director for an advertising agency. Lives in Oakland.

Johnny Bonnel: Songwriter and lead singer for Swingin' Utters, Filthy Thievin' Bastards, and Druglords of the Avenue.

Johnny Genocide: Vocalist and guitarist for No Alternative.

Johnny Strike: Guitarist and singer for Crime.

Jon Ginoli: Singer/guitarist/songwriter for queer rockers Pansy Division. He lives in San Francisco. His memoir, *Deflowered: My Life in Pansy Division*, has been published by Cleis Press.

Julie Generic: Creator of *Weird Weather* zine, artist, shitworker at the Farm for four years, poster hanger, wanderer. Currently writing book on S.F. punk, '77–'87, with Jayed from the Feederz. Single mom. Likes to laugh. A lot.

Kamala Parks: Former drummer for Kamala & the Karnivores, Cringer, the Gr'ups, Naked Aggression, and Hers Never Existed. Still living and working in the East Bay and looking to play music with others who don't mind playing with an old fart.

Kareim McKnight: Onetime Cloyne Court denizen. Clinic defender for Women's Choice movement. Co-founder of Direct Action Against Racism, Roots Against War, and Not in Our Name. Worked with October 22 to address police brutality in Los Angeles, organizing in Watts and South Central. Lives in Oakland.

Kate Knox: Co-founder of B.O.B. Co-founder and longtime inhabitant of the Maxi Pad. Has been working at Holden High (formerly CCAS), a school for alternative teens, since 1987.

Kegger aka Kelly Beardsley: Member of Hags S.F. and former bike messenger. Sober and driving BART trains.

Kelly King: Longtime East Bay punk and Flipper fan. Painter by trade and father of four.

Kevin Carnes: Detroit native moved to the Bay Area in 1984. Gilman member. Founding member and drummer of Beatnigs fronted by Michael ranti. Founding member of Broun Fellinis. Has recorded with Soulstice, Consolidated, Crack Emcee, Eric McFadden, Storm Inc., and George Clinton. Is currently working with Lady Miss Kier and Shauna Hall.

Klaus Flouride: Bassist for Dead Kennedys and guitarist for Jumbo Shrimp. Producer of Hi-Fives, Ape, and Bad Posture.

Kriss X: Ass-kicker, hell-raiser, current member of all-woman motorcycle club the Devil Dolls.

Krist Novoselic: Bassist for Nirvana, Sweet 75, No WTO Combo, Eyes Adrift, and the reformed Flipper.

Kurt Brecht: Vocalist for DRI. Author of several books, including *Notes from the Nest.*

Larry Boothroyd: Bassist for Victim's Family and Triclops!.

Larry Crane: Ex-Vomit Launch bassist. Now editor of *Tape Op Magazine*, recording studio owner.

Larry Livermore: Musician, writer, Gilman Street volunteer, co-founder of Lookout! Records.

Lars Frederiksen: Guitarist and vocalist for Rancid, front man of Lars Frederiksen and the Bastards.

Lenny Filth aka Lenny Johnson, Lenn Rokk: Guitarist for Isocracy and Filth. Onetime Ashtray dweller.

Leslie Fuckette: Former Fuckette. Now an emergency room trauma nurse in hospitals throughout the Bay Area.

Liz Highleyman: Longtime activist came to S.F. from Boston for the '89 Anarchist Gathering. Now a freelance medical writer and journalist focusing on HIV/AIDS, global justice issues, civil liberties, GLBT/queer history, and sexuality and gender issues.

Lochlan McHale: Southern California punk turned Bay Area punk. Owner of Funeral Records. Producer who works with at-risk youth. Member U.S. Thugs and Rumblers Car Club.

Lorraine (last name withheld): Oregon to East Bay transplant. One of the notorious Mad Punx. Currently infiltrating an international pharmaceutical corporation.

Lynn Breedlove: Former half-naked yeller for Tribe 8. Now man with tits and jerk of all trades. Comic, novelist, filmmaker.

Marc Dagger: Singer of Urban Assault. Co-founder of S.F. Skins.

Marcus DA Anarchist aka Chief Blackdawg: Born in San Francisco. Benevolent co-founder of the PyratePunx, which now has 30 chapters worldwide and a record label. Dedicated to the punk community for over two decades.

Marshall Stax: Bass player for Blatz, drummer for Subincision, longtime volunteer sound engineer for Gilman. Has been a KALX DJ since 1976.

Martin Brohm: Four-stringer for Isocracy and Samiam and former dog whisperer to the stars. Now loving the good life on a hill in El Cerrito, looking down at all the little people he used to make it to the top.

Martin Sorrondeguy: Longtime *MRR* shitworker. Singer of Los Crudos and Limp Wrist. Founder of Lengua Armada Discos. Documentary filmmaker. Prominent figure in straightedge and queercore scenes.

Martin Sprouse: From punk rock to independent furniture designer, with stops along the way: *Leading Edge* fanzine, *Maximum RocknRoll*, 924 Gilman, Blacklist, and Pressure Drop Press.

Matt Buenrostro: Singer, songwriter, guitarist of Sweet Baby. Now working with hundreds of teenage girls.

Matt Freeman: Bass player and founding member of Operation Ivy and Rancid.

Matt Wobensmith: Creator of Outpunk. Former shitworker at *Maximum RocknRoll* and Epicenter. Currently software engineer.

Max Volume: Guitar builder to the Gods. Guitarist for Big Bear Oatems/ Little Junior Brownhouse, 1967–1972, the Klingons, 1972–1978, the Runz, 1978–1979, False Idols, 1979–1980, the Naked Lady Wrestlers, 1980–right now.

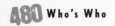

Merle Kessler aka Ian Shoales: Author, performer, and founding member of comedy group Duck's Breath Mystery Theater.

Michael Guarino: Former prosecutor for the Los Angeles City Attorney's office.

Michael Hoffman: Got his punk rock cherry popped by Lynn Breedlove.

Mike Avilez aka Cyco Logic Loco: Singer of Oppressed Logic since 1994. Bass player for Last Round Up, Retching Red, Strung Up, and many others. Banned from 924 Gilman, 1996–2000. Currently security guard at Gilman. Clean and sober, and still playing music, booking shows, and talking shit.

Mike Filth aka Mike-O the Psycho: Bass player for Filth, Strychnine, and Fields of Shit. Still alive at 40. Drugs are so crappy, can't even OD. It is a punk's nightmare.

Sheriff Mike Hennessey: Has served as sheriff of San Francisco for 30 years. He is a big fan of punk rock.

Mike K: Primarily a toilet cleaner based in San Francisco. Since the 1980s he has been a witness to, and sometimes participant in, the "radical" punk community. He maintains a long-standing blood vendetta and commitment to the destruction of American Empire and its quisling agents.

Mike LaVella: Publisher of *Gearhead*. Bass player for Half Life.

Mike Tsongas: Longtime San Francisco and Powell Street Punk. Today a proud father and poet.

Miranda July: Debuted the last name "July" on a flyer for her first play, performed at Gilman Street. Now a writer, performer, and filmmaker living in Los Angeles.

Murray Bowles: Chronicler of the Lost. Punk photographer and fiddler by night, mild-mannered software engineer by day. Co-perpetrator of East Bay Menace Records.

Nick 13: Lead singer, songwriter, guitarist, and founding member of Tiger Army. He has contributed background vocals to countless AFI tunes. And appeared in a few movies in recent years.

Nick Frabasilio: Longtime East Bay activist. Slingshot contributor and collaborator.

Nicki Sicki: Member of Legionnaire's Disease, Dirtbag, Afterbirth. Front man of Sick Pleasure and Humungus. Currently singing with his band Verbal Abuse.

Nils Frykdahl: Virulent anti-humanist and itinerant housepainter. A founder of the Rock Against Rock Museum. Onetime Barrington Hall dweller.

Ninja Death: S.F. punk. Deadly Sparks team member. Singer for Emetics. Baker Street denizen. Now working as a licensed mortician.

Noah Landis: Oakland born and raised. Guitarist and singer for Christ on Parade, 1985–1990. Currently keyboardist for Neurosis. Bassist for Everything Must Go. Co-founder of Sonic Art Recording Studio. Recording engineer for many East Bay punk bands.

Nosmo King: Onetime bassist for Negative Trend, Toiling Midgets, Fifth Column, and the bike-messenger band Noize Boyz. Jak's Team for life.

Oran Canfield: Juggling prodigy and underage Farm dweller. He currently plays drums in Child Abuse. His memoir, *Long Past Stopping*, was recently published by HarperCollins.

Orlando X: A fixture in the East Bay punk scene for over three decades. OX, as he is fondly known, was front man for Special Forces, United Blood, and Intrepid AAF. He DJs regularly and works at Amoeba on Haight Street when he's not traveling the globe visiting friends and family.

Patrick Hughes: Former *MRR* and Epicenter shitworker.

Patrick Tidd: Former drug-addicted BTU knucklehead. Now a BTU knucklehead addicted to adrenaline working as a framing contractor and whitewater raft guide, and raising five kids in Oakland and Mount Shasta.

Paul Casteel aka Dogsbar King: Onetime bass player for Impatient Youth, singer for the Black Athletes. Founding member of House of Wheels and Touch Me Hooker. Jak's Team since 1981—Jak #6.

PB Floyd: Longtime member of the Slingshot Collective, which publishes a quarterly, independent, radical newspaper in the Berkeley.

Penelope Houston: Balances her dark folk rock solo career with fronting the reformed Avengers and glorious library day job.

Portia: Onetime Powell Street punk and nasty little death rocker (never to be confused with "goth"). Friend of Hell House and the S.F. Skins. Currently an attorney, living in the East Bay with a private criminal defense practice.

Rachel DMR: Founding member of DMR. Now an equestrienne who lives the horsey life when not working or consulting for Bay Area architectural design firms. She lives with her twin sister in Oakland, staying in touch with her punk roots and friendships that have lasted several decades.

Rachel Rudnick: Former *MRR* shitworker. Wrote lyrics for Christ on Parade's "Another Country." Enjoys baking and fostering kittens. Still really bad at Scrabble.

Ralph Spight: Guitarist and vocalist for Victim's Family. Currently lives in San Francisco and makes a living teaching Green Day songs to suburban kids between shows with his new band, the Freak Accident.

Randy Rampage: Bass player for DOA.

Ray Farrell: Rather Ripped Records. Co-founder of *Maximum RocknRoll* Radio. On to SST, Geffen, and eMusic. Now in technology, guiding record labels through digital royalty process.

Ray Vegas: Longtime guitarist for Social Unrest. Onetime bassist and guitarist for Attitude Adjustment.

Rebecca Gwyn Wilson: Onetime denizen of the Rathouse. Contributor to Lawrence Livermore's zine *Lookout!* and, later, *Juxtapoz*. She is a former bike messenger, activist stripper, and a UC Berkeley graduate. Now lives in Oakland with husband Paul Casteel and two children.

Richard the Roadie: Toured with many bands, 1991–2004. Shitworker at Gilman, Epicenter, and Blacklist. Presently union trade-show installer by day, printer at 1984 Printing by night. Even more crappy tattoos now.

Robert Eggplant: Founding member of Blatz and the Hope Bombs. Onetime member of the S.P.A.M. Records collective, which organized Geekfest. He still volunteers at Gilman and has been publishing his zine *Absolutely Zippo* since 1987.

Robert James Hanrahan: Deaf Club/Walking Dead cultural instigator and political collaborator.

Rozz Rezabek: Front man of Negative Trend and Theater of Sheep. Continues to write *LoverLegendLiar*, his yet unpublished memoir of scandalous seminal obscurity and 15 minutes that lasted way too long.

Ruth Schwartz: Mordam Records founder. Now motivational speaker and business coach.

Ryan Mattos aka Mad Toast: Guitarist for Ceremony. Contributor to Rivalry Records. Onetime roadie for Nerve Agents.

Sammytown: Singer for Fang and the Resistoleros. Madonna Inn dweller.

Sara Cohen: Old friend of yours, present enemy of theirs. Settled down with the bass player from that one band. High school dropout with a Ph.D. in sociology, living and teaching in Seattle and raising a teenager.

Scott Kelly: Singer of Neurosis. Still breaking guitars and making babies.

Sergie Loobkoff: Toiled in vans for much of his life in bands such as Samiam, Sweet Baby, Soup, Knapsack, and Solea. Now an art director, living in downtown Los Angeles.

Sham Saenz: *Punk rocker* {pəngk´räkər} n. A worthless person (often used as a general term of abuse); a criminal or hoodlum.

Shawn Ford: Co-Flounder of Shred of Dignity Skaters' Union. Now living with his very own family that he made all by himself in Hawai'i, and teaching ESL at Kapi'olani Community College and the Basics of Home Brewing at the University of Hawai'i at Manoa.

Sothira Pheng: Singer and songwriter for Crucifix. Currently singer and bass player for Proudflesh.

Spike Slawson: Lead singer for Me First and the Gimme Gimmes. Bassist for Swingin' Utters. Bass player and singer for Re-Volts.

Steve DePace: Drummer of Flipper and Negative Trend.

Steve Tupper: Presently serving a life sentence running Subterranean Records.

Stormy Shepherd: Founder of Leave Home Booking, which works with many Bay Area bands, including Rancid, NOFX, AFI, and Me First and the Gimme Gimmes, as well as Tiger Army, the Damned, the Vandals, and the Offspring.

Suzanne Stefanac: Former roommate and legal assistant to Jello Biafra.

Tammy Lundy aka Tammy MDC: Longtime booker, roadie, and driver for MDC. Founder of Team Herpes. Partner to Mikey Donaldson of Offenders, MDC, and Sister Double Happiness for 16 years.

Ted Falconi: Guitarist for Flipper.

Tiger Lily aka Lily Chou: Spastic KALX DJ. Editor of *My Letter to the World* zine, 1993–2001, and *JetLag RocknRoll* online travel guide. Photographer of bands, places, pastries, and Domokun.

Tim Armstrong: Singer, songwriter, and guitarist for Rancid, Operation Ivy, and the Transplants. Co-founder and operator of Hellcat Records. Living in the East Bay.

Tim Tonooka: Founder of *Ripper* zine.

Tom Flynn: Founder of Boner Records, and former member of Fang, Special Forces, Duh, and Star Pimp. Now looks upon most other characters in this book with smug superiority.

Tom Jennings: Founder of *Homocore* zine. Co-founder of Shred of Dignity warehouse. Early coordinator at Gilman. Creator of FidoNet. Car nut and technical artist.

Toni DMR: Founding member of DMR. Managed to survive those years, as well as a broken neck, cancer, and chemo. Currently a surgical technologist who coordinates transplant teams, harvesting organs from dead bodies to save lives.

Wendy-O Matik: Spoken-word performer. Author of *Redefining Our Relationships: Guidelines for Responsible Open Relationships*. Pushing the boundaries on firmly rooted notions in mainstream society on relationships, love, and sexual politics.

Winston Smith: Radical collage artist since the 1970s. Created Dead Kennedys logo, album covers for Dead Kennedys, Green Day, and George

Carlin, to name a few. Work has appeared in *Playboy* and *The New Yorker*.

X-Con Ron aka Ron Posner: Onetime owner of Fogtown Skate Shop and Concrete Jungle. Longtime guitarist and founding member of MDC.

Zarah Manos: Former coordinator of Gilman Street. Now lives and works in Oakland.

Zeke Jak: S.F. punk. Jak's Team since 1988. Metal worker and machinist with Survival Research Laboratories.

SOURCE INDEX

Chapter 3: Baby, You're So Repulsive

Dirk Dirksen quotes "The reason I became the MC" and "Out of that, the huge X's," from *The Josh Kornbluth Show*, KQED-TV San Francisco, 2006.

Dirk Dirksen quotes "We premiered something like 25 plays of authors" and "I had my nose broken I think seven times," from "What We Talk About When WE Talk About Punk," Citysearch, February 1999, by Alexa Weinstein, used with permission from Alexa Weinstein.

All other Dirk Dirksen quotes from interview conducted on KALX by California Kid, November 20, 1997, used with permission from Alan Parowski.

All Chip Kinman quotes from interview for *Unknown Legends of Rock 'n' Roll*, Richie Unterberger, 1997 (Backbeat Books), used with permission from Richie Unterberger.

Chapter 5: Giddyup Mutants

All Dirk Dirksen quotes from interview conducted on KALX by California Kid, November 20, 1997, used with permission from Alan Parowski.

Excerpts from "Cramps/Mutants: Napa State Hospital," Howie Klein, *New York Rocker*, July 1978, used with permission from Andy Schwartz and Howie Klein.

Chapter 7: You Are One of Our Lesser Audiences

All Chip Kinman quotes from interview for *Unknown Legends of Rock 'n' Roll*, Richie Unterberger, 1997 (Backbeat Books), used with permission from Richie Unterberger.

All Dirk Dirksen quotes from interview conducted on KALX by California Kid, November 20, 1997, used with permission from Alan Parowski.

All Randy Rampage and Joey Shithead quotes from an interview for upcoming documentary directed by Susanne Tabata, used with permission from Susanne Tabata.

Quote from police sergeant, from personal collection of Chester Simpson, used with permission from Chester Simpson.

All Johnnie Walker quotes from interview with www.jive95.com, used with permission from Norman Davis.

Chapter 9: Fresh Fruit for Rotting Vegetables

Interview with Jello Biafra from *Maximum RocknRoll* 11, January 1984, used with permission from *Maximum RocknRoll*.

All Jello Biafra quotes in *Frankenchrist* trial section from *High Priest of Harmful Matter—Tales from the Trial*, Jello Biafra spoken-word CD, used with permission from Jello Biafra.

All Michael Guarino quotes from *This American Life* 285, David Segal, March 25, 2005, produced by Chicago Public Radio and distributed by Public Radio International, used with permission from David Segal.

Excerpts from court case from Dead Kennedys et al., Plaintiffs and Appellants, *v.* Jello Biafra, Defendant and Appellant; 094272; (San Francisco County Super. Ct. No. 998892), public domain.

Quote from "Punk Rock on Trial," RJ Smith, *Spin*, February 2000, used with permission from RJ Smith.

Chapter 10: No One's Listening

All Johnnie Walker quotes from interview with www.jive95.com, used with permission from Norman Davis.

Chapter 14: We Are the Kings Now

Lyrics from "Annihilation" by Crucifix, used with permission from Sothira Pheng.

Chapter 15: Better Living Through Chemistry

Excerpts from *The People's History of Berkeley*, used freely due to GNU free documentation license.

Chapter 17: Blitzkrieg Bop

Excerpt from "Part Two: S.F. Skins Respond," interview conducted by Tim Yohannan, *Maximum RocknRoll* 18, October 1984, used with permission from *Maximum RocknRoll*.

Excerpt from "Northern California Scene Report," Tim Yohannan, *Maximum RocknRoll* 15, July 1984, used with permission from *Maximum RocknRoll*.

Excerpt from "Nazi Skinheads: The Hate Behind the Headlines," Cary Tennis, *Calendar Magazine*, January 1, 1989, used with permission from Cary Tennis and *SF Weekly*.

Chapter 18: Gimme Something Better

All Creetin K-oS quotes from "Nothing Here Now but K-oS," interview by Jason Honea, used with permission from www.punkglobe.com.

Chapter 19: Berkeley Heathen Scum

Lyrics for "Berkeley Heathen Scum" by Fang, used with permission from Sammytown.

Excerpt from "Dixie Lee Carney/June 14th, 1965–August 6th, 1989," *Maximum RocknRoll*, 77, October 1989, used with permission from *Maximum RocknRoll*.

Chapter 21: Goddamn Motherfucking Son of a Bitch

Excerpt from "Bob Noxious of the Fuck-Ups," Tim Yohannan, *Maximum RocknRoll* 8, September 1983, used with permission from *Maximum RocknRoll*.

Chapter 22: High Priest(s) of Harmful Matter

Excerpt from "Scene Report Bay Area," Tim Yohannan, *Maximum RocknRoll* 1, July 1982, used with permission from *Maximum RocknRoll*.

Chapter 24: Beers, Steers and Queers: The Texas Invasion

All Nicki Sicki quotes from "Q&A Subject: Nicki Sicki," Jay Unidos, *Urban Guerrilla Zine* (UGZ) 11, 2001, used with permission from *UGZ*.

X-Con Ron quote "At first the band was called . . ." from web.mac.com/erposner1/MDC/MDC_PUNK.html, used with permission from Ron Posner.

Lyrics from "John Wayne Was a Nazi" by MDC, used with permission from Dave Dictor and MDC.

Chapter 25: Welcome to Paradise

All David Solnit quotes from *Intoxicated Culture: A Political History of the California Punk Scene*, Jeff Goldthorpe, 1990 (unpublished), used with permission from Jeff Goldthorpe and David Solnit.

All Nicki Sicki quotes from "Q&A Subject: Nicki Sicki," Jay Unidos, *Urban Guerrilla Zine* (UGZ) 11, 2001, used with permission from *UGZ*.

Chapter 27: Crossover

All Wes Robinson quotes and excerpts from "Wes Robinson—For a Good Time, Call (415) 841-2678," Cliff Carpenter, *Maximum RocknRoll* 3, November 1982, used with permission from *Maximum RocknRoll*.

Chapter 28: Let's Lynch the Landlord

All Jeff Goldthorpe quotes from *Intoxicated Culture: A Political History of the California Punk Scene*, Jeff Goldthorpe, 1990 (unpublished), used with permission from Jeff Goldthorpe and Chris Carlsson, of www.shapingsanfrancisco.com.

Chapter 29: Fucked Up Ronnie

Tim Yohannan quotes from *Maximum RocknRoll* 15, August 1984, used with permission from *Maximum RocknRoll*.

Tammy Lundy quotes "When we were in Madison, Wisconsin . . ."; "I was approached by . . ."; and "Biafra at one point . . ." from "Rock Against Reagan Tour '83," by Tammy MDC, *Maximum RocknRoll* 7, July 1983, used with permission from *Maximum RocknRoll*.

All Jeff Goldthorpe quotes from *Intoxicated Culture: A Political History of the California Punk Scene*, Jeff Goldthorpe, 1990 (unpublished), used with permission from Jeff Goldthorpe.

Chapter 30: White Trash, Two Heebs and a Bean

Lyrics to "I'm Telling Tim" used with permission from Fat Mike.

"Punk Voter Comments to the FEC," Fat Mike (Burkett), www.punkvoter. com, April 7, 2004, used with permission from Fat Mike.

Liner notes from *Heavy Petting Zoo* used with permission from Fat Mike.

Jesse Michaels quote "Fat Mike took his power," from www.punkvoter. com, used with permission from Jesse Michaels.

Chapter 37: You Put Your Chocolate in My Peanut Butter

Yeastie Girlz lyrics used with permission from Jane Guskin and Cammie Toloui.

Chapter 41: Unity

Lyrics to "Hedgecore" used with permission from Jesse Michaels.

ACKNOWLEDGMENTS

Outrageously important thanks to our transcribers from all over the U.S. and Canada: Paul Bartle, Bill Brent, Sean Castillo, Geraldine Convento, Beau Dowling, Chia Evers, Emma Gibbons, Ianna, Phylis J. Iqbal, Susan Jonaitis, Julie, Rochelle Lodder, Sarah Niersbach, Alana Parvey, Molly Rice, Pete Richards, Hope Richardson, Katrina Robinson, Sam, Aaron Sikes, Patty Spaniak, and especially Michelle Zulli and Naomi Hospodarsky. And to Susie Bright and Craig Newmark for helping spread the word.

More thanks to Anna Brown, Jesse Luscious, Chris Appelgren, and Dwayne Bonedog for opening their archives. To Martin Sprouse, Al Ennis, and Jay Unidos for reading through early drafts. To Jim Fitzgerald for hooking it up. To Alexis Washam and Kristen Scharold from Penguin, and in particular Karen Anderson, who saw the potential before anyone. And to the folks at Mission Creek Café and Lost Weekend Video, who let us barge in to do interviews with zero advance warning.

Jack would like to thank Peter Plate, John Marr, Bucky Sinister, and Patrick Hughes, among many others, for ideas and encouragement. My family, who remain supportive even though they don't really know what the hell I'm doing. And Christie Ward, for everything under the sun.

Silke would like to thank Sham Shaenz and Ben Econochrist, who helped us get the ball rolling, and the DMR Twins, who have never let it drop. Also my cousins, Arleda, James, and Finn, who gave me a place to rest my bones and nourish my heart during those marathon interview days; my parents, who lived through the fury and chaos of my youth and never loved me less; Audra Angeli-Slawson, who decided not to kill me in 1985; Andrew Flurry, who was my best friend then and remains so now; and Patrick Richards, who helped clear my head.

ABOUT THE AUTHORS

Jack Boulware is the author of *Sex, American Style* and *San Francisco Bizarro*. His freelance writing has appeared in the *New York Times Magazine*, the *Washington Post*, *Playboy*, *Maxim*, Salon, and the *San Francisco Chronicle*, among others. For ten years he was a columnist and features writer for *SF Weekly*. He is co-founder of San Francisco's annual Litquake literary festival.

Silke Tudor is a San Francisco–born writer who has contributed to the *Village Voice*, *Spin*, and *Tattoo Savage*. For ten years she was a columnist and nightlife editor at *SF Weekly*, and produced the annual *SF Weekly* Music Awards. She recently moved to New York and toured the world with the *Billy Nayer Show*.